# PRACTICING
# CLIENT-CENTERED THERAPY

SELECTED WRITINGS OF BARBARA TEMANER BRODLEY

edited by
Kathryn A. Moon, Marjorie Witty,
Barry Grant, and Bert Rice

*PCCS Books*
Ross-on-Wye

First published 2011

PCCS BOOKS
2 Cropper Row
Alton Road
Ross-on-Wye
Herefordshire
HR9 5LA
UK
Tel +44 (0)1989 763900
contact@pccs-books.co.uk
www.pccs-books.co.uk

**Practicing client-centered therapy: Selected writings of Barbara Temaner Brodley**

British Library Cataloguing in Publication Data.
A catalogue record for this book is available from the British Library.

ISBN 978 1 906254 26 1

Cover designed in the USA by Tom Rutherford
Printed in the UK by Ashford Colour Press, Gosport, Hants

# Contents

# Foreword

## Susan Pildes
### Client-centered therapist, consultant and teacher

I slammed my car door shut and leaned against it for a moment to collect myself. I was in front of Barbara's house in Chicago's South Shore neighborhood on a fall day in 1974. I felt happy. And I felt relief. The previous week I had watched her teach at the Counseling Center in Hyde Park. I went up to her afterward and asked her if I could meet with her at her office. After listening to her talk, I wanted her to be my therapist, and I wanted her to teach me to be a client-centered therapist. I kept these immodest hopes under my hat and we made an appointment to meet the following week. As we climbed the stairs and sat down facing each other in her second-floor office, I KNEW something. I knew that this person would be able to help me as her client, and I knew that if I had it in me to be a therapist, she would help me to become a good one. It was the truest knowing I ever had up to that point. I was 29 years old. She was 41. There has been no time in the intervening years that I have ever questioned that knowing. I have been her client, her student, her colleague, her friend. My family has trusted her to help us whenever things turned hard. In later years, I helped take care of her when she was sick. I arrived at the hospital minutes after she died on December 14th, 2007 – a sudden turn that took her away from her beloved and devoted family, and from us all.

But what we have now is this wonderful book – this book that is the combined effort of so many good people in the U.S. and in Great Britain. In it you will find significant papers that Barbara wrote on counseling and psychotherapy. The papers begin just prior to her graduate work in Human Development at the University of Chicago, extend through her teaching years at the Illinois School of Professional Psychology, and continue through the decades that follow when she was free to work on her own. From the time she entered graduate school until illness finally quieted her, she wrote about psychotherapy. She wrote for her own clarity and she wrote for students and therapists who were interested in client-centered thinking. She wrote and she taught in ways that further clarified the absolutely radical ideas of Carl Rogers. Her main message was this: that the "Necessary and Sufficient

Conditions" ARE both necessary AND sufficient. And, until she could no longer marshal the strength, her expressed thoughts focused on how therapists could do effective, ethical work.

The book you hold in your hands contains essays that will add to your understanding of Carl Rogers' work. Dr. Rogers once called Barbara "my spiritual daughter" because he knew how thoroughly she understood what he was saying about the growth of all people, even or especially the most burdened. They both wrote about each of us, persons trying to live authentically in a world so often not attentive to human need. For Barbara, though she saw today's world as doomed, she perceived in it a heedless beauty so wild in its extravagance and complexity that it could only be understood as nature itself, evolving endlessly through time.

# Foreword

# Jerold D. Bozarth

## Professor Emeritus, University of Georgia

Barbara Temaner Brodley was an icon in the person-centered community. She and I met in 1957 when we were involved in a pilot study designed to rehabilitate individuals hospitalized in Illinois State institutions. We worked at different locations but learned the client-centered approach from working with patients who had been given little hope of leaving the hospitals.

Barbara was a client-centered practitioner and a theorist. She educated, consulted and inspired significant numbers of nondirective therapists over 50 years. As a therapist over this time span, she met with more than a half dozen clients a day, six days a week. Barbara said that she did not understand how therapists became burned out being with clients. The task of therapy for Barbara was a joy.

Barbara was a radical purist of Rogers' theory of client-centered therapy. She sought to experience the client's truth; that is, as she put it: "... moments in therapy when the client is speaking absolutely, when his expression is completely and exactly what is most importantly going on in him." She was attentive to "experiencing the warmth, the pain, the static and confusion, the creative awareness" of the other person (Propst, 1962/2011). She, perhaps single-handedly, kept alive the central place of the construct of nondirectivity as the principle espousing the client as being her or his own best expert. Although she advocated the "Necessary and Sufficient Conditions" (Rogers, 1957) as nondirective attitudes, she distinguished the "Empathic Understanding Response Process" (Temaner, 1977/2011) as the predominant form of client-centered therapy. She facilitated abundant empirical examinations of therapy sessions of client-centered therapy.

This collection of her papers reflects the substance and nature of her work and convictions. Each chapter is worthy of examination and contemplation for any person interested in psychotherapy.

## REFERENCES

Propst, B. S. [Brodley] (1962, March 30). *Why do I want to be a therapist?* Memo to John Shlien. [This volume, Chapter 1]

Rogers, C. R. (1957). The necessary and sufficient conditions for therapeutic personality change. *Journal of Consulting Psychology, 21*, 95–103.

Temaner, B. [Brodley] (1977). The empathic understanding response process. Chicago Counseling and Psychotherapy Center. *Chicago Counseling Center Discussion Paper.* [This volume, Chapter 12]

# Acknowledgments

A surprisingly great number of people have had a hand in making this book possible. If we have forgotten anyone who has contributed to this book over the more than 10 years of its gestation, please forgive us!

Jerold Bozarth, Susan Pildes, Tony Merry, John Shlien, Nat Raskin, Marvin Frankel, Lisbeth Sommerbeck, Garry Prouty and Fred Zimring supported and encouraged Barbara to publish a collection of her work.

Suggestions and assistance at various junctures along the way have come from Alberto Segrera, Barbara Bogosian, Brian Burgess, Brian Levitt, Bruce Allen, Chuck Stuart, Claudia Kemp, Elizabeth Freire, Elmyra Walden, Emilie Pulver, Françoise Ducroux-Biass, Germain Lietaer, Gillian Proctor, Gerald Bauman, Grace Klein, Hope Sanchez, Irene Fairhurst, Ivan Rice, Javier Armenta, Jerome Wilczynski, Jerry Krakowski, Jin Wu, João Hipólito, Kevin Kukoleck, Laura Sklarsky, Noriko Motomasa, Paul Colley, Sue Wilders, Tanya Komleva and Tiane Graziottin.

We especially thank the PCCS Books group, Maggie Taylor-Sanders and Pete Sanders, our incredibly wonderful, patient, and creative copy-editor Sandy Green, and Heather Allan – who have been remarkably patient and generous through a decade of decision-making, cost-overruns, and hard work.

We are grateful to Tom Rutherford for his wonderful book cover.

This book would not have been possible without the support of Jerry Temaner, Noah Temaner Jenkins, Marco Temaner, Olive Louise Jenkins, and Robert Brodley.

We also thank our families who supported us in the many hours we spent selecting and editing articles.

Three of the editors wish to acknowledge Kathryn Moon's enormous contribution. Her dedication to the accuracy, style and structure of the book are only outdone by her day-in-day-out commitment to bringing this manuscript into its final form.

Most of all, we thank our indomitable, lion-hearted, and generous therapist-consultant-colleague, Barbara Scott Propst Temaner Brodley, whose presence and work has inspired us and many others. We hope this is the book she would have wanted.

# Dedication

The editors dedicate this book to Olive Louise Jenkins,
Barbara's granddaughter, who brought her joy unbounded.

# Editors' introduction

Barbara Temaner Brodley studied, practiced, taught, researched, and wrote about client-centered therapy for more than 50 years. Her practice and teachings bear the stamp of her brilliance, critical self-observations, discipline, and art. Her writings illuminate the intersections of client-centered ethics, theory, and practice and are a profound guide to developing, recognizing, understanding, and deepening the therapeutic attitudes and practice of the revolution that is client-centered therapy. We regard her writings as the rare gift of a brilliant master therapist who painstakingly and lovingly sought to articulate and clarify the practice of client-centered therapy. This collection of Barbara's writings is an indispensable guide to anyone wishing to become a client-centered therapist and to all, experienced and inexperienced, who are interested in developing their psychotherapy practice.

Barbara was an expositor of the paradigm shift within the counseling and psychotherapy field that was theorized by Rogers in the 1950s. Her writings depict and defend the critical significance of the nondirective attitude as the foundational hallmark of the client-centered approach. For Barbara, holding and expressing the nondirective attitude "asserts the idea of the inherent and precious value of human persons. It asserts the values of respect towards and trust in persons, egalitarian and democratic values, and the value of freedom" (Brodley, 1997, p. 18/2011).

Barbara's understanding of client-centered therapy is based on Rogers' classic publications, notably, "The Attitude and Orientation of the Counselor," Chapter Two of *Client-Centered Therapy* (Rogers, 1951), "The Necessary and Sufficient Conditions for Therapeutic Personality Change" (Rogers' 1957), and "A Theory of Therapy, Personality, and Interpersonal Relationships, as Developed in the Client-Centered Framework" (Rogers, 1959). It is in these works that Rogers most clearly describes the attitudinal basis of client-centered therapy and articulates its nondirective nature.

From a very early paper, "Client-Centered Psychotherapy as a Complex Task" (Propst, 1966), through the "Empathic Understanding Response Process" (Temaner, 1977/2011) to "Empathic Understanding and Feelings in Client-Centered Therapy" (Brodley, 1996/2011) and "Unconditional Positive Regard as Communicated through Verbal Behavior in Client-Centered Therapy" (Brodley & Schneider, 2001/2011), Barbara progressively refined her understanding of exactly how the therapeutic attitudes of empathy, acceptance, congruence, and the nondirective attitude are enacted in practice. She showed how the attitudes are melded together and embodied in all the therapist does.

Barbara was a keen student of Rogers' therapy work. She once commented that her work was a "committed exegesis" of Rogers' theory of therapeutic change. She made the remark with an ironic smile, since the term "exegesis" is associated with theology and Barbara openly inveighed against all psychologies, religions, or politics that subverted the inner authority and autonomy of sovereign human beings.

Barbara closely examined audio recordings and transcripts of Rogers' therapy and demonstration sessions. In a decades-long project, she and Germain Lietaer collected every recording and transcript of Rogers that they could find, and created transcripts when none existed. This work culminated in a journal article (Lietaer & Brodley, 2003) and an informal email publication (Brodley & Lietaer, 2006) of all of Rogers' available sessions and transcripts. Many of the articles in this book reference various of Rogers' transcripts. Since the release of the Brodley and Lietaer (2006) versions of the transcripts occurred subsequent to almost all of Barbara's writings, we have used brackets to update and supplement Barbara's original references to recordings and transcripts.

Barbara was passionately committed to preserving client-centered as a distinct therapy. Rogers' work has been the source of diverse schools of therapy – e.g., focusing and experiential – that are, as Barbara argued, different from client-centered therapy in their values as well as in their practice. All of Barbara's work, we can see in retrospect, was devoted to articulating and justifying the view that client-centered therapy is a distinct form of practice.

Barbara was a courageous exponent of nondirectiveness, which she saw as having been lost in the early 1970s, as Gendlin's experiential focusing approach was touted as an advance over the client-centered approach. She objected to this and other revisions of Rogers' theory and stressed that without the nondirective attitude, the core conditions were necessarily altered in character. Her rejection of the once standard, ecumenical position that everyone who follows Rogers is doing basically the same kind of therapy sparked debate. The significance of nondirectiveness to Brodley was profoundly ethical. She saw nondirectivity as the heart of client-centered therapy. Client-centered therapy, as she understood it, is a way, perhaps the only way, of working with people that fully respects their autonomy.

Perhaps Barbara's most important contribution to the literature on client-centered therapy was that she rigorously drew out the implications of nondirectiveness for all aspects of practice. She believed that the nondirective attitude necessitated a willingness to answer clients' questions, address requests for accommodations and changes in therapy, and respond from one's own frame of reference when clients requested a personal response. These are expressions of the nondirective attitude resulting in a high degree of empathic attunement and responsiveness to clients. In her writings, particularly, "Client-Centered Therapy: An Expressive Therapy" (Brodley, 2002/2011), "Reasons for Responses Expressing the Therapist's Frame of Reference in Client-Centered Therapy" (Brodley, 1999/2011) and "Criteria for Making Empathic Responses in Client-Centered Therapy" (Brodley, 1998/2011), she eloquently articulates how nondirective therapists can find their own subjective freedom as therapists, while retaining discipline and responsibility in therapeutic relationships.

She felt that the therapeutic attitudes are, for many beginners, more aspiration than reality, and specific guidance is useful before the "philosophy and the therapeutic attitudes have been understood and assimilated well enough to guide the therapist's practice" (Brodley, 1991, p. 1/1993/2000). She rightly regarded herself as a person in whom client-centered philosophy and attitudes were deeply integrated. She reflected on and observed how she handled certain situations, such as making therapist-frame responses, and then articulated the principle or guiding idea behind her response. The section in this book, "Implementation of the Values and Attitudes in an Expressive Client-Centered Therapy", can serve as a "how to" for novice therapists.

Barbara's writings explicating client-centered therapy amount, we believe, to an explication of how to be a therapist. Her writings are a vitally important guide to doing therapy in a way that avoids the still near-ubiquitous belief that the therapist has superior knowledge into how others should lead their lives.

REFERENCES

Brodley, B. T. (1991). *Instructions for beginning to practice client-centered therapy.* Unpublished classroom handout. Illinois School of Professional Psychology. Revision published (1993) as The therapeutic clinical interview: Guidelines for beginning practice. *Person-Centred Practice 1*(2), 15–21. Reprinted (2000) in T. Merry (Ed.), *Person-centred practice: The BAPCA reader* (pp. 103–109). Ross-on-Wye: PCCS Books. (This volume, Chapter 17)
Brodley, B. T. (1996). Empathic understanding and feelings in client-centered therapy. *The Person-Centered Journal, 3*(1), 22–30. (This volume, Chapter 8)
Brodley, B. T. (1997). The nondirective attitude in client-centered therapy. *The Person-Centered Journal, 4*(1), 18–30. (This volume, Chapter 5)

Brodley, B. T. (1998). Criteria for making empathic responses in client-centered therapy. *The Person-Centered Journal, 5*(1), 20–28. (This volume, Chapter 14)

Brodley, B. T. (1999). Reasons for responses expressing the therapist's frame of reference in client-centered therapy. *The Person-Centered Journal, 6*(1), 4–27. (Slightly revised in this volume, Chapter 15)

Brodley, B. T. (2002). Client-centered: An expressive therapy. *The Person-Centered Journal 9*(1), 59–70. (This volume, Chapter 13)

Brodley, B. T., & Lietaer, G. (Eds.). (2006). *Transcripts of Carl Rogers' therapy sessions, Vols. 1–17*. Available from germain.lietaer@psy.kuleuven.be and kmoon1@alumni.uchicago.edu

Brodley, B. T., & Schneider, C. (2001). Unconditional positive regard as communicated through verbal behavior in client-centered therapy. In J. D. Bozarth & P. Wilkins (Eds.), *Unconditional positive regard* (pp. 155–172). Ross-on-Wye: PCCS Books. (This volume, Chapter 9)

Lietaer, G., & Brodley, B. T. (2003). Carl Rogers in the therapy room: A listing of session transcripts and a survey of publications referring to Rogers' sessions. *Person-Centered & Experiential Psychotherapies, 2*, 274–291.

Propst, B. S. (1966). Client-centered psychotherapy as a complex task. University of Chicago Counseling Center. *Discussion Paper, 12*(9).

Rogers, C.R. (1951). *Client-centered therapy.* Boston: Houghton Mifflin.

Rogers, C. R. (1957). The necessary and sufficient conditions of therapeutic personality change. *Journal of Consulting Psychology, 21*, 95–103.

Rogers, C. R. (1959). A theory of therapy, personality, and interpersonal relationships, as developed in the client-centered framework. In S. Koch (Ed.), *Psychology: A study of a science. Vol. III: Formulations of the person and the social context* (pp. 184–256). New York: McGraw-Hill.

Temaner, B. [Brodley] (1977, March). The empathic understanding response process. Revision of paper presented to Changes on March 6. Chicago Counseling and Psychotherapy Center. *Chicago Counseling Center Discussion Paper.* (This volume, Chapter 12)

# Chapter 1

# Why do I want to be a therapist?

MEMO TO JOHN SHLIEN

**March 30, 1962**

Oh God, why do I want to be a therapist? It is so difficult! It seems the flow of talk between two people, focused on one of them, should be the naturalest and most practiced thing in the world – a breeze. But I know enough to know it isn't. It is many hard things, like shoveling coal sometimes, sometimes like being squeezed into a small box, or floating on the surface of the ocean, or being pulled under. I have felt like I was turning into a scraggly limbed tree with only my voice box unmetamorphasized. And I have felt, occasionally, just *there* and resonating to the other person. But all these different kinds of feelings probably reveal how definitively I am "in training" to become a psychotherapist, and am not yet one.

I think my motives are partly in relation to what being a psychotherapist means for me now, on the basis of my present experiences in being one, and are partly in relation to what I vaguely imagine the experience will be when I have reached a certain level of excellence in the performance that is still beyond me. If I thought I would always be a therapist as I am now I might not be so "motivated," for it is painful now, out of clumsiness and ignorance, not out of the intrinsics of the function. Or will it always be painful? Well, I think there are kinds of pain. Some are OK because they come out of deeply touching something and risking something for something of importance. But the kind of pain I get now seems to me to come mostly from fury at myself for not understanding, for being self-involved (and stuck in it) when I want to be other-involved, and for not being able to think clearly and quickly enough or express myself lucidly and appropriately enough.

What are my motives? I know what they are not! Not because I want to HELP others! I don't want to help others to get along better in the world, feel better, or even to realize their complex of capacities. No! That isn't true. I do want these things to happen to my clients or patients, but that still isn't my motive. It is part of what I expect to happen if I function well as a psychotherapist, but it is not my motive. My motives are something about me, have to do with something *for* me.

My motives have to do, mostly, with my experience, or imagined experience of the therapeutic procedure … the pleasures of the interaction.

1.  The closeness. I want the closeness to the other person. I want to feel the other person's experience – the warmth, the pain, the static and confusion, the creative awareness. But, at the same time, I want to know my own existence is in no way dependent upon the other person's feelings, attitudes, or ways of being in the world. This is a completely unsticky closeness to me. It is unlike any other, at least for me. A kind of indifference to my own being permits a certain unique freedom that I want to feel. In any other relationship I can only feel such freedom when the other person happens to be meeting my own conditions, and then I, in effect, limit his freedom. I don't understand this about me very well, but I think I am afraid to be dependent upon another person. I don't believe, at least steadily, that I deserve the thereness of the other person, and I am easily jeopardized if they seem to be there for me and then something occurs that contradicts my expectations, or seems a countersign. I become wild. So, as you might expect, I don't get close often. As a psychotherapist I don't even feel inclined to become dependent on the client, so I feel safe to get close and let the person get close to me. So, one of my motives for becoming a psychotherapist is to experience closeness of a kind that seems safe to me.

2.  Using myself. My expectations and my actual experience as a therapist tell me that being a therapist involves intensively using my most prized capacities, the ones I especially want to exercise. Almost simultaneously intelligence, esthetic sensibility, the creative use of language, expression of feeling, reservoirs of thought-out past experiences – are all being fused in the flow of communication and attention toward the client. In other ways, in my living, my use of myself is knotted and hindered in expression. Psychotherapy is a form of productivity for me that I feel more readily capable of than other forms that I also value. Perhaps being a psychotherapist will have less importance to me if I can clear my way in other areas of creativity, I don't know. Perhaps the knots in me will continue to show up in my performance as therapist, too. If so … I don't know.

3.  Experiencing truth. This is hard to express. There are moments in therapy when the client is speaking absolutely, when his expression is completely and exactly what is most importantly going on in him. That is what I mean by truth. And I love such an event; it exhilarates me and satisfies me. This is the special treasure I imagine to discover again and again as a therapist.

4. Knowledge and understanding. I want to conceptualize such things as personality, the nature of man, the processes of self-discovery and development; and functioning as a psychotherapist supplies an important kind of data to me for this purpose. The client's behavior in therapy is a rich fabric to think about and out of which to develop hypotheses for the tests of science. I can't stand thinking out of a thin context of facts. So, from my point of view, being a therapist puts me in the position of having access to a sufficiency of reality upon which to dwell and through which to seek understanding of man.

My motives for becoming a psychotherapist are all colored by my conviction that I can be adequate in the job in a way I am not sure I can be adequate in any other important function. I hope my conviction is not an illusion.

The Ideal Motivation for becoming a psychotherapist I can only state in negative terms. It seems to me that there is a great variety of possible "good" motives, but, whatever they are, they should be in the absence of a personal deprivation that is hoped to be made up by being a therapist. Ideal motivation is from abundance, I believe. Insofar as my own motivation is out of deprivation … and it is … or seems to be (it is hard to tell, when the deprivation is there, what is getting confused because of it), it deviates from this ideal, and will have sad consequences in the quality of my functioning and in my satisfaction from being a psychotherapist.

# Chapter 2

# A Chicago client-centered therapy:
# Nondirective and nonexperiential

My purpose in writing this paper is to publicize and emphasize the continued existence of a nondirective, client-centered therapy, currently practiced by many therapists who have been influenced by Rogers and some of them influenced, as well, by me.

My title "A Chicago Client-Centered Therapy" is tongue-in-cheek, because I do not think it is a benign idea to call a therapy by a location. Although my therapy was born and developed in Chicago, it has also developed from Rogers' theory in other places. I'd hoped this title would stimulate interest.

I shall write in the first person to summarize this therapy as I believe I practice it. I don't want to represent other therapists who may function almost, but not totally, the way I do. I shall also be assuming the reader is familiar with Rogers' writings about his theory of therapy.

I consider Rogers' own therapy behavior, available in many transcripts, the basic model for any "classical" client-centered therapy. I believe my "Chicago" client-centered therapy is almost identical to Rogers' therapy, and is one of several subclasses of "classical" client-centered therapy that are nondirective and show relatively small differences in practice. One of the other subclasses emphasizes the behavioral principle of empathic following more than my therapy. Another gives more latitude to the therapist's making idiosyncratic responses from the therapist's frame of reference. Another subset seems to define empathy with more emphasis on feelings than my therapy.

My personal "Chicago client-centered therapy" originated in Rogers' writings and therapy during his tenure in Ohio and Chicago, and it evolved in Chicago after Rogers departed from the city. It is strictly nondirective in regard to the therapist's attitudes which are expressed in behavior, does not rely upon Gendlin's conception of "experiencing" (Gendlin, 1974) in its theory

---

Barbara presented this paper in Fargo, North Dakota on July 24, 2006 during the annual meeting of the Association for the Development of the Person-Centered Approach. As such the paper is not a finished essay, but as it is her last paper, we wished to see it included in this collection.

or practice (Brodley, 1990/2011), nor adopt any of the other process-directive offshoots from Rogers' therapy, for example those of Greenberg, Rice, & Elliott (1993).

I shall summarize my personal history of Chicago client-centered therapy. I shall show my therapy's similarity to Rogers' client-centered therapy by reporting a study (Brodley, 2002/2011) comparing our two therapies. To clarify my approach, I shall describe ways it differs from some other nondirective client-centered therapies, and I'll summarize two surveys of my clients' perceptions of my presence and personality when doing therapy. The results emphasize some differences between my presence as a therapist and my presence in other contexts. Finally I'll summarize a description of my therapy.

HISTORY OF MY EXPERIENCE

From 1953 to 1955 I studied Rogers' writings and had long discussions about client-centered therapy with Rudyard Propst, a psychologist and therapy student of Rogers who became my husband. After completing my second BA (in psychology) at the University of Chicago in 1955, I began five years' work in a large state "mental" hospital, first as an industrial therapist and then as a rehabilitation counselor. Immediately upon starting work, I commenced doing psychotherapy with patients without any prior practical experience – only having absorbed theory, plus the model of Rudyard's interactions with me, and examples of therapy from Rogers' writings.

During the five years working full-time at the hospital, I interviewed several thousand patients – including one- or two-time sessions with some patients, and had many long-term therapy relationships. In 1956 I took the year-long evening practicum in client-centered therapy from Bill Kell, a student of Rogers, and began seeing outpatients in the evening, using the office of my physician father-in-law.

My therapy with hospital patients at the beginning was based on my intellectual understanding of Rogers' nondirective client-centered therapy (Rogers, 1942, 1951) and on many client-centered interactions with Rudyard concerning my personal problems. I had no apprehensions or fears about doing therapy and I slipped easily into the Rogerian attitudes and the activity of therapy with all diagnostic types of patients, mostly psychotic persons, creating no apparent problems for them or for me. Patients were receptive to me, and the very unusual "Rogerian-like" and democratic superintending psychiatrist, Kalman Gyarfas, M.D., supported my work as a therapist.

I quickly saw that my interactions with patients were therapeutic for most of them. Clients changed temporarily within sessions, becoming more coherent and relating to me in a more rational manner before the end of sessions. Some of the within-session changes persisted, and between sessions staff reported my patients to be less belligerent, personally cleaner, dressing more conventionally, more cooperative with staff, and more functional in their work assignments within the institution. Many who had previously been kept under constant supervision were able to have grounds passes; others were able to get passes to visit outside the hospital, and in many cases, to go to school or find work and be discharged.

In 1960 I returned to the University of Chicago to study for my doctorate in clinical psychology and human development. I took my second practicum in client-centered therapy at the University of Chicago Counseling and Psychotherapy Research Center. Subsequently I was a clinical intern and then a "junior" staff member for a total tenure of seven years.

During all those years, Rogers was at the University of Wisconsin and spending time also in California, so I only spent time with him in a few brief seminars and parties. My teachers and mentors at the Center were John Shlien, Jack Butler, Fred Zimring, Laura Rice, Dick Jenney and Charlotte Ellinwood. Dick was my therapist for three years and later I worked with Charlotte for a year. As a therapist at the Counseling Center, I worked with individual adults, adolescents, couples, and children as young as three years of age.

Until I started my private practice in 1967, I also worked part-time as a therapist in a student health center, a geriatric home, a clinic for patients with brain injuries and language disorders, and at an inpatient unit for male alcoholics. During the years of my private practice I have also worked as an emergency psychotherapist in a unit in a general hospital set up for patients with environmental illnesses, and as a teacher and consultant at a private agency, the Chicago Counseling and Psychotherapy Center, that some staff and students started when the University disbanded its clinical psychology program and closed Rogers' Counseling Center. From 1980 to the present I have taught client-centered therapy as an adjunct professor at Argosy University, Chicago (formerly known as the Illinois School of Professional Psychology), holding classes, groups, and supervising doctoral research.

## NONDIRECTIVENESS IN MY CHICAGO CLIENT-CENTERED THERAPY

When I started working with patients in 1955, I did not have access to Rogers' developing theoretical statements published in 1957 and 1959. I had especially studied Chapter 2, "The attitude and orientation of the counselor" in *Client-Centered Therapy* (Rogers, 1951), and the case of Mr. Bryan in *Counseling and Psychotherapy* (Rogers, 1942) including Rogers' informative critique of his work with Mr. Bryan. This literature, and Rudyard's tutoring, influenced me to conceptualize therapy as providing unconditional acceptance and empathic understanding in the subjective context of a nondirective attitude, and to be responsive to – not only to empathically understand – clients' questions and requests by addressing or answering them.

I had not consciously identified the characteristic of therapy that Rogers later referred to as "congruence." I wanted to feel authentic, not play a role, and I did feel natural and comfortable with most of my psychiatric patients while working with them.

Upon my return in 1960 to the University of Chicago to study for my doctorate, events there increased my conscious commitment to the nondirective attitude. The faculty at the Counseling Center (even Laura Rice, at that time) were not in any way suggesting or, as far as I knew, practicing a shift in Rogers' therapy to include directive intentions in the practice. Some of the students who had entered ahead of me at the Center, however, were proselytizing Gene Gendlin's theory of "experiencing." They argued that Gendlin's process directivity improved client-centered therapy (e.g., Gendlin, 1969, 1974, 1981).

This paradigm shift was unacceptable to me. First, it wrongly assumed a specific feeling process as the essence of therapy; second, it inserted focusing procedures into the therapy. I thought that Gendlin's ideas contradicted the nondirective essence of Rogers' client-centered therapy. I think this essential principle is a necessary feature of any therapy rightly called "Client-Centered." I wrote Counseling Center Discussion papers (Propst, 1966; Temaner, 1977/ 2011) to try to counter Gendlin's influence among my colleagues. Over the years I have written articles (Brodley, 1990/2011, 1994/2011, 1996/2011, 1997/2011, 1998/2011, 1999a/2011, 1999b/2011, 2000a/2011, 2000b/ 2011, 2006a, 2006b) and taught many students, emphasizing the inherent nondirectiveness of client-centered therapy and explaining that it shapes all of a therapist's expressions of the therapy.

## EVIDENCE THAT MY THERAPY IS SIMILAR TO ROGERS' CLIENT-CENTERED THERAPY

I always thought that my therapy was identical to Carl Rogers' therapy. But it was only after listening to or watching 20 or more tapes of Rogers doing therapy, and reading more than 100 of his transcripts that I felt sure that my work is very close in intentions and in style, with a few slight differences, to that of Carl Rogers.

As a part of my interest in a comparison, and to give it a more scientific basis, I conducted a study using transcripts of 22 sessions by Rogers and 20 sessions of mine to compare our practices of empathic understanding (Brodley,

2002/2011). First, I'll summarize findings that support the similarity of my therapy to Rogers' therapy.

### Total words spoken by the therapist
The two sets of interviews are similar in the percentage of total words spoken by Rogers and myself to clients – 29% by Rogers and 27% by me, primarily with empathic responses.

### Percentage of empathic responses
Studies of transcripts of Rogers' therapy behavior from the mid-1940s until his death in 1987 (Brodley & Brody, 1990; Brody, 1991; Brodley, 1994/2011; Nelson, 1994; Brodley, 1996/2011; Diss, 1996; Merry, 1996; Bradburn, 1996; Kemp, 2004) reveal that approximately 90% of Rogers' responses are empathic following responses. My 2002 study shows that all of our combined 42 sessions contained a mean of 91% empathic following responses, with the range of 85% to 100%. Only 9% of our responses were made from our own frames of reference. We appear to be similar in the extent to which we communicate from our own frames of reference during sessions in which we are predominantly empathically understanding and following our clients.

### Words for feelings
Comparing Rogers' and my use of "words for feelings" (e.g., "afraid," "hurt," "joyful"), I used two methods. Determining percentages of these words to all words used showed 1.1% of all words by Rogers were words for feelings, and 1.3% of all words I used were those kinds of words – similar frequencies. Counting natural interactions in which the therapist used words for feelings resulted in finding them in 30% of Rogers' natural units and in 31% of mine.

### Clients' confirmations of accuracy
Our clients confirmed all but 1% of Rogers' and my empathic responses as accurate – either explicitly or implicitly (revealed by the way they proceed developing their narratives). Rogers and my clients clearly confirm that almost all our empathic responses are perceived as accurate whether our responses contain words for feelings or not. We are frequently understanding and communicating other experiences that involve subtle or complex states or cognitive components.

### Figures of speech
Frequencies of responses containing figures of speech were high and similar. In approximately two-thirds of our empathic responses (Rogers 61%, mine

66%) we verbalized our understanding of our clients' experiences in an idiosyncratic and lively manner by using figures of speech (e.g., "in a black hole," "clam up," "before your eyes").

### Responses with affective features
Words-for-feelings, words or phrases alluding to feelings, and figures of speech (e.g., "In expressing some of the *stress* of this and some of your *upset* feelings, *people jump in* with solutions that *don't feel good to you*") are the main ways client-centered therapists capture their clients' feeling experiences and what is happening to or impacting their clients. In both Rogers' sample and my sample, 85% of the therapists' natural interaction units contain at least one word-for-feeling or at least one word or phrase alluding to feelings and/or at least one figure of speech. When I combined these salient means for expressing our understanding of clients' feelings, I found us identical in our frequency of responding to clients with affective elements in our empathic responses.

### Responses without affective features
Rogers and I both produced 15% of our empathic understanding responses devoid of affective features, e.g., "It's what follows from earlier choices ...." Instead, these responses include elements of the client's wants or interests, or are statements of facts or information, or statements that express conceptual, rational or other cognitive experiences. These affectless responses were confirmed by our clients as accurate understandings of them.

### Responses representing the client as a proactive or reactive actor or agent
One class of words that represent the client as an agent, not as passive or unreactive, are words with the base "want." For example, "You want her to get out of your life...." Nine percent of Rogers' responses included statements using the term "want" words and 8% of my responses included "want."

Clients' remarks such as "I am trying ..." also express the agency and intention of the speaker. Four percent of Rogers' responses include statements including "try" words, and 2% of my responses include such words, as in "You try and try, but nothing happens ...." Adding frequencies of "want" and "try" together, 13% of Rogers' responses and 10% of mine include either of these words.

### Sentence units expressing the client's agency
Most of the clients' statements to Rogers and to me indicate our clients are active agents, either proactive or reactive. For example, "*It feels* oftentimes that *it's just too much for me. Then I build up notions ... I mix it up* ...."

Correspondingly, empathic responses by both Rogers and by me express the quality of our clients' agency. Ninety-three percent of the empathic sentence units in the Rogers sample, and 92% in mine, contain expressions of our clients as agent or actor, either proactive or reactive.

## Agency to the external and agency to the internal

Clients' narratives may be about their reactions (their agency) in relation to something or someone outside themselves, e.g., "I want to get him to stop doing that," or in relation to something within their inner experience, "I feel deeply vulnerable and hurt." Empathic responses in both therapists correspond to these directions in our clients' narratives. Empathic understanding responses may be about a client's feelings, thoughts or reactions in relation to something or someone outside of self ("You were feeling ignored by your father"), or in relation to something within their inner experience ("Those sensations give you a whole other level of stress").

Comparison of Rogers' responses and my responses reveal similar frequencies. Thirty-nine percent of Rogers' empathic understanding responses express clients' agency in relation to inner experiences and 34% of my empathic understanding responses express the same thing. Similarly 61% of Rogers' empathic understanding responses express clients' agency in relation to outer experiences, and 65% of my empathic understanding responses express the same thing. In both therapists our clients confirmed our accuracy in empathically understanding them. It appears that both sets of clients are expressing more about their thoughts, feelings and reactions to persons and situations outside of themselves (two-thirds of the time), than to their internal, subjective world (one-third of the time).

### EVIDENCE THAT MY THERAPY DIFFERS SLIGHTLY FROM ROGERS'

**Empathic responses including the words "feel," "feeling," "feels," "felt"**
"Feel" words, e.g., "You feel it's a mystery to you ..." and "It feels it was clear..." occur in 37% of Rogers' empathic responses and in only 26% of mine. This 11% difference is consistent with the fact that I consciously tend to avoid using these words to describe my client's experiences if the client's object has to do with thinking, believing, imagining or other cognitive activities. This is because I think it is more accurate and because I think the nondirective attitude precludes me from systematically directing my client's attention to inferential subjective feelings. I prefer to use the words that explicitly describe the client's mental activity, rather than point to feelings.

My difference from Rogers in this matter shows up in our frequencies of combining "feel" words with cognitive words within an empathic response.

Forty-eight percent of Rogers' responses that contain "feel" words also include specific words for cognitive experiences. In contrast, only 4% of my responses that contain "feel" words also contain specific words for cognitive experiences, a difference of 44%.

### First-person empathic responses
At times, Rogers and I both use the first person "I" when representing our clients in empathic responses, e.g., "I need maturity to live with that fear within myself." It is an immediate or dramatic way to express an empathic response, expressing it exactly as we think the client would express it, given what the client has expressed immediately prior to our response. Rogers, however, uses the first-person form more frequently than I do. Rogers expressed the form in 29% of his empathic responses, while I expressed it in only 14% of my empathic responses, a difference of 15%.

### Words or phrases alluding to feelings
Although Rogers and I use words for feelings with almost the same frequency – Rogers in 30% of empathic understanding responses and I in 31% of empathic understanding responses – we differ in our use of words or phrases alluding to feelings, "unsafe," "confused," "intimate." I use words or phrases that allude to feelings in 59% of my empathic understanding responses and Rogers uses them in 45% of his empathic understanding responses, a difference of 14%. Despite our similarity in making empathic understanding responses with words for feelings, this difference in making words or phrases *alluding to feelings* in our empathic understanding responses suggests I perceive my clients as communicating their feeling experiences more frequently than does Rogers.

### Specific words for cognitive processes
Rogers expressed more words for cognitive processes, such as "think," "consider," "implies," than I did in empathic responses. Rogers expresses such words in 35% of his empathic understanding responses and I express them in 28% of mine. It is a small difference that could reflect a difference in frequency of these kinds of experiences in our clients.

### Self-representations as expressions of tentativeness
Rogers and I both express our tentativeness in empathic understanding by including brief statements from our own frames of reference, before, within, or at the end of empathic understanding responses. For example, "I don't know if I get this right, but it seems …." Rogers explicitly expresses his tentativeness in 20% of his empathic responses, whereas I explicitly express tentativeness in 9%

of mine, a difference of 11%. Such explicit expressions of uncertainty, of course, are not strategy. Nevertheless, there may be a serendipitous effect on our clients, giving them a sense that we are personal in our participation, by owning and acknowledging our imperfections in understanding.

## CHARACTERISTICS OF CHICAGO CLIENT-CENTERED THERAPY

My "Chicago client-centered therapy" is based on Rogers' (1957) three therapeutic conditions experienced by the therapist. I believe these conditions can be viewed as his basic instructions for the therapist. These "instructions" are expressed as experiences, not in terms of any behavior. The sixth condition states the client must perceive or experience the therapist's attitudes of unconditional positive regard and empathic understanding of the client's internal frame of reference for therapeutic change to occur. This condition implies that the therapist must be communicating or expressing the three therapist conditions. The manner of the therapist's communication is open to the therapist and the client situation he is encountering within limits that follow from the nondirective principle.

Chicago client-centered therapy as a practice can be described more specifically by explaining certain features of 18 categories of theory or behavior: empathic understanding, congruence, unconditional positive regard, the relationship, responses from the therapist's frame of reference (T-frame responses), responses to clients' questions and requests to the therapist, the therapist's spontaneous comments from his or her own frame of reference, the rationales for therapists' self-disclosures, socializing behavior, touching the client, psychotropic medications, diagnoses, arrangements with clients, the nondirective attitude, the therapist's goals, the mechanisms of therapeutic change, the therapy's benefits, and the irrelevance of theories of personality or process in client-centered therapy practice.

### Empathic understanding of the client's internal frame of reference
Empathic in this approach, as in Rogers', refers to an attitude. It means being focused on the other person, attuned to nonjudgmentally appreciating the inner experiences of other persons. Empathic understanding refers to a combination of cognitive and affective symbolizations (subjective or expressed) of another person's inner experiences. "[O]f the client's internal frame of reference" refers to the primary target (Zimring, 2000) of a therapist's attention as he or she listens to the many things a client may express.

Rogers (1959) describes the "internal frame of reference" as the "emotional components and meanings … and the causes thereof" (pp. 210–211), not only "feelings." In fact Bradburn's (1996) research on a sample of

25 of Rogers' therapy transcripts has shown that Rogers *did not express any affective features* in 24% of his following responses to his clients. Other studies have shown that words for feelings occur only in approximately 25% of Rogers' empathic responses (Brody, 1991; Brodley 1994/2011, 1996/2011; Merry, 1996; Nelson, 1994). Both statistics support the fact that Rogers was not responding *only* to his clients' feelings.

Therefore, following Rogers' approach, clients' feelings are only part of what I attend to in trying to understand. I am trying to understand the client as an agent or actor, as an active and reactive person, and as a source of meanings, feelings, reactions and other experiences about his or her self or about the external world. I feel I don't *empathically* understand a client until I am able to grasp the client's personal reactions to what he or she is talking about. Understanding the information they produce is not enough for success in *empathic* understanding.

I most often (in approximately 90% of my responses) empathically follow by making empathic understanding responses, when I respond to self-narrating clients. Empathic responses are usually verbal, but they may be vocal gestures or expressive behaviors. When they are deliberate verbal responses, they usually represent my attempt to check the accuracy of my inner understandings directly with the client about what the client has been immediately expressing or narrating, or *apparently intending* to express (Rogers, 1986; Brodley, 1998/2011).

I express empathic responses without having any goal to influence the client to explore any specific topics, or to explore in any specific manner, but I do hope that at least some of my responses stimulate the client to implicitly or explicitly confirm, deny or modify my understandings in the immediate interactive situation. This is so I can know how well I am understanding the client.

Although I am not intending to influence the client in regard to his or her narrative content or processes of self-reflection, empathic responses do tend to influence the client to reflect upon what he or she has been expressing. Empathic understanding in my approach is not aimed to stimulate feelings or "focusing" (in Gendlin's sense), although it may have that effect on clients. The specific effects of empathic understandings are not predictable, although their frequent effect on clients is to stimulate them to continue to narrate (Brodley, 1991/2008).

## Congruence

"Congruence" refers to the wholeness and integrated condition of the therapist and the ability of the therapist to be accurately aware of his or her feelings, thoughts and other subjective experiences. It also refers to *the ability* of the therapist to be honest in all his or her verbal and expressive behavior. This does not mean "congruence" is a rationale or justification for any of my explicit therapist self-representations. I think "congruence" never refers to the behavior itself – the words. Congruence refers to the accuracy of the words in representing subjective experiences – the congruence of words with their subjective symbolization – their honesty.

Communications may be congruent (i.e., accurate or honest) communications. I believe that a therapist's congruence, however, is not a reason, or an occasion, for communication nor is it the communication itself. I cannot justify speaking from my own frame of reference in order to "be congruent."

Congruence is basically a person's capacity for accurate awareness of inner experiences and the personally integrative effect of this subjective accuracy. It is also what produces the appearance of transparency, although self-disclosures may also contribute to this appearance. Whether I choose to communicate from my own frame of reference must depend upon other reasons or justifications or be left as without reason or justification.

## Unconditional positive regard

I tend to substitute the word "acceptance" for Rogers' term "unconditional positive regard." In either case it is an attitude toward a client as a person inherently deserving of respect and understanding. It involves warmth towards the person regardless of what my personal judgment outside of the therapy situation about the client's behavior, feelings or ideas might be.

I think warm acceptance towards clients is probably the crucial and most ubiquitous aspect of effective psychotherapy. I think my warm acceptance is expressed in my tone of voice, my intonation, my manner and overall presence, and by things I do not think or say. As best I can recall, never by explicitly reassuring my client.

## The relationship

The relationship refers to a client-centered manner of interaction between me and my client and the emotional effects of the qualities of the interaction in the client and in me, granted our different perspectives on our interaction. Within the interview, the relationship, defined by Rogers' therapeutic conditions, facilitates the client's courage to face pain and anxiety, to extend his or her intelligence as a tool for solving problems, and ultimately generates compassion towards self. Between sessions the relationship is a mentally enduring context for clients as they take steps to express their changing sense of self and others.

## Responses from the therapist's frame of reference

I rarely make responses from my frame of reference (therapist-frame) that I intend to direct the client or influence his or her behavior, feelings or ideas. I maintain my nondirective attitude when I make a response from my own frame of reference. In an earlier paper I have discussed the reasons for therapist-frame statements in nondirective client-centered therapy (Brodley, 1999a/2011). The situations where I think therapist-frame statements may occur in client-centered therapy are: (1) arrangements and terms of the therapy; (2) addressing questions and requests; (3) appearance of the possibility of a question; (4) empathic observations; (5) corrections for loss of acceptance or loss of empathy, or for incongruence; (6) spontaneous insights and ideas; (7) emotionally compelling circumstances; (8) prior information; (9) spontaneous agreements; (10) evaluative reactions; (11) impulses to exteriorize; (12) correcting misunderstandings; and (13) the view that the therapist is responsible as a potential source of information concerning clients' well-being. I believe the art of therapist-frame remarks in client-centered therapy should be fundamentally affected by the nondirective attitude, which I'll discuss below.

## Responses to clients' questions and requests

I systematically treat clients' questions and requests as expressions of clients' self-determination and self-direction. I believe this is consistent with Rogers' practice, as a study by Kemp (2004) has demonstrated. Her analysis of 129 of Rogers' transcripts revealed his most frequent responses to his clients' questions were direct answers, sometimes followed by empathic understanding responses. Rogers directly answered 89% of his clients' questions that asked for his opinion, evaluation or perspective. Treating clients' questions and requests as expressions of their self-determination I address them directly, whether by answering the client or otherwise addressing the client from my own frame of reference, and often, as well, responding empathically.

I think the socially structured and conditioned power differential between my clients and me is inevitable, although clients differ in their perceptions of the extent of the difference in power. Clients' vulnerabilities from their self-defined subjective feelings of "subordinate" or "inferior" also augment our power differential. For both reasons, I try to avoid contributing to the client's experience of subordination in the relationship. Thus I tend to avoid responding only empathically which appears to ignore or dismiss questions or requests as such. I see addressing or answering clients' questions and requests as an expression of nondirectiveness, and as an expression of the value of personal equality in client-centered therapy.

Depending upon what I say, and my way of addressing specific questions and requests, I do risk – more or less – suggesting to the client that I feel only a conditional acceptance. Thus, sometimes my comments may appear to be contradicting or undermining the client-centered basic intentions of providing acceptant empathic understanding.

Taking therapy time for therapist-frame remarks also takes time from the client's self-determined narration. Therapists' remarks may unintentionally stimulate a client to take a different narrative path than otherwise. I weigh these concerns in addressing clients' questions from my frame of reference against the risk of inhibiting the client's sense of freedom and autonomy in the relationship. My experience with the particular client and my accumulated sense of the client's ability to accurately understand me influence my manner of responding. In any case, I feel confident about the constancy of my acceptance towards clients and my ability to correct for misunderstandings. Consequently, I am more concerned about giving the impression that I am curtailing clients' self-determination by avoiding answering questions than concerned that the client may misunderstand and feel conditional acceptance.

## Therapists' spontaneous comments

The frequency with which "Chicago" client-centered therapists make spontaneous comments such as self-disclosures, comments about the client, emotional reactions about the client, explanatory or interpretive remarks about the client, agreements or disagreements with the client, or suggestions has not been studied. But it is likely to vary from therapist to therapist. I think such therapist-frame responses by client-centered therapists are usually infrequent and unsystematic (Raskin, 1988).

When they occur, I think they should not be rationalized. There is no way to predict their impact on the individual client, so I think it should simply be admitted that they happen – for good or ill of the client. Certainly they are not intended to hurt the client although they may have that effect.

I know that I spontaneously communicate from my own frame of reference – represent myself – more frequently with some clients than others. This variation is primarily because clients vary in their explicit wish for my point of view or feelings independent of specific requests. Some of my clients make a request that I express my ideas or personal reactions freely with them. In these cases I make such responses more frequently than with clients who do not request this, but still they are infrequent. Statements from my own frame of reference of all kinds in a sample of responses to sessions with 20 of my clients ranged from 0% to 15%.

I think all responses from the therapist's frame, in varying degrees, risk distracting the client from his or her own path, as well as by having a directive effect on the client's narrative, or undermining the client's sense of safety in the relationship by pointing up the therapist as a person who evaluates. In contrast, empathic understanding responses pose less risk of these effects and do not imply an evaluative mentality in the therapist, although clients may assume he or she is silently judging.

I do not intend my therapist-frame responses to structure or guide the interview, although they certainly involve that risk. On rare occasions they may represent a lapse in my empathic attitude. However, I do not intend to communicate goals for my client when I spontaneously express these kinds of responses. Instead, they represent looseness in my empathic discipline. These responses may benefit the client or the relationship in some way, but they are not produced for that effect and even if the client praises them, it is difficult to know when they may have caused harm to the client or the relationship.

This license that I allow myself may include responses that confuse the client or, in contrast, be ones that the client experiences as empathic. Most therapist-frame remarks contain some knowledge of the client based on the ongoing empathic interaction. Consequently, they are not often experienced as irrelevant to the client.

I cannot honestly justify this lack of discipline in making any spontaneous utterances. I have had, however, the impression, over the years, that many clients appreciate knowing something about their therapist's thoughts and that it supports their comfort with and trust in the therapist, even though it may temporarily cause a disruption or disturbance.

I've absorbed this impression as an emotional support for my own license in regard to this type of "spontaneous" behavior. However, clients' positive reactions do not provide its justification, partly because the positive or negative impact of therapist-frame remarks is not predictable and is hard to identify.

In any case, for whatever reason at the time, if I make some remark from my own frame of reference, I subsequently maintain or restore Rogers' therapeutic attitudes in the interaction. Whether it is a temporary lapse in my nondirective attitude or a response to my client's question, or whether it appears to be having a constructive or a destructive impact on the client, I proceed by accepting and empathically understanding the client.

Ordinarily spontaneous responses do not involve a lapse in my nondirective attitude although they may sometimes involve a lapse in my empathic attitude. My aim is to maintain the nondirective attitude regardless of my immediate forms of response with the client.

## Therapist self-disclosures

Other than answering with self-disclosures in response to a client's question concerning the therapist, I have no rationale for self-disclosures. I do volunteer responses about myself sometimes, nevertheless, and I classify them as spontaneous therapist-frame responses. Sometimes making a statement about myself may function as an indirect way of expressing an empathic understanding. But like all therapist-frame responses, they risk confusing, distracting, leading, or stimulating the perception that I am evaluating, the client. On the other hand, like other therapist-frame statements, they may be appreciated by some clients as giving a welcomed small window to my inner or nontherapeutic self. I do not justify self-disclosures by this outcome, in part because their positive or negative impact can't be predicted in advance and they do risk disruptions in the relationship.

## Socializing

I do not have a personal reason for socializing with clients and I make no *a priori* assumption about clients' preference for socializing or not socializing. It is left up to the client. Some clients take the initiative to socialize entering or leaving sessions, or even within a session. When this is what the client does, I am responsive and participate, but I try to do so in a manner that is not likely to stimulate a prolongation of this type of interaction. My aim is to be receptive to the unique client but also to preserve the client's scheduled time. I try not saying things that stimulate more social conversation or raise topics that may be of interest to the client and thus inadvertently direct the material of the session. There is no guarantee that my benign intention is in fact the consequence for the client. Socializing may influence the direction of the session.

Outside of the therapy situation, when I accidentally meet a client, I engage as I would with a friendly acquaintance, introducing the client if necessary, and behave as with any acquaintance.

## Touching the client

In most instances of touching (simple touch to an arm, embracing the client, sitting with my arm around the client, etc.), my clients initiate the contact or specifically request it. Whether or not I touch the client, even if requested, is a matter of my ease with this client, the behavior, and my willingness to do it. I do not view touching as categorically inappropriate. In fact, I have rarely refused or avoided touching.

## Psychotropic medications

I do not volunteer an opinion in response to the simple information that my client is already using psychotropic medications. When clients who are not medicated ask about taking medications I provide information or try to direct the client to other sources of information – books, the web, a better-informed colleague. If my client wants my opinion, I offer it with information about the experiences or academic sources that are the bases for the opinion.

## Diagnoses

Like most other client-centered therapists, I do not need to make diagnoses or diagnostically "conceptualize" clients in order to proceed with therapy. It is not a "treatment" but a relationship that focuses on the client's concerns. I believe client-centered therapy is highly likely to be helpful to any client who wishes to have it or even clients who "fall into it." Through our interactions in the therapy I learn to make adjustments in my manner of working with clients.

In general, people need many things to facilitate their well-being, so my clients may have other help or treatments as well as client-centered therapy. I make tentative diagnoses occasionally for one of two reasons. The client may request a diagnosis. In this case I answer or address the request honestly, acknowledging the limited extent of my expertise in diagnosis. The other reason for discussion of diagnoses comes up when the client discusses or manifests a problem that I think may be helped by some other type of helper or service and I choose to discuss the possibility of a referral with the client. In this latter situation, if the client accepts the suggestion, he or she usually remains in therapy while pursuing the other kind of help.

## Arrangements with clients

Arrangements refer to frequency, times, length of sessions, location of sessions, taping, telephone sessions, extra sessions, changes in arrangements, payments, vacations, etc. I negotiate these practical matters with clients but obviously options are always limited by factors determined by both persons. The client, or the client's situation, determines the duration and the end of therapy.

I do not employ the concept of "termination." I remain open to clients to return for more sessions, if they choose. Before and after therapy starts, clients usually initiate discussions about arrangements. These discussions involve sequences of empathic following and, like all other interactions, are shaped by my empathic, accepting, nondirective and congruent attitudes as well as providing information.

## The nondirective attitude

All "classical" client-centered therapists view nondirectiveness as inherent in Rogers' client-centered therapy. Although he did not make it explicit in his 1957 and 1959 theory statements, I view Rogers' descriptions of the three therapist-offered conditions as instructions for the therapist and in these instructions nondirectiveness seems self-evident. Rogers expressed his theory in a way that shows no room for any kind of directive attitude by the therapist.

There are many beneficial reasons for maintaining the nondirective attitude in this approach (Brodley, 1997/2011; Merry & Brodley, 2002). In general terms, it protects clients' feelings of safety in the relationship, their self-determination, autonomy, and sense of self. It tends to protect the relationship from conflicts and adversarial interactions that would undermine the client's experience of the therapeutic conditions.

I think that any experience of subordination risks harm. Even when a person rationally chooses and accepts it, as from a physician or lawyer, and even when it is not abusive, being a subordinate has an impact on persons that at least temporarily diminishes their sense of personal power, sense of control over themselves, and their personal value. I think these effects may not always be completely conscious, but nevertheless affect the person and his or her behavior. This makes it all the more important, in the context of therapy, to not contribute to clients' feelings of inferiority or weakness by imposing directive behaviors that risk undermining clients' good feelings about themselves.

My nondirective attitude almost always shapes all the ways I behave and communicate with my clients. My behavior within a therapy relationship is usually very different than the "same" behavior outside that relationship because I often have goals for others in my outside relationships.

### The therapist's goals

I make a distinction between my generic goals and my immediate goals as a therapist. I think there are certain goals involved in choosing to engage in therapeutic work, and other goals that are directly and immediately experienced in relationship and interaction with the client. My goals or aims for engaging in therapeutic work include the general goal of contributing to the well-being of clients, especially when they are undergoing disturbing experiences. That goal is part of my experiential context, although not a conscious concern, while doing therapy. My immediate goals in the therapy interaction, however, are not goals for clients but goals for myself in relation to the client – specifically to experience empathic understanding, unconditional positive regard, personal congruence, and to feel a freedom from goals for the client (see Rogers in Baldwin, 1987/2004). I have no goals for my clients and I avoid adopting my clients' goals for myself. I want to remain open to my clients' changes.

### The mechanisms of change

If there is any general mechanism for therapeutic change in my therapy, it is the person's inherent actualizing tendency (Rogers, 1980; Brodley, 1999b/ 2011) and the person's unique capacities. The actualizing tendency takes many different, unpredictable, paths within the individual who experiences the safety, understanding and acceptance of the client-centered relationship.

In any given individual the mechanisms of change may involve insights, making historical connections, increasing openness and self-awareness, emotional experiences, physical activity, artistic activity, sexual experiences, religious experiences, relationships, altruistic experiences, educational experiences, other social experiences or other experiences than these mentioned. I don't observe that there is only a single mechanism in the changes in client-centered therapy but many different processes, even in the same client. Whatever mechanisms of change occur with particular clients, I believe they should not become a focus of my efforts with the client.

## The benefits of the therapy
Clients have told me about, and I have observed, hundreds of benefits, hundreds of changes in my clients. In general terms, Rogers' descriptions of the variables and processes of clients moving towards functioning more fully (Rogers, 1961) says it for me.

## The irrelevance of theories of personality or process in client-centered therapy practice
Rogers' and other theorists' explanations of personality development, of the genesis of psychological disturbance, or their theories of processes in psychological change are *all irrelevant* to the practice of client-centered therapy. For example, even taking Rogers' own theories of the process of change in client-centered therapy (Rogers, 1959, 1961) as instructions for what the therapist should focus on undermines the nondirective essence of client-centered therapy.

Gendlin made this mistake when he developed the theory of experiencing and elevated it to a fundamental directive feature of his "experiential therapy" (that became his "focusing therapy") that he originally thought was an improvement on client-centered therapy rather than a fundamental departure. Client-centered therapy may have many different under-theories that in other approaches would alter the practice of therapy. It is a more accurate grasp of client-centered therapy to keep in mind that taking theories of personality, etc., as instructions for the therapy does not apply.

CLIENTS' PERCEPTIONS OF MY PERSONALITY WHILE DOING THERAPY

My years of practicing have influenced my behavior outside of therapy partly because I think the values of client-centered therapy are applicable in non-therapy situations. Granted, differences in the goals of "outside therapy" situations draw on personal qualities and behaviors that are not appropriate in therapy. Nevertheless, I think I became more likely to express empathy, acceptance, and transparency outside therapy, since I began to adopt the philosophy of persons that Rogers (1951) wrote about.

I feel certain that my personality and my communicated presence while doing therapy show qualities that I believe I show at times outside of therapeutic relationships. However, I also know that outside of therapy, I show, at times, other personal qualities that never appear in my relations with clients. I speculate that this is true of other therapists, in general, regardless of approach because the task of therapy is narrower than the tasks of living one's life.

To get information about the perceptions clients have of me when I am doing psychotherapy, I have conducted two small studies to assess some of my clients' perceptions. The first one (Brodley, 2000b/2011) asked eight clients for words to describe my presence while doing therapy. A second one* asked 25 former clients I worked with as much as 40 years ago and a few as recently as two years ago for word, phrase, or sentence descriptions of my personality or personal qualities while doing therapy.

From the first study, in response to my request to eight clients for words describing my presence I received 45 responses. Twenty-six of the responses appeared to relate to the basic concepts of Rogers' theory: congruence, unconditional positive regard, empathic understanding of the client's internal frame of reference, and nondirectiveness. Eight other words described me as showing consistency or reliability, and 10 responses expressed other personal qualities. All responses suggested positive or desirable qualities in a therapist.

The second study received responses from 25 former clients who were asked, by email, for words, phrases, or sentences that they felt described my personality while doing therapy with them. Forty percent of the 150 words were the words: "warm," "accepting," "interested," "calm," "caring," "respectful," "consistent," "genuine," and "open." The word "warm" was mentioned most frequently, by 12 clients.

Forty-nine words were mentioned by more than one client. According to categories I made out of the words: 22 words communicate understanding or empathy; 41 words communicate congruence, integration, or authenticity; 28 words communicate acceptance, warmth, or unconditional positive regard; 20 words suggest nondirectiveness; 10 words suggest cognitive qualities; and additional words suggest miscellaneous other qualities. All of the words or phrases mentioned by my former clients appear to refer to positive, desirable qualities in a therapist.

As mentioned above, I have other qualities that show up sometimes outside of therapy relationships but never in them. Some of these that I have

---

* Editors' note: Although this study was undertaken, its results have not previously been published.

observed in myself are "mean," "aggressive," "selfish," "judgmental," "cold," "resentful," "jealous," "defensive" and "unhappy." I think all of the words mentioned by clients to describe my presence or personality when doing therapy are also more or less true of me, at times, outside of therapy. But along with these positive qualities that I show in my life, I expose negative personal qualities outside of therapy – ones that could hurt my clients if I displayed them. Fortunately my negative potentials don't get stimulated when I am engaged in client-centered therapy.

I think the responses from my clients, in both surveys, suggest that I am successfully communicating Rogers' therapeutic attitudes and other qualities that contribute to my therapeutic impact. Granted my clients may have omitted some unflattering words that would have been mentioned if the survey had been "blind," but it seems to me that it is a simple, easy-to-do, survey method that might be useful to other therapists to assess their personal impact on their clients.

## SUMMARY DESCRIPTION OF MY THERAPY

I take some general information from clients, which I explain is for research I plan to do about my therapy in the long run. I have been doing this since starting my private practice 39 years ago. I ask for very basic information about age, marital status, place of birth, some details about family members, client's education and work history. I make it clear to my client that this information is for future research and request that the client give it to me for my sake, that I don't need it for the therapy.

It is information which I don't feel I need in order to work with the person. When working in clinical settings I did not need and often never read diagnostic or history information before working with a patient/client.

After requesting the information, before my new client starts to talk about him- or herself, and after I have volunteered any information that hasn't been covered in our telephone contact, I ask if my client has any questions of any kind to ask me now. After that interaction, I tell my client that I would like them to feel they are free to ask me any kind of question at any time in our sessions. I tell them I am open to questions in hopes of breaking a common "set" that clients expect they are to solve their own problems and not ask for answers from their therapist.

I have called my therapy "the plain style" to myself and students for many years because it is superficially simple – I don't have any goals for my clients so I am mostly *following* with empathic understanding in my encounters with self-narrating clients. I think I tend to err, particularly in an early interview when I am beginning to tune in to my client, in the direction of being over-detailed and taking too much time in making my empathic responses. However, I adapt the qualities of my speech to my individual client as we go along, wanting to be accurately understood by them as much as possible.

I think all understanding of speech, expressive behavior, or writing involves interpretive mental processes. All empathic responses involve this sense of interpretation. Even if an empathic response is a literal repetition of the client's words, the interpretive element is revealed in the way the therapist expresses the words. I am similar to Rogers in the way I use my own language and my own figures of speech in expressing my empathic understandings.

My aim in making empathic responses is only to check my understanding, unless my client has asked for a repetition of what he or she has said. I am not listening for the client's edge of awareness. I would consider that a directive intention and I don't want to have goals for my clients. If my empathic understanding is revealed to be "at the edge," that is simply a result of my constant attentive listening, my ability to understand implied meanings, and the client's openness at the moment.

In empathic understanding I don't aim particularly to understand my client's feelings or to evoke emotional or feeling experiences in my clients. These things happen spontaneously, or serendipitously. My empathic understanding is based on my idea that true empathic understanding is based particularly on understanding the relation to the client of what the client is talking about. This results in understanding the client from the client's point of view as a source of perceptions, feelings, wants, efforts and other active and reactive experiences. To be empathic requires attunement to the personal meanings, feelings, and whatever else expresses the client's agency in any way.

If clients are not talkative, I feel acceptance towards them and relaxed comfort. When clients are silent, I speak, in some cases, but only to determine whether my stance of silent attention is acceptable to the client.

I am accommodating to clients' questions and requests, taking care to express myself in a manner that is unlikely to stimulate conditions of worth, threat, or a sense of being challenged in my clients. I do not intend to be challenging, having no goals for clients and thus no basis for such behavior.

I don't want to contribute to any adversarial qualities in my therapy relationships. I am very open to requests for self-disclosures and I never challenge a client's interest in personal information about me.

I am not jealous or threatened if my client wishes to see another type of helper and some of my clients do have appointments with others while working with me. I am also open to working with clients who are also seeing another psychotherapist, although other therapists, outside the person-centered community, tend to reject that arrangement. Some of my clients initiate homework of various kinds, and discuss it in therapy although I do not take on the client's goals of the homework and do not monitor it (Brodley, 2006b).

I tend to be open, animated and expressive as a therapist. I talk with my hands, use a lot of figures of speech, often swear (unless I learn a client is disturbed by swearing) and I have been told that my eyes are very communicative in therapy. Although my work is primarily disciplined, I am not so disciplined that I can't behave in a surprising or unjustifiable manner at times. I want to continue to express the license I do, unless I see evidence that I am doing harm to my client's sense of safety or being understood. When in the relationship with a client I feel free, spontaneous and very happy.

CONCLUSION

It is outside the purview of this paper to discuss the extent that my "Chicago client-centered therapy" is practiced by other therapists. I am pretty sure it is practiced the same way by many other therapists, especially some of my students, given inevitable differences due to personalities. I hope it is clear that the therapy I practice is very adaptable to clients, and that the practice of Rogers' therapeutic conditions and the nondirective attitude is a matter of art, not rules.

REFERENCES

Baldwin, M. (1987). Interview with Carl Rogers on the use of the self in therapy. In M. Baldwin & V. Satir (Eds.), *The use of the self in therapy* (pp. 45–52). New York: Haworth Press. [Reprinted (2004) in R. Moodley, C. Lago, & A. Talahite (Eds.), *Carl Rogers counsels a Black client: Race and culture in person-centred counseling* (pp. 253–260). Ross-on-Wye: PCCS Books]

Bradburn, W. M. (1996). *Did Carl Rogers' positive view of human nature bias his psychotherapy? An empirical investigation.* Unpublished doctoral clinical research project. Illinois School of Professional Psychology, Chicago (now Argosy University, Chicago).

Brodley, B. T. (1990). Client-centered and experiential: Two different therapies. In G. Lietaer, J. Rombauts, & R. Van Balen (Eds.), *Client-centered and experiential psychotherapy in the nineties* (pp. 87–107). Leuven, Belgium: Leuven University Press. [This volume, Chapter 23]

Brodley, B. T. (1991, May). The role of focusing in client-centered therapy. Unpublished paper. Presentation for a dialog with A. Weiser Cornell at the annual meeting of the Association for the Development of the Person-Centered Approach in Coffeyville, Kansas, May 23–27. Slightly revised in French version (2008) Rôle du focusing dans la thérapie centrée sur la personne. (F. Ducroux-Biass, Trans., F. Ducroux-Biass & K. Moon, Eds.), *Approche Centrée sur la Personne: Pratique et recherché, 7,* 79–91.

Brodley, B. T. (1994). Some observations of Carl Rogers' behavior in therapy interviews. *The Person-Centered Journal, 1*(2), 37–48. [This volume, Chapter 25]

Brodley, B. T. (1996). Empathic understanding and feelings in client-centered therapy. *The Person-Centered Journal, 3*(1), 22–30. [This volume, Chapter 8]

Brodley, B. T. (1997). The nondirective attitude in client-centered therapy. *The Person-Centered Journal, 4*(1), 18–30. [This volume, Chapter 5]

Brodley, B. T. (1998). Criteria for making empathic responses in client-centered therapy. *The Person-Centered Journal, 5*(1), 20–28. [This volume, Chapter 14]

Brodley, B. T. (1999a). Reasons for responses expressing the therapist's frame of reference in client-centered therapy. *The Person-Centered Journal, 6*(1), 4–27. [This volume, Chapter 15]

Brodley, B. T. (1999b). The actualizing tendency concept in client-centered theory. *The Person-Centered Journal, 6*(2), 108–120. [This volume, Chapter 11]

Brodley, B. T. (2000a). Client-centered: An expressive therapy. In J. E. Marques-Teixeira & S. Antunes (Ed.), *Client-centered and experiential psychotherapy* (pp. 133–147). Linda a Velha, Lisboa, Portugal: Vale & Vale. [Reprinted (2002) in *The Person-Centered Journal 9*(1), 59–70; this volume, Chapter 13]

Brodley, B. T. (2000b). Personal presence in client-centered therapy. *The Person-Centered Journal, 7*(2), 139–149. [This volume, Chapter 10]

Brodley, B. T. (2002). Observations of empathic understanding in two client-centered therapists. In J. C. Watson, R. N. Goldman, & M. S. Warner (Eds.), *Client-centered and experiential psychotherapy in the 21st century: Advances in theory, research and practice* (pp. 182–203). Ross-on-Wye: PCCS Books. [This volume, Chapter 26]

Brodley, B. T. (2006a). Non-directivity in client-centered therapy. *Person-Centered & Experiential Psychotherapies, 5*, 36–52.

Brodley, B. T. (2006b). Client-initiated homework in client-centered therapy. *Journal of Psychotherapy Integration, 16*(2), 140–161.

Brodley, B. T., & Brody, A. F. (1990, August). *Understanding client-centered therapy through interviews conducted by Carl Rogers.* Unpublished paper presented at the annual conference of the American Psychological Association, Boston.

Brody, A. F. (1991). *Understanding client-centered therapy through interviews conducted by Carl Rogers.* Unpublished doctoral clinical research project. Illinois School of Professional Psychology, Chicago (now Argosy University, Chicago).

Diss, J. W. (1996). *Facilitative responses leading to client process disruption in Carl Rogers' therapy behavior.* Unpublished doctoral clinical research project. Illinois School of Professional Psychology, Chicago (now Argosy University, Chicago).

Gendlin, E. T. (1969). Focusing. *Psychotherapy: Theory, Research and Practice. 6*, 4–15.

Gendlin, E. T. (1974). Client-centered and experiential psychotherapy. In D. A. Wexler & L. N. Rice (Eds.), *Innovations in client-centered therapy* (pp. 211–246). New York: Wiley.

Gendlin, E. T. (1981). *Focusing* (2nd ed.). New York: Bantam Books.

Greenberg, L. S., Rice, L. N., & Elliott, R. (1993). *Facilitating emotional change: The moment-by-moment process.* New York: Guilford Press.

Kemp, C. M. (2004). *Responses to clients' questions in client-centered therapy.* Unpublished doctoral clinical research project. Chicago School of Professional Psychology.

Merry, T. (1996). An analysis of ten demonstration interviews by Carl Rogers: Implications for the training of client-centered counselors. In R. Hutterer, G. Pawlowsky, P. F. Schmid, & R. Stipsits (Eds.), *Client-centered and experiential therapy: A paradigm in motion* (pp. 273–284). Frankfurt am Main: Peter Lang.

Merry, T., & Brodley, B. T. (2002). The nondirective attitude in client-centered therapy. *Journal of Humanistic Psychology, 42,* 66–77.

Nelson, J. A. (1994). *Carl Rogers' verbal behavior in therapy: A comparison of theory and therapeutic practice.* Unpublished doctoral clinical research project. Illinois School of Professional Psychology, Chicago (now Argosy University, Chicago).

Propst, B. S. [Brodley] (1966). Client-centered psychotherapy as a complex task. University of Chicago. Counseling Center. *Discussion Papers, 12(9).*

Raskin, N. J. (1988). Responses to person-centered vs. client-centered: *Renaissance, 5*(3&4), 2–3.

Rogers, C. R. (1942). *Counseling and psychotherapy.* Boston: Houghton Mifflin.

Rogers, C. R. (1951). *Client-centered therapy.* Boston: Houghton Mifflin.

Rogers, C. R. (1957). The necessary and sufficient conditions for therapeutic personality change. *Journal of Consulting Psychology, 21,* 95–103.

Rogers, C. R. (1959). A theory of therapy, personality and interpersonal relationships, as developed in the client-centered framework. In S. Koch (Ed.), *Psychology: A study of a science. Vol. III: Formulations of the person and the social context* (pp. 184–256). New York: McGraw-Hill.

Rogers, C. R. (1961). *On becoming a person.* Boston: Houghton Mifflin.

Rogers, C. R. (1980). *A way of being.* Boston: Houghton Mifflin.

Rogers, C. R. (1986). Reflection of feelings. *Person-Centered Review, 1*(4), 375–377.

Temaner, B. [Brodley] (1977). The empathic understanding response process. Chicago Counseling and Psychotherapy Center. *Chicago Counseling Center Discussion Paper.* [This volume, Chapter 12]

Zimring, F. (2000). Empathic understanding grows the person. *The Person-Centered Journal, 7*(2), 101–113.

# Chapter 3

## Why are there so few client-centered therapists when so many people around the world acknowledge Carl Rogers' influence?

I think there are two main reasons. First, client-centered theory has been misunderstood and is perceived as too limited to be able to meet the full range of experiences and situations encountered with clients. This perception is largely the consequence of client-centered therapy being identified as "making reflections," "making listening responses," or "making empathic responses." The misunderstanding is that client-centered therapy is a technique or the application of a technique. Of course, any technique is limited in what it can accomplish.

Client-centered therapy is rarely understood as a way of working with clients that is distinguished by the therapist's striving consistently to live out the Rogerian values of respect for and trust in persons and the therapeutic attitudes. The misunderstanding exists despite Rogers' exquisite clarity on this matter in his writings and lectures.

An important factor in the misunderstanding of client-centered therapy as a technique lies in the nature of the illustrations of the therapy that have been used by Rogers and others. Most of the illustrations of the therapy which have been offered (including live demonstrations, films, audiotapes, excerpts of sessions transcribed and used in articles) have consisted almost totally of the empathic understanding response process. This process, of course, is the one client-centered therapists engage in with their clients as a natural and optimal realization of the therapeutic attitudes that provide the interpersonal conditions for the client's change and growth. Therefore the empathic understanding process should have been illustrated as often as it has been. But there have been few illustrations of client-centered work that show other forms of response, such as answering questions or therapist self-disclosures. There have been even fewer illustrations of responses that give explanations or interpretations or advice to the client, or of the multitude of

From the Roundtable Discussion: Why do you think there are so few person-centered practitioners or scholars considering that literally thousands of persons throughout the world attest to the enormous impact Carl Rogers has had on their personal and professional lives? Published (1988) in *Person-Centered Review*, 3(3), 353–390. Reproduced with permission.

other responses that can occur in reaction to clients' requests and questions and to many different states of experiencing.

The mistaken idea of client-centered therapy as "making reflections" or "doing active listening" has been taught by therapy/counselor educators for years. Since the limited illustrative material has tended to support this misunderstanding, the combination of a wider range of forms of response in illustrations (in demonstrations, tapes, and articles), along with explanations of the way in which these responses fit the theory, could help clarify the truth about client-centered therapy and show its true range.

The second main reason for there being so few client-centered practitioners is that the approach is in conflict with the beliefs and procedures advocated, taught, and enforced by the psychology, psychiatry, social work, and counseling professions. When therapists do come into contact with an accurate portrayal of client-centered therapy, it often feels to them that this approach will involve taking on too much conflict with their supervisors and colleagues. It also requires more intellectual independence, more resistance to conventional force, and more self-confidence than many therapists, especially new therapists, have achieved.

Client-centered therapy is in no way an application of a formula to a person. But the formula approach is the essence of standard psychotherapy practice and education. Client-centered therapy, in contrast, is a disciplined expression of the therapist's character. It is a disciplined living out of certain values and attitudes in a personal relationship with the client. The relationship is deliberately experienced by the therapist as a unique relationship with a unique person. Generalizations about types of persons and about types of psychological problems and categorization of techniques and interventions are intrinsic to the "treatments" advocated by the psychotherapy institutions. These conceptions and "treatments" are totally irrelevant to and actually undermine the practice of client-centered therapy.

The procedures of diagnosing a client's problem, conceptualizing what the client should feel or do to be more healthy, and the application of a strategy consisting of techniques and interventions to correct the problem to achieve the goal conceived by the therapist *is* what most therapists are doing. Although procedures are often couched in "humanistic" language and may appear related to client-centeredness, if one looks more closely at what is conceptualized and recommended, it is apparent that it is the usual diagnosis and "treatment" approach. This psycho-technological formula approach has been professionally legitimatized and therefore is the one therapists learn to believe they must do to be fully helpful and responsible to their clients.

The process of working with clients and meeting all situations that arise in a client-centered way is disciplined, independent, individualistic, and personal. It is a creative process that is usually spontaneous, although therapists often engage in considerable reflection afterwards. It also requires that therapists trust themselves much more than their teachers, "supervisors," and training institutions have ever trusted them.

Those readers who are client-centered practitioners know that the work is a profound and unique process with every client; that it involves struggling for clarity about one's own feelings; an understanding of and a commitment to Rogerian values and therapeutic attitudes in ways that are felt as well as understood cognitively. In short, what client-centered therapy *is* requires that practitioners discover for themselves what it actually is, and then prepare themselves to function in deep conflict with the standard and legitimatized approaches to therapeutic work. This is hard to do.

# THE ETHICAL FOUNDATION OF
# CLIENT-CENTERED THERAPY

# Chapter 4

# Ethics in psychotherapy

**A. In applying the concept of ethics to the psychotherapy situation, "ethics" may be defined two different ways:**

*1. Ethics defined as "conforming to professional standards of conduct. What is professionally right or fitting."*
I am not going to discuss this sense of ethics in psychotherapy, although I think persons doing counseling or psychotherapy ought to know what the relevant professions advocate or require. Personally I dislike the concept of "professional." To me it seems to lead to a lot of unethical activity. It is:

- Authoritarian
- Exclusive
- Self-justifying
- Self-protective
- Does not guarantee any real competence to carry out so-called professional functions

What is professionally right or fitting often means how to maintain an image to make the professional group attractive to the public in order that the group will get clients and money.

Also, "professional" usually implies self-regulation of the group over its members, and that seems wrong to me. I believe the consumers should have the main role in regulation.

Also, "professional" usually implies unnecessary qualifications that have nothing to do with carrying out the function well. In the case of counseling and psychotherapy, having the usual degrees assures nothing.

---

This is an outline for a January 8, 1975 presentation at the Chicago Counseling and Psychotherapy Center. Although Barbara never turned the outline into a paper, we believe it is a unique and important contribution to the discussion of ethics in psychotherapy. We have made minor edits to make it easier to read, while refraining from resolving ambiguities in what Barbara wrote.

*2. Sense of ethics that I plan to discuss here is defined as "relating to moral action; the principles of right and wrong in behavior."*

Ethics in psychotherapy has to do with the principles of right and wrong relating to the behavior of the psychotherapist as it affects a client and others through the service given the client.

**B. Ethical principles, issues of right and wrong behavior, are inherent in the therapy situation, regardless of the type of psychotherapy or theory employed. Why ethical issues are intrinsic to therapy:**

1.  As in all human relationships, harm or good can be done.

2.  Ethical questions in therapy carry special weight because structurally and inherently the relationship is not between equals. This is complicated because the need of the client for help is what defines the inequality – one is looking to the other: there is a one-way relationship and the vulnerability of the client is the basis for service. (Later I will discuss how one should try to work against this inevitable inequality.) At the same time the client is not equal to the therapist, he or she may be obviously superior to the therapist in intelligence, general competence, and even in specific areas of concern which are the basis of seeking help. An ethically difficult situation for the therapist – he is being looked up to when he knows he can't do as well as the client. A set-up for the abuse of power. The therapist has to be able to take the truth.

3.  There is an implicit contract between the client and therapist: The therapist claims to provide a service and there are expectations that follow naturally from that claim that regulate the therapist's behavior. It seems to me that *the therapist always claims to provide the service of helping, that is, to be successful in helping, or he will give an adequate and acceptable accounting for the failure to the client.* Money paid for services only underlines this obligation, but it exists even if the service is free.

4.  The specific function of the therapist is to change a person's inner and outward life. It is a very special kind of service which can involve affecting the total conduct of a person's life and have endless ramifications. Thus the therapist has a special responsibility to be effective and responsible for what he is doing. He can't legitimately say "My job is therapist, I help people," because being a therapist simply puts one in the position of being able to do a great deal of harm or good – depending. The special weight of the job shows up in the way humor is inappropriate. A gardener may say he is a lousy gardener and draw a laugh if said in the right way, but therapists simply cannot make comparable statements, (except perhaps in the idiom

of black humor which is arousing and flaunting moral outrage). The therapist can't joke about his function because we feel his special responsibilities.

Because he is affecting people's lives significantly and directly, he has the responsibility to be good, to act properly. He must be good enough to be offering himself as one who can help.

5. Regardless of whether or not the therapist likes to think so, what the therapist does and does not do influences the feelings and life of the client. The therapist identifies himself as special and is perceived as a special kind of person – one who is to be confided in, trusted, listened to in a serious way, one who has some command of an art, and wisdom. So the therapist has special power in relation to the client; this gives therapist behavior a special weight and meaning to the client. The information the therapist shares or does not share, his tone, the words he uses, the process of interaction he creates has a great impact on the client. And the therapist must accept responsibility for this power, even if he does not think it is valid or he wishes to minimize it.

## C. The ethics of Rogerian psychotherapy

Rogerian psychotherapy is an inherently ethical process, in the sense that it is a process of freeing the basic nature of the person which is conceptualized as "Good" and "Constructive." Ethicality is in this way built into the theory, and although it is not usually expressed or taught in ethical terms, what is good for the client, and what helps to make him good, is exactly what is required of the therapist to be effective (Rogers as a philosopher of interpersonal relations).

It is helpful to examine two different models of psychotherapy to see the ethical implications. The first, and most usual, is the *pathology-cure model* which permits a variety of techniques, which can be shown in themselves to be wrong, destructive, hurtful, but are justified because they exercise or rid the person of his pathology. The second model is the *Rogerian model* (because I think he first most clearly conceptualized it and carried it further than anyone else). In this model, means and ends must be ethically consistent. One cannot justify some technique because it "works" in the narrow sense if it also does harm. For example, one cannot justify showing power over a client, or being condescending, or trying to arouse anger or having a sexual relation with the client for the sake of limited helping aims.

The two models differ in three main ways: (1) The conception of the person in the world; (2) the conception of a "problem"; and (3) the conception of the causes of the trouble that leads a person to seek help.

## 1. The pathology-cure model

a. The person has a character structure that may have evolved and been shaped, but is relatively static in adulthood.

b. Problems conceived as the introduction of a pathological process, even if the seeds planted in early childhood. The pathological process may be brought out by different factors, such as situational stress, genetic factors, and physical pathology, but in any case the pathological process warps or disguises the basic character structure.

c. Therapy is usually called "treatment" and it is thought of as a process of extirpation of the pathology. This may be a lengthy process, usually because of the notion of defenses of the person to preserve the pathology. It is a "doing something to," even if relatively passive.

d. Therapy teaches a dependency on an expert for help, although sometimes conceptualizations (interpretations) are applied independently, but not creative solutions, rather further extrapolations or generalizations.

## 2. The Rogerian model (client-centered and others)

a. Conception of individual range of capabilities more or less realized at any given time. Also concept of person's optimal access to and utilization of his inner resources. Functioning is uneven, variable and highly individualed because of process of interaction with person's world. The person is an interactive unit or interactive whole, and parts and interactions affect whole.

b. Concept of the person having a basic tendency to growth, to develop himself, to develop others and an appreciation of his interdependence on his social and physical environment. Self-interest is inherently interest in others and the environment.

c. Two major causes of problems:
   i. Inadequate present personal, social, or physical environment; opinion; environmental forces that undermine capabilities or undermine processes of utilization directly, and situationally (e.g., constraining marriage, misdirected education, threatening situations, and overwork).

   ii. Environmental forces that undermine capabilities or utilization processes (thinking openly about oneself) are introjected and carried along in the person. These can be attitudes towards self, beliefs, dogma, which are handicapping and unnecessarily limiting.

d. Therapy involves movement towards optimal functioning of capabilities and utilization of inner resources, especially openness. It is an unsnarling and freeing process, a finding of the proper conditions for this particular individual.

e. Therapy teaches a process the client can carry on alone.

### 3. Ethically, different implications of two models

a. Therapist has the sense that there is much less danger of doing harm to person if one holds a relatively static concept of character. While person in process is being affected for good or bad all the time, and therapist feels that.

b. Means can justify ends in the pathology-cure model because the important thing is to get rid of the pathology. There is no pathology in Rogerian model and every means is an end in itself because it is taken in and alters the person.

c. In pathology-cure model the therapy is recognized as becoming a problem in itself, e.g., the transference, the problem of dependence on the therapist. This is not necessary, not expected and does not occur in the Rogerian model; although help may be freely sought repeatedly it is not viewed as an inappropriate dependence but as a right to use resources to help with problems that living brings.

## D. The aims of Rogerian therapy, specifically client-centered therapy

The major aim is to increase the individual's ability to be conscious of his own thoughts and feelings, to increase his experiencing which is available to awareness, (and can be sorted out; feelings become more complete; develops organizations of meaning).

A general direct effect of the major aim is to help the person to have more control over the conduct of his own life and to be able to take more responsibility for his effect on others.

Indirectly:

1. Increasing effectiveness. The person can utilize inner experiences as crucial information in processing input from environment, in understanding things, and in making decisions.

2. Increasing independence. The person increases his independence in the sense of becoming the locus of decisions affecting him and guiding the conduct of his own life.

3. Increasing interdependence. The person increases his interdependence by becoming more open to information concerning others; he has a greater

capacity for sharing with others, sensitivity to the feelings of others. In general he is less "defensive" and benefits from his openness to and experience of others.

## E. The means used by a client-centered therapist to implement aims (based entirely on conceptualization in Rogers' 1957 paper "The Necessary and Sufficient Conditions of Personality Change")

1. Therapist attempts to understand, empathically, what client is saying and feeling and communicates his understanding to the client. This process causes an opening up and development of thought and feeling in the client.

2. Therapist attempts to maintain congruence in the relationship with the client, i.e., the therapist strives to be honest with himself and with the client.

   Also, the therapist must feel acceptance, caring, even love for the client to help him, but he can't make this happen directly. In Rogers' terms the extent to which the therapist feels unconditional positive regard for the client will positively affect the client's progress, but the therapist does not have direct control over this aspect of his performance.

3. *Other things the therapist does that have to do with the set-up of therapy – with the culture, society and the individuality of the therapist.* It is necessary to come to terms with these things, as it is necessary to have a comfortable space to interact in, but these things have ethical consequence. These things have to do with the context of therapy, the real world in which it is embedded, for example the clinic, private practice, hospital, community center that allow the client and the therapist to get together. Some of these factors are anti-therapeutic; they undermine the client-centered therapy process. They become our ethical concern because they must be taken into account and, sometimes, explicitly, corrected for.

   I am going to give examples of categories of such things which I have found coming up often as a problem and concerning which I think a therapist often has to make some decision about what to do or not do. In other words, these are things the therapist has to take responsibility for.

   a. *The authoritarian status of the therapist.* Regardless of the democratic values and nonauthoritarian approach of the therapist, clients often approach the therapist with expectations which are usually valid with psychotherapists, physicians, lawyers, social workers, and others who have power over people who need some life-relevant service.

   There are some actions by the therapist which can counterweight the authoritarian image and re-educate the client, in this sense. Of course, the client-centered therapist would be gradually changing this impression simply by functioning as a client-centered therapist.

i. The therapist can make his authority concrete and specific by informing clients of his training, background as it is relevant, and about formal credentials or lack of them and his view of their relevance. Clients usually do not ask these questions; they trust their source of referral or trust the institutional setting or feel they have to, and shouldn't ask lest it be taken as a challenge.

ii. The therapist can correct the "formal" address of the client if he uses it and you do not. Do not assume the client prefers the formal designation, he may not feel he has a choice – that you might not like to be called by your first name – because it is typical of authorities such as teachers, doctors, nurses, etc., to address clients or patients by their first names and they don't want the same treatment.

iii. The therapist can make a point of admitting not understanding something, admit ignorance instead of letting certain kinds of things pass because in a way it doesn't matter that one doesn't understand them, e.g., technical concepts, things about a job, or medical problems. It is sometimes valid to say "I don't follow that, but I'm not sure I need to in order to get your point ...." The reason for being conscientious about this is that the client may assume you are following him, especially after having the experience of your understanding responses and requests for clarification on strictly personal content.

b. *The psychogenic premise.* This refers to the assumption that problems, troubling or upsetting experiences, and malfunctioning spring from the psyche of the individual and are inappropriate to the situation or exaggerated responses. I don't think the therapist should hold this premise, but rather a more open one. But, regardless of what the therapist feels about this, it is very likely that a client will assume you hold the psychogenic premise to the exclusion of other explanations, and the clients will tend to hold the viewpoint themselves. This culture has indoctrinated people, and not only well-educated ones, into the idea of things being "caused by the mind." The source of this idea is largely from psychoanalytic ideology floating around and it is extremely influential and affects the attitudes and behavior of many people the client has been exposed to while growing up. The influence is to seek explanations in early childhood experiences and more generally in a very narrow version of the psychogenic premise.

c. *Many symptoms and troublesome experiences may have other causes.* Examples of other causes that I have experienced as very important in the context of therapy that clients have not considered because of focus on psychogenesis:

i. *Pollutants* – chemicals in the environment at home or work such as the use of cleanser or other cleaning materials that make a person feel sick, headachey, itchy, like he has a chronic cold, nauseated, nervous and even anxious.

ii. *Allergies to common substances* – such as marijuana, cigarettes, prescribed or over-the-counter drugs, alcohol. Sugar and many common foods which can cause irritability, nervousness, headache, fatigue, etc.

iii. *Physical problems* – such as lack of sleep or overwork, that can cause chronic fatigue and depression; back problems that are not taken seriously but can cause headache and general tension states; lack of exercise which would be an outlet for energy and tension.

iv. *Lack of information, ignorance* – such as in sexuality, for example, not knowing how to masturbate effectively or not understanding conception.

v. *Incorrect information* – for example, women who view themselves as unresponsive sexually or as inadequate often think they should be capable of orgasm during intercourse, or they think taking sexual initiative will be legitimately unacceptable.

vi. *Inadequate or detrimental personal or institutional situations* – The objective features of a client's situation are often the cause of things he experiences as psychogenic because he is not taking their inadequacy and its natural effect on him into account. A therapist can ignore the way realities can affect people and mistakenly encourage the client to emphasize his own culpability by focusing on the psychological reasons for a problem. Examples include adultery, when betrayal and sneaking around is necessary for a sexual relation, because it almost inevitably distorts feelings. Living with a critical person, one who says he loves and respects but cannot resist finding fault. And almost all social institutions as they now exist, such as schools which put students in false and dependent positions which promote inadequate behavior, and hospitals and other medical facilities which demand helplessness, or passivity and can punish the person.

It has come gradually to me that the therapist must suggest these possibilities to the client, to check them out, if they seem relevant because of the prejudice of the psychogenic bias, and the client's assumption of that bias in the therapist.

d. *The impersonal, non-person, status of the therapist* – This is similar to the authoritarian expectation but worth talking about separately. It involves the client as seeing the therapist as "not personally involved" and therefore "not personally there" which are two different things. It involves seeing the therapist as a functionary and as operating out of rules and role rather than himself, a self that includes ways of focusing on another and being helpful. This can gradually change through functioning as a client-centered therapist – understanding, accepting, being honest – but sometimes a more direct effort on the part of the therapist is helpful. The client may be holding back from making demands, such as asking for the therapist's opinion or for sharing his relevant experiences, or just asking questions.

To alleviate this problem it sometimes helps if the therapist will volunteer his background at the beginning. I often include some personal information, which is especially relevant because clients have to pass through my house with husband, children and others there. I also offer my therapy-relevant background, to some extent, and I explicitly inform the client I am willing to tell him anything about myself or my experiences he might think is useful or even if he is curious.

4. *Within the framework of client-centered therapy essentially all other activity is ineffective, counter-therapeutic, and unethical.* In other words, the responsibility of the therapist is to be what will effect the positive change in the client, and these things are inherently good, good for the client and the therapist is "a good person" in the situation. In fact, effective client-centered therapists are "their best selves" in therapy. One can be a touchstone or model for oneself in other situations.

Aside from the particular behaviors and concerns that follow from the SITUATION of therapy referred to above in E.3 (Other things the therapist does that have to do with the set-up of therapy), *everything the therapist should be trying to do falls into the categories of* understanding and communicating understanding *and* maintaining congruence, or honesty in the situation.

Common examples of extraneous, irrelevant, and thus unethical behavior:

a. Attempting to "show off" oneself in any way, to impress the client, to point to one's accomplishments, knowledge or expertness (this can be in the "form of humble pie" – showing how humble and democratic one is) for the sake of enhancing one's self.

b. Attempting to *covertly* influence the client in any way. (Explicit attempts to influence or guide the client are sometimes helpful.) To determine an emphasis in what the client is saying, but to give the impression you *found* it in the client's words. This is very tempting and very bad practice because it *undermines the growth of the client's sense of the process of self-understanding if you deceive him into thinking he has discovered or sensed something that you have actually done. Engaging in the process of client-centered therapy teaches a process that the client can carry on alone. It is very important for the client to have an accurate representation of the process including the weights of his role and that of the therapist.*

c. Attempting to feel good at the client's expense – to try to show power over the client, to make the client feel the therapist's powers; these efforts generally emphasize, implicitly, the client's relative "inability," "lack of awareness," "lack of skill or integrative powers," his helplessness. Ways of doing this include:

- Catching the client in an inconsistency
- Reminding the client of the fact that he has talked about something before
- Making interpretive integrations out of the blue (inspirations)

Many of the things that are presented here as unethical are similar to completely valid and helpful behaviors. The difference depends largely on what the therapist is *up to* when he does it, and whether he is taking responsible care in presentation.

d. Pretense of empathy. In Rogers' theory, "empathic understanding" of the client's frame of reference and communication of this is the primary means to effect change. Rogers is clear that it is not always possible to have this with a client.

When Rogers talks about "empathic understanding" he is talking about the real thing, a *felt caring, understanding.*

*Pretense of empathy* occurs with the therapist when he feels little although he may understand, or he may actually have feelings of coldness or dislike toward the client generated by the client's statements. But the therapist feels he must sound empathic, feelingful, caring, when he just doesn't have it.

Hopefully, real empathy will be felt and communicated often in the therapy process with a client. Rogers believes the effectiveness and velocity of change in therapy will be greatly increased, the greater the proportion of empathic understanding, and my experience corresponds to that.

Practical problems in pretense of empathy:

i. Therapist is not doing what he appears to be doing – is deceiving, more or less. This is confusing to the client, undermines trust and distracts the client.

ii. Therapist is harboring feelings that undermine his own control, jamming his own processes.

iii. Therapist communicates insincerity – as a *model.*

Clients can be thought about as falling on a continuum:

From those people one cannot "accept," "abide," "tolerate," "like," and probably should not work with unless able to be completely honest with the person about the problem for the therapist in the client's presentation.

To those people whose feelings, experiences, and values are almost totally congenial and make very quick, feelingful sense to the therapist.

Most clients are more or less away from these poles. To the extent a particular client is away from the congenial pole, then much of the therapist's work is a less than empathic, more just a purely intellectual understanding, which is very helpful, if it is direct and lacking any pretense to feelings not present.

*To sum up this section,* inherent in the techniques of client-centered therapy are ethical processes. And failures to function within that framework in the senses of imposing other aims on those of understanding-communicating it and being dishonest are unethical activities.

*But*: it is important to add that one need not be a perfect therapist technically to be a good one and an effective one: there are honest and ethical errors. One can falter in understanding, lack empathy, and actually feel complicated and negative feelings, if one is honest with oneself and does not try to deceive the client.

## F. Ethical considerations that are related to the person of the therapist (as contrasted to the cultural-situation factors)

### 1. Therapist must agree with the aims of the client in respect to their ethicality

The therapist should not take on a client whose aims are felt to be immoral unless he clarifies willingness to work with the client in the hope that he will change his aims.

Aims of client can be in political, interpersonal, familial, professional, economic spheres – they must be *adequately* acceptable to the therapist. The factor of *unconditional positive regard* can only be met for clients whose values are humanist and democratic, and truth-seeking.

Choice for the therapist:

a. Tell client you cannot help to foster X aim, but you will work with him (assuming you can accept him otherwise).

b. Tell client why you can't accept him and can't work with him. Refer him (e.g., client who wants skill in manipulating self and others).

*Note*: Distinguish unethical feelings and their exploration from putting an unethical plan into effect.

Depending on nature of action (adultery vs. child-batterer) client may be carrying on certain ethically bad actions but trying to understand, change them. Therapist can see the harm but faith in client's aims (and evidence of work toward aims) allows adequate acceptance of person.

### 2. Therapist must never gossip about clients

There can be many valid uses of information taken from therapy with a client, for example, to illustrate a construct, to show how something actually occurs in current life, etc., but gossip is to titillate, amuse, and to enhance oneself "by knowing." This is a betrayal of the client, an abuse of the relationship. Client is implicitly *trusting*, although he will usually not mind your making responsible use of things about him. Gossiping has a bad effect on a therapist. He *knows* he has betrayed the client, and he has put himself into incongruence – (guilt, bad faith). Rule-of-thumb: say only what you would be comfortable for the client to overhear you say about him. An exception to this rule is when a therapist is speaking to his or her consultant.

### 3. Therapist should not hide behind the therapeutic, noncommittal, "understanding" process, in or out of the therapy situation

For example, it is common to say "You feel ..." when the person is asserting something *is* such and such a way or fact. If the assertion is unreflected upon *and* is open to question the therapist can honestly introduce his view that the client feels a certainty that is about something open to question. For example:

Client: She tries to hurt me.

Therapist: It seems to me that she may likely be trying to get reassurance and as soon as she gets it she forgets, ignores her responsibilities to you. Then she's hurting you, but not necessarily trying to. What makes you think she's trying to hurt you?

Therapist: You are stating that as if it were a certainty, while I can imagine other views – why do you state it that way, do you have other reasons than what you have mentioned?

The *understanding process,* the use of the *"reflection of feeling,"* is the most powerful tool and the most frequently used one in client-centered therapy. It must not be misused as a way of disguising or hiding opinions of the therapist. At the same time, judgment must be used about the timing of bringing out contrary feelings of therapist. For example:

Client: Talking about his feeling or guilt in a situation where the therapist feels sure others have been at fault.

Therapist: A reflection is often the best immediate type of response, a later one can bring in the contrary viewpoint – it is irrelevant at that moment.

**4. The problem of moving into a personal relationship (friend, lover) as long as the person is likely to need you as a therapist**

Clients (and therapists) are *at their best* – they are more fair-minded, more reflective, more understanding, tolerant and accepting, more accommodating and intelligent – in therapy than anywhere else.

*The client's presentation of his worst characteristics is responsible, humane, critical, undefensive, and reflective in the therapy situation. Demands upon the client by the therapist are very circumscribed.* Therapist can deceive himself into thinking this very attractive client can "hold up" in other situations, at least with him. And can deceive himself into thinking he can be as accepting and understanding in his natural habitat as he is in the more limited therapy situation. It's very unlikely that the therapist can do so because getting out of [the therapy situation] *leads to a loss of the functional equality of client and therapist built up by the therapist. The inequality reasserts itself. The client loses a good therapist and is likely to get hurt when he finds he cannot hold up his end of a relationship* (even if the therapist friend is not holding up his end either).

It is much easier and more workable to take a person you already know, love, have sex with, work with, into therapy than to go in the other direction. You both already know about the limitations of each other in the personal relationship and can find the therapist exchange an improvement for both people, as well as having effects that reverberate back into the original, ongoing relationship.

## G. Other ethical issues

*1. Attempt to create a functional relation of equality with client*
In fact, as has been discussed above, you are not equals in the situation.
Client: Feelings of helplessness, in need, feels inadequate to cope alone at least about some aspect. Self-esteem in jeopardy by seeking help.

Therapist: Feels capable of helping, feeling of strength and adequacy in the situation, at least enough to justify being there.

In taking the attitude of an equal, one utilizes expertise and knowledge for the sake of the client and without emphasizing the client's dependence. The client has a right to your help (or someone's help if not yours). His predicament is natural under life's circumstances, and all people have a right to help when they need it. And those who are fortunate enough to be trained and/or gifted enough to help have the responsibility to help.

### 2. Attend to the effects of the client's behavior on others, particularly where you are having an effect on that behavior

Attention to impact on children, spouse, parents, friends. Try to find a way to help client to be responsible towards them, as he changes relationship. Often therapist is helping client to free himself from burdensome entanglements and obligations, but therapist has to be alert to, and speak to, victimization of these people.

### 3. Do not set, nor limit, goals of client

Greatest danger is in limiting client's goals, especially if they are more demanding of self than therapist would be under same circumstances. Tendency to dissuade by flattery. Therapist must be very realistic about himself and be at peace with his limitations, in therapy situation, at least.

### 4. Seek nothing from the process except serving aims of client and improving your own skill

Finally, it is a good idea to share an evaluation of the therapy process with the client, periodically. Create a conscious consideration of whether or not job is getting done.

To summarize very briefly: if one has a guiding understanding of client-centered therapy, its aims and means and accepts responsibility for one's power in the situation, one is very likely to be, ethically speaking, doing and being good.

### REFERENCE

Rogers, C. R. (1957). The necessary and sufficient conditions of therapeutic personality change. *Journal of Consulting Psychology, 21*, 95–103.

# Chapter 5

# The nondirective attitude in client-centered therapy

Client-centered[1] therapists are unique in the extent of their commitment to be of help without disempowering their clients. The theory of the person-centered approach (Rogers, 1980) is based on the hypotheses that all humans have innate power and capabilities for personal growth and have pro-social tendencies. Further, that these capabilities can be realized more fully under the facilitative interpersonal conditions of congruence, unconditional positive regard and empathic understanding. In the theory of therapy, clients' potentialities for healing and further growth are freed and accelerated when they perceive the congruent therapist's acceptant empathy and when the therapist at the same time avoids disempowering attitudes and behaviors in the relationship.

Client-centered therapists' commitment to avoid client disempowerment during the processes of helping is realized and is expressed through their adherence to the nondirective attitude. The nondirective attitude, in client-centered theory, adheres within the meld of the basic therapeutic attitudes. It is a quality intrinsic to the therapeutic attitudes. It influences the therapist to protect the client's self-determined processes that promote the client's self-empowerment. And it fosters the avoidance of therapist intentions and behaviors that might disempower the client. This paper is intended to clarify the meanings and some of the implications of the concept of the nondirective attitude in client-centered therapy as they apply to the therapist. Implications for the client will be discussed in another presentation.*

---

1. Client-centered therapy and person-centered therapy refer to the same therapy. The term "client-centered" will be used in this paper.

---

* Editors' note: This issue may have been presented but we are not aware of any fully formed paper on this subject.

---

Published (1997) in *The Person-Centered Journal, 4*(1), 18–30. Revision of a paper presented at the annual meeting of the Association for the Development of the Person-Centered Approach (ADPCA), Kendall College, Evanston, Illinois, May, 1994. Reproduced with permission from *PCJ*.

## DEFINITIONS

Webster (1979) defines the verb "to direct" as "to manage the affairs of; guide, conduct, regulate; control; give authoritarian instructions and ordain (that a thing be done); order, command" (p. 516). In the adjectival form, "directive" is defined as "tending to or intending to direct" (p. 516). Obviously, "nondirective" means something opposite to the meanings of "to direct" and "directive." Thus, the "nondirective attitude" literally refers to an attitude in which one is not intending to manage the affairs of others, not intending to give guidance, not intending to conduct, regulate, command or control others. Clearly, the client-centered nondirective attitude is not a paternalistic attitude; and it is an anti-authoritarian attitude.

The nondirective attitude can be defined, also, in positive terms. The positive meanings of the concept require reference to the values that inform the attitude. The philosophical orientation of client-centeredness (Rogers, 1951, Chapter 2), primarily asserts the idea of the inherent and precious value of human persons. It asserts the values of respect towards and trust in persons, egalitarian and democratic values, and the value of freedom understood partly in terms of John Stuart Mill (1859) "... that of pursuing our own good in our own way, so long as we do not attempt to deprive others of theirs, or impede their efforts to obtain it ..." (in Lerner, 1961, p. 266). The nondirective attitude in client-centered work exists in the therapist's intentions to experience the values of respect and trust as consistently and deeply as possible and to act in relation to clients only in ways that express these values.

The nondirective attitude is intrinsic to and necessary for true client-centered work. Without proper cognizance and inner experiencing of the nondirective attitude, the therapist is inadequately prepared to function in a client-centered way with a wide range of clients with their surprising and varied characteristics and expectations. Without it the therapist has insufficient inner guidance as well as inadequate criteria for response limitations in interaction with clients. Without the guiding and the limiting role of the nondirective attitude, for example, congruence can be construed as self-disclosure, unconditional positive regard can be construed as praise of the client, and empathic understanding can be construed as the therapist's imaginings about the client.

Some therapists, who work from Rogers' basic philosophical orientation and the theory of the therapeutic attitudes, but without cognizance of the nondirective attitude, evolve somewhat different forms of therapy in which particular directive principles are brought into the therapeutic process.[2] The

---

2. Examples of therapies based on Rogers' theory which also utilize directive principles are E. Gendlin's experiential therapy (Gendlin, 1973; Brodley, 1990), Friedman's experiential therapy    ... contd.

49

popularity of these deviations and the related loss of focus on the value of client-centered work is one reason for my attempt to bring attention to the nondirective attitude. The nondirective attitude needs to be explicitly incorporated into client-centered theory and practice. It is necessary in order to preserve and further develop a relatively pure and highly effective form of client-centered therapy so it can continue to be available as a choice for therapists and clients.

## SOME HISTORY

Many therapists have been influenced by Rogers' philosophical orientation (Rogers, 1951, Chapter 2) and generic theory of therapy (Rogers, 1957). Some mistakenly have identified pure client-centered work with a rigid and limited responsiveness they associate with nondirectivity (see Lietaer, 1997). Rogers recognized this misunderstanding, it disturbed him, and it was one of his reasons for abandoning the term "nondirective." After the early 1950s Rogers' only use of the term is in his references to the history of client-centered therapy.

Nondirective, understood as an *attitude* rather than as the name of his early conceptualization of client-centered therapy or as the name of a technique in that early therapy, was never explicit in Rogers' writings. In *Client-Centered Therapy* (Rogers, 1951), the nondirective attitude comes across implicitly in the therapist's intentions to give all of his or her attention to the client in order to acceptingly and empathically understand. It is also implicit in the client-centered operational philosophy placing high value upon respect for and trust in the client. The term is explicit in the title of Raskin's (1947/2005) paper, "The Nondirective Attitude." Raskin, in this paper, coined the concept. Rogers (1951) commented that Raskin's paper gives "a vivid description ... of the counselor's function" (p. 29). Raskin wrote:

> There is [another] level of nondirective counselor response which to the writer represents *the* nondirective attitude .... At this level, counselor participation becomes an active experiencing with the client of the feelings to which he gives expression ... [he tries] to get under the skin of the person .... And in struggling to do this, there is simply no room for any other kind of counselor attitude ... (cited in Rogers, 1951, p. 29)

---

contd. ... (Friedman, 1982) and F. Gerbode's traumatic reduction therapy (Gerbode, 1992, 1994). In Gendlin's and Friedman's approaches, experientially focused process of client self-explication and self-expression is considered the essence of, and necessary for, therapeutic change. Consequently the therapist has a responsibility to intervene and to promote that specific client process if it is not occurring spontaneously. In Gerbode's approach, the therapist gives instructions and guides the client through specific procedures in order to dispel the emotional charge and other symptoms of post-traumatic conditions.

But this citation from Raskin's paper is the sole reference that I have found where Rogers explicitly acknowledges the concept of a "nondirective attitude." Nevertheless, it remains implicit in Rogers' theory of therapy and writings about therapy until his death. Also, it is ubiquitous in his own therapy.

Examination of Rogers' own therapy behavior shows that he is systematically and very consistently nondirective in his relations with his clients and in the manner of his empathic responding to clients (Brodley & Brody, 1990; Brody, 1991; Nelson, 1994; Brodley, 1994/2011; Merry, 1994/ 1996). For example, in a sample of 31 of Rogers' interviews, 90% of his responses are nondirective, empathic following responses (Brodley, 1994/ 2011). Most of the other 10% of responses – those made from his own frame of reference – are also nondirective and have empathic qualities.

Indeed, there are some exceptions to nondirectivity in available examples of Rogers' therapy (Bowen, 1996; Brodley, 1996a). But directive responses are rare exceptions and constitute only a very small portion of Rogers' behavior in the few sessions where they can be found.[3] Whatever Rogers' reasons for the exceptions, they are exceptions. Rogers' own therapy behavior, from the 1940s until his last demonstrations in 1986, almost entirely manifests the nondirective attitude.

## IMPLICATIONS

Implications, for the therapist, of the nondirective attitude in client-centered therapy occur in two different arenas. One arena is the personality and subjective life of the therapist. The other is the arena of behavioral expression of the attitude. In regard to the arena of therapist personality and subjective life, the social, cultural and professional contexts of the therapist are additional determinants, and often are obstacles.

## THE THERAPIST IN CONTEXT

The therapist who adopts client-centered values must be – by nature or nurture – a nonpaternalistic, an anti-authoritarian, a democratically oriented personality and be able to resist the prevailing cultural climate of authoritarian values. Client-centered values are in conflict with the systemic paternalistic and authoritarian values of the institutions and practices that permeate all

---

3. In the instances where directivity appears in Rogers' own therapy behavior, it may be that Rogers was experimenting with some directive intentions or, alternatively, Rogers may have allowed himself to drift from his otherwise very pure nondirectivity – a loss of discipline – perhaps following some idea or impulse in those moments, or they are instances of idiosyncratic therapist freedom and not meant to be explained beyond invoking that principle.

cultures which have formal psychotherapeutic practices (as well as most cultures that do not).

The therapist who is inclined to adopt the philosophical orientation and practice of client-centeredness is pushing his or her nonpaternalistic and nonauthoritarian tendencies further away from societal norms. The therapist, as well, is almost inevitably functioning in the context of the prevailing authoritarian and paternalistic clinical culture. Consequently he or she must often tolerate relative isolation from like-minded colleagues and persist in a life of considerable incongruence with the social context of work. Tolerance for criticism, tolerance for conflict, capability for independent thinking and propensities for maintaining integrity, maintaining valued principles and self-direction while in a marginal position are necessary characteristics of, or ones that need to be developed by, client-centered workers.

## A PHENOMENOLOGY OF THE NONDIRECTIVE ATTITUDE

The phenomenology of nondirectivity as it is lived in the therapist's subjective experience involves the development of specific kinds of sensibility and sensitivity. This sensibility is difficult to describe and undoubtedly varies with the individualities of therapists. The following description is based on my own phenomenology as well as upon impressions I have gleaned from other client-centered therapists. It is not meant as a model, but is intended to illustrate how a nondirective phenomenology can have both a guiding and inhibiting character.

The guiding character of the client-centered therapist's nondirective sensibility seems to exist as a *drive to understand* – empathically and accurately – without interfering in, or contributing additional meanings to, the client's flow of thoughts and feelings. It is a drive to understand what it is the client is intending to express or communicate on a moment-to-moment basis. The drive feels like a vivid interest to take in what it is the client is pursuing in his or her narrative. The therapist feels this drive-like interest even before experiencing concrete understandings. It also involves a motivation to differentiate the therapist's own input or own shades of meaning (subjectively and prior to communication) from those the client appears to be transmitting. It is an interest in knowing the other as the other perceives and knows him- or herself.

The nondirective sensibility also feels like a *drive to respond with attunement*. It is a desire to be close to, to feel and to respond with acknowledgment of the client's intonations and other expressive behaviors that convey specific meaning and feeling. It also involves awareness of, and concern for, the client's autonomy and right to self-direction. These attunements shape the therapist's expression. The attunement element seems inextricably bound to *responding and being responsive* to the client while respecting the client's autonomy and self-direction.

The nondirective guiding sensibility also involves a feeling of humility. In the process of empathic understanding the therapist feels tentativeness, and some degree of uncertainty, in respect to the understandings achieved. Empathic understanding responses are always imbued with the question to the client: "Is this (meaning or feeling) accurate according to your sense of what you were intending to express to me?" The humility in the client-centered sensibility is based on respect for the client and on the belief that the client is the expert and authority on his or her own experiences and truths.

There is also an inhibiting sensibility that is an aspect of the phenomenology of the nondirective attitude. It shows up in the absence of paternalistic or authoritarian kinds of reactions to clients. This inhibiting sensibility is not a form of incongruence.[4] Congruent inhibition most likely involves a preconscious sorting out of paternalistic or authoritarian responses in the therapy situation. I suspect this to be the case because many client-centered therapists, including myself, have paternalistic and directive reactions in other situations. If such reactions begin to occur, of course, inhibition is a conscious and careful process. It involves their full identification and consideration, not a knee-jerk type of reaction.

In addition to the guiding and inhibitory processes that seem to be involved in the nondirective attitude with one's own clients, there are subjective responses to the therapy work of other therapists that seem to arise from having a nondirective phenomenology. These responses are feelings of pleasure and well-being when witnessing nondirective empathic processes between another therapist and client. Respect for the client, protection of the client's autonomy and consequent empowerment of the client is apparent in nondirective processes, making them enjoyable to behold. Disturbed reactions occur as well, when witnessing directive processes in the work of other

---

4. This is a complicated issue. Inhibiting contradictory attitudes, in this context, means one is not experiencing them at the time with the particular client. Thus they cannot be affecting the interaction. The therapist is not incongruent, however, even if experiencing attitudes that are inconsistent with empathy and unconditional positive regard as long as he or she is acceptant toward him- or herself in having those reactions, and is able to accurately symbolize the experiences in awareness.

Inhibiting expression of contradictory attitudes while being able to accurately symbolize them to oneself is not incongruence, although it is desirable that the therapist remain open to disclosing the contradictory attitudes if they persist with the client. Inhibition of the experiences of attitudes that are contradictory to the therapeutic attitudes allows the therapist to reflect on them and their stimuli and to seek consultation rather than impulsively voicing them. Therapeutically problematic incongruence involves being unaware of, but betraying in words or expressive behavior, attitudes contradictory to the therapeutic attitudes (Brodley, 1996b). There are other interpretations of congruence and incongruence (see Lietaer, 1993).

therapists. These responses, both positive and negative, are an immediate kind of experience and, depending upon the nature of the perceived directive behaviors, variably intense.

## BEHAVIORAL IMPLICATIONS OF THE NONDIRECTIVE ATTITUDE

The most frequent and most natural behavioral implication of the nondirective attitude occurs in the therapist's *empathic following* of a client who is talking voluntarily to the therapist and expressing his or her thoughts, feelings and concerns about his or her self and life. These responses are expressions of the therapist's acceptant, nonjudgmental, and empathic following and understanding of the client's self-directed communication and its experiential meanings. I have termed the whole interactive pattern "the empathic understanding response process" (Temaner, 1977/2011). It is also referred to by Barrett-Lennard (1981) as "the empathy cycle."

The therapist's empathic, following, verbal responses, along with his or her expressive behavior of face, gestures by hands and arms, body language, posture and movements, the therapist's tone of voice and phrasing of sentences – all together express the therapist's nondirective attitude in response to the self-representing client. These empathic responses and concomitant behaviors together express all of the therapeutic attitudes.[5] Rogers (1951) described this basic expression of the therapeutic attitudes.

> It is the counselor's function to assume, in so far as he is able, the internal frame of reference of the client, to perceive the world as the client sees it, to perceive the client himself as he is seen by himself, to lay aside all perceptions from the external frame of reference while doing so, and to communicate something of this empathic understanding to the client. (1951, p. 29)

Empathic responding is an optimal form of client-centered implementation because it can nondirectively express all of the therapeutic attitudes.[6] It is a

---

5. Empathic understanding without therapist congruence and therapist acceptance is not what is meant in Rogers' (1957, 1959) theory. Unconditional positive regard is not perceivable and/or receivable by the client if it is not infused with or coexistent with the informedness of empathic understanding and the validating quality of therapist genuineness. Congruence as the wholeness and authenticity of the therapist may be admirable and be an ideal state, but its therapeutic potency requires its integration with enlightened acceptance, which is the combination of unconditional positive regard and empathic understanding. Rogers' therapeutic attitudes are a totality – one holistic therapeutic attitude in practice.

6. Acceptant, authentic, empathic understanding is inherently a nondirective phenomenon. On the one hand, acting on agendas or goals for the client is not unconditional acceptance. On the other hand, behaving nondirectively without empathic understanding, acceptance and  ... contd.

straightforward and respectful response to the client's hope and intention, when talking about him- or herself, to be understood. People usually want and expect to be understood when they talk to another person. This is more so in the context of therapy. Thus, in following the client – through acceptant, empathic understanding of the client in the moment – the client-centered therapist is being responsive to the client's wishes and expectations, not imposing a form of response on the client.

The behavior expressing empathic understanding in client-centered therapy is basically an interactive, relational activity. It is not a series of unrelated discrete responses to client's utterances. Instead, it is a process in which the therapist tries to accurately represent his or her experiences of the client's intended communications, followed up by the client validating, correcting, modifying, and elaborating on his experiences, and the therapist's further empathic understanding.

In empathic interaction processes, the therapist's verbal statements of empathic understanding are always tentative. They imply the sincere question "Is my understanding accurate?" The therapist intends his or her specific empathic responses to check with, or find out from the client whether or not the therapist's communicated understanding is accurate according to the client (Brodley,1984/1985 [for revision see Brodley, 1998/2011]; Rogers, 1986).

The client's responses that verify, deny or qualify the therapist's accuracy of understanding are essential to empathic understanding. The therapist's verbal empathic responses, along with qualities of his or her voice and gestures, contribute to the client's perception of the therapist's authenticity and acceptance and communicate the therapist's intentions to be respectful and to not be controlling or directive. The client's responses of validation, correction and further development of thoughts and experiences tend to confirm the therapist's sense that his or her authentic inner attitudes of acceptance, understanding and nondirectivity are being communicated as intended. The interaction is mutually supportive towards more of the same kind of interaction – the client continuing to narrate and communicate with the therapist and the therapist trying to accurately, acceptingly, empathically understand.

Therapeutic change, according to Rogers (1957, 1959), occurs when the client perceives the therapist's therapeutic attitudes. Perception of the therapeutic attitudes by the client usually appears to involve the client's consciousness of the therapist's intent to understand and the client's

---

contd. ...    authenticity is not an expression of the client-centered nondirective attitude. It is more likely a passive or indifferent attitude expressed in noninterference. The nondirective attitude adheres to felt values of respect and trust, democratic and egalitarian values, and the valuing of freedom. These are all active, caring values, not passive or indifferent ones.

consciousness of the therapist's accuracy of empathic understanding. Clients' responses, such as "exactly," "yes," "well, not quite as …," "no, I meant …," etc., seem to demonstrate their consciousness of the therapist's intention to empathically understand.

Spontaneous client statements usually do not reveal whether or not clients are equally conscious of the therapist's attitudes of acceptance, genuineness and nondirectiveness. In many client/therapist interactions the attitudes may be subceived (see Rogers, 1959, pp. 199–200) and in this way contribute to the therapeutic climate. Whether or not the client consciously appreciates them, their impact on the client is one of a mixture of qualities that are important in having therapeutic effect. Aspects of the therapeutic impact of the behaviors that are shaped by the nondirective attitude are client's perceptions of the therapist's respect for and trust in the client. This respect and trust is implied in the empathic interaction with its inherent protectiveness of the client's autonomy and self-direction.

Empathic responding is both rightly and wrongly identified with client-centered therapy. It is rightly so identified because it can be an authentic, appropriate, optimal realization of the therapeutic attitudes and responsive to the client's hope of being understood. It is sometimes wrongly identified with client-centered therapy when it is thought to be the only form of response consistent with the nondirective attitude.[7]

## RESPONSIVENESS TO QUESTIONS AND REQUESTS

Responsiveness to clients' questions and requests is the second major behavioral implication of the nondirective attitude.[8] Students sometimes

---

7. In client-centered work there are occasionally responses that express the therapist's frame of reference (in addition to responses to questions and requests). There are forms of response in client-centered work which are consistent with the nondirective attitude and the other therapeutic attitudes, but which are not the direct result of these attitudes. Therapist responses that are expressed out of persistent feelings (usually aimed to correct for therapist incongruence when other avenues for correction are not effective) and spontaneous responses (Brodley, 1987) cannot be considered behavioral implications of the nondirective attitude nor of the basic therapeutic attitudes. These forms of response result from therapists needing a leeway or elbowroom that protects their authenticity as persons in relationship. Personhood is a more fundamental characteristic of the therapist than his or her therapisthood. It is an idiosyncratic component in client-centered therapeutic relationships tempered by therapeutic theory. Such idiosyncratic responses, when they occur, are shaped in part by the therapist's motivations to preserve empathy and acceptance and manifest these characteristics although they are expressed from the therapist's frame of reference. In any case, these forms of response are necessarily infrequent in client-centered work. In a sample of Rogers' work with regular clients they constitute a mean of 4% of his responses (Brodley, 1994/2011).

8. [Editors' revision: In her doctoral research Claudia Kemp (2004) examined how Rogers responded to clients' questions.]

assume that it is outside the scope of client-centered work to answer clients' questions or to honor clients' requests. Although incorrect, this conclusion is understandable because such behavior does risk influencing clients' choices, risks deflecting clients from their own exploratory process and risks undermining their self-direction. To avoid these risks of directive effects when their clients ask questions or make requests, some students of the approach tend to limit themselves to responding empathically to clients' feelings or motivations.

Empathic responses, sometimes, may be an adequate response to a client's questions or requests. When a client asks a question or makes a request, the therapist may feel the need to be sure he or she understands the client's subjective experience that has stimulated the question or request. Or, the therapist may want to be sure the client meant the question as a question. In either case, an empathic response may be an adequate response from the client's point of view.

From the context of a question, the therapist often has enough information about the client's immediate frame of reference to have a basis for an accurate empathic understanding response, or at least for an empathic guess. Indeed, a client may feel a therapist's empathic response is more helpful than whatever answers the therapist might provide. If, however, the therapist's response to a client's intended question or request is limited to an empathic response, the client's intention – to be answered – has been ignored. The experience of being ignored, particularly if it occurs frequently, tends to diminish any person's sense of self and their sense of personal power in the situation.

There is a therapeutic problem even when clients do not object to their questions being left unanswered. Clients may interpret an empathic response as an avoidance of the question and further, as indication that the therapist should not be asked questions. When this is the client's interpretation, the client's freedom of expression in the relationship has been diminished. An instance of avoidance of a client's question or request may not inhibit or disturb the client. If questions and requests are deflected by empathic responses frequently or systematically however, the effect is likely to be one of disempowering the client to some extent. Any disempowerment of the client in client-centered therapy is viewed as counter-therapeutic.

Systematic avoidance of clients' questions and their requests is, effectively, a form of control over the therapeutic process and over the client. It diminishes the client's freedom to bring out his or her felt needs in the relationship. Diminished freedom may be the consequence of not responding directly to questions or requests even if the therapist is highly empathic to the client's motives and feelings and feels committed to empowerment.

The nondirective attitude in client-centered work implies that questions and requests should be respected as part of the client's rights in the relationship. These rights are the client's right to self-determination of his or her therapeutic content and process, and the client's right to direct the manner of the therapist's participation within the limits of the therapist's philosophy, ethics and capabilities. The result of the therapist's respect towards these client rights is a collaborative therapeutic relationship (see Natiello, 1994).

This conception of the client's rights in the relationship is radically different from that of other clinical approaches. In other approaches, to a greater or lesser extent depending upon the theory, the therapist paternalistically decides whether or not it will be good for the client to have his or her questions answered or requests honored (Glickhauf-Hughes & Chance, 1995). The client-centered approach eschews decision making for the client. Decisions are collaborative, with the client almost always leading the process.

While being responsive to questions and requests the therapist also continues to maintain congruence and continues to experience and implement the therapeutic attitudes of unconditional positive regard and empathic understanding. The therapist continues, as in the empathic understanding response process, to respond to the client in the question or request situation from the client's internal frame of reference. But responsiveness to questions and requests also involves the therapist in responding to the client from the therapist's own internal frame of reference. Addressing questions and honoring clients' requests is, consequently, a more complex implementation of the therapeutic attitudes than the empathic understanding implementation.

The client-centered therapist aims to maintain the attitudes of congruence, unconditional positive regard and empathic understanding even in situations of bringing his or her frame of reference, own self and/or specific capabilities or expertise into the foreground of interaction with the client. The situation of answering questions or accommodating to requests makes the therapist's moment-to-moment attention to and attunement to the client more difficult to maintain. This is because it is being interrupted by a focus on the therapist's own internal frame of reference.

While the therapist is responding authentically and deeply to the client's question or request throughout the interaction that deals with these, the therapist must focus into him- or herself and attune to his or her own experiencing processes and cognitive processes. Attunement to the client and the client's frame of reference is to some extent interrupted when the therapist is accommodating and trying to make his or her responses coherent, empathically relevant to the client, and at the same time self-integrated responses – not-off-the-top-of-the-head responses. Difficult as it may be, responding directly to questions and requests can be and should be from the therapist's empathic and personal depths as much as pure empathic following.

## THE THIRD MAJOR BEHAVIORAL IMPLICATION

The third major behavior implication of the nondirective attitude has to do with ways the therapist does *not* behave in client-centered therapy specifically in order to avoid disempowering the client in the relationship. In effective client-centered therapy the therapist experiences acceptant empathic understanding and maintains an integrated, congruent state as consistently as possible. Maintaining this combination of attitudes and behaving consistently with and expressively of them constitutes the therapist's active role in the relationship. Not less important, however, is the task of avoiding directive intentions and avoiding behaviors that the client is likely to interpret as implying the therapist has goals for the client.

The basic definition of the nondirective attitude states that the therapist does not intend to manage, give guidance to, conduct, regulate, or control the client. In more specific terms the client-centered therapist does not intend to diagnose, create treatment plans, strategize, employ treatment techniques, or take responsibility for the client in any way. These authoritative intentions are the usual ones that are based on the standard psychotherapy paradigm in which the client is viewed as sick and the therapist is viewed as responsible for the client's diagnosis, treatment plan and cure. There is a profound difference in a therapeutic relationship between the situation of the therapist having the standard paradigm goals for clients and the client-centered relationship in which the therapist has no such goals.

In client-centered work there is only the very general therapy goal of effectively helping the client by providing the therapeutic attitudes in the relationship, and doing so without hurting or disempowering the client. In the collaborative therapeutic relationship of client-centered work the therapist keeps him- or herself free of all other goals and intentions for clients and only rarely engages in behaviors that typically express these goals and intentions.

The client-centered therapist does not usually take a history,[9] does not question the client for the purpose of establishing a diagnosis, does not ask leading or probing questions, does not volunteer interpretations or

---

9. Psychotherapy is carried out in many settings having varying institutional requirements. Taking a history, doing a diagnostic history or making notes of a treatment plan, etc., when required by the institution do not preclude functioning as a client-centered therapist. One way to combine extra- and counter-therapeutic requirements with client-centered therapy is for the therapist to be clear about the distinction, communicate the distinction to the client and to temporarily separate the nontherapeutic activities from pure therapy time.

explanations about the client to the client, does not advise, does not volunteer reassurance, does not evaluate the client's ideas or plans, does not try to control the manner or style of expression in which the client presents him- or herself, does not decide for the client about the frequency of sessions, the length of the therapy, nor guide the process of stopping therapy.[10]

The client, however, may make requests or initiate experiments during which the therapist engages in some of these behaviors. Or the therapist may on rare occasions, unsystematically,[11] volunteer some of these behaviors. Without abandoning the philosophical orientation of client-centeredness and while still committed to the therapeutic attitudes and the nondirective attitude, the client-centered therapist remains free to behave in whatever way his or her best judgment or therapeutic instincts lead or demand of him or her. The client-centered therapeutic relationship with each client is viewed as unique, complex and unpredictable. The client's manner and processes of change are unique to the individual, so there can be no formulas or rules to follow.

The client-centered values and attitudes, however, result in the therapist tending to have certain subjective experiences, tending to engage in certain behaviors, and tending to avoid certain other behaviors. The therapist's experiences and behaviors are determined by values and his or her perceptions

---

10. It might be argued that the restrictions placed on the behavioral repertoire of client-centered therapists betray the basic principles of respect for, and trust in clients as actualizing beings. Why wouldn't clients, if they are inherently self-actualizing beings, override directive therapist behaviors and protect their own autonomies? In actual practice, some clients do just that. In fact, the evidence that all therapies often help their clients tends to support that principle. Clients often benefit from directive therapists, apparently selecting the elements of empathy, compassion, and acceptance and, perhaps, the modules of wisdom dispensed by such therapists to support their own growth and healing. There is no evidence, however, to give us confidence that such benefits are not contaminated within the whole person in ways that undermine the person. The issues of outcome are very complex. Emphasis on the protection of autonomy, self-determination and self-direction of the client in client-centered work is based on the view that the reason for therapy is some degree of damage to the client's self (Rogers, 1959) which may be expressed in inadequate self-protection, inadequate self-regulation and inadequate self-determination. Responding honestly to clients' questions, accommodation to clients' requests, and spontaneous therapist responses – any of which might risk interference in or undermine clients' vulnerable sense of self – involve a flexibility that, hopefully, compensates for the protective feature of client-centered work which might otherwise, paradoxically, undermine clients' independence and empowerment. There is no certainty about this matter. We make our choices about what to emphasize in selecting therapeutic theories as the basis for our practice. Then we observe the results as impartially as we can and modify our theory and practice if it doesn't work as we expect.

11. Raskin (1988) introduced the concept of spontaneous and nonsystematic forms of response (such as the therapist offering reactions, suggestions, asking questions, etc.) in client/person-centered therapy, while maintaining the same basic respect for the self-directive capacities of the client and for the client as "architect of the process" (p. 2). In Raskin's view the therapist is being systematically directive when he or she has a preconceived notion of how to change the client and "work[s] at it in a systematic fashion" (p. 3).

of the moment, not by rules. Consequently it cannot be being true to the practice to assert that behaviors associated with directivity are impossible in the context of client-centered work. The client-centered therapist's freedom, however, is embedded in value-determined disciplines. It is both a creative and a disciplined freedom.

## SUMMARY

The implications of the nondirective attitude for the therapist in client-centered therapy are in the arenas of the therapist's subjective life and in his or her communicative behavior during therapy. In the subjective arena, the nondirective attitude and therapeutic congruence together require a long process of self-scrutiny and self-definition in order to be able to counter early learnings, as well as to counter social/contextual pressures towards paternalism and authoritarianism. In the arena of therapeutic behavior, the nondirective attitude contributes to the form of response made to self-exploring, self-expressing clients – the empathic understanding response process (Temaner, 1977/2011). It contributes to accommodative responsiveness to client's questions and requests. And it contributes to avoidance of behaviors that might undermine the client's autonomy and self-determination.

Client-centered theory and its practice are clarified by understanding the important role of the nondirective attitude in the therapist's intentions and by maintaining that attitude in the context of providing the therapeutic attitudes of congruence, unconditional positive regard and empathic understanding. Rogers' theory of therapy is a theory for client empowerment and the nondirective attitude is primarily the therapist's inner guide for protecting that empowerment.

## REFERENCES

Barrett-Lennard, G. T. (1981). The empathy cycle: Refinement of a nuclear concept. *Journal of Counseling Psychology, 28*, 91–100.

Bowen, M. (1996). The myth of nondirectiveness: The case of Jill. In B. H. Farber, D. C. Brink, & P. M. Raskin (Eds.), *The psychotherapy of Carl Rogers* (pp. 84–94). New York: Guilford Press.

Brodley, B. T. (1984). Criteria for making empathic understanding responses in client-centered therapy. In A. S. Segrera (Ed.), *Proceedings of the First International Forum on the Person-Centered Approach*. México, Distrito Federal, Mexico: Universidad Iberoamericana. [Excerpted (1985) in *Renaissance, 2*(1), 1–3. under altered title. Revision (under altered title) published (1998) in *The Person-Centered Journal, 5*(1), 20–28; this volume, Chapter 14]

Brodley, B. T. (1987). *A client-centered psychotherapy practice*. Paper prepared for the Third International Forum on the Person-Centered Approach, La Jolla, California.

Brodley, B. T. (1990). Client-centered and experiential: Two different therapies. In G. Lietaer, J. Rombauts, & R. Van Balen (Eds.), *Client-centered and experiential therapy in the nineties* (pp. 87–107). Leuven, Belgium: Leuven University Press.

Brodley, B. T. (1994). Some observations of Carl Rogers' behavior in therapy interviews. *The Person-Centered Journal, 1*(2), 37–48. [This volume, Chapter 25]

Brodley, B. T. (1996a). Uncharacteristic directiveness: Carl Rogers' session with an angry and hurt client. In B. H. Farber, D. C. Brink, & P. M. Raskin (Eds.), *The psychotherapy of Carl Rogers* (pp. 310–321). New York: Guilford Press.

Brodley, B. T. (1996b, May). *On congruence.* [Unpublished] Paper presented at the annual meeting of the Association for the Development of the Person-Centered Approach, Kutztown University, Kutztown, PA.

[Brodley, B. T. (1998). Criteria for making empathic responses in client-centered therapy. *The Person-Centered Journal, 5*(1), 20–28; this volume, Chapter 14]

Brodley, B. T., & Brody, A. F. (1990, August). Understanding client-centered therapy through interviews conducted by Carl Rogers. Paper presented in the panel, *Fifty years of client-centered therapy: Recent research.* American Psychological Association Annual Conference, Boston.

Brody, A. F. (1991). *Understanding client-centered therapy through interviews conducted by Carl Rogers.* Unpublished doctoral clinical research project, Illinois School of Professional Psychology, Chicago (now Argosy University, Chicago).

Friedman, N. (1982). *Experiential therapy and focusing.* New York: Half Court Press.

Gendlin, E. T. (1973). Experiential psychotherapy. In R. Corsini (Ed.), *Current psychotherapies* (pp. 347–352). Itasca, IL: Peacock.

Gerbode, F. (1992). *Traumatic stress reduction.* Paper presented at the annual meeting of the Association for the Development of the Person-Centered Approach, Menlo Park, CA.

Gerbode, F. (1994). *Trauma and personal growth.* Unpublished manuscript, Institute for Research in Metapsychology, Menlo Park, CA.

Glickhauf-Hughes, C., & Chance, S. E. (1995). Answering clients' questions. *Psychotherapy, 32*(3), 375–380.

[Kemp, C. M. (2004). *Responses to clients' questions in client-centered therapy.* Unpublished research project, Chicago School of Professional Psychology.]

Lerner, M. (Ed.). (1961). *Essential works of John Stuart Mill.* New York: Bantam Books.

Lietaer, G. (1993). Authenticity, congruence and transparency. In D. Brazier (Ed.), *Beyond Carl Rogers* (pp. 17–46). London: Constable.

Lietaer, G. (1997). *From nondirective to experiential: A paradigm unfolding.* Unpublished manuscript.

Merry, T. (1994, September). *An analysis of ten demonstration interviews by Carl Rogers: Implications for the training of client-centered counselors.* Paper prepared for the Third International Conference on Client-Centered and Experiential Psychotherapy, Gmunden, Salzkammergut, Austria. [Published (1996) in R. Hutterer, G. Pawlowsky, P. F. Schmid, & R. Stipsits (Eds.), *Client-centered and experiential psychotherapy: A paradigm in motion* (pp. 273–284). Frankfurt am Main: Peter Lang]

Natiello, P. (1994). The collaborative relationship in psychotherapy. *The Person-Centered Journal, 1*(2), 11–18.

Nelson, J. A. (1994). *Carl Rogers' verbal behavior in therapy: A comparison of theory and therapeutic practice.* Unpublished doctoral clinical research project, Illinois School of Professional Psychology, Chicago, Illinois (now Argosy University, Chicago).

Patterson, C. H. (1984). Empathy, warmth and genuineness in psychotherapy: A review of reviews. *Psychotherapy, 21*(4), 431–438.

Patterson, C. H. (1990). On being client-centered. *Person-Centered Review, 5*(4), 425–432.

Raskin, N. J. (1947). The nondirective attitude. Unpublished manuscript. [Published (2005) in *The Person-Centered Journal, 12*(1–2), and (2005) in B. E. Levitt (Ed.), *Embracing non-directivity* (pp. 327–347). Ross-on-Wye: PCCS Books]

Raskin, N. J. (1988). Responses to person-centered versus client-centered? *Renaissance, 5*(3&4), 2–3.

Rogers, C. R. (1951). *Client-centered therapy.* Boston: Houghton Mifflin.

Rogers, C. R. (1957). The necessary and sufficient conditions of therapeutic personality change. *Journal of Consulting Psychology, 21*, 95–103.

Rogers, C. R. (1959). A theory of therapy, personality and interpersonal relationships, as developed in the client-centered framework. In S. Koch (Ed.), *Psychology: A study of a science. Vol. III: Formulations of the person and the social context* (pp. 184–256). New York: McGraw-Hill.

Rogers, C. R. (1980). The foundations of a person-centered approach. In *A way of being* (pp. 113–136). Boston: Houghton Mifflin.

Rogers, C. R. (1986). Reflection of feelings. *Person-Centered Review, 1*(4), 375–377.

Temaner, B. [Brodley] (1977). The empathic understanding response process. Chicago Counseling and Psychotherapy Center. *Chicago Counseling Center Discussion Paper.* [This volume, Chapter 12]

Webster, N. (Ed.). (1979). *Webster's new twentieth century dictionary* (2nd ed.). New York: Simon & Schuster.

# Chapter 6

# Client-centered values limit the application of research findings: An issue for discussion

In this paper I discuss the view that the values of client-centered theory and practice should significantly limit the role of research findings in a client-centered therapist's efforts to develop the practice and theory. Values should probably place limits on the use of research findings by therapists from any orientation, but the issue is especially obvious in client-centered therapy because it is based explicitly on values. Early in his writings on client-centered therapy, Rogers (1951) asserted that the "philosophical orientation of the counselor" is crucial in therapist development. He wrote that the therapist "can be only as 'nondirective' as he has achieved respect for others in his own personality organization" (p. 21). He was explicit about the underlying role of values.

> How do we look upon others? Do we see each person as having worth and dignity in his own right? If we do hold this point of view at the verbal level, to what extent is it operationally evident at the behavior level? Do we tend to treat individuals as persons of worth, or do we subtly devalue them by our attitudes and behavior? Is our philosophy one in which respect for the individual is uppermost? Do we respect his capacity and his right to self-direction, or do we basically believe that his life would be best guided by us? To what extent do we have a need and a desire to dominate others? Are we willing for the individual to select and choose his own values, or are our actions guided by the conviction (usually unspoken) that he would be happiest if he permitted us to select for him his values and standards and goals? The answers to questions of this sort appear to be important as basic determiners of the therapist's approach. (p. 20)

Revision of a paper presented at the annual meeting of the Association for the Development of the Person-Centered Approach, Cleveland, Ohio, August, 2002 and published (2003) in *Person-Centred Practice, 11*, 52–55. This revision published (2005) in S. Joseph & R. Worsley (Eds.), *Person-centred psychopathology* (pp. 310–316). Ross-on-Wye: PCCS Books.

If one concurs with Rogers' view of the role of values, what should a client-centered therapist do with research findings that appear to suggest the efficacy of directive procedures or that omit or de-emphasize empathic understanding and acceptance of the client? A common response to such a question says "since these techniques are effective ... they should be used" (Bergin, 1970, p. 271). My contrary contention is that, "yes, one should mention these findings when discussing research, but ignore them in respect to theory and practice because research findings are not messages from a bank of truth."

The dominating context of this discussion is psychologists' and counselors' general belief that research findings are necessary to legitimize therapeutic practice and to improve theory. Rogers, himself, supported Thorndike's dictum that "anything that exists, exists in some quantity that can be measured" (quoted in Gordon, Grummon, Rogers, & Seeman, 1954, p. 13), and he fostered many empirical studies of client-centered therapy as well as pioneering the use of transcripts of sessions in psychotherapy research (Kirschenbaum & Henderson, 1989).

Some writers (Levant, 2004; McFall, 1996; Messer & Wampold, 2002; Peterson, 2004) qualify their general emphasis on empirical research by asserting that evidence-based practice should be integrated with clinical expertise. Some respond that it is true – so far, scientific procedures have not answered all the questions. But they argue that a wider range of questions and appropriate methods would keep therapy practice based on science and be best for clients (Beutler, 2004; Chambless, 2002; Rounsaville & Carroll, 2002).

Opinions vary about the role of not strictly scientific clinical expertise in modifying therapy. Still, all current writers on the subject appear to believe in and promote a scientific basis for therapy. None challenge the use of research for modifying practice, or assert the limiting role of values in incorporating research findings into therapy practice or theory.

Many of Rogers' descendents within the person-centered community use research findings to justify directive procedures and to change Rogers' theory. Outstanding examples are Gendlin (1969), Greenberg, Elliott and Lietaer (1998), Hendricks (2002) and Sachse and Elliott (2002). Rogers' own history as an innovative researcher and his encouragement of individualistic therapist development would seem, to some, to support letting the research chips fall where they may, even if it means abandoning nondirective client-centered therapy. Rogers' behavior as a therapist, however, belies that impression.

Indeed, Rogers was a pioneer in psychotherapy research (Cain, 2002), but the research he fostered on outcome, on the concomitants of change, and on the specific processes involved in change (Rogers & Dymond, 1954; Halkides, 1958; Rogers, 1959, 1961a, 1967) does not appear to have had much influence on his own therapy practice other than to give it support. His therapy sessions in the 1980s are little changed from those in the mid-1940s (Bozarth, 1990, 2002; Brodley, 1994/2011; Cain, 1993).

Rogers recorded, transcribed, and studied his and his students' therapy behavior starting in 1940 (Rogers, 1942; Kirschenbaum, 1979). He critiqued his early therapy behavior in relation to his theory and on that basis made changes that are evident after 1942 (Brodley, 1994/2011, 2004), but there is no evidence that any value-conflicting research findings available before his death influenced his therapy. He acknowledged that changes might be needed on the basis of research findings (Rogers, 1957, 1967) but he did not change his own behavior with his individual clients on those grounds.

An example of Rogers' fidelity to his values can be found in his response to a study of his own therapy. In the late 1950s Rogers listened to many of his therapy tapes and observed stages in clients' processes and manner of representing themselves as they improved (Rogers, 1961a). The pattern of therapeutic movement he observed in his clients was their response to his nondirective, congruent, offering of unconditional positive regard and empathic understanding to his clients – behavior consistent with his theory. For this good reason Rogers did not interpret his own process research findings as instructions for directive procedures.

Some other therapists originally in the client-centered milieu did use this and other research to adopt directive procedures. For example, reports by Tomlinson and Hart (1962), Gendlin, Beebe, Cassens, Klein and Oberlander (1968), Gendlin (1969), Klein, Mathieu and Kiesler (1969), Friedman (1982), and Mathieu-Coughlan and Klein (1984) showed their shift to an experiential process-directive therapy in part on the basis of Rogers' process findings.

A great deal of research shows the efficacy of client-centered therapy. For example, Truax and Carkhuff (1967) reported research results from 10 separate studies involving 850 clients. Those results "overwhelmingly support" Rogers' hypothesis that therapist congruence, unconditional positive regard and empathic understanding result in constructive personality change (Friedman, 1982, p. 34). Rogers often reported such confirming studies and it appears that Rogers embraced research findings when they tended to support his values about persons and about therapy. However, he did not do this in a cavalier manner. In fact, Rogers (1961b) expressed a theoretical justification for the role of values in adopting scientific findings. He wrote:

> What I will do with the knowledge gained through scientific method ... is a matter of subjective choice dependent upon the values which have personal meaning for me. (p. 223)

Rogers' client-centered therapy remained nondirective and empathic (Bozarth, 2002; Brodley, 1994/2011; Merry, 1996; Van Belle, 1980) in respect to both content and process. After all the challenging research, his subsequent therapy remained consistent with his values.

Until the end of his life (early in 1987) Rogers continued to think that values determine what kind of therapy he would do, and that it is best to be aware of those values as one incorporates research findings. In a 1986 interview (Rogers & Russell, 2002) Rogers asserted, "Whatever philosophical views I hold I clearly implement in practice" (p. 188) and said that client-centered therapy is "an approach that simply lives a philosophy and puts its trust in the capacities of the client ..." (p. 259).

Rogers held to his description of client-centered therapy, written in 1946, for the rest of his career. He wrote:

> The therapist must ... give up the temptation to subtly guide the individual, and must concentrate on one purpose only; that of providing deep understanding and acceptance of the attitudes consciously held at this moment by the client .... (p. 421)

The obvious difference in Rogers' later-in-life therapy that I have observed from videos is that he manifests a less formal, less clinical, presence with his clients. He changed in his nonverbal, expressive behavior, but Rogers continued to exclusively communicate his nondirective, empathic intentions with clients with only rare exceptions to this purity (Brodley, 1996).

Rogers expressed his values in an interview late in his life (Baldwin, 1987/2004), stating that the "suitable goals" in the therapy interaction are for the therapist's self. He said,

> I want to be as present to this person as possible. I want to really listen to what is going on [in the client]. I want to be real in this relationship ... The goal has to be within myself, with the way I am ... "Am I really with this person in this moment? Not where they were a little while ago, or where they are going to be ...." This is the most important thing. (pp. 47–48)

Also, in 1986, a few months before his death, Rogers expressed his nondirective client-centered attitudes, commenting to an interviewer:

> When the situation is most difficult, that's when a client-centered approach is most needed and ... what is needed there is a deepening of the [therapeutic attitudes] and not trying something more technique-oriented. (Rogers & Russell, 2002, p. 258)

Research is useful. Outcome research can show some of the specific ways a therapy is helpful. It may also be useful for political or social purposes. For example, it may be used to justify a therapy to certification boards, or it may contribute to clients' decisions about who they would like to help them, by looking at the measures of benefits shown by research. Descriptive research using transcripts and tapes may help therapists evaluate the immediate effects of their behavior on clients or show how consistent or inconsistent their behavior is in relation to their theory.

Research results, however, should not be viewed as providing an objective truth (Rogers, 1961b) as grounds for modifying a practice – especially if the research results have implications that contradict the underlying values of the therapy. Psychotherapy research, itself – in its questions, in its methods, in the interpretation of results – and any move to apply results to a therapy – is influenced by the researcher's specific values and attitudes (Lietaer, 2002).

Consequently, one may legitimately argue that it is absurd to give credence to any research in respect to applying it to psychotherapy, given the proven role of the researcher's theoretical allegiance. Studies looking at theoretical allegiance are consistent in finding large effects (Messer & Wampold, 2002). There is as much as 69 percent of the variability in effect sizes of treatment comparisons attributable to researcher theoretical allegiance (Luborsky et al., 1999, 2002). Given such powerful researcher contamination of findings, it is hard to understand why therapists and others trust psychotherapy research results at all.

CONCLUSION

Psychotherapy should be viewed as fundamentally a practical art and recognized as an ethical activity (Schmid, 2002; Grant, 1985). Consequently, a therapist should place severe limits on his or her use of research in the theory and practice of therapy. Therapy, and the research applied to a therapy – both – always express the therapist's values and attitudes about persons whether the therapist is conscious of this or not. Conversely, therapists should be aware of how their operational values may be impacted if they adopt changes in their therapy on the basis of research findings.

REFERENCES

Baldwin, M. (1987). Interview with Carl Rogers on the use of the self in therapy. In M. Baldwin & V. Satir (Eds.), *The use of self in therapy* (pp. 45–52). New York: Haworth Press. [Reprinted (2004) in R. Moodley, C. Lago, & A. Talahite (Eds.), *Carl Rogers counsels a Black client: Race and culture in person-centred counseling* (pp. 253–60). Ross-on-Wye: PCCS Books]

Bergin, A. E. (1970). Some implications of psychotherapy research for therapeutic practice. In J. T. Hart & T. M. Tomlinson (Eds.), *New directions in client-centered therapy* (pp. 257–276). Boston: Houghton Mifflin.

Beutler, L. E. (2004). The empirically supported treatments movement: A scientist-practitioner's response. *Clinical Psychology: Science and Practice, 11*, 225–229.

Bozarth, J. D. (1990). The essence of client-centered therapy. In G. Lietaer, J. Rombauts, & R. Van Balen (Eds.), *Client-centered and experiential psychotherapy in the nineties* (pp. 59–64). Leuven, Belgium: Leuven University Press.

Bozarth, J. D. (2002). The evolution of Carl Rogers as a therapist. In D. J. Cain (Ed.), *Classics in the person-centered approach* (pp. 43–47). Ross-on-Wye: PCCS Books.

Brodley, B. T. (1994). Some observations of Carl Rogers' behavior in therapy interviews. *The Person-Centered Journal, 1*, 37–48. [This volume, Chapter 25]

Brodley, B. T. (1996). Uncharacteristic directiveness: The case of Rogers and the "anger and hurt" client. In B. A. Farber, D. C. Brink, & P. M. Raskin (Eds.), *The psychotherapy of Carl Rogers* (pp. 310–321). New York: Guilford Press.

Brodley, B. T. (2004, July) *Rogers' responses to clients' questions in client-centered therapy: Some findings from a dissertation research by Claudia Kemp.* Unpublished paper presented at the annual meeting of the Association for the Development of the Person-Centered Approach, Anchorage, Alaska.

Cain, D. J. (1993). The uncertain future of client-centered counseling. *Journal of Humanistic Education and Development, 31*, 133–139.

Cain, D. J. (2002). Preface. In D. J. Cain & J. Seeman (Eds.), *Humanistic psychotherapies: Handbook of research and practice* (pp. xix–xxvii). Washington, DC: American Psychological Association.

Chambless, D. L. (2002). Beware the dodo bird: The dangers of overgeneralization. *Clinical Psychology: Science and Practice, 9*, 13–16.

Friedman, N. (1982). *Experiential therapy and focusing.* New York: Half Court Press.

Gendlin, E. T. (1969). Focusing. *Psychotherapy: Theory, Research and Practice, 6*, 4–15.

Gendlin, E. T., Beebe, J., Cassens, J., Klein, M., & Oberlander, M. (1968). Focusing ability in psychotherapy, personality and creativity. In J. M. Shlien (Ed.), *Research in psychotherapy. Vol. 3,* (pp. 217–241). Washington, DC: American Psychological Association.

Gordon, T., Grummon, D. L., Rogers, C. R., & Seeman, J. (1954). Developing a program of research in psychotherapy. In C. R. Rogers & R. F. Dymond (Eds.), *Psychotherapy and personality change* (pp. 12–34). Chicago: The University of Chicago Press.

Grant, B. (1985). The moral nature of psychotherapy. *Counseling and Values, 29*, 141–150.

Greenberg, L. S., Elliott, R., & Lietaer, G. (1998). *Handbook of experiential psychotherapy.* New York: Guilford Press.

Halkides, G. (1958). *An experimental study of four conditions necessary for therapeutic change.* Unpublished doctoral dissertation, University of Chicago.

Hendricks, M. (2002). Focusing-oriented/experiential psychotherapy. In D. J. Cain & J. Seeman (Eds.), *Humanistic psychotherapies: Handbook of research and practice* (pp. 221–252). Washington, DC: American Psychological Association.

Kirschenbaum, H. (1979). *On becoming Carl Rogers*. New York: Dell.

Kirschenbaum, H., & Henderson, V. L. (Eds.). (1989). *The Carl Rogers reader* (pp. xi–xvi). Boston: Houghton Mifflin.

Klein, M. H., Mathieu, P. L., & Kiesler, D. J. (1969). *The Experiencing Scale: A research and training manual. Vol. 1.* Madison, WI: University of Wisconsin.

Levant, R. F. (2004). The empirically validated treatments movement: A practitioner/ educator perspective. *Clinical Psychology: Science and Practice, 11,* 219–224.

Lietaer, G. (2002, July) Paper presented on panel: Open discussion on person-centered research, at the Carl R. Rogers Symposium, La Jolla, CA.

Luborsky, L., Diguer, L., Seligman, D. A., Rosenthal, R., Johnson, S., Halperin, G., Bishop, M., & Schweizer, E. (1999). The researcher's own therapeutic allegiances: A "wild card" in comparisons of treatment efficacy. *Clinical Psychology: Science and Practice, 6,* 95–132.

Luborsky, L., Rosenthal, R., Diguer, L., Andrusyna, T. P., Berman, J. S., Levitt, J. T., Seligman, D. A., & Krause, E. D. (2002). The dodo bird verdict is alive and well – Mostly. *Clinical Psychology: Science and Practice, 9,* 2–12.

Mathieu-Coughlan, P. L., & Klein, M. H. (1984). Experiential psychotherapy: Key events in client-therapist interaction. In L. N. Rice & L. S. Greenberg (Eds.), *Patterns of change* (pp. 213–248). New York: Guilford Press.

McFall, R. M. (1996). Manifesto for a science of clinical psychology. *The Clinical Psychologist, 44,* 75–88.

Merry, T. (1996). An analysis of ten demonstration interviews by Carl Rogers: Implications for the training of client-centered counselors. In R. Hutterer, G. Pawlowsky, P. F. Schmid, & R. Stipsits (Eds.), *Client-centered and experiential psychotherapy: A paradigm in motion* (pp. 273–284). Frankfurt am Main: Peter Lang.

Messer, S. B., & Wampold, B. E. (2002). Let's face facts: Common factors are more potent than specific therapy ingredients. *Clinical Psychologist: Science and Practice, 9,* 21–25.

Peterson, D. R. (2004). Science, scientism, and professional responsibility. *Clinical Psychology: Science and Practice, 11,* 196–210.

Rogers, C. R. (1942). *Counseling and psychotherapy.* Boston: Houghton Mifflin.

Rogers, C. R. (1946). Significant aspects of client-centered therapy. *American Psychologist, 1,* 415–422.

Rogers, C. R. (1951). *Client-centered therapy.* Boston: Houghton Mifflin.

Rogers, C. R. (1957). The necessary and sufficient conditions of therapeutic personality change. *Journal of Consulting Psychology, 21,* 95–103.

Rogers, C. R. (1959). A theory of therapy, personality and interpersonal relationships as developed in the client-centered framework. In S. Koch (Ed.), *Psychology: A study of a science. Vol. III: Formulations of the person and the social context* (pp. 184–256). New York: McGraw-Hill.

Rogers, C. R. (1961a). A process conception of psychotherapy. In *On becoming a person* (pp. 125–159). Boston: Houghton Mifflin.

Rogers, C. R. (1961b). Persons or science? A philosophical question. In *On becoming a person* (pp. 199–224). Boston: Houghton Mifflin.

Rogers, C. R. (1967). *The therapeutic relationship and its impact: A study of psychotherapy with schizophrenics.* Westport, CT: Greenwood Press.

Rogers, C. R., & Dymond R. F. (Eds.). (1954). *Psychotherapy and personality change.* Chicago: The University of Chicago Press.

Rogers, C. R., & Russell, D. E. (2002). *Carl Rogers, the quiet revolutionary: An oral history.* Roseville, CA: Penmarin Books.

Rounsaville, B. J., & Carroll, K. M. (2002). Commentary on dodo bird revisited: Why aren't we dodos yet? *Clinical Psychology: Science and Practice, 9,* 17–20.

Sachse, R., & Elliott, R. (2002). Process-outcome research on humanistic therapy variables. In D. J. Cain & J. Seeman (Eds.), *Humanistic psychotherapies: Handbook of research and practice* (pp. 83–115). Washington, DC: American Psychological Association.

Schmid, P. F. (2002, July) *The characteristics of a person-centered approach to therapy and counseling: Criteria for identity and coherence.* Presentation given at the Carl R. Rogers Centennial Celebration, La Jolla, CA.

Tomlinson, T. M., & Hart, J. T. (1962). A validation of the process scale. *Journal of Consulting Psychology, 26,* 74–78.

Truax, C. B., & Carkhuff, R. R. (1967). *Toward effective counseling and psychotherapy: Training and practice.* Chicago: Aldine Press.

Van Belle, H. A. (1980). *Basic intent and therapeutic approach of Carl R. Rogers.* Toronto, Canada: Wedge Publishing Foundation.

# THE THEORY OF
# CLIENT-CENTERED THERAPY

# Chapter 7

# Congruence and its relation to communication in client-centered therapy

Lack of attention to the theoretical definition of congruence, and the practice of misidentifying congruence as candor, leads to distortions in client-centered therapy and in person-centered group situations. In individual and other forms of client-centered therapy, the distortion shows up when therapists systematically state their own reactions to, or thoughts about, clients and justify the practice as a form of living the therapeutic attitude of congruence in the relationship. In regard to peer groups, the distortion appears when interpretations, accusations and insulting communications are justified as "being congruent." It is necessary to grasp the theoretical definition of congruence in order to have an accurate picture of client-centered therapy (Haugh, 1998). In particular, according to Rogers, communications relating to congruence have specific restrictive and therapeutically relevant characteristics.

In this paper I shall attempt a partial exegesis of Rogers' writings on the concepts of congruence and experience. Understanding Rogers' definition of experience is necessary for understanding congruence. I shall also explain a theoretical basis for client-centered therapists (and practitioners of other applications of the person-centered approach) to adopt an attitude that leads to particular forms of communication relating to their congruence.

## THE MEANING OF CONGRUENCE

The meaning of congruence in Rogers' writings changed somewhat over the years, and the different versions can provide rationales for different interpretations and applications of the concept. In effect, the precise meaning of congruence remains somewhat ambiguous. Additionally, Rogers' theory of therapy (1957, 1959) and his theory of interpersonal relationships (1959) present different functions of congruence. Thus, Rogers provided the grounds

First published (1998) in *The Person-Centered Journal*, 5(2), 83–116. Reproduced with permission from *PCJ*. Subsequently published (2001) in G. Wyatt (Ed.), *Rogers' therapeutic conditions, Vol. 1: Congruence* (pp. 55–78). Ross-on-Wye: PCCS Books.

for different interpretations of the concept and for different roles for congruence in psychotherapy and in work with groups within the client-centered framework.

Rogers did not use the terms "congruence" or "incongruence" at all in his 1951 book which introduced client-centered therapy. He did define adjustment and maladjustment in terms that he later used in his definitions of congruence and incongruence. Rogers (1951) defines adjustment in his chapter presenting a theory of personality and behavior in his proposition XV:

> Psychological adjustment exists when the concept of the self is such that all the sensory and visceral experiences of the organism are, or may be, assimilated on a symbolic level into a consistent relationship with the concept of self. (p. 513)

Proposition XIV expresses Rogers' definition of maladjustment:

> Psychological maladjustment exists when the organism denies to awareness significant sensory and visceral experiences, which consequently are not symbolized and organized into the gestalt of the self-structure. When this situation exists, there is a basic or potential psychological tension. (p. 510)

In the definitions of congruence above, Rogers refers to a person's openness to awareness of all organismic valuing experiences occurring at a given moment such that the person can accurately symbolize the experiences. The meaning Rogers gives to experience, in both definitions, involves sensory and visceral events that are amenable to consciousness. Experience does not refer to events that are inevitably and permanently unconscious.

The term "adjustment" and the term "congruence" appear to refer to the same phenomena.

They refer to the capability for, and the activity of, accurate symbolization of experiences in awareness. In Rogers' theory of therapy (1957, 1959), congruence is defined differently than adjustment only in the sense that it refers to more temporary and situational states. In the theory of therapy, congruence is characterized as one of the three qualities that the therapist experiences in order to contribute to clients' therapeutic change.

In Rogers' generic theory (1957, 1959), the role of congruence is stated in the third of his six necessary and sufficient conditions for therapeutic personality change as follows:

The second person, whom we shall term the therapist, is congruent or integrated in the relationship. (1957, p. 96)

Rogers explains therapeutic congruence as follows:

> ... the therapist should be, within the confines of this relationship, a congruent, genuine, integrated person. It means that within the relationship he is freely and deeply himself, with his actual experience accurately represented by his awareness of himself ... It should be clear that this includes being himself even in ways which are not regarded as ideal for psychotherapy. His experience may be "I am afraid of this client" or "My attention is so focused on my own problems that I can scarcely listen to him." If the therapist is not denying these feelings to awareness, but is able freely to be them (as well as being other feelings), then the condition (congruence) we have stated is met. (1957, p. 97)

This explanation of congruence emphasizes the therapist's personal as well as personality *integration*, in the context of the therapy relation. Keeping this emphasis, Rogers (1959) defines congruence:

> ... when self-experiences are accurately symbolized (in awareness), and are included in the self-concept in this accurately symbolized form, then the state is one of congruence of self and experience ... terms which are synonymous ... [are] integrated, whole, genuine. (1959, p. 206)

Congruence is thus theoretically defined in terms of Rogers' distinction between self and experience, not in terms of the therapist's behavior. In the theory of therapy, in both the first and second published forms, Rogers (1957, 1959) asserts that for successful therapy to take place, only the therapist's conditions of unconditional positive regard and empathic understanding must be perceived by the client. (Thus they must be communicated or expressed by the therapist.) In neither theoretical statement is it posited that the client must perceive the therapist's congruence. This implies it *need not* be communicated, although it is a necessary condition for therapy.

Congruence is a condition for therapy in the sense that it must be a state or condition *within the therapist*. This state permits the therapist to succeed in his intentions to experience unconditional positive regard and empathic understanding in relation to a client. It does so by permitting the therapist to experience an unconflicted and undistracted dedication to acceptant empathy.

The state of congruence also refers to the therapist's subjective, inner condition as one that results in an appearance of authenticity or transparency.

The therapist's integrated, authentic appearance facilitates the client's clear and trustworthy perceptions of the therapist's attitudes of unconditional positive regard and empathic understanding.

Congruence refers to wholeness and integration within, or of, oneself. The congruent therapist's openness to accurate awareness and symbolization of experience is the "ground" or "field" which underlies and coexists with the salient "figure" of the attitudes of unconditional positive regard and empathic understanding. Rogers states the connection between congruence and the other two therapeutic attitudes as follows:

> ... for therapy to occur the wholeness of the therapist in the relationship is primary, but a part of the congruence must be the experience of unconditional positive regard and the experience of empathic understanding. (Rogers, 1959, p. 215)

In order to understand how congruence in client-centered therapy functions in real therapy practice, it is important to understand Rogers' general position about the continua of the three therapeutic conditions. Rogers (1957) asserts that the three therapist conditions, which are all subjective states and attitudes, are not absolutes, but occur on continua. His theory predicts that to the extent the therapist experiences these three therapeutic attitudes while with the client, and if the client perceives the unconditional positive regard and the empathic understanding, to that extent the client will experience therapeutic change.

The therapist (or other kind of practitioner) experiences the therapeutic attitudes only to some degree, not absolutely, in a relationship. The totality of all of the therapist conditions occurs more or less frequently, but not constantly, in any given therapy encounter. The conditions must be present to some degree for therapy to be effective, and the specific degree required is probably dependent upon the needs of the individual client.

In practice, the coexistence of congruence, unconditional positive regard and a pure *intention* to empathically understand (with some inaccuracies in specific understanding from time to time) may function as effectively for many clients as does the pure intention fulfilled by perfectly accurate empathic understanding. In any case, Rogers' theory does not require absolute constancy of the therapeutic conditions for effective therapy to take place. In fact, Rogers does not consider constancy of the therapeutic conditions to be a human possibility. He states, for example, in relation to congruence:

> It is not to be expected that the therapist is a completely congruent person at all times. Indeed if this were a necessary condition there would be no

therapy. But it is enough if in this particular moment of this immediate relationship with this specific person he is completely and fully himself, with his experience of the moment being accurately symbolized and integrated into the picture he holds of himself. Thus it is that imperfect human beings can be of therapeutic assistance to other imperfect human beings. (Rogers, 1959, p. 215)

Given the inevitable imperfections of therapists in providing the therapeutic conditions, a question then arises. If a therapist has a choice about it when functioning imperfectly, which therapeutic condition has priority over the others?

Rogers asserts that the most important therapeutic condition, the one to be given priority, is congruence (1959, p. 215). In practical terms, the therapist should attend to his feelings if he realizes he is functioning imperfectly. If, at moments, the therapist is not unconditionally accepting or not empathically understanding, he should attend to these experiences and allow accurate symbolization of these experiences in his awareness.

For example, a therapist's congruent experience during a therapy session may include experiences of failing to empathically understand. A lapse in empathy might occur because the therapist is distracted from the client's internal frame of reference. Alternatively, such a lapse might occur because the therapist is experiencing a personal agenda for the client. The therapist's experience of congruence during a session might include experiences of feeling judgmental or critical or disapproving instead of feeling unconditional acceptance towards his client. In the instance of judgmental feelings, Rogers' opinion is that the therapist should remain open and attentive to his own experiences. The therapist should accurately symbolize them to self, rather than deny such experiences to awareness or distort them in awareness and, as a consequence, become incongruent. Denial or distortion in awareness of experiences results in the therapist being unintegrated and not whole, not congruent, in the therapy relationship.

In therapy practice, momentary distractions or momentary judgmental thoughts and reactions, if accurately symbolized in awareness, can be recognized and *accepted* by the therapist who gives priority to his own congruence. They are simply moments during which one of the therapeutic attitudinal conditions is not experienced. They are instances of personal fallibility and are material for introspection or consultation.

For example, a therapist is distracted from empathic attention to the client and the client's narrative by preoccupation with a family problem. Consequently, the therapist is not engaging in empathic understanding of the client at those moments. The client, however, may be continuing to perceive the therapist as empathic. The therapist becomes aware of being distracted, accepts the lapse and refocuses attention empathically towards the client. In this scenario, the therapist has temporarily failed to empathically understand, has remained acceptant towards the client, is self-acceptant and is congruent. To the extent that there was a lapse in empathic understanding, the therapist did not experience all of the therapeutic conditions. The therapy is assumed to be less effective for that client during the moments of lapse.

The most important thing to keep in mind concerning congruence is that it is a *relation*, not an entity or a content of experience. Rogers refers to congruence in terms of an integrated state or wholeness of the person. That is a holistic way of referring to how crucial aspects of the person are related to each other. The theoretical definition of congruence as accurate representation of experience by inner symbols is about the *relation* between the contents of experience and the symbols representing the contents. The congruence is the relation, not the contents. Similarly, as congruence is a state, it is a state defined by the relation between parts of the person.

### CONGRUENCE IN REGARD TO COMMUNICATION

The issue of congruence in regard to communication arises practically in certain situations. One situation is when the therapist is congruent but not experiencing unconditional positive regard or empathic understanding. For example, the therapist experiences irritation in reaction to something the client has said. This experience is contrary to unconditional positive regard. Under what circumstances and in what way should the therapist tell the client about his nonacceptant feelings? Rogers acknowledges "the puzzling matter as to the degree to which the therapist overtly communicates this reality in himself to the client" (1957, pp. 97–98). He further remarks:

> Certainly the aim is not for the therapist to express or talk out his own feelings, but primarily that he should not be deceiving the client as to himself. (p. 98)

The aim is to *not deceive* the client. But the therapist also does not want to interfere with the client's own narrative and self-exploration or become the focus of the interaction if it is not for the client's benefit. There are two practical variables in this issue, particularly if the nontherapeutic experience occurs only briefly. One has to do with the extent to which the particular therapist's inner reactions are telegraphed in facial expressions, in other gestures, or in tone of voice. The second is the extent to which the particular client is attuned to the therapist's nonverbal expressions.

In the case of many therapists, their momentary distractions or preoccupations or momentary unacceptant reactions cannot be perceived or detected by an observer. They remain private. The therapist may be inhibiting expression or not. An inhibited therapist may be perceived as transparent. Obscurity of inner reactions, however, need not result from the therapist trying to inhibit or control his expressiveness. The therapist who does not telegraph momentary inner states may be relaxed and unguarded. Such a person simply does not tend to manifest brief or undramatic vicissitudes of inner life when self-acceptant about them. Even the highly attuned client is unlikely to be able to perceive such passing inner reactions, if the therapist who has private reactions remains self-acceptant and congruent when experiencing counter-therapeutic subjective reactions.

Authenticity does not require the therapist to be free of the variety of evaluative reactions that are characteristic of subjective experience. Nor does it imply the therapist's inner experiences are not inherently private in the therapy context. The contents of subjective awareness are fleeting, evaluative and varied. There could be no personal authenticity if it required a simplicity and constancy of inner reactions. Logically, authenticity must involve a person having acceptance toward, and perspectives on, the inherent variety and the evaluative nature of subjective life (Bargh, Chaiken, Raymond & Hymes, 1995; Bargh, 1997).

The second variable is the degree of client attunement to therapist expressiveness. For example, the therapist frowns slightly, realizing he does not understand something the client is expressing. The client perceives this and interprets it as disapproval, or at least as a puzzling contrast to the acceptance she is accustomed to and upon which she depends in the therapy relationship. The interaction that occurs subsequent to this situation depends upon the client's ability to question the therapist or upon the therapist's awareness of his own expressive display. Sometimes a client feels able to ask about the therapist's feelings. The therapist, in aiming to be consistent with Rogers' dictum "that he should not be deceiving the client as to himself," might respond by disclosing his inner experience (Rogers, 1957, p. 98).

An alternative situation occurs when a client does not ask the question. In this situation, the therapist is aware that the spontaneous, expressive behavior was likely to be perceived and experienced by the client as disturbing to the client. Then, in aiming to be consistent with the general client-centered aim to communicate clearly to clients, as well as with Rogers' dictum to not deceive, the therapist might choose to disclose inner experience. The reason would be one of wanting to be clear and unambiguous to the client. The therapist wants to correct for the ambiguity that may have been created.

A relaxed and congruent therapist is unlikely to telegraph momentary and fleeting, nontherapeutic, subjective feelings or thoughts into his involuntary expressive behavior. The congruent therapist, however, might choose to communicate about such thoughts or feelings if they happen to have been involuntarily expressed and perceived by a client. The aim in communicating about them would be to correct for an appearance of ambiguity that might have confused or disturbed the client. The characteristics of such communications are extremely important and will be discussed later.

Therapists may also have persistent nontherapeutic experiences when interacting with their clients. Rogers (1957) addresses these situations. Referring to the therapist, he states:

> At times he may need to talk out some of his own feelings [either to the client, or to a colleague, or supervisor] if they are standing in the way of ... [acceptance and empathy] .... (p. 98)

Much later, in an interview (Baldwin, 1987/2004), Rogers dropped mention of talking first with colleagues or supervisors and stated:

> When I am with a client, I like to be aware of my feelings, and if there are feelings which run contrary to the conditions of therapy and *occur persistently*, then I am sure I want to express them ... [to the client]. (p. 46)

These statements, particularly the latter one, *appear* to imply that Rogers (or any therapist choosing to follow Rogers' theory and guidance) can responsibly say what he is thinking or feeling to his clients (as that is usually understood) when persistently not experiencing unconditional positive regard or empathic understanding. This meaning seems very unlikely, given the fundamental value of respect and acceptance towards clients that underlies client-centered work.

Rogers' statement "I am sure I would want to express them" does not necessarily mean he would simply say what he thinks or feels to his clients under the circumstances of persistent nontherapeutic feelings. The reason for his wanting to express his feelings to his clients must have to do with fostering the therapeutic relationship and benefiting the client under these imperfect therapist conditions. In this light, it would seem that Rogers' statement, "I want to express them," refers to having an interaction with the client that might correct for or compensate for the lapse in therapeutic conditions.

Rogers is referring to new moments in the relationship that occur after the therapist's counter-therapeutic experiences. For example, in respect to annoyed reactions to a client or after becoming distracted. The new moments include the therapist's accurate symbolization in awareness (i.e., congruence about the counter-therapeutic experiences) and some communication about the contents of that awareness. They also include the therapist's therapeutic intentions to acceptantly and empathically understand. In these new moments of intention to voice feelings, the therapist would aim to be consistent with a fundamental part of the therapeutic theory:

> ... a part of the congruence of the therapist must be the experience of unconditional positive regard and the experience of empathic understanding. (Rogers, 1959, p. 215)

At the moments of addressing the client to disclose his counter-therapeutic feelings he would also be in touch with both the counter-therapeutic subjective reality and his more pervasive attitudes of acceptant empathy. Or at least he would be in touch with his *intentions* to relate to the client with acceptant empathic understanding. The therapist's manner of addressing the client would be influenced by those intentions. Thus, the thoughts and feelings would not be communicated in an undisciplined manner – one that might hurt or threaten the client.

There are several possible beneficial consequences that may result when the therapist chooses to communicate persistent counter-therapeutic feelings to his client. First, the communication process that ensues between therapist and client can, and often does, dispel the therapist's discordant feelings, distraction, etc. For example, imagine the situation when the therapist has been feeling annoyed by a client who has corrected the therapist's empathic responses. Perhaps the therapist is interpreting the client to be critical of the therapist for not having accurately understood. Something in the client's tone of voice seems to the therapist to betray an unspoken irritation or criticism. If the therapist's annoyance is persistent and he consequently chooses, as Rogers would, to acknowledge those feelings, the interaction might lead to clarification of the client's behavior.

The client's ambiguous behavior might reveal the client's own frustration about not communicating more effectively. If this is what the therapist learns from the client, reoccurrence of the client's previously annoying behavior can be given the correct interpretation – the client's discomfort with self. As a consequence of that knowledge, the therapist no longer perceives criticism and is not annoyed. The therapist also has a better general empathic understanding of the client as a result of the interaction.

Therapist disclosure of counter-therapeutic feelings specifically may result also in a deeper empathic understanding of the client's feelings about the therapist. Using the same example, the therapist's disclosure leads to the client's disclosure that she has been feeling irritated at the therapist, but not because of his inaccurate responses. Assuming the therapist's capacity for an acceptant understanding of this fact, it might well lead to an opening up of feelings and thoughts about the therapist and the client's disappointed expectations of the therapist. Or it might lead down another path, towards the client's phenomenology of expectations and disappointments. There are many possibilities, but in any case, the therapist's empathic knowledge of the client may be deepened as the result of his disclosure of annoyance. Additionally, renewed understanding dispels the therapist's annoyance.

Another beneficial result that may be served by a therapist's disclosure of counter-therapeutic feelings is that the disclosure may contribute to the therapist's transparence. Rogers introduced the term "transparent" to refer to the therapist's congruent, acceptant and understanding presence that makes possible the client's perceptions of him as whole, authentic and trustworthy (Rogers, 1961, p. 49, p. 339). Lietaer (1993) interprets transparency as referring to the therapist's self-disclosing communications. I differ with Lietaer and interpret the concept of transparence similarly to Haugh (1998), as a characteristic perceived by the client that is likely to result from the therapist's congruent state. It most often does not involve therapist self-disclosures, although it may involve them. Rogers (1980) stated that a therapist is transparent when the therapist:

> ... is openly being the feelings and attitudes that are flowing within at the moment ... the client can see right through what the therapist *is* in the relationship; the client experiences *no holding back* [italics added] on the part of the therapist. (p. 115)

The value of the therapist's transparence in clients' perceptions is its contribution to the therapist's perceived trustworthiness and dependability. Transparence contributes to the client's perception of the therapist's authenticity when the therapist appears to be acceptantly empathic. Returning to the earlier example of the client's experience of the therapist's disclosure of annoyance (assuming this is done in a therapeutic manner): because it reveals a negative response, it may reassure the client that the therapist's negative feelings, if and when they come up, will be brought out. Thus the client can trust the authenticity of the therapist's appearance of acceptance.

At about the same time (circa 1961) that Rogers introduces the term "transparence" as an aspect of congruence, he somewhat shifts the meaning of congruence to a looser definition, to that of matching. Rogers (1961) states:

> ... [congruence] has been developed to cover a group of phenomena ...
> to indicate an accurate matching of experiencing and awareness. It may
> be still further extended to cover a matching of experience, awareness
> and communication. (p. 339)

His point is clear. Rogers states that the term "congruence" refers not only to
accurate symbolization in awareness of experiences, but it also refers to
communication that accurately represents the accurate symbolization of
experiences.

Rogers has included the idea of matching communication to inner
symbolization into the meaning of congruence. This is along with the prior
matching of symbolization in awareness with experience that was implied by
the idea that inner symbolization accurately represents experience. The term
"matching" could always have been used loosely in respect to the relation
between experience and symbolization in awareness. "Matching" is colloquial
for accurate symbolizing of experience.

Previously, Rogers (1959) emphasized the theoretical bases of congruence
in his theories of personality development, disintegration and reintegration.
Also, in the therapy context, communication springing from congruence
was limited to special circumstances of fleeting nontherapeutic experiences
and especially to circumstances of persistent feelings counter to acceptance
or empathic understanding. The contents of congruent experience were not
referred to as congruence.

## CONGRUENCE IN THE THEORY OF INTERPERSONAL RELATIONSHIPS

Rogers' shift to the term "matching" in regard to congruence coincides with
his second published discussion of his general law of interpersonal relationships
(1961, pp. 338–346). He had not used the term, but his remarks carried the
sense of "matching" in the earlier statement of that theory (1959, pp. 234–
240). In the earlier statement of that theory the matching meaning is revealed
when Rogers refers to the *congruence* of distorted perceptions with the self-
structure by a vulnerable person, in his discussion of a deteriorating
relationship (1959, pp. 236–237):

> ... Since X is vulnerable, he tends to perceive Y's responses as potentially
> threatening ... Hence he tends to *perceive them in distorted fashion*, in
> ways which are *congruent* with his own self-structure. (p. 237)

In this matching usage of the word "congruent," Rogers implies that
conditions of worth, affecting the self-structure, may result in distortions of

a person's perceptions of external reality. This usage of "congruent" can appear to be legitimately extrapolated into the idea that whether or not the symbolizations in awareness are distorted (in relation to experience), communication can be viewed as congruent communication when it matches symbolizations. This idea can be extended further to the view that *saying* whatever it is a person symbolizes to self at a given moment is an act of being congruent. It may be that this portion of Rogers' writings is what has led to the distortions in practice mentioned in my introduction.

Rogers also appears to be using the term "congruent" to mean "matching" (without using the term) in the first publication of his "tentative law of interpersonal relationships" (1959, p. 240) a few pages after the last quote above. Rogers states the law, in part, as follows:

> [T]he greater the communicated congruence of experience, awareness, and behavior on the part of one individual, the more the ensuing relationship will involve a tendency toward reciprocal communication with the same qualities, mutually accurate understanding of the communications, improved psychological adjustment and functioning in both parties, and mutual satisfaction in the relationship. (p. 240)

Rogers' wording in this statement is slightly ambiguous in so far as it suggests that the contents of experience, of awareness and behavior are congruence. This is not what Rogers must mean. Congruence always refers to a *relation* and careful reading of his wording suggests Rogers meant "congruence" as the relation between experience, awareness and behavior. In the basic therapeutic meaning of congruence as "integration" or "wholeness," the meaning has to do with a harmonious and effective relation between various aspects of the person. In the strict definition, congruence refers to the accurate relation between the contents of experience and the symbols in awareness. In application to behavior, congruent communications refer to communications that accurately represent inner symbols – again a relation.

Note that *communication* of congruent experience is being given a leading role in Rogers' theory of interpersonal relationships. This is a deviation from the role of congruence in psychotherapy. In therapy, congruence is viewed as the most important therapeutic condition, but is meant as a description of the therapist's inner, subjective state or condition while he is acceptant and empathically understanding.

Returning to congruence in the interpersonal law, Rogers' theory predicates the possibility of distortion in a person's interpretation of external reality. Distortions may occur as a consequence of conditions of worth or as a consequence of the experience of threat. Perceptions of external reality, also, may be simply in error from the perspective of consensual validation. Regardless of the consensual validity of perceptions, persons are congruent if their symbols in awareness are accurate to the experienced perceptions. Accurate symbolization in awareness of distorted perceptions of external reality are none the less congruent.

Rogers' view of human nature recognizes the powerful influence of personality and of immediate emotional influences on persons' interpretations of external events. Nevertheless, human nature is adaptive to external reality and consequently needs means to correct for distortive tendencies. In effect, humans have scientific natures according to Rogers (1961). In the extreme of his view, Rogers commented:

> Science is not an impersonal something, but simply a person living subjectively another phase of himself. (p. 223)

Persons make inferences or make interpretations of external events and then test their perceptions by taking some action that tends to validate or qualify the original perceptions. Congruent symbolization in awareness followed by congruent communication promotes accurate understandings between persons.

Obviously, Rogers cannot be using congruence to mean simple matching in the interpersonal theory. Rogers' general law of interpersonal relations must be employing the strict meaning of congruence between experience and awareness. The theory refers to an unrestricted accuracy of awareness in respect to experience that permits accurate symbolization.

It should be understood that accurate and undistorted perceptions of inner experience say nothing, however, about the accuracy or adequacy of the perceptions and interpretive processes involved in generating experiences in relation to consensual reality. Nor do they require true knowledge of the intentions of another person whose behavior is being perceived. Whatever they are, the interpretive factors in perceptions that lead to subjective experiences determine the qualities and affective valences of experiences.

Consequently, it may be said that experiences and their accurate symbolizations are experientially true whether or not they spring from the realities of situations from a consensual viewpoint or the viewpoint of the intentions of a person whose behavior is being perceived. Regardless of the adequacy status of a person's perceptions in respect to external criteria for truth, if a person's self-concept is flexible and open to experience, that person will be able to accurately symbolize his or her experiences in awareness. Or, if the person's self-concept is restrictive then certain experiences will be denied to awareness or distorted. Respectively, the person is congruent or incongruent.

This is quite apart from determinations of consensual reality or reality from another person's perspective.

Another reason for interpreting Rogers' meaning of congruence in his law of interpersonal relationships as strictly within his theory, not as simple matching, has to do with the fact that his interpersonal theory is designed to foster better understanding, improved adjustment and mutual satisfaction among people. How is it possible that in this context Rogers could be advocating the behavior of saying what one thinks and feels in a given moment? Such behavior often includes judgments, criticisms, insults, accusations, interpretations of other people, etc. All of these behaviors are generally recognized as destructive. They are usually destructive to communication, to personal well-being and to satisfaction between people. Could Rogers be naive? No, he most likely means something else by congruent communication.

Understanding Rogers' view of communications in relation to congruence requires clarification of his usage of experience in that context. It also requires understanding of his views about the processes involved in accurate symbolization of experience.

### THE COROLLARY CONCERNING CONGRUENT COMMUNICATIONS

Rogers' conception of congruence between experience and awareness, and between these two elements and communication, has a particular and not always recognized meaning. Rogers (1961) states:

> There is an important corollary of the construct of congruence, which is not at all obvious. It may be stated in this way. If an individual is at this moment entirely congruent, his actual physiological experience being accurately represented in his awareness, and his communication being accurately congruent with his awareness, *then his communication could never contain an expression of external fact*. If he were congruent he could not say, "That rock is hard"; "He is stupid"; "You are bad"; or "She is intelligent." The reason for this is that we never *experience* such "facts." Accurate awareness of *experience* would always be expressed as feelings, perceptions, and meanings from an internal frame of reference ... I never *know* that the rock is hard, even though I may be very sure that I experience it as hard if I fall down on it ... If the person is thoroughly congruent then it is clear that all of his communication would necessarily be put in a context of personal perception. This has very important implications. (p. 341)

Rogers' corollary introduces the idea of an *attitude of personal perceptions* that has direct implications for the nature of congruent communications. To understand the implications specifically for the nature of the communication that might follow from this corollary, we need to understand Rogers' meaning of experience and the meaning of "always be expressed as feelings, perceptions, meanings from an internal frame of reference."

## THE MEANING OF EXPERIENCE

The concept of experience, as a noun, is complex in Rogers' most precise theoretical writings. He indicates he is referring to something synonymous with the whole phenomenal field (Rogers, 1959, p. 197) which includes all perceptions, thoughts about these perceptions, the person's responses to his perceptions including thoughts, sensations, feelings and personal meanings. He describes experience as "all that is present in immediate awareness or consciousness" including "... memory and past experience ..." (p. 197). He also includes "... events of which the individual is unaware, as well as all the phenomena which are conscious" (p. 197). The many elements that are aspects of experience also include the person's assessment of what is real and judgments about what is good or bad in moral or ethical terms. This plethora of elements that are included in the term experience as phenomenal field suggests Rogers' definition is similar to the common English definition:

> [A]nything observed or lived through; an actual living through an event; personally undergoing or observing something or things in general as they occur; individual reaction to events, feelings, etc. (Webster, 1979, p. 645)

In Rogers' and in general usage, experience refers to something happening in or to an individual. In addition, it is from the individual's point of view or frame of reference.

Rogers, however, also appears to give experience a second, much stricter and narrower meaning. Rogers writes of an individual being "entirely congruent" and "... his actual *physiological* experience being accurately represented in his awareness" (1961, p. 341). Although experience is influenced by memory and past experiences, Rogers specifies that these influences are "... active in the moment ... restricting or broadening the meaning given to various stimuli" (Rogers, 1959, p. 197). Also, experience "includes events of which the individual is unaware" (p. 197). But it does not include events such as "neuron discharges" that are not directly available to awareness through introspection. He further states that he has used phrases such as "sensory and visceral ... [and] organic" to convey what is referred to by experience. Experience, in Rogers' narrower definition, of events that are amenable to awareness and symbolization is apparently being differentiated from relatively complex thoughts or cognitions that are part of the wider definition of the term.

The stricter and narrower of Rogers' usages of the term "experience" seem to refer to physiological events that can be sensed. He uses the words "sensory" and "visceral." He is referring to perceptible physical events occurring in the individual's body that can be felt at moments with immediacy. Also, they are pregnant with implicit meanings, which can be identified and symbolized through a process of introspective attention.

The particular qualities of feeling that appear to be basic in Rogers' stricter usage of experience are those in dimensions of satisfactory/unsatisfactory, safe/threatening, pleasurable/unpleasurable. These are qualities of the inherent human capability to organismically value perceptions in respect to their organismic meanings and as signaling well-being or ill-being for the individual. Recent research by Bargh et al. (1995) suggests that all perception is evaluatively tinged as pleasing or displeasing. His findings indicate that the simplest perceptions are not neutrally experienced. The research supports Rogers' conception of the organismic valuing process. It appears that this process is the basic object of awareness in the narrower meaning of experience, in respect to congruence.

Experiences, in Rogers' stricter usage, can be more or less complex experiences in the sense that adequate symbolization of their basic qualities can bring about more or less complex awarenesses through the introspection process. Examples of relatively simple verbal symbolizations of basic experiences are: "I'm scared," "I'm elated," "I'm bored," "I'm disgusted," "I'm comforted," "I'm joyful." Basic or primitive experiences such as "I'm scared" may be elaborated through introspection into more complex experiences and understandings about the situation that provokes a basic reaction of fear. Through introspection, the statement "I'm scared" might become: "When you moved towards me so fast, and seemed so angry, I was afraid you were going to hit me. I felt sick and weak and scared. I still feel afraid of you. I don't want to be near you."

Translating basic affective experiences into subjective language or speech will use the language and discriminations available to the individual according to their culture, education and level of language development.

Introspection of experiences, still referring to Rogers' strict usage, may depart from the immediate character of the experiences in the process of understanding the circumstances of the experience and its implications. Memory of the stimulating situations, identification of the particular perceptions, discrimination of their evaluative qualities, assumptions and interpretations that were intrinsic to the perceptions, and historic associations may fill out the person's understandings of the basic affective experiences. Similar cognitive and associative processes may be brought into the exploration of the implications, to the individual, of the experiences. Whatever processes are brought into the introspection process while attending to the basic experience or sequence of experiences, the person is plumbing her own phenomenology and using her own criteria for assessing reality.

All experiences and all thoughts about things intrinsically exist from a person's idiosyncratic perceptual framework. Persons make distinctions, however, consciously or unconsciously, about what is "out there" in contrast to what is due to the variable of oneself. These distinctions are relevant to understanding Rogers' (1961) idea that a communication of accurate awareness of experience never involves a statement of external fact. And that it would always be expressed as "feelings, perceptions, meanings from an internal frame of reference" (p. 341).

Developments in awareness concerning an experience are likely to occur through introspection. The congruent voicing of the experience, nevertheless, must involve a conscious discrimination of the experience as an *affective event with its personal meanings* as distinguished from the opinions and ideas the person may have about events and persons that are part of the context for the experience.

For example, a person might voice their congruence concerning an experience as follows: "I feel very angry with you, so angry I feel like hitting you because you told that story about me." This statement could be a communication that matches the person's accurate symbolization in awareness of the experience. It also includes the circumstances the person perceives as arousing their anger, because the point of the communication is not only to let their feelings be known, but to engage in conversation that might bring about some restitution, for example, an apology. Or result in some kind of more satisfying experience with their friend in the future. The communication notably does not include interpretation of the friend's motives or character. Presumably the element "told that story …" is consensually valid.

Often, however, an experience is evoked by an event that involves a more complex interpretation of the situation. For example, a person sees an acquaintance coming towards them on the street. As they pass, the acquaintance seems to glance at the person and goes on their way. Later, when they meet again, the person says to the acquaintance: "I was very hurt when you didn't greet me the other day. At first I was afraid you might be angry with me because I haven't called you in a while. But then I got angry because you ignored me. And I've been stewing about it ever since." The person has interpreted the acquaintance as deliberately ignoring the person. The behavior of passing without greeting, however, might or might not have been that. The statement "ignored me" is an interpretation of intentions. The attribution of "ignored" is stated as a fact about the acquaintance, which is not consistent with Rogers' dictum about communications related to congruence. If the last statement were modified to say "But then I got angry because *it seemed to me* you saw me and ignored me …" it could be considered a communication that voices the person's accurate symbolization of the experience. In the modified statement there is only a tentative interpretation of the acquaintance's behavior, and the speaker acknowledges the interpretive factor in the perception.

In the modified statement the person translated the "ignore" perception into the consensual observation: "you didn't greet me," and distinguished the consensual observation from the interpretation of it: "It seemed to me you saw me and ignored me …." Communication that is intended to be about congruent experience often might need to be first processed to discriminate spontaneous interpretive elements (that would result in assertions of fact such as "you ignored me") from the affective experience and from the consensual elements in the stimulating or contextual perception. An attitude of personal perceptions is not always easy to realize.

THERAPEUTIC CONGRUENT COMMUNICATIONS

The basic context and concern for this discussion of experience and congruent communication is, of course, client-centered psychotherapy and person-centered peer groups. In these situations, the therapist (in the former) and the participants (in the latter) are attempting to create an interpersonal environment that is therapeutic and that may promote growth for themselves and others. Rogers' theory of therapy asserts that congruence, unconditional positive regard and empathic understanding are attitudes that, when experienced often and together, in context of a relationship, create a therapeutic and growth-enhancing climate. Recall that Rogers' early statements of his theory did not assert or imply that the contents of congruent experiences are definitely to be communicated in therapy. Congruence was presented as a condition of wholeness and integration, wherein the therapist is able to accurately symbolize experiences in awareness.

Differently, Rogers' theory of interpersonal relationships gives congruence a communication function. This theory applies particularly to situations where both or all parties involved are participating in order to represent themselves as well as to function constructively in relation to other persons. Thus, this theory seems to apply to person-centered peer groups because participants function in such groups to represent themselves as well as to provide therapeutic conditions for others. In so far as participants in a person-centered group are functioning as individuals serving their own purposes (exploring problems, raising issues, expressing reactions to other participants), the general theory of interpersonal relationships can be appropriately applied.

The attitude of personal perceptions cannot influence all communications that serve group participants' momentary personal goals. Communications that act out destructive impulses may occur in therapeutic or group situations although they are errors in respect to the purposes of those situations. Destructive intentions are contrary to the attitude of personal perceptions as a corollary of congruence. Some participants in group settings may communicate with a form of personal perceptions while experiencing destructive intentions. This may be confusing and augment the destructive impact. If, however, participants have constructive intentions and wish to self-disclose or comment from their personal perspectives, then an attitude of personal perceptions implemented by appropriate forms would apply. In any case, constructive or otherwise, communications in therapy, or in groups, cannot accurately be accounted for or be justified on grounds of congruence.

Rogers' corollary about the nature of congruent communication was incorporated by Gordon (1984) and by Guerney (1977) in their interpersonal training programs. Gordon developed techniques for congruent communications in his training of people for constructive family and professional conversations. Guerney (1977) developed techniques for teaching the role of the "expresser" to family members. Both psychologists probably understood Rogers' corollary in terms of an attitude of personal perceptions, but their approaches focused upon and taught techniques.

Rogers illustrated empathic understanding in many demonstration interviews and discussed empathy in many of his writings. In several demonstration therapy interviews, Rogers communicates from his frame of reference. He self-discloses or makes observations about his client in some interviews in response to their questions and does so, on occasion, spontaneously. Rogers illustrated his theory of therapy by publishing interviews and by filming demonstrations. He did not, however, explain or classify the occasions for, or the form of, communications that would be consistent with his theoretical concept of congruence in the context of psychotherapy or peer groups. More recently, Lietaer (1993) has ventured to put forward some reasons the client-centered therapist might self-disclose, make comments, or give feedback in the context of his discussion of transparence. The writer (Brodley, 1999/2011) has also ventured to clarify reasons for such responses in client-centered therapy.

In some studies of Rogers' therapy behavior (Bradburn, 1996; Brodley, 1994/2011; Brodley & Brody, 1990; Brody, 1991; Diss, 1996; Nelson, 1994), several rating categories have been employed to cover a variety of statements made from the therapist's internal frame of reference. Some responses captured by these categories might be viewed as instances of Rogers communicating congruently.

Although congruence has not been employed as a category of therapist behavior in this writer's studies, in client-centered work there are two categories that may include responses that can be interpreted as congruent communications. The first category contains responses in reaction to certain kinds of clients' questions or requests. The second is a category of responses from the therapist's frame of reference that are unsolicited by the client, that are spontaneous and unsystematic. Some responses within these categories may conform to Rogers' conception of communications that express the therapist's congruence. They may communicate some of the contents of the therapist's accurately symbolized experience.

The first category of responses are ones in reaction to clients' questions or requests when the appropriate response requires the therapist's introspection to determine his immediate feelings. An interaction illustrating this follows:

Client: What do you feel about what I just said?

Therapist: You want to know my personal reaction about what you told me or about my reaction towards you?

Client: Both, I guess. I'm afraid your feelings about me will be different now you know I do that. I'm afraid you're disgusted by me.

Therapist: I don't feel disgusted at all. My feelings aren't changed. I do feel a deep sadness that you want to hurt yourself.

Client: Don't you feel it's sick?

Therapist: I don't feel that. My thought about it is it's something that has come out of your suffering. Although it hurts you, it also relieves you.

Client: It's really hard to believe you aren't disgusted with me.

Certain statements from this interaction seem to express the attitude of personal perceptions and may be considered congruent communications: "I don't feel disgusted," "My feelings aren't changed" and "I feel a deep sadness."

The second category of responses, which may express some of the contents of the therapist's experiences in a congruent manner, consists of responses unsolicited by the client but which are reactive to something emotionally unusual or intense that has happened to the client. The responses are spontaneous, unsystematic, and emotionally expressive. Examples are as follows:

The client has arrived at the session and announced her much-loved mother died. The therapist responds, "Oh, I'm terribly sorry!"

The client reports she just got the job she was hoping for. The therapist responds, "I'm so glad! Congratulations!"

The client vividly describes a horrible accident. The therapist responds, "Ohhh, my god!"

The responses "I am terribly sorry" and "I'm so glad" are communications that match the therapist's accurate symbolizations in awareness of the two experiences. "Ohhh, my god!" expresses, but does not verbally represent, the inner experience. Presumably, at the time, the experience is not expressible in articulate language. They all seem to be congruent communications that conform to Rogers' corollary.

## A THEORY OF ATTITUDES

Client-centered therapy and the person-centered approach, in its various applications, are based on a theory of attitudes (Brodley, 1997 [see 2000/2011]). Understanding the theory, one realizes that the development of practitioners is a development of their character, especially as attitudes express character. Development of the ability to practice in a client-centered way requires students to reflect upon their implementations in the light of Rogers' (1951) philosophy of the person. The student experiments with implementations of the therapeutic attitudes and observes the effects both from the inside and the outside. How does he feel about engaging in the behavior of the experiment? How much does the experiment appear to conform to the concepts of the theory? How does the experiment impact the client (or participant, or student, as the case may be)?

Implementations of the therapeutic attitudes are not the attitudes themselves. They may, however, effectively express the attitudes. It has been an understandable mistake to identify attitudes with behavior. But it should be recalled that *an attitude is always a subjective experience*, either *an intention* or *a state of mind* that shapes communication and other behavior.

In the case of unconditional positive regard, its attitudinal nature is so obvious and salient it seems strange to refer to implementations at all. The expression of unconditional positive regard is rarely in most client/person-centered therapeutic relations communicated by explicit statements such as "I accept you and care about you regardless of your ..." (filling in the dots with some behavior about which the client feels self-hatred).

Unconditional positive regard is almost always transmitted indirectly or by nonverbal expression. The trust clients develop, that they are accepted by their therapist, is stimulated by the therapist's empathic understandings that do not shy away from the painful or socially unacceptable material that the client discloses. The client's perception of the therapist's acceptance is also transmitted indirectly by the absence of judgmental statements, and by a tone of voice and manner that are shaped by the acceptant attitude.

Although there may be rare examples of direct communication of unconditional acceptance, it is so infrequent that there is no class of responses that can be pointed to as implementations or techniques to communicate acceptance. Empathic responses, or responses that attempt to address clients' questions, can be shown to be imbued or saturated with acceptance. But these are not statements of acceptance and are certainly not, themselves, the attitude.

In respect to the empathic attitude, there are direct communications – implementations or techniques – that express the attitude. These are primarily empathic understanding responses. There are also some comments expressed from the therapist's frame of reference that communicate empathy. These responses are not, however, themselves the empathic attitude.

Client-centered therapists become more able to implement their acceptant, empathic attitudes as they develop. Their implementations become more purely expressive of the therapeutic attitudes. Therapists also become more confident in their ability to respond accurately and naturally. Their clients perceive them as more accurate in their understandings. Clients less often correct the therapist and more often make comments that the therapist understands "exactly." In this process of personal therapeutic development, maintaining congruence, and experiencing the attitudes of unconditional positive regard and empathic understanding become highly consistent qualities in therapists' personality make-up, at least in relation to clients.

There are a number of familiar interpretations and misunderstandings that are held about the concept of empathic understanding as an attitude and as a practice. Some such misunderstandings about empathic understanding are that they are: "saying back what the client is saying"; "picking up on and responding to feelings"; "focusing the client to be more attuned to her experiencing"; "trying to respond to what is just beneath the surface." These are common misunderstandings of the empathic attitude particularly among teachers who are acquainted with theory but who have not developed themselves as client-centered therapists. It usually takes students quite a lot of trying to implement the concept, then observing effects of the implementations on practice clients, and introspectively reflecting upon their own experiences, to develop a functional understanding of the concept. *Much* more time and practice are needed in order to have the conceptual clarity to teach empathic understanding to others.

Empathic understanding has been given a great deal of attention in the training of therapists. Even so, there remains a significant range of different interpretations or understandings about it. Rogers' concept of congruence is more difficult to understand and difficult to live in relation to clients, students and others. The question even remains as to whether it is accurate to say it is implemented at all in the context of therapy. It certainly is not being *implemented* when the therapist is experiencing acceptant empathic understanding. It is, rather, a state or condition of the therapist underlying those attitudes.

In the context of acceptant empathic understanding, therapist disclosure of personal feelings and thoughts usually would be a distraction to the client's work. When would the therapist appropriately self-disclose? When would one not? For what purpose would the therapist disclose? Frequent self-disclosures would result in the therapist's feelings dominating the conversation and it would no longer be therapy.

CONGRUENT COMMUNICATIONS

Congruence, as Rogers defined it in his theory of psychotherapy, is *an integrated, whole state of the therapist in which he is capable of accurate symbolization in awareness of all experiences.* In respect to communication, the voicing of personal experiences while maintaining an attitude of personal perceptions may be referred to as "expressing congruent communications" or as "communicating congruently." These terms avoid the suggestion that congruence refers to the contents of experience or the contents of communications.

The idea of congruent communications, itself, is a fiction or at least a generous inference. It is very difficult to determine with certainty one's own congruence. Conditions of worth do not promote full and accurate awareness and conditions of worth are ubiquitous. Much less may the congruent state of another be determined with any certainty. In any case, congruence should be distinguished from communication of the contents of experience. Congruent communication may be better thought of as honest communication that also expresses the attitude of personal perceptions. This might avoid confusion of congruence, a relation, with contents.

Congruent communications of self-experiences refer to communications voiced explicitly from the therapist's frame of reference. Also, they refer to personal feelings and personal meanings rather than statements purporting to be statements of facts. Congruent communications usually would also include some description or statement of the perceptions that set the stage for the revealed experiences. These descriptions or statements of perceptions would also explicitly refer to their source in the evaluations or interpretive processes of the speaker.

The following is an example of communication of a therapist's experiences in a therapy session: The therapist is unusually tired and realizes that the client is becoming less articulate. This calls the therapist's attention to the fact that he has been less attentive and has been less closely following the client for a few minutes. In order to be authentic in relation to the client ("not be deceiving the client as to himself"), and to correct for this lapse in his empathic understanding, the therapist undertakes the following conversation:

Therapist: Have I seemed to be less attentive than usual?

Client: Yes, I guess so, but I wasn't so sure about what I was trying to say either.

Therapist: I'm feeling tired and I just realized I've not been tuned in to you as well as I usually am. I've been a bit distracted.

Client: Maybe I was making it harder because I wasn't very coherent.

Therapist: I really don't think I experienced you that way, I just feel kind of tired and vaguely distracted. I am very sorry about that – I am aware of it now, so I think I can listen better, more like I normally do. Would you be willing to go on with what you were telling me?

Client: OK ...

The client may have been losing her train of thought because she was aware of the therapist's distracted presence. In the example, the client also blames herself for the therapist's unusual behavior, even when he explains it has to do with his tiredness. This phenomenon is very common. Clients often feel at fault when the therapist appears to deviate from acceptance or empathy. One of the reasons the therapist might choose to self-disclose his problem could be to try to prevent misunderstandings.

In the example, the particular parts of the interaction that show congruent communication are the therapist's statements: "I'm feeling tired," "I've not been tuned in to you," "I've been distracted," "I'm very sorry," "I am aware of it now." The other elements of the self-disclosure express the therapist's intentions and wishes and are also important for the therapeutic character of the interaction.

Another example of a communication of the therapist's experiences takes place in a person-centered peer group. One participant has been the focus of criticisms by several persons in the group but has also been defended by some others.

> Participant: I'm very confused right now. So many people have been saying things about me. Some of the comments were criticisms and accusations, but I also heard some support. So many things were said so fast, I've been sitting here having a whole lot of different feelings. I know I feel hurt and angry but a bit touched and grateful too. I don't know what all else. I'm confused and upset. More than anything, I guess, I'd like to get out of here.

She communicates her experiences, in terms that appear to express the attitude of personal perceptions, in the following: "I'm very confused," "... having a whole lot of feelings," "I feel hurt and angry but a bit touched and grateful," "I'm confused and upset" and "I'd like to get out of here."

Congruent communication of experiences requires responses that are explicitly from the speaker's frame of reference. They are largely affective responses, as well. References to the stimulating circumstances are often part of the whole statement, but they are expressed carefully to avoid assuming general agreement about the interpretation of events and to avoid interpretation of other persons' motives.

Communication of one's self according to the attitude of personal perceptions also avoids retaliatory remarks. Congruent communication of experiences, according to Rogers' (1961) theory, takes place in the context of an effort to create constructive interactions. This is regardless of the character of previous interactions. Consequently it takes care and discipline and self-control.

Therapists working with clients, and participants in person-centered groups, are free to experiment with forms of self-representation. Self-disclosures are not restricted to communications about the contents of presumed congruence. However, if one truly wants to communicate congruently, then one should be guided by the meaning of the concept of congruence and the attitude of personal perceptions expressed in Rogers' corollary.

The *attitude of personal perceptions*, expressed in Rogers' corollary, does not refer to techniques. It is likely that communications expressing the attitude will be in the first person. Simply making first-person remarks, however, does not guarantee the attitude. First-person statements – "I statements" – may communicate congruent experiences. Also, "I statements" may refer to the speaker's frame of reference but include accusations, interpretations or other assertions of fact. Such statements that begin "I feel" may have a less assertive communicative quality than they would otherwise. They are, nevertheless, assertions of fact, not congruent communications.

In client-centered contexts, many other kinds of statements besides communications of congruence may be appropriate and often are necessary for adequate self-representation or for responding to others. In client-centered therapy, for example, the most frequently observed form of communication (Brodley, 1994/2011) is the broad category of *empathic following responses*. This category includes pure empathic understanding responses, questions for clarification, empathic fragments, "I-form statements" where the therapist is speaking in the first person representing the client, informational following responses and metaphorical following responses which use the clients' own metaphors. This broad form of empathic understanding is common in other applications of the person-centered approach as well as psychotherapy. All of these kinds of statement attempt to characterize what the therapist has understood as the client's intended communications. They are expressed to find out whether or not the therapist's inner understandings are accurate according to the client (Rogers, 1986; Brodley, 1998/2011).

There are responses that are *comments from the therapist's frame of reference*, in addition, within the therapy context. They are not following responses. Comments from the therapist's frame are often saturated with empathic knowledge or empathic speculation about the client. An example of this is a response from the therapist's frame of reference that is an inference about the client's behavior. The therapist remarks, "you seem to be sitting on the edge of your seat and ready to go" in response to a client's description of a plan. The therapist's attitude inquires as to the validity of the statement from the client's frame of reference, when making observations about the client. Clients sometimes perceive empathy-laden responses as if they were empathic following responses, although they spring from the therapist's frame of reference.

Other comments from the therapist's frame are self-disclosures such as "I must be sure to stop on time, so I may be looking at the clock towards the end of the session." Some self-disclosures may be communications of congruent experiences. They could be spontaneous reactions such as "Tears are welling up in me" in response to a moving poem the client has quoted. Self-disclosures could be explanatory statements such as "I was preoccupied for a moment and didn't hear what you were saying" to correct for the therapist appearing to listen when it was not the case. The most common kind of comment from the therapist's frame of reference are introductions or endings of empathic responses which express the therapist's degree of uncertainty or tentativeness about the accuracy of his or her understandings. An example of this is the introduction "I'm not sure if this is right, but do you mean …?"

In addition to these categories of statements to clients, client-centered therapists may occasionally (albeit only rarely), and unsystematically, volunteer an *interpretation* or an *explanation about the client*, or ask a *leading or probing question*, or assert an *agreement* with a client. All of the mentioned categories of responses occur as therapists' verbal communications in response to clients who are self-expressing and self-representing. They may occur, also, in response to clients' questions or requests.

FOUR REASONS FOR COMMUNICATION OF THE THERAPIST'S FEELINGS

Responses that congruently communicate the therapist's experiences exist in the client-centered therapist's response repertoire. These responses are expressed from the attitude of personal perceptions. They often include therapist self-disclosures that emphasize the therapist is expressing *an opinion, an impression* or *an interpretation*. I shall not discuss all possible reasons for congruent communications or other therapist self-disclosures in this paper. I have presented reasons for responses from the therapist's frame of reference elsewhere (Brodley, 1999/2011). Four situations that constitute reasons for the therapist to make such responses have been mentioned that seem clearly consistent with Rogers' theory.

One is the situation when a client perceives, or the therapist believes the client perceives, inconsistency of meaning among the therapist's behaviors. The reason for the congruent communication in this situation is in order that the therapist can remain clear, unconfused to the client, and be likely to have the quality of transparency.

The second is the situation of the therapist having persistent experiences that are counter to the therapeutic attitudes of unconditional positive regard or empathic understanding. This is the most likely reason for making such a response and the one Rogers mentions.

I feel conservative in respect to this rationale. I recommend considerable introspection and talking feelings out with a colleague or consultant before voicing the therapist's problems to a client. I recommend this conservative approach to congruent communications because I think clients should not be distracted from self-direction by being presented with the therapist's problems unless there is no other way to solve the problem. I have observed, also, that therapists who have counter-therapeutic feelings tend to be unprepared to cope with clients' complex and unexpected reactions to disappointing information from the therapist.

The third situation occurs when the client asks a direct question or makes a request. A self-disclosure or an honest expression of the therapist's opinion is appropriate in order to be respectful towards the client and allow the client to be the architect of the therapy.

The fourth situation is where there are simply spontaneous eruptions of disclosure of the therapist's feelings. These are unsystematic, infrequent and brief responses coming from the therapist's personal presence and responsiveness.

In all of these situations we assume the therapist remains faithful to the aim to function therapeutically. The therapist attempts to communicate his own feelings and personal meanings in ways that do not undermine or confuse the client. In situations where the therapist chooses to communicate his experiences, or his opinion or perspective about something, he is, also, at the same time, attempting to experience unconditional positive regard and empathic understanding. This attempt exists even when the context of congruent communication or the self-disclosure of opinion involves experiences that are counter to the therapeutic attitudes of acceptant empathy. Communications about personal experiences or self-disclosures of opinions in client-centered therapy require discipline.

CONCLUSION

The respectful, democratic and egalitarian orientation of client-centered work is intrinsic to the therapist's character and the therapist's attitudes. These qualities influence all behavior with clients. We emphasize that we are speaking from our own perspectives and inner experiences, in contrast to speaking from the authority of our credentials or our status as therapists. We have this emphasis when making empathic responses and whenever we respond to clients from our own frames of reference. We avoid declarations of fact. Instead we emphasize personal perspectives. We convey our tentativeness when we do express statements of fact. We give the client the anatomy of our reasoning, or give our evidence, when we make statements of explanation or interpretation. We invoke our attitude of personal perspectives when we wish to communicate about our congruent experiences. All of these efforts contribute to the client's sense of being respected as a person.

Client-centered behavior may appear spontaneous to an observer and it may feel spontaneous to the therapist. It is, however, very disciplined behavior. It appears spontaneous when the values, attitudes and concepts about the work have become part of the therapist's character and lived attitudes. A therapist's capability to maintain a congruent state is fundamental and essential to all therapeutic qualities and endeavors.

**REFERENCES**

Baldwin, M. (1987). Interview with Carl Rogers on the use of the self in therapy. In M. Baldwin & V. Satir (Eds.), *The use of the self in therapy* (pp. 45–52). New York: Haworth Press. [Reprinted (2004) in R. Moodley, C. Lago, & A. Talahite (Eds.), *Carl Rogers counsels a Black client: Race and culture in person-centred counseling* (pp. 253–260). Ross-on-Wye: PCCS Books]

Bargh, J. A. (1997). The automaticity of everyday life. In R. S. Wyer, Jr. (Ed.), *The automaticity of everyday life: Advances in social cognition, Volume X* (pp. 1–61). Mahwah, NJ: Erlbaum.

Bargh, J. A., Chaiken, S., Raymond, P., & Hymes, C. (1995, May). *The automatic evaluation effect: Unconditional automatic attitude activation with a pronunciation task.* Paper presented at the annual conference of the American Psychological Association, New York.

Bradburn, W. M. (1996). *Did Carl Rogers' positive view of human nature bias his psychotherapy? An empirical investigation.* Unpublished doctoral clinical research project, Illinois School of Professional Psychology, Chicago (now Argosy University, Chicago).

Brodley, B. T. (1994). Some observations of Carl Rogers' therapy behavior in therapy interviews. *The Person-Centered Journal, 1*(2), 37–48. [This volume, Chapter 25]

Brodley, B. T. (1997, July). *Client-centered: An expressive therapy.* Paper presented at the Fourth International Conference on Client-Centered and Experiential Psychotherapy. Lisbon, Portugal. [See Brodley, 2000]

Brodley, B. T. (1998). Criteria for making empathic responses in client-centered therapy. *The Person-Centered Journal, 5*(1), 20–28. [This volume, Chapter 14]

Brodley, B. T. (1999). Reasons for responses expressing the therapist's frame of reference in client-centered therapy. *The Person-Centered Journal, 6*(1), 4–27. [This volume, Chapter 15]

[Brodley, B.T. (2000). Client-centered: An expressive therapy. In J. E. Marques-Teixeira & S. Antunes (Eds.), *Client-centered and experiential psychotherapy* (pp. 133–147). Linda a Velha, Lisboa, Portugal: Vale & Vale. Reprinted (2002) in *The Person-Centered Journal 9*(1), 59–70; this volume, Chapter 13]

Brodley, B. T., & Brody, A. F. (1990, August). *Understanding client-centered therapy through interviews conducted by Carl Rogers.* Paper presented at the annual conference of the American Psychological Association, Boston, MA.

Brody, A. F. (1991). *Understanding client-centered therapy through interviews conducted by Carl Rogers.* Unpublished doctoral clinical research project, Illinois School of Professional Psychology, Chicago (now Argosy University, Chicago).

Diss, J. W. (1996). *Facilitative responses leading to client process disruption in Carl Rogers' therapy behavior.* Unpublished doctoral clinical research project, Illinois School of Professional Psychology, Chicago (now Argosy University, Chicago).

Gordon, T. (1984). Three decades of democratizing relationships through training. In D. Larson (Ed.), *Teaching psychological skills: Models for giving psychology away* (pp. 151–170). New York: Brooks/Cole.

Guerney, B. G. (1977). Basic skills of relationship enhancement programs. In *Relationship enhancement* (pp. 25–53). San Francisco: Jossey-Bass.

Haugh, S. (1998). Congruence: A confusion of language. *Person-Centred Practice, 6*(1), 44–50.

Lietaer, G. (1993). Authenticity, congruence and transparency. In D. Brazier (Ed.), *Beyond Carl Rogers* (pp. 17–46). London: Constable.

Nelson, J. A. (1994). *Carl Rogers' verbal behavior in therapy: A comparison of theory and therapeutic practice.* Unpublished doctoral clinical research project, Illinois School of Professional Psychology, Chicago (now Argosy University, Chicago).

Rogers, C. R. (1951). *Client-centered therapy.* Boston: Houghton Mifflin.

Rogers, C. R. (1957). The necessary and sufficient conditions for therapeutic personality change. *Journal of Consulting Psychology, 21*, 95–103.

Rogers, C. R. (1959). A theory of therapy, personality and interpersonal relationships, as developed in the client-centered framework. In S. Koch (Ed.), *Psychology: A study of a science. Vol. III: Formulations of the person and the social context* (pp. 184–256). New York: McGraw-Hill.

Rogers, C. R. (1961). *On becoming a person.* Boston: Houghton Mifflin.

Rogers, C. R. (1980). The foundations of a person-centered approach. In *A way of being* (pp. 113–135). Boston: Houghton Mifflin.

Rogers, C. R. (1986). Client-centered therapy. In J. L. Kutash & A. Wolf (Eds.), *A psychotherapist's casebook: Theory and technique in practice* (pp. 197–208). San Francisco: Jossey-Bass.

Webster, N. (1979). *Webster's new universal unabridged dictionary.* New York: Simon and Schuster.

# Chapter 8

# Empathic understanding and feelings
# in client-centered therapy

Experienced client-centered therapists and other students of Carl Rogers' theory of therapy agree that the client-centered conception of empathic understanding gives emphasis to the client's feelings in the therapy process. In the process of empathic understanding response interactions the therapist is highly attuned and responsive to the client's feelings. In that process the therapist "… senses accurately the feelings and personal meanings that the client is experiencing …" (Rogers, 1980a, p. 116).

The precise meaning of "feelings" and the precise function of the language of feelings, however, are not fully articulated by Rogers or others when describing empathic understanding in client-centered therapy. The meaning and the function of "feelings" in empathic understanding are, consequently, somewhat confusing to students. The approach is particularly misunderstood when Rogers is interpreted to be advocating that the therapist respond to the "hot" emotions or feelings in the client's communication (Zimring, 1990, p. 436).

In fact, Rogers' conception of empathy is different and more complex than simply responding to feelings. Rogers stated:

> … being empathic is to perceive the internal frame of reference of another with accuracy and with the emotional components and meanings which pertain thereto … it means to sense the hurt or the pleasure of another as he senses it and to perceive the causes thereof as he perceives them …
> (Rogers, 1980b, p. 140)

In other words, client-centered empathy refers to empathic understanding of the client's entire presented internal frame of reference which includes perceptions, ideas, meanings and the emotional-affective components connected with these things as well as the client's feelings and emotions per se.

Several studies (Brodley & Brody, 1990; Brody, 1991; Brodley, 1994/ 2011; Merry, 1996; Nelson, 1994; Bradburn, 1996; Diss, 1996) attempt to

Published (1996) in *The Person-Centered Journal*, 3(1), 22–30. Corrected version of an incomplete paper published (1992) in *The Person-Centered Journal*, 1(1), 21–32. Reproduced with permission from *PCJ*.

elucidate Rogers' conception of client-centered therapy by examining Rogers' empathic responses in samples of Rogers' own therapy interviews. The results of the Brodley and Brody (1990) and the Brody (1991) studies, along with a subsequent analysis by the writer of several additional interviews by Rogers, show that Rogers uses feeling words – words that explicitly designate feelings or emotions – in only 24% of his empathic following responses. Obviously, more is involved in Rogers' empathic behavior than responses designating feelings.

In addition to words for the clients' feelings, Rogers uses words in his empathic responses that are not precisely feeling words, but are words that express dispositions (such as "prefer," "alienate," "seduce"), evaluations (such as "denigrate," "value," "assess") and volitions (such as "determine," "resist," "reject"). Words that express dispositions, evaluations, and volitions occur in approximately 48% of Rogers' empathic responses – twice as many such words than words for feelings.

On the basis of the research findings and careful reading of Rogers' writings, it appears to be more accurate, when discussing client-centered empathy, to not overgeneralize the meaning of "feelings." It seems to be more faithful to Rogers' theory, as it is enlightened by his therapy behavior, to clarify that Rogers' conception of empathic responses emphasizes *the client's perceptions and the ways in which the client as a self is an agency or an active force and a source of meanings, reactions and other experiences.* The client represents self as source, of course, in his or her expressions of feelings as well as other experiences.

The studies of Rogers' therapy behavior (e.g., Brody, 1991) reveal that approximately 90% of Rogers' empathic following responses either explicitly or implicitly communicate that Rogers is understanding the client as a source of reactions and meanings. Approximately 70% of Rogers' total empathic following responses are found to be explicit in expressing the client's reactions and meanings. Approximately 20% are implicit or indirect. Thus, 90% of Rogers' empathic following responses either use specific words that express the client's self as a source of reactions (words for feelings, dispositions, evaluations, volitions or other forms) or meanings, or they communicate self as a source of experiences implicitly or indirectly.

An example of interaction between Rogers and a client wherein Rogers' empathic response includes no words for feelings but nonetheless expresses the client as a source of experiences:

Mrs. Roc: Inside my head I'm rushing around and saying "*Oh*, I want my mama. *Oh*, what's wrong? *Oh, help me.*" And I guess I have the hook instead.

Rogers: But there is just that pleading feeling in you, "*Mama*, somebody, help me, do things for me, take care of me." And you feel the only substitute you have for that is, is the hook in your head.

(Rogers, 1955a) [See also Brodley & Lietaer, 2006, Vol. 10, Mrs. Roc, p. 53]*

An example from another client includes no words for feelings:

Vivian: ... feeling I have to entertain and then I get taken care of. Yeah, that's it, an "entertain" analogy. And not quite knowing what to do after the introductions. And feeling I just can't ... just *be*.

Rogers: That's the essence of it, that you ought to be entertaining or you ought to have something well in mind. The notion of just *being* ... that doesn't seem possible. (Rogers, 1984)

[see also Brodley & Lietaer, 2006, Vol. 16, Vivian, Interview, p. 4]

The studies by the writer and Brody also show that Rogers' clients correct his empathic responses less than 1% of the time. From this observation, and from the observation that Rogers' clients frequently acknowledge the accuracy of his empathic responses, and from observations that clients manifest productive narrative and expressive processes following Rogers' responses (Diss, 1996), we infer that Rogers' empathic responses are perceived as accurate by his clients most of the time. It seems justified to further infer that Rogers' clients feel understood largely because he is picking up on the way they are expressing their selves as sources of reactions and experiences.

Feelings are only a portion of the experiences clients express about their selves. In a recent analysis of 25 of Rogers' therapy interviews, Bradburn (1995, personal communication) found that 27% of Rogers' clients' statements were *without* affective features. These clients' statements expressed personal meanings, perspectives and information. Thus, for the sake of accurate empathic understanding, it is appropriate that the therapist not read in feelings when empathically following the client.

In therapy interactions, as the client narrates and lays out his or her life situations, there are (interspersed before, within or after the information about situations, events, people and things) communications expressing the client's

---

* Editors' note: In the course of many years, Barbara transcribed and supervised others in transcribing Rogers' therapy and demonstration sessions. In this paper she refers to transcripts that were in the process of being "polished" through multiple listenings to the tapes. It is uncertain at which point of evolution she quoted from the various transcripts. The transcript work culminated in a joint effort with Germain Lietaer resulting in a journal article (Lietaer & Brodley, 2003) and an informal email publication (Brodley & Lietaer, 2006).

subjective reactions. Clients' descriptions of situations, events, people and things are important aspects of their phenomenal field. It is thus important that the descriptions be understood and respected in empathic interactions. It is, however, not until the client has in some way revealed his or her particular relation to the situations, etc. that the therapist has the basis for true empathic understanding.

It may clarify this point to give examples of different client communications which offer different kinds of information relevant to the question of what allows understanding to be truly empathic understanding. Rogers produces empathic responses that are purely information about situations, events, people or things in approximately 5% of his empathic following responses (Brody, 1991; Brodley, 1994/2011). Pure information responses are, usually, responses to client statements which are, equally, purely informational. Such client statements do not reveal the client's reactions or the client's personal relation to what he or she is talking about. The following is an example of a purely informational statement:

Client: He called me up at work and wanted to see me again.

Obviously, this statement, by itself, does not communicate what the call means to the client. Nor does it communicate the client's feelings or other reactions to the call. It is possible, and sometimes is the case, that such a purely informational type statement by a client does suggest the client's reactions. This occurs when the client has previously informed the therapist about the meaning or impact this event has had in the past or about the meaning or impact the client has predicted it would have if it were to occur in the future. Standing alone, however, the statement does not tell the listener what it means to the client, nor does it reveal the client's reactions.

The client-centered therapist might offer a following type of response to the statement above that research (Brodley & Brody, 1990) has classified as a "pure information" empathic following response – such as "He called." As mentioned above, Rogers occasionally produces this type of response. It appears to serve almost the same role as "umhum," "OK," "yeah," and nonverbal nodding responses. Any of which simply signal to the client that the therapist is attentive, is attempting to follow, and is understanding in a general sense.

A slightly different client statement, giving information that could be the basis for true empathic understanding is as follows:

Client: He *finally* called me up and wanted to see me again.

The emphasized *finally* communicates something of the client's reaction to the event. It does not express enough information, however, for the therapist to know exactly what experiences (meanings, feelings, other reactions) are alluded to. The therapist, nevertheless, might make a true empathic response to this communication, although it would be limited in its differentiation of meaning. The therapist might respond by saying *"Finally!"* which could communicate to the client the therapist's sense that the client had some strong feelings and that the client had been waiting to hear from the man.

Alternatively, the therapist might simply absorb the *"finally,"* maintain empathic attention to the client and wait for more material that might communicate the client's reactions, thoughts, feelings or whatever other expression of the client's self might be involved. The client's *"finally"* in any case would have increased the therapist's experience of empathic understanding.

The following example of a client statement expresses information that is differentiated in respect to the client's reactions and, consequently, makes it possible for the therapist to more fully empathically understand the client in the moment.

Client: He called me up at work and wanted to see me again. (Pause) *Finally!* (Pause) I was so busy I couldn't talk, but I was emotionally all over the place and couldn't concentrate for the rest of the afternoon. (Pause) *I'm such a sap!* He's a complete asshole, but I'm still dying to see him.

Putting aside the organization of the client's meanings and the question of the main thrust of the client's agency in this example, the elements that could contribute to *true* empathic understanding of the client are: *"Finally!"* (because of the vocal emphasis); "emotionally all over the place"; "couldn't concentrate"; *"I'm such a sap!"*; "He's a complete asshole" (inferentially); "I'm dying to see him." Notably, none of these statements directly and explicitly state the client's *feelings*, although the entire statement is pregnant with feelingful expression and allusion to feelings.

There are a number of different possible empathic following responses which a therapist might make to check his or her understanding of what the client has been expressing in the above statement. One possible response is:

Therapist: You feel you're a fool to want a person who upsets you so badly, but ... you do want him!

An alternative response that might express the therapist's inner empathic understanding in response to the client statement above is:

Therapist: You got what you were waiting for, but it brings with it a lot of mixed feelings.

Only the client can tell us which, if either, of these responses is the more accurate. It is likely that the client would accept either response as representing the therapist's sincere intentions of trying to understand. The client's statements revealed her various experiences in relation to the situation of the call. These expressions of her *self* permit the therapist to have an experience of, and to communicate, empathic understanding.

Most of Rogers' responses to his clients express his immediate grasp of the meanings the client is attributing to situations or the client's reactions to what he or she is talking about. Exceptions, as noted above, are a small percentage of Rogers' responses which are purely informational following responses, such as "He called you."

Purely informational responses are forms of empathic following that occasionally occur in a client-centered therapist's sequence of empathic understanding interactions with a client. Clients, however, would not be likely to experience the feeling of being empathically understood if this informational form were the only form of response the therapist expressed in the extended interaction.

According to client-centered theory (Rogers, 1959), the client's perception of the therapist's acceptant empathic understanding is necessary for therapeutic change. The therapist fosters this perception through many interactions by empathically following the client's narrative. The perception is fostered most particularly when the therapist is understanding the aspects of the client's communication in which the client is expressing his or her relation to the situation. This occurs when the client is expressing self-agency. Self as the source of meanings, or reactions, or experiences in relation to the situations being disclosed.

THE THERAPIST'S INTENTIONS AND EFFECTS OF EMPATHY

The client-centered therapist's immediate intention when making an empathic response is to check, test or verify the accuracy of his or her subjective empathic understanding (Brodley, 1985 [see revised version, 1998/2011]; Rogers, 1986). This is done by the therapist communicating his or her inner understanding to the client for the client's verification, correction or modification. The communication may be through words, gestures, body language or vocal intonations. The form of communication is only important in that it must be one the client is able to perceive in order to evaluate its accuracy. The client is viewed as the expert, the authority, about his own intentions, meanings and feelings.

There are two frequently observed effects of accurate and acceptant empathic understanding when they are perceived by clients. One is that the client elaborates, develops and reveals more of his or her phenomenal world to the therapist. The other is that clients tend to become more consistently and intently focused on, and express themselves from, the experiential source of what they are talking about. In other words, there is a frequent focusing effect of client-centered empathic work; although this is not the intention of the therapist when making empathic responses (Brodley, 1991).

From the point of view of Rogers' process theory of change in client-centered therapy (Rogers, 1956, 1958, 1961, 1980b; Gendlin, 1964), the focusing effect of empathic following is desirable and considered therapeutic. Although the focusing effect is notable and may be considered theoretically desirable – it is serendipitous in the existential interaction. The client-centered therapist does not deliberately intend to produce the focusing effect. It is not the motivating reason the therapist makes an empathic response.

The client-centered therapist's empathic intention is to acceptantly understand. Rogers himself is very clear in his writings that he has no goals for his clients (Baldwin, 1987/2004, p. 47/p. 256). His therapy behavior is highly consistent with this nondirective principle although there are some infrequent exceptions (Brodley, 1994/2011). Theoretically, and usually in practice, client-centered therapists' immediate interaction goals are strictly goals for themselves – to experience and offer the attitudinal conditions of congruence, unconditional positive regard and empathic understanding in the relationship with their clients. This is an implication of the nondirective attitude which is intrinsic to client-centered therapy. The focusing effect of empathic understanding is, consequently, serendipitous even though predictable.

## THE CONNECTIONS BETWEEN TRUE EMPATHY, FEELINGS AND EXPERIENCING

The therapist's acts of true empathic understanding, in themselves, tend to stimulate clients to be in touch with the underlying experiential source of their self-disclosures and self-representations. The client hears the therapist's empathic response and checks with his or her inner source. In this way the client is attuned to find out whether or not the therapist's communicated perceptions of the client's meanings and feelings are consistent with what the client was trying to express. Rogers asserts that this checking within phenomenon, observed in clients when they are empathically understood, is based on a natural and basic characteristic of human functioning. He states:

> ... at all times there is going on in the human organism a flow of experiencing to which the individual can turn again and again as a referent in order to discover the meaning of those experiences. (Rogers, 1980b, p. 141)

People are not aware that they are checking with their subjective flow of experiencing when they reflect upon their feelings, their reactions and upon what things mean to them. Such self-reflection is spontaneous, not self-conscious, and is a natural process for most people. Regardless of whether or not clients are aware of the process of referring to their own experiencing in the particular instances, the client-centered therapeutic attitudes promote and enhance this natural process.

The fundamental empathic activity in client-centered therapy is the therapist's intention to subjectively experience the client's intentions in his or her communications. In order to be sure subjective understandings are accurate, the therapist attempts to find out from the client. This desire to verify inner experience of understanding brings about the therapist's communications of empathic understanding, often in the form of empathic understanding responses. The therapist's attempts to find out if his or her subjective understandings are accurate or not according to the client stimulate the client toward an attunement to the qualities and contents of his or her own experiencing. The key element in the therapist's stimulation of the client towards attunement to his or her own experiencing is the therapist's attunement and responsiveness to the client's self-agency – to the client's perceptions, feelings and other elements of the client's self as a source of experiences.

It is generally the case, if we are trying to understand another person empathically, that we find ourselves making statements that include references to the other person as a self who is an active force, an actor or agency in the creation of meanings and reactions. We make statements that include elements such as "you want," "you feel," "you think," "you know," "you reject," "you wonder," "you were full of conflicting reactions," "you expect," "you believe," etc. Although not intended to have this effect, in making these references we stimulate the other person to attend to his or her self as a source – a source of wants, feelings, perceptions, etc. These references to the person's self as an actor or agency and as a source tend to attune the person to his or her phenomenological source – what Rogers calls "experiencing" (Rogers, 1959).

One cannot authentically, with personal authority, agree or disagree with an empathic statement unless one attends to the experiential source of meanings and feelings. Without the authority of one's inner sense of meanings, agreement or disagreement is at most a purely logical conclusion, or it is based on conventional beliefs and is not a personal truth. In client-centered therapy empathic responses always implicitly contain the question to the client "Do you feel this is an accurate understanding of what you have been intending to express to me?" The combination of the fact that the therapist is seeking validation of his or her empathic understanding and also that it is in the nature of empathic responses to be communicating about activities of the client's *self* tends to stimulate the client to attend to inner experiencing.

The client's checking-within process, that tends to be stimulated by the therapist's empathic responses, is a spontaneous focusing activity on the part of the client. Such focusing acts recur over and over in the client-centered empathic following process. To the extent the therapist does *not* shift away from acceptant and empathic attitudes (and in that way distract the client with external foci such as the therapist's ideas about the client), the process of empathic following facilitates the client's focus on his or her phenomenological experiencing.

## ROGERS' USE OF THE WORD "FEELING"

Another observation from research that contributes to clarifying the connection between empathy, experiencing and feelings in client-centered therapy is that Rogers uses the words "feel," "feels," "feeling" or "feelings" in more than half of his empathic following responses (Brodley & Brody, 1990). He does so in responses that *do not*, as well as in responses that do, include words or phrases that communicate specific feelings. Following are examples of Rogers' usage of "feel," etc. in some of his empathic understanding responses in therapy interviews:

Rogers: You feel there's so little chance of anyone else really understanding you.

(Whiteley, 1977) [See also Brodley & Lietaer, 2006, Vol. 12, Dione, 2nd Interview, p. 99]

Rogers: You'd like to be aware of your feelings about these demands, right at the time they happen instead of having bright thoughts afterwards.

(Rogers, 1955b) [See also Brodley & Lietaer, 2006, Vol. 10, Miss Mun, p. 60]

Rogers: You feel at a stage. And when you work through some of the other things in the background, that may straighten out too.

(Rogers, 1947) [See also Brodley & Lietaer, 2006, Vol. 4, ETT, Session 12, p. 141]

Rogers: A really contradictory feeling that "I don't want to be a person who just gives in to all demands" and, yet, feeling "that's the only chance I have of being loved."

(Rogers, 1955b) [See also Brodley & Lietaer, Vol. 10, Miss Mun, p. 64]

These examples of Rogers' empathic responses illustrate that he uses the words "feel," etc., in several ways. One way he uses these words is as synonyms for "think," "believe," "imagine," "know" or "perceive," etc. This synonymous usage of the word "feel" carries the message that there are emotions or feelings or emotional components associated with the client's thoughts, beliefs, etc., although the emotions or feelings have not been explicitly stated. A second way Rogers uses the words "feel," etc., in his empathic responses, is to refer to an inner experience – to something in the realm of subjective experiencing – of the client without naming it. For example:

Rogers: You'd like to be aware of your feelings ...

A third way Rogers uses "feel," etc., in his empathic responses is to refer to an experience that Rogers does express in the particular empathic response, although the experience is not expressed with any word for feeling. For example:

Rogers: A ... feeling that "I don't want to be a person who just gives in ..."

In this usage of "feeling," what is referred to in the client's experience is not expressible (at least at that moment) with a word for feeling, possibly because the experience is too complex or because it may involve feelings for which, in English at any rate, there are no specific words.

Another way Rogers uses the words "feel," etc., is as introduction to an empathic following response. The empathic response itself may or may not include words for feelings, dispositions, evaluations, volitions or other kinds of agency words. Introductions with "feel," etc., are heuristic or at least expressive of the way the remainder of the empathic response refers to experiencing. For example:

Rogers: You feel there is so little chance ...

Each of the usages of the words "feel," etc., which are so frequent in Roger's empathic responses, express Rogers' attunement to the experiential source of feelings and meanings. The frequent expression of these words tends to attune the client to the client's own experiencing. The usages take advantage of the way in which "feel," etc. allude to the source of responses within a person's self in the English language. This is not to suggest that Rogers is deliberately trying to direct or instruct his clients to attend to experiencing. Rather, true empathic responses communicate the client's self-agency and express the empathic attitude. This pattern of behavior in client-centered work has the effect of attuning clients to their feelings and to other facets of their own experiencing.

## SUMMARY

Client-centered empathy is not intended to discriminate the client's feelings out of the matrix of the client's communication and self-expression. The therapist's experience of empathic understanding includes understanding of the client's feelings, dispositions, evaluations, volitions, personal meanings, perspectives, explanations and information. The therapist gives the client's narratives respectful attention and follows all elements in them. The therapist, however, does not achieve true empathic understanding until understanding the elements expressive of the client as a self and particularly as a self-agency. The client's perception that the therapist understands these elements is crucial to the client feeling empathically understood.

A focusing effect is a natural and ubiquitous effect upon clients when they perceive they are truly empathically understood. The empathic interaction stimulates the person who feels understood in this way to attend to their own experiencing and to represent himself or herself more acutely from their experiential source. The therapist's recognition of the client as agency – actor and reactor – in empathic responding, and the client's perception of this recognition by the therapist, are keys to the focusing effect.

In addition to the focusing effect of empathic recognition of the self-agency of clients, the ways in which Rogers uses the words "feel," "feels," "feeling," "feelings" in his empathic responses tend to allude to, and also attune the client to, his or her experiencing. Both of these features of Rogers' empathy – empathic recognition of self-agency and the usages of "feels," "feeling," etc. – help to clarify client-centered therapy and its concept of empathic understanding.

It is crucial for correct understanding of client-centered therapy, however, to realize that the focusing effects stimulated by empathic behavior are and should remain serendipitous. The therapist does not deliberately attempt to focus clients on their experiencing processes. If the therapist implements such a goal for the client, he or she is stepping outside of client-centered therapy.

## REFERENCES

Baldwin, M. (1987). Interview with Carl Rogers on the use of self in therapy. In M. Baldwin & V. Satir (Eds.), *The use of self in therapy* (pp. 45–52). New York: Haworth Press. [Reprinted (2004) in R. Moodley, C. Lago, & A. Talahite (Eds.), *Carl Rogers counsels a Black client: Race and culture in person-centred counseling* (pp. 253–260). Ross-on-Wye: PCCS Books]

Bradburn, W. (1996). *Did Carl Rogers' positive view of human nature bias his therapy? An empirical investigation.* Unpublished doctoral clinical research project, Illinois School of Professional Psychology, Chicago (now Argosy University, Chicago).

Brodley, B. T. (1985). Criteria for making empathic understanding responses in client-centered therapy. *Renaissance, 2*(1), 1–3. [See Brodley,1998/2011 revision in this volume, Chapter 14]

Brodley, B. T. (1991, May). *The role of focusing in client-centered therapy.* Presented in a dialogue concerning the role of focusing, between Ann Weiser Cornell and Barbara Brodley at the Annual Meeting of the Association for the Development of the Person-Centered Approach, Coffeyville, KS.

Brodley, B. T. (1994). Some observations of Carl Rogers' behavior in therapy interviews. *The Person-Centered Journal, 1*(2), 37–48. [This volume, Chapter 25]

Brodley, B. T. (1998) Criteria for making empathic responses in client-centered therapy. *The Person-Centered Journal, 5*(1), 20–28. [This volume, Chapter 14]

Brodley, B. T., & Brody, A. F. (1990, August). Understanding client-centered therapy through interviews conducted by Carl Rogers. Paper presented for the panel *Fifty years of client-centered therapy: Recent research,* at the American Psychological Association annual meeting in Boston.

[Brodley, B. T., & Lietaer, G. (Eds.). (2006). *Transcripts of Carl Rogers' therapy sessions, Vols. 1–17.* Available from germain.lietaer@psy.kuleuven.be and kmoon1@alumni.uchicago.edu]

Brody, A. F. (1991). *A study of ten interviews conducted by Carl Rogers.* Unpublished doctoral clinical research project, Illinois School of Professional Psychology, Chicago (now Argosy University, Chicago).

Diss, J. W. (1996). *Facilitative responses leading to client process disruption in Carl Rogers' therapy behavior.* Unpublished doctoral clinical research project, Illinois School of Professional Psychology, Chicago (now Argosy University, Chicago).

Gendlin, E. T. (1964). A theory of personality change. In P. Worchel & D. Byrne (Eds.), *Personality change* (pp. 102–148). New York: Wiley.

[Lietaer, G., & Brodley, B. T. (2003). Carl Rogers in the therapy room: A listing of session transcripts and a survey of publications referring to Rogers' sessions. *Person-Centered & Experiential Psychotherapies, 2*(4), 274–291.]

Merry, T. (1996) *An analysis of ten demonstration interviews by Carl Rogers: Implications for the training of client-centred counsellors.* In R. Hutterer, G. Pawlowsky, P. F. Schmid, & R. Stipsits (Eds.), *Client-centered and experiential psychotherapy: A paradigm in motion* (pp. 273–284). Frankfurt am Main: Peter Lang. [Originally presented (1994) at the Third International Client-Centered and Experiential Conference, Gmunden, Austria, August]

Nelson, J. A. (1994). *Carl Rogers' verbal behavior in therapy: A comparison of theory and therapeutic practice*. Unpublished doctoral clinical research project, Illinois School of Professional Psychology, Chicago (now Argosy University, Chicago).

Rogers, C. R. (1947). *Transcript of Rogers' session with Mrs. Ett*. Carl Rogers Memorial Library, Center for Study of the Person, La Jolla, CA.

Rogers, C. R. (1955a). *Transcript of Rogers' session seven with Mrs. Roc*. Carl Rogers Memorial Library, Center for the Study of the Person, La Jolla, CA.

Rogers, C. R. (1955b). *Transcript of Rogers' session seventeen with Miss Mun*. Carl Rogers Memorial Library, Center for Study of the Person, La Jolla, CA.

Rogers, C. R. (1956, October 20). *The essence of psychotherapy: Moments of movement*. Paper presented at the first meeting of the American Academy of Psychotherapists, New York.

Rogers, C. R. (1958). A process conception of psychotherapy. *American Psychologist, 13*, 142–149.

Rogers, C. R. (1959). A theory of therapy, personality, and interpersonal relationships as developed in the client-centered framework. In S. Koch (Ed.), *Psychology: A study of a science. Vol. III: Formulations of the person and the social context* (pp. 184–256). New York: McGraw-Hill.

Rogers, C. R. (1961). A process conception of psychotherapy. In *On becoming a person* (pp. 125–159). Boston: Houghton Mifflin.

Rogers, C. R. (1980a). The foundations of a person-centered approach. In *A way of being* (pp. 113–136). Boston: Houghton Mifflin.

Rogers, C. R. (1980b). Empathic: An unappreciated way of being. In *A way of being* (pp. 137–163). Boston: Houghton Mifflin.

Rogers, C. R. (1984). *Transcript of Rogers' interview with Vivian*. Carl Rogers Memorial Library, Center for the Study of the Person, La Jolla, CA.

Rogers, C. R. (1986). Reflection of feelings. *Person-Centered Review, 14*, 375–377.

Whiteley, J. M. (Producer). (1977). *Carl Rogers counsels an individual on anger and hurt* [Film]. American Personnel and Guidance Association.

Zimring, F. (1990). A characteristic of Rogers' response to clients. *Person-Centered Review, 5*, 433–448.

# Chapter 9

# Unconditional positive regard as communicated through verbal behavior in client-centered therapy

Barbara Temaner Brodley
and
Carolyn Schneider

Any experienced client-centered/person-centered therapist will testify that unconditional positive regard is usually communicated by implication when the therapist is engaged in empathic understanding response process (Temaner, 1977/2011). As Bozarth (2000, personal communication on email) has stated:

> The consistency of empathic understanding response communicates the acceptance of the client's frame of reference to the extent that acceptance of the client is clearly implied.

Acceptance of the client is communicated indirectly through the therapist's impartial, expressed whole understandings of the client as well as through the therapist's syntax, choice of words and general manner of communication. During speech it is also conveyed through the therapist's tone of voice, intonation and body language when making empathic responses. It is also implicitly communicated by the *absence* of certain kinds of communications from the therapist's frame of reference, including certain kinds of communications commonly found in other therapy approaches (Tomlinson & Whitney, 1970) such as interpretations, leading questions, confrontations, and suggestions.

This paper aims to illustrate how unconditional positive regard is communicated through the verbal interactions of client-centered therapy, as examined in transcripts. Our method employs transcript segments of client-centered interviews conducted by Carl Rogers. Auditory and visual features of therapist behavior are crucial aspects of the communication of

This chapter was previously published (2001) in J. D. Bozarth & P. Wilkins (Eds.), *Rogers' therapeutic conditions: Evolution, theory and practice: Vol. 3 Unconditional positive regard* (pp. 155–172). Ross-on-Wye: PCCS Books.

unconditional positive regard, but a written paper aiming to illustrate limits one to the study of the verbal features of interaction. Such an examination, nevertheless, reveals much about how the acceptant attitude gets across to the client.

Rogers (1957/1989, 1959a) stated in his therapy theory that therapeutic impact requires that "the therapist is experiencing unconditional positive regard toward the client" and "the client perceives, at least to a minimal degree" (p. 213) the therapist's unconditional positive regard and empathic understanding. Lietaer (1984) distinguishes the concept of unconditional positive regard into three parts: positive regard, nondirectivity and unconditionality. These three parts function together, along with the empathic attitude, within the therapist, affecting his or her communications while relating to clients. Bozarth (1996, 1998) and Wilkins (2000) recognize unconditional positive regard as the fundamental therapist-cause of change in the client on the basis of Rogers' theories of personality development and the processes of its distortion (1959a). Many writers (e.g., Bozarth, 1998; Brodley, 1998/2001/2011; Haugh, 1998; Merry, 1999; Wilkins, 2000; Wyatt, 2000) interpret congruence as the underpinning for empathic understanding and unconditional positive regard. Most client/person-centered therapists view the therapist's empathic understandings as the prominent, although not exclusive, vehicle for communicating unconditional positive regard in their therapy.

The primary difficulty in the practice of unconditional positive regard is the reality of therapists' judgmental and evaluative reactions to their clients' experiences, desires and behaviors. One of client-centered therapists' tasks is to put aside their personal opinions and morality when attempting to experience acceptant empathic understanding in relation to clients. There is no leeway for any kind of prejudice in consistently effective client-centered work. Unconditional positive regard, however, involves putting aside approving reactions as well as criticisms. It is an attitude of acceptance of the person that includes feelings of warmth, caring and compassion toward the client but not approval of, or agreement with, the client's beliefs, choices or predilections. The client-centered therapist who maintains unconditional positive regard tends to convey steady evaluative neutrality in relation to clients' behaviors and narrative contents along with warmth (Merry, 1999) towards the client. The practical difficulty is most often perceived in terms of a therapist's negative reactions, but there is a lesser although not insignificant difficulty in maintaining warm neutrality rather than telegraphing endorsement of clients' feelings and behaviors. A therapist may find it difficult to maintain an unconditionally acceptant attitude towards a client when he or she discloses or shows experiences, or desires, or behaviors that are repugnant or morally unacceptable to the therapist. Under certain circumstances the therapist may find it equally difficult not to experience or display pleasure, appreciation or approval in reaction to the manner in which the client is presenting self. There may be, of course, exceptions to the therapist's evaluation-neutral presence, which have been explained elsewhere (Brodley, 1999/2011). There are no absolutes in the method.

Client-centered therapists consciously cultivate a capacity for unconditional acceptance towards clients regardless of the client's values, desires and behaviors. The unconditional positive regard capacity involves the ability to maintain a warm, caring, compassionate attitude and to experience those feelings towards a client regardless of their flaws, crimes, or their moral differences from oneself. Unconditional positive regard, however, is almost never a deliberate communication in client-centered therapy. A statement such as "I accept everything you tell me with a sympathetic or compassionate feeling and I never feel critical towards you" is not an impossible, honest comment in client-centered therapy work. If something of that kind is honestly expressed, it is most likely in response to a direct question from the client.

For the most part, unconditional positive regard is communicated by certain qualities in the therapist's presence (Baldwin [interview of Rogers], 1987/2004; Brodley, 2000/2011) and by the absence of certain other qualities such as annoyance, criticism. These unconditional positive regard qualities are the result of a philosophical orientation and learned disciplines. The most fundamental attitudes in client-centered work are attitudes of respect and trust in relation to clients. They are theoretically interpreted to follow from the therapist's belief in the actualization tendency principle, and from the ubiquitous nondirective attitude (Raskin, 1947/2005; Brodley, 1997/2011) that is inherent in client-centered therapy. The latter attitude carries the therapist's intention to protect the client's self-determination, autonomy and sense of self, thus contributing to the absence of certain kinds of counter-therapeutic responses to clients. These basic attitudes are consistent with and contribute to the therapist's unconditional positive regard. The qualities communicated are the therapist's consistent acceptant understanding of the client's experienced and communicated internal frame of reference, the therapist's consistency in expression of warm interest in the client, and the therapist's consistent attention to the client's self-representations. Unconditional positive regard is also communicated by the *absence* of communications that display challenge, confrontation, interventions, criticisms, unsolicited guidance or directive reassurance or support. Whether it is intended or not, all of these omitted types of communication, if expressed, are likely to be perceived as the therapist's expression of conditional approval or explicit disapproval.

The therapist's unconditional positive regard is a fundamental attitude that colors the therapist's entire behavior in relation to the client. This behavior includes conversations that deal with arrangements for the therapy, responses to clients' questions and any statements the therapist may initiate from his or her own frame of reference, as well as the therapist's empathic understanding responses. The therapist's unconditional positive regard is likely to be experienced by the therapist and felt by the client as the therapist's *acceptance* of the client. *Acceptance* is also implied in the therapist's empathic understanding *responsiveness* that may be contrasted to a benign inexpressiveness that clients often perceive as disinterest. Regardless of the client's attitudes and feelings that are manifest in his or her narrative, the client-centered therapist attempts to internally experience what the client appears to intend to communicate, and tries to understand that material from the perspective the client is giving to it. This *empathic orientation* to the client means the therapist understands and is receptive to whatever the client is feeling or however the client is construing experiences. Empathic orientation includes accepting the client's shifts in point of view, his or her atypical interpretations of commonly consensual perceptions, ambivalence, inconsistencies or contradictions and it also includes psychotic experiences – delusions, hallucinations and blatant distortions in perception.

The first transcript segment will show a typical client-centered interaction with a voluntary, self-disclosing client. It is an example of client-centered empathic understanding response process (Temaner, 1977/2011), as it appears midway into the seventeenth session conducted by Rogers (1954).*

## Illustration I

C38: Of course I know that she isn't able to be that way any longer ... but for a minute I thought "well, I really miss her and I sort of need a mother at this point, and yet it's impossible."

T38: Even though it's factually impossible, the feeling was "gee, I miss her. I *wish* she were here to take care of me and look after me."

C39: Uh um. Yet at the same time I felt, well a little later I thought, "Maybe that wasn't what I needed, maybe it was a more adult sort of ... companionship in some way, rather than a mother." But I needed something, or somebody.

---

* Editors' note: In the course of many years, Barbara transcribed and supervised others in transcribing Rogers' therapy and demonstration sessions. In this paper she refers to transcripts that were in the process of being "polished" through multiple listenings to the tapes. It is uncertain at which point of evolution she quoted from the various transcripts. The transcript work culminated in a joint effort with Germain Lietaer resulting in a journal article (Lietaer & Brodley, 2003) and an informal email publication (Brodley & Lietaer, 2006).

T39: You really didn't feel sure in yourself whether what you wanted was someone to really give you close mothering ... or whether you wanted some more grown-up kind of relationship.

C40: And then in another sense I felt (sighs) well, maybe it's just something I have to go through alone.

T40: Maybe it's just hopeless to wish that that could really be in a relationship with anybody ... Maybe I have to be alone.

C41: Uh um ... the thing that's sort of thrown me this week is that ... well, I feel better about the physical condition compared to last week. I talked to my doctor and I sort of made friends with him, which makes me feel a little better (laughs). So we're not sort of quietly fighting without saying anything, and I think I have more confidence in him. I read an article about this and it said it's very hard to diagnose so I don't hold that against him any longer. But he feels he has to be sure that this is what it is, and so they're giving me X-rays and I'm frightened because I kind of feel they're having to be sure that it isn't cancer and that really frightens me terribly.

T41: Uh um. Uh um ... It's, "If it's really something like that, then it just feels so alone."

C42: And it's really a frightening kind of loneliness because I don't know who could be with you in that.

T42: Is this what you're saying? "Could anyone be with you in a fear or in a loneliness like that?"

C43: (Cries)

T43: It just really cuts so deep.

C44: I don't know what it would feel like if there was somebody around that I could feel as though I did have someone to lean on. I don't know whether that would make me feel better or not. I kind of think this is something that you just have to grow within yourself, to stand it. It will take two weeks I guess before they know. Would it help to have somebody else around? Or is it just something that you just have to really be intensely alone in? I just felt that way this week, just dreadfully, dreadfully all by myself.

T44: Uh um ... Is the feeling as though you're so terribly alone, in the universe almost, and whether ...

C45: Uh um.

T45: Whether it even, whether anyone could help, whether it would help if you did have someone to lean on or not, you don't know.

C46: I guess sort of, basically, that would be a problem you would have to do alone. I mean you just couldn't maybe do it with anybody, you just couldn't take anybody along with some of the feelings, and yet it would be sort of a comfort, I guess, not to be alone.

T46: It surely would be nice if you could take someone with you a good deal of the way into your feelings of aloneness and fear.

C47: I guess I just have.

T47: Maybe that's what you're feeling right this minute.

[See also version in Brodley & Lietaer, 2006, Vol. 10, Miss Mun, pp. 65–66]

In this segment the client moves from wishing for the comfort of her deceased mother, through her questioning whether it would help her deal with her fear if she were not alone in facing a diagnosis of cancer, to the immediate sense that Rogers has been a companion. Throughout the process Rogers has empathically followed the client without expressing an opinion, without giving explicit support, and without giving any promise of accommodating her wishes. Without the visuals and soundtrack, which give more vivid evidence of Rogers' emotional attunement and compassion, his wording communicates his intention to closely understand her feelings. In his responses he includes her tentativeness and indecisiveness in his empathic understanding responses (T38, 40, 44, 45, 47). The client's comment in C47 expresses her feeling that Rogers has been a supportive presence.

Another example of empathic understanding process to illustrate unconditional positive regard is a segment near the end of an interview conducted by Rogers (1983). This session took place 30 years after the first segment. Rogers is with a client who has expressed fears about relationships.

### Illustration II

C62: I think two things, in being caught up in a relationship. I know it could take me in a lot of new directions, really new uncharted courses could be very exciting ... and I guess I'm a bit afraid about where that might lead me. It might lead me to very new, very unknown things, but ... something that excites me, that idea, 'cause I know it would only be positive I think. But I think I'm afraid of being led, being swept away, and being led to where I don't want to go and not feeling control to pull away.

T62: Your whole face lights up with the idea of a close relationship that might open up new and uncharted possibilities, but wow, that's also scary.

C63: Yeah, the feeling of getting ... tied down.

T63: You might lose control again or might be controlled.

C64: Not lose control but be controlled, yeah. Being tied up ... just the image I have is like an octopus, holding me, you know. I just can't get loose.

T64: Uhm hm.

C65: Being taken where I don't want to go, where I'm not ready to go.

T65: That's one picture you have of a relationship ... is of an octopus. Many tentacles that would just hold you tight.

C66: Yeah, just can't get free. See, that was really exactly the relationship with my mother. And now I think that's why I've got to have complete distance with her because if I let one tentacle touch, it's too much (laughs).

T66: You're so super-sensitized to that, that one touch of that tentacle – one of those tentacles – is more than you can take.

C67: Yeah. Well the one tentacle I could take but the others I couldn't and I know that you don't get one without getting all eight (laughs). It's ... Yeah, that's very much – that very much captures the relationship with my mother.

T67: You're in the grip of an octopus.

C68: Yeah. And you just can't get close at all. But – I have a tendency, particularly I think with women to see them as all potential octopuses ...

T68: It really does make it hard to see women any other way than that.

C69: Yeah. It's not a conscious thing, but ...

T69: Sort of some deep thing in you that feels, "Look out, this might be another octopus."

C70: Uhm hm. Yeah. Well, I'm not really conscious of that. But I know that's the feeling there. Yeah, I'd just be ... pounced upon if I let myself – you know – and then, I mean further than I want ... I mean maybe I want just four tentacles and not all eight (laughs). Yeah. I like that image.

T70: You wouldn't mind a few but not the whole eight.

C71: Yeah ... taking it in small doses. What I'm capable of handling. Make it in proportion to what I want; what I'm ready for.

T71: Sounds like you might like to be held, but not gripped.

C72: Yeah, yeah. And then be able just to say, "OK, that's enough now." Just, you know ...

T72: Shed the tentacles.

[See also Brodley & Lietaer, 2006, Vol. 15, Daniel Interview, pp. 74–76]

This client expresses his sense that he would have exciting benefits from being open to a relationship but is afraid of being controlled. He then realizes his fearful response to relationships comes out of his experience of his mother whom he pictures as an octopus whose eight tentacles will grip him if he allows a single one. He then continues with his wish to have only some tentacles, a metaphor for some degree of attachment, and to be released when it is too much for him.

Rogers, again, stays close to his client's expressed meanings. The material is provocative and might be perceived by some therapists as an opportunity to support the client's more daring feelings. Rogers' acceptance is implied many ways including by the absence of reassurances, suggestions or interpretations and by his use of the client's metaphor in his empathic responses (T65, 66, 67, 69, 70 and 72).

Interactions with clients who are critical of the therapist's methods, or who express anger at the therapist, or who make responses indicating they are not being accurately understood may be experienced as difficult and undermine the therapist's unconditional positive regard. The following interview (Rogers, 1984) took place at a training conference with a voluntary demonstration client who was not comfortable with the nondirective approach or with Rogers. The segment starts at the beginning of the interview.

## Illustration III

C1: I began to realize how frightened I am of the nonstructured nature of this interaction. (Pause) And I have to ask myself why. It's easy for me to come up with a problem; I have no trouble talking. In fact I use talking as a way of controlling situations. I think the nondirectiveness of your approach is very frightening to me.

T1: Sounds as though the fear of not knowing where this might go ... and the fact of your being in charge of the direction. Both of those things are really scary.

C2: That's right. It's like I would like you to take over now and ask me lots of questions ... and I don't want to have to do much work. In fact, the fantasy was ... I would rather have volunteered for a hypnotist (laugh) than for you. (T: Mhm) So it's saying something about my not wanting to be as active as I probably will have to be with you.

T2: It really does say something about the deep fear you have of initiating something entirely on your own.

C3: Yes ... It's very contradictory. Because if you look at my life, the one thing that would be most apparent is my independence and my initiative. So it's a contradiction. (T: Uhm hm) But down deep I am very frightened of nonstructure, and yet resist structure when it's imposed.

T3: Mhm. How do you understand that? That in dealing with the external world you're quite willing to take initiative and organize things and so on, but when it comes to revealing your internal self, then that becomes much more frightening.

C4: Yes. (Pause) I should tell you that I'm a behavior therapist.

T4: (Laughs) I did know that.

C5: You did know that (laughs). I prefer to work directively. So coming here was an experiment (T: Uhm hm) for me, and I've been very uncomfortable with the nondirective aspects of the workshop and the interview ... It just highlights this problem.

T5: So when I said it was a risk, that's an understatement.

C6: It's a real risk ...

The client responds, explaining some facts about her background including the dissolution of her marriage, having to raise her children alone and support her family. She expresses the feeling of being gypped in her life. Then she continues:

C7: There's a feeling of being lost without a structure, a structure of family, a husband, somebody to come to every night after work. (T: Uhm hm) Someone who is just there.

T7: That does bring a real sense of loss even to think about that.

C8: That's right. That's right. So I guess having to structure this interview is like more of the same. I just don't feel comfortable in sitting and letting things happen. 'Cause when they happen, they haven't turned out so positively.

T8: So this interview is part of the whole sense of being lost.

C9: Yes. Yes. I feel very lost in my life.

T9: And the same carries over to the interview a little bit.

[See also Brodley & Lietaer, 2006, Vol. 16, Vivian Interview, pp. 2–3]

Rogers responds empathically throughout the client's expression of feelings and views that are challenging to his method in the same neutral and understanding manner as he has done about external material in the previous segments. A bit further on, there is a long pause and the client complains:

C10: I feel that you're waiting for me to say something else (small laugh). I have trouble with silences.

T10: Uhm hm. (Pause) I don't have that trouble. I'm perfectly willing to wait until you know what you wish to say.

C11: (Pause) I'm just feeling very hot – my cheeks are burning. And I'm not sure that I know what I want to say.

T11: Uhm, hm. I wonder if you aren't sort of experiencing that sense of being lost right now ... "What the hell do I do?"

C12: That's right, exactly.

[p. 4]

Although Rogers does not accommodate the client by helping her to find a topic, his T10 is responsive in the form of a self-disclosure acknowledging his difference with her feelings and then a response that is a combination of a reassurance and letting her know the direction remains with her. His T11 is an empathic guess based on her previous expression of feeling lost and in a first-person form. It is an intense response about her predicament. Rogers reveals no impatience with her, no sense of feeling discomfort or disapproval of her condition throughout the interaction. Then the client reflects further on herself:

C13: I just have trouble just sitting quietly. (Long pause)

T13: I think I see in your eyes a sense of "please, please guide this!"

C14: Do something (laughing), that's right.

T14: "Do something."

C15: Do something. Uh (pause) yes, I've had a hard time with you this workshop. My feelings for you have, uhm, been on a roller coaster. (T: Uhm hm) Uhm, I wondered, I had curiosity about how you could just sit there and just ... what did you do while all this was going on with yourself because ... there was so much going on and I kept wanting something to happen. I was very angry at you for not realizing how many people were in pain, or not creating a plan. Uhm, uhm, at one point, if I could have been more active, I would have just ranted and raved at you and I was in a fury. I didn't do that. Uhm, and I think it was partly the group, but then it's very hard for me to be angry with someone who sits there so benignly. Uhm, and, uh, wants things to sort of be nice and good and, then it became harder for me to be angry at you when you said ... were nice to me or uhm, started making contact ... So I really had a hard time with you. Uhm, I keep wanting more of a response than you give.

T15: So you've been very angry with me in the workshop ... Perhaps not expressed, but nevertheless the feelings have been there ... (C: Yes) Being very angry toward me ... "Why the hell don't you do something, why the hell don't you see what's going on?" (C: Yes) And part of that anger carries over right here.

C16: That's right, right now ...

T16: "Why the hell don't you do something?"

C17: *Do* Something. Uhm, (pause) yeah, do something, be ... don't just let people sit and struggle (pause and sigh).

T17: And it isn't only "Why do you let people sit and struggle," it's "why do you let me sit and struggle?"

C18: Yeah. Why are you letting me sit and struggle like this? You set up this interview, interview me! Uhm, it's a contradiction that I have with ... in terms of my feelings with you. And then I say, "What's the use." I mean you are who you are, this is the way you are and I have a hard time dealing with it, so what's the point of even expressing the anger since it's not going to do any good. Nothing will change, nothing will change.

T18: It's hopeless, you can't change our relationship.

C19: That's right, if I yell and scream at you it's not going to change.

[pp. 4–5]

In this segment Rogers obviously accepts her anger and vigorously acknowledges it in first-person-form empathic responses (T15, 16, 17). Rogers does not defend himself or his method, he simply continues to try to understand her feelings. In a segment not quoted the client continues to complain that Rogers has not provided supportive arrangements in the workshop. She goes on:

C20: I'm not feeling the rage I felt ... At one point I was furious ... What I'm feeling now is ... Obviously, my problems with you really relate to my problems in dealing with my father who was not a responsive person. (Pause) And one of the problems that I have is that you are very different than my father in that you would accept whatever choices I made. And my father doesn't respond ... hardly ever responds, but when he does respond, it's with disapproval – "I don't like what you're doing" (pause).

T20: So you really are, in a sense, dealing with your father in dealing with me, and yet it's with a different father who is more willing to accept.

C21: And it's confusing. It's confusing (pause).

T21: It makes it very hard to know how the hell to relate to me.

C22: That's right. Exactly.

[pp. 5–6]

Rogers' response (T20) represents her interpretation that she is responding in part to Rogers out of her history of experiences with her father with his usual neutrality. He then expresses the intensity and anger aspect of her confusion by using "how the hell" in his next empathic response (T21). As may be observed in this segment Rogers does not side-step to his client's anger, even when it is directed at him. A study by Bradburn (1996) of Rogers' affect demonstrated that Rogers consistently responds to client's anger with acceptance and affective empathic responses.

The following illustration of unconditional positive regard is in a session with a client who is a patient in a psychiatric hospital (Rogers, 1958) who has been diagnosed with a paranoid schizophrenic disorder. There are several instances during the interview when the client perceived Rogers as not understanding her, and Rogers' responses express his unperturbed acceptance of the corrections and of the client.

### Illustration IV

C11: I think it means working all day in the laundry, too, and I'm not quite ready for that ... I asked the doctor [before] if he would move me so I could go to work in the laundry. (T: Uhm hm) And the transfer came today. I didn't ask to be transferred, though, at this time.

T12: It troubles you as to whether you're really ready to face some of the things that would be involved.

C12: I don't know, there isn't much to face. It's kind of confusing, I think.

T13: I see. It's more a question of facing the uncertainties, is that what you mean?

C13: I don't know what I mean (little laugh). I just know that ...

T14: Right now you feel kind of mixed up?

[See also Brodley & Lietaer, 2006, Vol. 11, Loretta, pp. 13–14]

Rogers' responses (T12 and T13) were probably too abstract for the client, given her mental condition, and thus were poor attunements to her in these instances. Consequently, he may have stimulated her confusion (C12 and C13). He continues to follow, however, going to the client's more immediate and concrete level in T14. The client continues, explaining a nurse's ambiguous behavior. Rogers responds to her:

T17: The explanation was doctor's orders and all that, but you can't help but feel, "Is she really trustworthy?" 'Cause here she seemed to ...

C18: No, I don't trust people anyway, anymore. (T: Uhm hm) That's why I don't want them to trust me. I either believe in them or I don't believe in them.

T18: Uhm hm. And all or none.

C19: And I don't think I believe in her very much.

T19: Uhm hm. And really with most people you feel, "I don't think I trust 'em."

C20: That's the truth, I don't trust 'em. Either believe 'em or I don't believe 'em or I don't ... I'm not quite certain whether I believe them yet or not. (T: Uhm hm) But I don't believe in trust anymore.

T20: Uhm hm. That's one thing that you feel has really dropped out for you, that's just to trust people. Not for you.

C21: No, I don't trust 'em. You can get hurt much too easily by trusting people.

T21: Uhm hm. If you really believe in someone, and let your trust go out to them, then ...

C22: I don't have any trust. That's why I can't let any out to 'em!

T22: Uhm hm. But evidently your feeling is that when that has happened in the past ...

C23: You just get hurt by it.

T23: That's the way you can get hurt.

C24: That's the way I have been hurt.

T24: That's the way you have been hurt.

[pp. 14–15]

The client apparently needs precise and relatively concrete responses in order to feel understood. In T21 Rogers expresses a hypothetical that implies the trust the client states she does not experience. When corrected (C22), Rogers makes a reconciling response by referring to the past (T22). In the segment Rogers errs in understanding several times (C12, 21, 23), but each time he accepts the correction and tries to understand exactly what she means. The audiotape of his voice supports the patience and sincerity in Rogers' attitude toward the client that is suggested by his words.

In another illustration, Rogers (1975/1984) interacts with a client who feels afraid of emotional risks in relationships, and the experience of that fear occurs in the therapy encounter.

## Illustration V

C7: I think I'm keeping myself in a kind of no-win situation where I'm really lonely and yet it's kind of like I'm keeping myself there because I've got a guard round me, and I'd kind of like to break out of that.

T7: It's as though you're in some way sort of responsible for your loneliness.

C8: Yes, I know that ...

T8: And that something you'd like to break out of that shell, or that safeguard that you've been hiding behind.

C9: Part of me does.

T9: Part of you does, OK, OK.

C10: Part of me says "noo way."

T10: So it really is a very ambivalent, two-way thing.

[see also Brodley & Lietaer, 2006, Vol. 12, Kathy Interview, p. 55]

The client then explains some history of her withdrawal and fear of getting hurt and continues:

C13: I've been aware of this for a long time too, but I never go beyond the awareness level.

T13: So that the knowledge isn't new, it is the question of what you do about it.

C14: That's right, that's right. How can one stay safe and still be open?

T14: The way you shake your head makes me feel, "I don't see any way."

[p. 56]

The client explains her caution in friendships and that she requires friendship before she would feel love or have a sexual relationship. Then she refers to her immediate relationship with Rogers:

C21: We've gotten to the point where I won't go beyond.

T21: Uh-huh. That's what I was sort of thinking, you've thought your way this far, but then where do you ...

C22: I've laid the cards out and that's all I want to play.

T22: So that, in this relationship it's like in your other relationships.

C23: That's right.

T23: "It goes so far and then let's stop. That's as far as I want to go." If you go any further, there's a risk, isn't it?

C24: Yes, it is.

T24: And I think your eyes tell me you're feeling that risk right now.

C25: (Pause) So here I am. (Pause) I feel like saying to myself, "Well, you got this far, it's not so bad (laughs). It's all right; I make the best of it."

T25: It's all right up to this point.

C26: Yeah, right.

T26: So let's laugh it off.

C27: Yeah, make a joke, talk about something else.

T27: Could ... very easy to run away from yourself.

[pp. 56–57]

But the client doesn't do that, she re-engages in her personal exploration. Rogers' acceptance of her reluctance to go on (C21, T22, 23, 24), and ambivalence (C10, T10), leaves the choices to her. But Rogers also doesn't shy away from subtle expressions of anger (Illustration III, C15, T15, T16) or states expressed as nervous laughter (C25, T26).

The next illustration is a segment from an interview Rogers (1959b) conducted with a teenage girl in a psychiatric hospital. The interview is not very coherent. The client is quite difficult to understand, but it illustrates Rogers' attempt to relate to the young woman regardless of the difficulty, and reveals his patience that is a form of acceptance of her. It begins with Rogers initiating contact and expressing his interest in her.

## Illustration VI

T1a: I've seen you [around the hospital] twice now. (C: Uhm hm.) I just thought that I would like to talk with you. I would be interested if you would tell me about yourself and your situation.

C1: Well, my situation is tough.

T1: Your situation is tough. (C: Yeah) Do you want to tell me a little about it?

C2: Well, it's mostly home and with my parents except when other people ... I don't know exactly what happened ...

T2: You're confused why it's so disruptive.

C3: Yes, it is.

T3: But it's hard to tell about.

C4: Yes it is. (T: Uhm hm) I think to drop it is an answer. Just drop it, or something.

T4: That's one possibility is to just drop it. Uhm hm.

C5: Just forget about it.

T5: Ah … if you could just put it out of mind. (C: Yeah) Uhm hm. And then sometimes that seems like …

C6: The only possible thing to do.

T6: The only possible thing to do. You might like to forget it and drop it. But …

C7: Once you get away with murder, once you get more away with other …

T7: Is. Uh, that … and this is your parents you're speaking of? (C: Yes) That when they get away with …

C8: Or anyone.

T8: Or anyone. (C: Yes) That "When they get away with murder once, why, boy, then they try it again."

C9: Yeah. Yeah.

Observer: Do you feel that's true with your parents?

C10: No, not naturally, 'cause (inaudible) when she got beat up … She's been meddling in other peoples' affairs.

T10: Uhm hm. And I guess you don't like her when … (C: No, I don't) … she meddles in other peoples' affairs. That makes you …

C11: Pretty disgusted.

T11: Disgusted. Uhm hm, Uhm, hm. (Pause) Could you tell me any more about that?

C12: Well, it would incriminate me quite a bit.

T12: I see. If you really told, that would … It would kind of incriminate you.

C13: Yes. It would.

T13: Kind of put you in a bad light if you really … (C: Yes it would) told about it.

C14: Except my mother and father.

T14: I see. So you feel you would hardly um, dare tell your side of it because it might incriminate you. You'd rather leave it up to your folks.

C15: Yes. (T: Uhm hm, Uhm hm) Does that settle that?

T15: Well, there might be … the thing is that, uh; I guess that settles part of it. But I was thinking that if there was anything that you were willing to tell me that would help me to know you better.

C16: Well, my heritage for one thing.

T16: About your heritage.

C17: I feel incriminated myself.

T17: You feel incriminated yourself.

C18: You see (inaudible) my son was in it?

T18: Your son was in it.

C19: Yeah (T: Uhm, hm) my grandmother told me my history and that ... (T: Hmm) She wants me to know her son's history. (Inaudible)

T19: Uhm hm. She brings in her son's history and your parents bring in your history? Hmm? And that's pretty rough.

C20: Yes it is.

T20: I'm not sure I quite understand that.

C21: Mine isn't any better than his.

T21: Yours isn't any better than his. (C: No) So that, in a sense, both histories sort of incriminate each other. (C: Yes) Uhm hm. Hmm. I guess what you're saying is that if the truth came out, or your parents told the whole story, it would make it look pretty bad for you. Is that ...?

C22: Yes that would (inaudible).

T22: So you feel that if the (C: History) story came out ...

C23: That would (inaudible).

T23: If the (inaudible).

C24: (Inaudible)

T24: Uhm hm. Uhm hm. But it does seem as though, if the true story came out, you're afraid that, that you'd be put away for life. (C: Uhm hm) Hmm, You must feel that the true story is pretty bad.

C25: The true story is ... (inaudible) and he gets away with everything (inaudible) 'cause I won't have anything to do with it.

T25: I see. So that when he gets out, you're going to have to sort of face up to the truth. (C: Inaudible) You won't have anything to do with it.

C26: No. I won't.

T26: So I guess it sounds like you did have something with him in the past. But not in the future you won't.

C27: No, not in the past, present or future, no. (T: Uhm hm) There's nothing to look forward to.

T27: You really feel there's nothing to look forward to.

[For a revised version with more complete information, see Brodley & Lietaer, 2006, Vol. 11, Elaine Interview, pp. 31–36]

Rogers has been encouraging the client to disclose about herself and she appears to be generally willing. She lets it be known she would prefer not to go further into a certain topic (C15) and Rogers accepts (T15). This is another example of his acceptance, his respect for the person and of his commitment to following the client:

C42: I do want to stop fighting so my father can (inaudible).

T42: Uhm hm, Uhm hm. That's one of the things you'd like.

C43: Yes I do. And all the way up to my friend's house. (T: Uhm hm.) Up to the house and let me clean up. That's what I wanted to do.

T43: The other thing you wanted to do was to clean it up as far as the road.

C44: There will be a highway. (Inaudible) It would be better not to talk about it. (T: Uhm hm) That's good.

T44: Are there other things you could tell me to help me know you a little better? 'Cause I don't know anything of your record or ...

C45: You probably already know.

T45: No. I really don't.

C46: You really don't know me.

T46: No. I really don't know you. Just what you've told me now is what I know of you.

C47: Mhm. It takes lots of expense and money (inaudible).

T47: It takes lots of expense and money to ...

C48: To carry on such a performance.

T48: Now there I'm not quite sure. You carry on such a performance ...?

C49: Well this is awfully embarrassing. (T: Hmm) 'Cause my father is connected to it too. I wouldn't want to say anything to ... (inaudible).

T49: But really, there is something that troubles you and all, but you don't like to bring it out because it may affect other people and you feel it might do them ...

C50: More harm and no good. More harm as far as my father's mom. (Inaudible) I can't do anything about it. My name and his name (inaudible). (T: Uhm hm) When we went through this as far as the performance, that settled me.

T50: So that you think you've settled.

C51: Yeah. At least I hope it is. 'Cause I know my dad wouldn't make a habit of it.

The session continues for the most part with intelligible remarks that Rogers responds to with empathic understanding responses. Rogers hears and understands more information in the client's remarks than are audible on the audiotape. The tape took many reviews to get to the present level because the client speaks very fast and with a rural dialect. But Rogers is also dealing with very unclear meanings and the client's idiosyncratic manner of speech even when she can be heard. It requires some guesswork and occasional admission to her that he has not understood.

Whatever Rogers is doing – trying to stimulate more conversation, making empathic responses, making guesses, or admitting he doesn't understand – he does it with a steady, respectful and acceptant responsiveness, as best he can, and he always accepts the limits the client puts on specific topics. This fifth illustration is not typical client-centered work, but neither is it unusual for its context. It is an example of a type of session involving incompletely coherent client statements requiring extreme patience and attentiveness. It is a type of session that occurs frequently when the therapist is working in a psychiatric hospital and initiates the relationship, and when the patient's illness makes clear or totally comprehensible communication difficult or impossible.

The final illustrative segment is from an interview (Rogers, 1986) that took place as a demonstration in front of a training group. The client initially expressed her problem as difficulty in stopping her habit of smoking. A short way into the session, her legs and body began to twitch, or involuntarily jerk, and that became the focus of the interaction. After starting to discuss her smoking, the client felt distracted by the group of observers. She then calmed herself with a deliberate breathing exercise.

## Illustration VII

C26: I can feel you have that calmness too. It's fine. (T: Uhm hm) I guess, I can be with me and with you without interrupting that feeling.

T26: Uhm, hm. We can be calm together and calm separately. (C: Uhm hm) And, each of us breathing okay.

(Pause 40 seconds)

C27: I'm aware of my body trembling, and my legs.

T27: Uhm hm. There is a nervousness there and your legs are just ...

C28: Uhm, hm. The breathing's okay.

T28: The breathing's okay.

(Pause 40 seconds)

C29: Jerkin' here. (T: Hmm?) My body jerked right here. (T: Uhm, hm. Uh, huh Uh huh) Do you want to see that (smiles)?

T29: Whatever you want to bring up is what I want to hear. (Pause) It was important to you that your body jerked at that point.

C30: (Laughs) I don't know why. (Pause 13 seconds) (She makes a fluttering gesture close to her body)

T30: You feel fluttering? (Fluttering gesture)

C31: Uhm hm. A jerk here. (She points to her midriff, her body jerks, she shakes her head)

T31: Uhm hm. Another jerk. (Pause 10 seconds) Can you say what those jerks mean to you?

C32: (She shakes her head in negative) It's a very uncomfortable feeling.

T32: Your body is just doing something that's out of your control.

C33: Hmm. (Nods) Well, I could control it (T: Yeah) but if I go with the process (T: Yeah) then ...

T33: But it just happens without your knowing why.

C34: Uhm hm. In the encounter group we had earlier this week, this happened. (T: Uhm hm) And I still don't know why. (Her body jerks)

T34: Uhm hm. Uhm, hm. You don't quite understand what happens when your body is, (inaudible) goes ...

C35: And I feel it just races around ... (inaudible). (She gestures toward her forehead)

T35: Yeah. Can you say some of the things that are racing around up there? (Gesturing towards his head)

C36: "What is this about?" "This looks stupid." You know, "What are you doing?" You know, uh, I've seen people who have seizures, you know? (T: Uh, huh. Uh huh) And that's my experience of what my body's doing. And it's ...

T36: Uh, huh. So, you are being stupid or having a seizure or "what in the world is going on?" You keep asking yourself.

C37: Yeah.

T37: Sort of critical of yourself.

C38: Hmm. Part of me is judging it as wrong and the other part is saying, "Shut up. Whatever this is, just go with it and be ..."

T38: Uhm hm. Part of you is saying, "Now stop it, it's stupid. This is ridiculous." And another part of you is saying, "Wait a minute. My body is doing something, if I can go with it, maybe I can learn something."

C39: Right.

[See also Brodley & Lietaer, 2006, Vol. 17, Lydia 1st Interview, pp. 94–96]

Rogers remains empathic throughout this unusual interview although he was probably surprised by the turn of events. Verbally, most of his responses are of the empathic understanding, following-type responses (T 26, 27, 28, half of 29, 30 in the form of a question for clarification, half of T31, T33, 34, 36, 37 and 38).

Other responses are attitudinally consistent but of a different type. In T29 he first addresses the client's question and immediately follows that with an empathic understanding response. In T31 he first empathically follows and then asks the client if she can verbalize the meaning of the movements. In this he is pursuing more empathic understanding of her experience through a leading question.

T32 is an empathically intended guess about what is happening. His following response (T33) accepts the client's clarification (C33). Rogers' T35 is similar to T31, it pursues understanding of the client's experience employing a leading question based on the client's gesture. There is nothing obviously evaluative in Rogers' remarks and nothing in his manner or tone of voice (seen and heard on the videotape) suggesting conditional acceptance or disapproval of the client. He tries to stay with the client and pursues empathic understanding of her communications and the behaviors she is attending to in the interaction.

CONCLUSION

The seven illustrative segments reveal Rogers responded with empathic understanding or other explicit following responses (such as questions for clarification and parroting-type responses) in 97 (84.3% of all) responses. He gave answers or an explanation in response to explicit or implied questions on five occasions. He made comments that were observations of clients' expressive appearance on six occasions. He requested that his client (only in Illustration VI) tell him something more about herself four times – twice after she stated she was finished with particular topics that he did not attempt to pursue.

In the illustrations he verbalized two leading questions (only to the client in Illustration VII). These were specifically about the meaning the client might be attributing to her involuntary behavior in order to better understand her phenomenology in the situation. He made one explicit statement of not understanding the client (in Illustration VI). These make a total of 18 responses that we are not classifying as empathic understanding or other type of following responses. This total is slightly less than 16% of the 115 therapist responses in the illustrations. It seems to us on the face of it, it would be difficult to successfully argue that any of these particular responses, all expressed from the therapist's frame of reference, had a likelihood of stimulating a sense of disapproval or conditional approval in these clients. Although we must admit we cannot be certain of our conclusion, having no way of assessing the clients' perceptions in the transcripts.

This paper has presented very typical and masterful examples of client-centered therapy by Carl Rogers to illustrate unconditional positive regard in the therapist's verbal behavior. It aimed to illustrate unconditional positive regard in good implementations of Rogers' theory of therapy with clients who are able to be in contact, who are able to some considerable extent represent themselves, and who are able to narrate about their experience. These are features of most clients, even psychotic clients, participating in psychotherapy. The paper shows how the unconditional positive regard attitude appears to come across – depending for evidence only on the verbal aspects of the communication – as unqualified acceptance of the person and with an absence of judgments or conditional acceptance.

Bozarth (2000, personal communication on email) has theorized:

> Empathic understanding is the total acceptance of the client's frame of reference at any given moment, and unconditional positive regard is the total acceptance of the individual as an individual at any given moment. In that sense, empathic understanding is a subset of unconditional positive regard.

This formulation appears to be supported by the observations we have made of the seven transcripts. The impact of Rogers' consistency in acceptance, as it is primarily expressed in empathic responses throughout the dialogues, as well as in his other forms of response, comes across as a total acceptance of the client.

## REFERENCES

Baldwin, M. (1987). Interview with Carl Rogers on the use of the self in therapy. In M. Baldwin & V. Satir (Eds.), *The use of the self in therapy* (pp. 45–52). New York: Haworth Press. [Reprinted (2004) in R. Moodley, C. Lago, & A. Talahite (Eds.), *Carl Rogers counsels a Black client: Race and culture in person-centred counseling* (pp. 253–260). Ross-on-Wye: PCCS Books]

Bozarth, J. D. (1996). A theoretical reconsideration of the necessary and sufficient conditions for therapeutic personality change. *The Person-Centered Journal, 3*(1), 44–51. [Also adapted as: A reconceptualization of the necessary and sufficient conditions for therapeutic personality change (1998) in *Person-centered therapy: A revolutionary paradigm* (pp. 43–50). Ross-on-Wye: PCCS Books]

Bozarth, J. D. (1998). *Person-centered therapy: A revolutionary paradigm*. Ross-on-Wye: PCCS Books.

Bradburn, W. M. (1996). *Did Carl Rogers' positive view of human nature bias his psychotherapy? An empirical investigation.* Unpublished doctoral clinical research project. Illinois School of Professional Psychology, Chicago (now Argosy University, Chicago).

Brodley, B. T. (1997). The nondirective attitude in client-centered therapy. *The Person-Centered Journal*, 4(1), 18–30. [This volume, Chapter 5]

Brodley, B. T. (1998). Congruence and its relation to communication in client-centered therapy. *The Person-Centered Journal*, 5(2), 83–116. [Reprinted (2001) in G. Wyatt (Ed.), *Congruence* (pp. 55–78). Ross-on-Wye: PCCS Books; this volume, Chapter 7]

Brodley, B. T. (1999). Reasons for responses expressing the therapist's frame of reference in client-centered therapy. *The Person-Centered Journal*, 6(1), 4–27. [This volume, Chapter 15]

Brodley, B. T. (2000). Personal presence in client-centered therapy. *The Person-Centered Journal*, 7(2), 139–149. [This volume, Chapter 10]

[Brodley, B. T., & Lietaer, G. (Eds.). (2006). *Transcripts of Carl Rogers' therapy sessions, Vols. 1–17*. Available from germain.lietaer@psy.kuleuven.be and kmoon1@alumni.uchicago.edu]

Haugh, S. (1998). Congruence: A confusion of language. *Person-Centred Practice*, 6(1), 44–50.

Lietaer, G. (1984). Unconditional positive regard: A controversial basic attitude in client-centered therapy. In R. F. Levant & J. M. Shlien (Eds.), *Client-centered therapy and the person-centered approach* (pp. 41–58). New York: Praeger.

[Lietaer, G., & Brodley, B. T. (2003). Carl Rogers in the therapy room: A listing of session transcripts and a survey of publications referring to Rogers' sessions. *Person-Centered & Experiential Psychotherapies*, 2, 274–291.]

Merry, T. (1999). *Learning and being in person-centred counselling*. Ross-on-Wye: PCCS Books.

Raskin, N. J. (1947) The nondirective attitude. Unpublished paper. [Published (2005) in *The Person-Centered Journal* 12(1–2) and (2005) in B. E. Levitt (Ed.), *Embracing non-directivity* (pp. 327–347). Ross-on-Wye: PCCS Books]

Rogers, C. R. (1954). *Transcript of Rogers' interview with "Miss M."* The Carl R. Rogers Archive, Congressional Archives, Washington, DC. [Also in The Carl Rogers Memorial Library, Center of the Studies of the Person, La Jolla, CA]

Rogers, C. R. (1957). The necessary and sufficient conditions of therapeutic personality change. *Journal of Consulting Psychology*, 21, 95–103. [Also published (1989) in H. Kirschenbaum & V. L. Henderson (Eds.), *The Carl Rogers reader* (pp. 219–235). Boston: Houghton Mifflin]

Rogers, C. R. (1958). *Transcript of Rogers' interview with "Loretta."* Archives of The American Academy of Psychotherapy. [Also in The Carl R. Rogers Archive, Congressional Archives, Washington, DC]

Rogers, C. R. (1959a). A theory of therapy, personality and interpersonal relationships, as developed in the client-centered framework. In S. Koch (Ed.), *Psychology: A study of a science. Vol. III: Formulations of the person and the social context* (pp. 184–256). New York: McGraw-Hill.

Rogers, C. R. (1959b). *Transcript of Rogers' interview with "Elaine."* The Carl R. Rogers Archive, Congressional Archives, Washington, DC. [Also in The Carl Rogers Memorial Library, Center for the Studies of the Person, La Jolla, CA]

Rogers, C. R. (1975). Transcript of Rogers' interview with "Ms. K." In E. L. Shostrom (Producer). *Three Approaches to Psychotherapy II. Client-Centered Therapy Part 1.* [Film]. Corona del Mar, CA: Psychological and Educational Films. [Also published (1984) in J. D. Bozarth, Beyond reflections. In R. F. Levant & J. M. Shlien (Eds.), *Client-centered therapy and the person-centered approach* (pp. 59–75). New York: Praeger; and The Carl R. Rogers Archive, Congressional Archives, Washington, DC]

Rogers, C. R. (1983). *Transcript of Rogers' interview with "Daniel."* The Carl R. Rogers Archive, Congressional Archives, Washington, DC. [Also in The Carl Rogers Memorial Library, Center for the Studies of the Person, La Jolla, CA]

Rogers, C. R. (1984). *Transcript of Rogers' interview with "Vivian."* The Carl R. Rogers Archive, Congressional Archives, Washington, DC. [Also in The Carl Rogers Memorial Library, Center for the Studies of the Person, La Jolla, CA]

Rogers, C. R. (1986). *Transcript of Rogers' interview with "Lydia."* The Carl R. Rogers Archive, Congressional Archives, Washington, DC. [Also in The Carl Rogers Memorial Library, Center for the Studies of the Person, La Jolla, CA]

Temaner, B. [Brodley] (1977). The empathic understanding response process. Chicago Counseling and Psychotherapy Center. *Chicago Counseling Center Discussion Paper.* [This volume, Chapter 12]

Tomlinson, T. M., & Whitney, R. E. (1970). Values and strategy in client-centered therapy: A means to an end. In J. T. Hart & T. M. Tomlinson (Eds.), *New directions in client-centered therapy* (pp. 433–467). Boston: Houghton Mifflin.

Wilkins, P. (2000). Unconditional positive regard reconsidered. *British Journal of Guidance and Counselling, 28*(1), 23–36.

Wyatt, G. (2000). The multifaceted nature of congruence. *The Person-Centered Journal, 7*(1), 52–68.

# Chapter 10

# Personal presence in client-centered therapy

*Abstract*
This paper presents two conceptions of "presence" found in Rogers' writings about client-centered therapy. The first conception is a naturalistic one emphasizing the openness and immediacy of the therapist in the relationship. The second builds on the first, adding an element of spirituality or mysticism. Expressing my rejection of Rogers' second conception, I discuss the phenomena of presence and compare Rogers' spiritual or mystical interpretations to my own naturalistic interpretations of similar experiences. Finally, I describe a small pilot study of presence that shows the concept can be meaningful to clients.

Over the course of his career, Carl Rogers ascribed two different meanings to the concept of "presence" in client-centered therapy.[1] The two conceptions have different implications for the practice and the development of theory. The first meaning Rogers gave to presence does not refer to the term but is implied by condition numbers one and six in his explicit (and generic) theory of therapy (Rogers, 1957). This conception refers to the therapist being in a relationship with his client. It also refers to the therapist's feelings of being *all there*, completely engaged and absorbed in the relationship with the client [Brodley & Lietaer, 2006, Vol. 12, Gloria Post-Session Commentary, pp. 19–20; Kathy, Introduction, p. 52 & Post-Session Commentary, p. 67].* The therapist is not distracted, nor preoccupied, but is focused on the client,

---

1. The writer views "client-centered therapy" and "person-centered therapy" as alternative terms for the same practice. "Therapy" and "counseling" are also interchangeable terms.

---

* Editors' note: In the course of many years, Barbara transcribed and supervised others in transcribing Rogers' therapy and demonstration sessions. In this paper she refers to transcripts that were in the process of being "polished" through multiple listenings to the tapes. It is uncertain at which point of evolution she quoted from the various transcripts. The transcript work culminated in a joint effort with Germain Lietaer resulting in a journal article (Lietaer & Brodley, 2003) and an informal email publication (Brodley & Lietaer, 2006).

Prepared for the Conference on Presence in Bratislava, Slovak Republic, 5–9 October, 1999. Published (2000) in *The Person-Centered Journal*, 7(2), 139–149. A version with a slightly different emphasis (2003) Presence in client-centered therapy, was published in *A Pessoa Como Centro: Revista de Estudos Rogerianos*, (6), 48–77. Reproduced with permission from *PCJ*.

empathically interested in the client, and congruent in relation to the client. This first meaning of presence emphasizes the idea that the therapist is *there* with the client, a genuine companion, "face-to-face" (Schmid, 1998). Additionally, the therapist is personally integrated and authentic – is what he or she *appears* to be.

Late in his life, Rogers posited presence as a *cause* of therapeutic change. During an interview of him concerning the role of self in therapy, Rogers (in Baldwin, 1987/2004) said:

> When I am intensely focused on a client, just my *presence* seems to be healing ... [w]hen my *self* is very clearly, obviously *present* ... and I think this is probably true of any good therapist. (p. 45)

In his late writings, Rogers also referred to *presence* as a cause of healing in groups as well as in individual therapy. Concerning a large group experience in South Africa, Rogers (1987) wrote dramatically:

> My understanding and my presence helped them to drain the infection, the festering pus out of their internal wounds, and to let the healing process begin. (p. 11)

The second meaning Rogers gave to "presence" emerged in the last 20 years of his life. He injected supernatural elements into the concept that had not been included in his earlier use of the term (e.g., Rogers, 1980a). This second meaning is based on the first meaning of presence, but adds spiritual or mystical elements.[2] Rogers (in Baldwin, 1987/2004) said:

> I am in a slightly altered state of consciousness in the relationship, then whatever I do seems to be full of healing. Then simply my presence is releasing and helpful. At those moments it seems that my inner spirit has reached out and touched the inner spirit of the other. Our relationship transcends itself, and has become part of something larger. (p. 50)

Rogers expressed this spiritual or mystical direction in several of his writings (e.g., Rogers, 1980a, p. 129). Granted, statements in his writings, such as "the transcendental core of me" (p. 129), *could* be interpreted as metaphors. This writer and others, however, believe Rogers' statements such as

---

2. These spiritual or mystical elements do not appear to have changed Rogers' therapy behavior. He did slightly increase the frequency of his therapist-frame responses (Brodley, 1994/2011) in his last 20 years, but this seems unrelated to his spiritual/mystical interpretation of some events in therapy.

"... experiences in therapy and in groups ... involve the transcendent ... the spiritual" (p. 130) make it clear that he intended us to understand he was interpreting certain experiences as supernatural. He was expressing a new spiritual or mystical direction in his thought and in his feelings about therapy (e.g., Van Belle, 1990; Hart, 1997, 1999; Schmid, 1998; Wood, 1998).

Rogers' spiritual or mystical interpretation of his own therapeutic experiences appears to have emerged, in part, out of his work with large community meeting groups (Rogers, 1980b). In discussing groups he refers to a "transcendent aspect" (p. 196), with "overarching wisdom of the group" (p. 196). He also refers to "the presence of an almost telepathic communication" (p. 196). He comments that his "relationship with others in the group transcended itself and became part of something larger" (p. 197). Also, he described "awareness of together being part of a broader universal consciousness" (p. 197). These and other statements suggest Rogers' intellectual movement was toward what Van Belle (1990) terms "mystical universalism," involving belief in a supernatural reality. Although Rogers was not conducting individual psychotherapy with regular clients during the final 20 years of his life, he gave frequent demonstrations of his way of doing individual client-centered therapy for training groups. During that last phase of his life's work, sometimes he interpreted one-to-one therapy as involving spiritual or mystical experiences as indicated in the quote above. Despite my great admiration for Rogers, I reject his mystical or spiritual interpretations of presence and his mystical or spiritual interpretations of experiences in therapy. I believe this development in Rogers' thought is interesting biographically. In my opinion, however, it should be ignored in the further development of client-centered or person-centered theory and ignored in the practice of client-centered therapy. I think Rogers' mystical or spiritual interpretations of therapy may lead to serious damage, even destruction, of the nondirective and client-centered essence of client-centered therapy.

The naturalistic meaning of presence, however, is relevant to understanding client-centered therapy. It may also lead to some research. In this paper I shall not explain my concerns about Rogers' mystical or spiritual ideas which I have written about in another place (Brodley, 2000). Instead I shall describe certain events that I view in a naturalistic light – ones similar to those that Rogers referred to as spiritual or mystical. I shall discuss the naturalistic meaning of personal presence and the role of natural presence in therapy. I shall also describe a short pilot study based on the idea of naturalistic therapeutic presence.

NATURALISTIC PRESENCE

Naturalistic presence can be viewed as a determinant of therapeutic change apart from the mystical context in which Rogers expressed it. From the early phase of Rogers' (1951) theory of therapy, clients' perceptions of the therapist were crucial to therapeutic effectiveness. Naturalistic presence is a concept that extends and elaborates on the crucial role in client-centered therapy of clients' perceptions of the therapist.

In remarks made very late in his life, Rogers described *being present* as a basic goal for himself as a therapist. Even then he expressed the idea of *presence* in terms of his non-spiritual theory of the "necessary and sufficient conditions" (Rogers, 1957) for therapeutic change. He said:

> I think that if the therapist feels "I want to be as *present* to this person as possible. I want to really listen to what is going on. I want to be real in this relationship," then these are suitable goals for the therapist ... The goal has to be within myself, with the way I am. (Rogers, in Baldwin, 1987/2004, p. 47)

Rogers' goal of *being present* fits into basic and naturalistic client-centered theory. Client-centered therapy includes the concept of naturalistic personal presence. The therapeutic benefit of *presence* results from the way the therapist lives, exudes and expresses the totality of the therapeutic attitudes. These attitudes come across as an aspect of the therapist's *self* in interactions with the client over time. The basic meaning of *presence* to Rogers is the therapist being in the relationship with the client. She or he participates wholeheartedly, experiencing the therapeutic attitudes and directing attention toward the client to empathically understand the client from the client's internal frame of reference. Presence is spontaneous. It involves no intentions or deliberate actions to produce an image.

NATURAL PHENOMENA

I have had experience as a client-centered therapist for over 40 years. When reading late Rogers, I notice that every situation in individual therapy, group therapy or encounter groups – that Rogers describes as having a spiritual or mystical aspect – all sound familiar to me. His experiences seem like experiences I have had many times while doing individual therapy, and with groups. However, I do not interpret my similar experiences as spiritual or mystical. Instead, I perceive and interpret these experiences naturalistically. I interpret no spirituality, no transcendent reality, nor any kind of supernatural reality or mystery in the experiences. Where Rogers interprets "transcendence",

I see normal human experiences, devoid of any supernatural implications. They are down-to-earth experiences that occur under certain conditions.

For example, some individuals in a group may come to have the feeling or impression that the group members are thinking in harmony. They may feel an emotional connection among all the persons who are present. Rogers quotes a participant who said people "felt, and spoke for one another ..., without the usual barricades of "me-ness" or "you-ness" (Rogers, 1980a, p. 129). This is a kind of experience that occurs from time to time in large groups that have characteristics such as the following.

Many of the participants share similar humanistic values or ideologies. They have been hashing out conflicts over many hours together. They have resolved some differences; they understand each other better. Some people have probably expressed emotionally intense experiences in the group that the others have witnessed. They may have described past personal sufferings. They may have cried, shouted, showed rage. They have expressed compassion towards the suffering of other participants. The group members are probably tired, *stressed* from the lengthy, often intense, discussions and *elated* by the extent they have overcome some conflicts. It is not a surprise that some people may have unusual feelings after such experiences. Their imaginations are aroused. Especially if the group has been going on for many hours for several days.

I also perceive normal phenomena – nothing spiritual, nothing mystical – in individual therapy experiences. For example, an experienced client-centered therapist is immersed in the phenomenology of a particular client for many hours over many sessions. The client has been expressing himself very thoughtfully and emotionally. He reveals that his *awareness* of things about himself and his life is increasing, becoming clearer and becoming richer. The therapist feels she is in a somewhat altered state of mind in the sessions. She feels very tuned in and connected with her client. She thinks the client is feeling the same way towards her. The interaction between them has a flowing quality. Under these and similar circumstances, sometimes a therapist may be able to mentally anticipate the client's narrative content. The therapist may find she is accurately anticipating some of the client's thoughts or emotions. Sometimes she even finds she has mentally anticipated exactly what the client says next. Or she says what the client says, simultaneously with him. Or the therapist experiences a mental image that the client subsequently describes to the therapist. These can be understood as natural phenomena. They express a close and effective therapeutic relationship based on acceptance and empathic understanding.

Rogers interprets experiences, similar to the ones I have experienced while conducting therapy, as illustrating a transcendent or spiritual reality.

He says he feels his and his client's "spirits touching." I recognize and feel closeness, but I never construe the events as "spirits touching" because I do not believe in the existence of inner spirits or supernatural contact between persons. Such events, that Rogers interprets spiritually, do not appear to me (nor to some other experienced client-centered therapists) to be supernatural, spiritual, transcendent, mystical, magical or esoteric. I do not believe any of my therapy experiences are related to a supernatural existence. They are normal psychological events that occur commonly under certain interpersonal circumstances. They are natural phenomena that emerge among members of a group, or emerge out of the therapist and client being engaged together in a particular manner.

The therapist's strong *presence* is a natural result of working well with some clients. In one of my therapy relationships, my client described the experience of perceiving a sense of light glowing from my body, especially from around my head. My "glow" made him feel happy and safe, when I entered the therapy room. We had a very good working relationship. I felt a strong sense of attunement with the client and I liked the client. He felt I was helping him. The client himself did not interpret the phenomenon of my *glow* as spiritual. He told me he thought his visual experiences of me were only in his perceptions. He thought they were the result of his perceptions of some of my personal qualities and his strong feelings about me.

Another client reported in a session late in our therapy, that it was the first time she was aware of anything in the room other than me. It had seemed to her that we were in a space surrounded by nothingness. Her focus had felt so totally attracted to me that she hadn't been aware of anything else for months! At that point she noticed some art objects and books in the room that had been there all along.

Another client remarked that she always experienced me as having a "joyful" expression. She said she perceived it even when she was talking about painful things and when I was understanding her pain. She told me my *joyfulness* gave her hope in the midst of the expression of her worst feelings. In this case I was very surprised, and concerned that my presence sometimes might give her the impression I was indifferent or distant from her. But she apparently did not take it that way. I do feel there is truth in her perceptions of me because doing therapy always makes me happy. Perhaps my happiness comes through to some of my other clients in their perceptions of my presence. Perhaps it contributes to my therapeutic effectiveness with them.

## BELIEFS

Belief in a mystically apprehended reality, in a religion, in spirituality, as well as in agnosticism or atheism, is a personal matter. When conducting therapy, religious or supernatural belief systems – like all of a therapist's individual opinions, beliefs and desires – must be discriminated from what clients are trying to communicate to us. We want to understand and respond to the client from his own perspective, unbiased by our own beliefs (Schwarz & Bonner-Schwarz, 1999).

Client-centered therapy facilitates the unique individual and his idiosyncratic way of moving towards therapeutic change. As a client-centered therapist I want to be vigilant about my own emotional and ideological investments. I do not want them to distort my empathic understandings nor inadvertently influence my clients. It is part of basic therapeutic responsibility to protect my clients from my private interpretations of reality unless the client requests I share with him such information.

## PERSONAL PRESENCE

Personal presence is a natural and universal phenomenon. All living persons involuntarily express or emanate a presence. A person's *presence* is interpreted by others as a manifestation of their self – their individuality. Presence is made up of physically perceptible qualities of a person that *are picked up by the senses of others* when others observe them. Presence is a set of perceptions of physical events in and on the body of a person. The observer's perceptions blend together into an impression. An observer is probably not aware of all the details that make up their impression of someone's presence because perceptions of presence tend to be holistic experiences. Thus *presence* basically refers to manifestations of a person that are perceived by the senses, but it also depends upon the observer's perceptual receptivity and the meanings the observer applies to his perceptions. The observer generalizes his whole impression of the person's *presence*. It is an appearance seeming to reveal the person's self, personality or character.

## THERAPEUTIC PRESENCE IN CLIENT-CENTERED THERAPY

Client-centered therapeutic presence is the result of the therapist's ability *to be present to the client*. This means the therapist gives himself to bringing forth certain of his capabilities in the relationship. These are capabilities for self-integration and self-awareness. They are capabilities for acceptance of another person and capabilities for empathic understanding of another person. The therapist is willing and able to be completely engaged with the client.

She is willing to be undistracted and deeply focused on the client in order to understand the client's inner world as the client reveals it.

These typical efforts of the client-centered therapist produce a presence that is perceptible, often noticed and, whether consciously noticed or not, is taken in by clients. The therapist, however, does not deliberately communicate therapeutic presence. It is the *inadvertent* effect of a client-centered therapist experiencing, and constantly maintaining, certain attitudes and expressing behaviors that convey those attitudes.

The sixth of Rogers' necessary and sufficient conditions of therapeutic personality change (Rogers, 1957) refers to the client's perception of the therapist's attitudes of unconditional positive regard and empathic understanding. The therapist's *presence*, the qualities that emanate from the therapist, are the medium for the client's perceptions of those conditions. Therapeutic *presence* probably also includes the other qualities that are part of the whole set of values involved in client-centered therapy. These include the therapist's respect for the client, and trust in the client and the therapist's transparence as a person in relationship with the client.

## PRESENCE NOT A FOCUS FOR TRAINING

Therapeutic presence is important in clients' perceptions and the therapeutic benefit of the therapy. However, there is not much of a practical nature implied by the concept of presence for functioning as a client-centered therapist or for training client-centered therapists. It may be a helpful construct in that it reminds the therapist *to be present*. It may remind him to develop an undefensive, open capacity that he can bring to therapy with clients. It probably does not add much to understanding how to function as a client-centered therapist.

Efforts to help therapists further develop the client-centered therapeutic attitudes should focus on helping them to understand the subtle meanings of the therapeutic attitudes. Training should focus on how a therapist may *experience* the therapeutic attitudes and on how a therapist may overcome personal obstacles to those experiences. Training should not focus therapists' attention on presenting a presence. If a therapist has developed the therapeutic attitudes and is relatively constant in experiencing them, she or he is likely to manifest a presence that has a perceptual potency to clients.

## PRESENCE IN RESEARCH

There is an implication of the "*natural presence*" concept for research. I doubt, however, that it contributes much to familiar methods of studying client-perceived qualities of the therapist such as those studied in relation to outcome (Rogers & Dymond, 1954). In any case, it is a slightly different angle on the issue of how the therapist is perceived by clients. Along these lines, using the concept of "*presence,*" I have conducted a small pilot study using some of my own clients' perceptions of me and their perceptions of a nontherapeutic person.

## A PILOT STUDY OF THERAPEUTIC PRESENCE

I asked eight (current and former) clients about their impressions of my *presence* while conducting therapy. I assumed that *therapeutic presence* is a *gestalt or holistic impression* that clients may experience and that could be discriminated into various qualities and described with words. The study's subjects are people who have experienced me functioning as their therapist in several or in many interviews. Some have also observed me giving demonstrations of client-centered therapy in front of a class or group.

### Method
First, I asked subjects to try to recall *my presence* as they perceived me when I was functioning as a therapist, and to write at least several words or phrases, but no more than 10 words, describing *my therapeutic presence*. Second, the same eight subjects were asked to produce as many as 10 words describing the presence of a person with a *non*therapeutic or *counter*-therapeutic presence. I asked them to recall a poor therapist they had experienced or observed.

### Results
#### Responses to therapeutic presence
I received in response to my inquiry *about my presence* 47 different words or phrases from the sample of eight clients. The subjects were all people familiar with client-centered theory, so it is not a surprise to find they use many words or phrases to describe me that relate to the therapeutic attitudes of the theory. They also use idiosyncratic words.

## 1. Words/phrases descriptive of my therapeutic presence that appear related to client-centered theory

### Words or phrases appearing to relate to the concept of Congruence:

| | |
|---|---|
| trustworthy | undisturbed |
| calm | relaxed |
| real | centered |
| calm posture | not "professional" |
| sit and move comfortably | |

### Words appearing to relate to Unconditional Positive Regard:

| | |
|---|---|
| caring | sympathetic |
| feeling | acceptant |
| nonjudgmental | pleased to see me |
| never judging | a source of goodwill toward me |

### Words appearing to relate to Empathic Understanding:

| | |
|---|---|
| interested | empathic |
| completely involved | remembers things about me |
| attentive | with me |

### Words appearing to relate to the Nondirective Attitude:

| | |
|---|---|
| allowing | indifferent to outcome |
| receptive | |

## 2. Words used to describe my therapeutic presence not related to the theory

### Consistency and reliability:

| | |
|---|---|
| consistency of qualities | formal (in the sense of a reliably |
| reliable | structured experience in terms of time, |
| consistent | space and behavior) |
| unambiguous | ready when I arrive |
| | prompt (for appointments and in returning calls) |

### Other personal qualities:

| | |
|---|---|
| alert | gentle |
| not self-focused | gentle voice |
| soft spoken | accommodating |
| warm smile | calming |
| not self-concerned | generous |
| kind eyes | |

*Responses to nontherapeutic presence*

The same eight subjects produced 47 words or phrases describing the presence of a person who seemed to them to be nontherapeutic or counter-therapeutic.

### 1. Words for nontherapeutic presence that appear related to the therapeutic attitudes

**Not Congruent:**

| | |
|---|---|
| scared child | phony |
| insecure | rigid postures |
| emotional | fake smile |
| defensive | not trustworthy |
| threatened | flaky |
| secretive | comical |

**Not showing Unconditional Positive Regard:**

| | |
|---|---|
| critical | judgmental tone |
| angry | judgmental |
| demanding | subtly making fun |
| demeaning | flip |

**Not showing Empathic Understanding:**

| | |
|---|---|
| distracted | betraying an attitude |
| closed | does not attend to me and what I |
| non-listening | am saying |
| preconceptions | taking up a lot of psychological |
| re-framing | space |

**Not Nondirective:**

| | |
|---|---|
| confrontational | coaxing |
| manipulative | pushing a perspective |
| directive | too sure of the value of what |
| paternalistic | is offered |

### 2. Words for other nontherapeutic qualities of the person

| | |
|---|---|
| unkind | voyeuristically observant |
| presumptuous | self-centered |
| arrogant | menacing |
| self-concerned | vindictive |
| not intelligent (simplistic) | trying too hard |
| self-invested | over-serious |

The clients in this study, who are at least slightly familiar with client-centered theory, produce a majority of theoretically relevant descriptive words or phrases for their perceptions of both *therapeutic presence* and *nontherapeutic presence.* The descriptors of my therapeutic presence included 57% of words or phrases that appear to relate to Rogers' therapeutic attitudes. The descriptors of a therapist with a counter-therapeutic presence included 65% of words or phrases that appear to negatively relate to the therapeutic attitudes. The subjects also described my *therapeutic presence,* and their recollection of a person with a *counter-therapeutic presence,* using idiosyncratic words. The descriptors for my therapeutic presence all express positive qualities. Those for the person with a counter-therapeutic presence all express qualities usually considered negative for a therapist.

The pilot study shows that a request for descriptive words or phrases for a therapist's *presence* has meaning to therapy clients. Clients who are familiar with the concepts of client-centered theory produce many descriptors that are related to the theory. Another study might explore whether client-centered clients who are unfamiliar with the approach produce similar descriptors. It is interesting that 17% of the words the clients used to describe my presence seem to describe consistency or reliability. These are qualities that I feel are important to me in working with clients. A future study might examine whether other therapists' clients use words to describe *presence* that relate to qualities their therapists consider particularly important in their therapy. There are many possibilities for studying *therapeutic presence* by asking clients for descriptors, such as comparing the presence-descriptors produced by clients of therapists from different orientations.

CONCLUSION

In my view, client-centered clients may perceive a distinctive naturalistic therapeutic presence when the therapist is congruent and is empathically and acceptantly focused on the client. The pilot study suggests that although therapeutic presence is a holistic perception, clients are able to distinguish their therapist's presence into aspects and describe it by words that refer to many different qualities.

Some of the therapist's physical manifestations that contribute to perceptions of presence are subtle, such as emotionally stimulated changes in skin tone or temperature. Some are more obvious, such as postural adjustments. A therapist's *presence* may stimulate a variety of different emotional and psychological impacts. Presence is perceived when the therapist's inner attitudes are expressed in perceptible physical events, and when the client is able to interpret those stimuli into perceptions of personal qualities. Presence may significantly contribute to therapeutic impact, as Rogers suggested.

## REFERENCES

Baldwin, M. (1987). Interview with Carl Rogers on the use of the self in therapy. In M. Baldwin & V. Satir (Eds.), *The use of self in therapy* (pp. 45–52). New York: Haworth Press. [Reprinted (2004) in R. Moodley, C. Lago, & A. Talahite (Eds.), *Carl Rogers counsels a Black client: Race and culture in person-centred counseling* (pp. 253–260). Ross-on-Wye: PCCS Books]

Brodley, B. T. (1994). Some observations of Carl Rogers' behavior in therapy interviews. *The Person-Centered Journal, 1*(2), 37–48. [This volume, Chapter 25]

Brodley, B. T. (2000). Presence in client-centered therapy. *A Pessoa Como Centro: Revista de Estudos Rogerianos,* (6), 48–77. [A different emphasis from the version published here: see the note on the title page of this chapter]

[Brodley, B. T., & Lietaer, G. (Eds.). (2006). *Transcripts of Carl Rogers' therapy sessions, Vols. 1–17.* Available from germain.lietaer@psy.kuleuven.be and kmoon1@alumni.uchicago.edu]

Hart, T. (1997). Transcendental empathy in the therapeutic encounter. *The Humanist Psychologist, 25*(3), 245–270.

Hart, T. (1999). Carl Rogers as mystic? *The Person-Centered Journal, 6*(1), 81–87.

[Lietaer, G., & Brodley, B. T. (2003). Carl Rogers in the therapy room: A listing of session transcripts and a survey of publications referring to Rogers' sessions. *Person-Centered & Experiential Psychotherapies, 2,* 274–291.]

Rogers, C. R. (1951). *Client-centered therapy.* Boston: Houghton Mifflin.

Rogers, C. R. (1957). The necessary and sufficient conditions of therapeutic personality change. *Journal of Consulting Psychology, 21,* 95–103.

Rogers, C. R. (1980a). The foundations of a person-centered approach. In *A way of being* (pp. 113–136). Boston: Houghton Mifflin.

Rogers, C. R. (1980b). Building person-centered communities: The implications for the future. In *A way of being* (pp. 181–206). Boston: Houghton Mifflin.

Rogers, C. R. (1987). Client-centered, person-centered. *Person-Centered Review, 2*(1), 11–12.

Rogers, C. R., & Dymond, R. F. (Eds.). (1954). *Psychotherapy and personality change.* Chicago: University of Chicago Press.

Schmid, P. F. (1998). Face to face: The art of encounter. In B. Thorne & E. Lambers (Eds.), *Person-centred therapy: A European perspective.* (pp. 74–90). London: Sage.

Schwarz, J., & Bonner-Schwarz, S. (1999). Person-centered therapy and spirituality: The art of knowing and self determination. *The Person-Centered Journal, 6*(1), 75–80.

Van Belle, H. A. (1990). Rogers' later move toward mysticism: Implications for client-centered therapy. In G. Lietaer, J. Rombauts, & R. Van Balen (Eds.), *Client-centered and experiential therapy in the nineties* (pp. 47–57). Leuven, Belgium: Leuven University Press.

Wood, J. K. (1998). Carl Rogers and transpersonal psychology. *The Person-Centered Journal, 5*(1), 3–14.

# Chapter 11

# The actualizing tendency concept
# in client-centered theory

*Abstract*
The paper discusses the actualizing tendency as a biological concept. It aims to clarify the meaning of "constructive" in actualizing tendency theory and resolve the apparent contradiction between human pro-social nature and antisocial behavior from the perspective of actualizing tendency theory.

In this paper I want to discuss and elaborate on the organismic actualizing tendency concept – a first principle in Rogers' theory of client-centered therapy and the person-centered approach. I aim to clarify the meaning of "constructive" as a fundamental feature of the actualizing tendency, explain how the constructive direction of the actualizing tendency is theoretically consistent with observations of destructive human behavior, and emphasize the biological, natural science character of the concept. My discussion is largely based on Rogers' writings, but it includes other ideas that I think are consistent with Rogers' thinking. Starting in the 1950s I was influenced by the organismic theory of Kurt Goldstein (1939/1963, 1940) as I was developing my understanding of Rogers. Along the way, Rogers', Goldstein's and my own ideas have merged and become difficult to extricate from each other. Nevertheless, my intention is to discuss the actualizing tendency and the organism in a manner that is consistent with Rogers' ideas.

THE CONCEPT

The actualizing tendency is the sole motivational concept in Rogers' theories of personality, client-centered therapy, and interpersonal relations and in applications of the person-centered approach. The concept of an actualizing tendency was first proposed by Rogers in the 1950s (Rogers, 1951, 1959); it continues to be discussed in books and articles on client-centered therapy and the person-centered approach (e.g., Barrett-Lennard, 1998; Biermann-

This paper, published (1999) in *The Person-Centered Journal,* 6(2), 108–120, is a revision of a paper published (1998) in *A Pessoa Como Centro, 2*, 37–49, in Portuguese and English. Reproduced with permission from *PCJ.*

Ratjen, 1998; Bozarth, 1998; Hawtin & Moore, 1998; Merry & Lusty, 1993; Schmid, 1996; Thorne, 1992; Van Kalmthout, 1998). Similar concepts have been proposed by other theoreticians (e.g., Bohart & Tallman, 1999; Goldstein, 1939/1963).

Rogers was sensitive to evidence of an inherent growth motivation from early in his career. He observed that psychotherapy clients do not benefit, or the gains are soon lost, when they have been guided, interpreted or directed. He observed that a self-determined client process appears to be most effective, suggesting an internal source of healing and growth. In an early book Rogers (1942) stated:

> Therapy is not a matter of doing something to the individual, or of inducing him to do something about himself. It is instead a matter of freeing him for normal growth and development. (p. 29)

The actualizing tendency concept emerged out of therapy experiences and Rogers (1951) posited the concept as an hypothesis to be tested. He wrote:

> [T]he counselor chooses to act consistently upon the hypothesis that the individual has a sufficient capacity to deal constructively with all those aspects of his life which can potentially come into conscious awareness … The counselor acts upon this hypothesis … being always alert to note those experiences (clinical or research) which contradict this hypothesis as well as those which support it. (p. 24)

It is "an *hypothesis* in human relationships" that "will always remain so" (p. 23), because it cannot be conclusively proved or disproved. Although the actualizing tendency is a hypothesis to be tested with each new client, it functions in theory as a first principle, axiom or basic assumption about organisms, including human organisms. In therapy, the actualizing tendency functions as an assumption that influences the way the therapist proceeds as a helper.

Rogers' actualizing tendency is a teleological concept – a final cause in Aristotelian terms – based on many observations of the behavior of humans and other creatures (e.g., Bertalanffy, 1952/1960; White, 1959). Understanding of the actualizing tendency concept is inextricable from understanding Rogers' biological concept of the organism. Schmid (1998) quotes Rogers: "I use the term organism for the biological entity. The actualizing tendency exists in the biological human organism" (p. 47).

The actualizing tendency is the organism's "one central source of energy" (Rogers, 1963, p. 6); it has constructive directionality, aiming toward realization and organismic perfection. It is intrinsic to the life of organisms and cannot be defined without including or implying the concept of the organism. Rogers (1980) wrote: "The actualizing tendency … cannot be destroyed without destroying the organism" (p. 118). Further:

> … All motivation is the organismic tendency toward fulfillment. There is one central source of energy in the organism. This source is a trustworthy function of the whole system rather than some portion of it: it is most simply conceptualized as a tendency towards fulfillment, toward actualization, involving not only the maintenance but also the enhancement of the organism. (p. 123)

The actualizing tendency is a meta-motivation that subsumes all specific motivations. All motives, needs and drives are an expression of the actualizing tendency (Rogers, 1959). All functions, all activities of the organism, are manifestations or channels of the actualizing tendency. Statements about the actualizing tendency are in effect statements about the nature of the organism and thus are also about human beings. As a person lives in the world, specific motivations and functions become organismically, experientially and behaviorally salient. The actualizing tendency is the person's energy and determines a *generally constructive* direction of his functions. The person's processes and specific aims, however, are determined by other causes as well as the actualizing tendency – by inborn potentials, by conditioning, by learning and by circumstances. Understanding the actualizing tendency concept simultaneously clarifies the concept of the organism in Rogers' theory. The following discussion summarizes the major characteristics of the actualizing tendency and of organisms, including human organisms.

INDIVIDUAL AND UNIVERSAL

The actualizing tendency is both individual and universal (Rogers, 1980). The expression of the tendency is always unique to individuals and at the same time it is a motivating tendency in all organisms.

HOLISTIC

The actualizing tendency is holistic (Rogers, 1959). The functioning of the actualizing tendency, and the functioning of the organism as a whole, is a changing gestalt. Different aspects of the person assume figure and ground relations (Goldstein, 1939/1963) depending upon the specific aims of the person, and depending upon the immediate demands of the environment.

The actualizing tendency functions throughout all of a person's systems. It is expressed in a variable and dynamic manner through the subsystems of the whole person while maintaining the person's wholeness and organization.

## UBIQUITOUS AND CONSTANT

The actualizing tendency is ubiquitous and constant (Rogers, 1963; Rogers & Sanford, 1984). It is the generic motivation for all activity, at all levels of function within the person, under all circumstances. It is the energy and direction to the moment-by-moment living of the person. It is intrinsic to the person's moving, to responding to stimuli, and to maintaining wholeness. To the person's feeling, thinking, striving, and self-preserving activity. The actualizing tendency is expressed through all of the person's capacities.

The actualizing tendency functions under all circumstances. It functions when circumstances are favorable and when they are unfavorable to the maintenance or enhancement of the individual. It is the life force of the individual organism. If the person is alive, the actualizing tendency is functioning. Rogers (1977) commented in this vein:

> This is the very nature of the process we call life. This tendency is operative at all times, in all organisms. Indeed it is only the presence or absence of this total directional process that enables us to tell whether a given organism is alive or dead. (p. 239)

## A DIRECTIONAL PROCESS

The actualizing tendency is a constructive directional process having two aspects. First, there is an overriding *organizational* directive process. The actualizing tendency is always directed toward maintaining a person's integrity and organization, thus preserving identity and life. It involves assimilation and differentiation processes while maintaining the wholeness of the person. Secondly, the actualization direction is towards *realization, fulfillment and perfection* of inherent potentialities as well as learned capabilities of the individual (Rogers, 1963). The actualization process is a selective process in that it tends to maintain and enhance the whole organism/person. Rogers (1977) wrote:

> Whether the stimulus arises from within or without, whether the environment is favorable or unfavorable, the behaviors of an organism can be counted on to be in the direction of maintaining, enhancing and reproducing itself. (p. 239)

## CHANGES IN TENSION

The actualizing tendency is primarily tension increasing (Rogers, 1959). The organism/person is not fundamentally a drive-reduction system. There is a dynamic equilibrium between organism and environment (Angyal, 1941) with energy and tensions shifting back and forth. According to Goldstein (1939/1963):

> Normal behavior corresponds to a continual change of tension, of such a kind that over and again that state of tension is reached which enables and impels the organism to actualize itself in further activities, according to its nature. (p. 197)

Organisms require reduction of tensions, especially in homeostatic and preservation mechanisms; tension reduction is a secondary, corrective reaction. From the perspective of the living organism, however, tension increase is most characteristic of its functioning. The organism is a system that increases tension levels to differentiate, grow, and further realize inherent capabilities. Changes in tension are channels for the actualizing tendency, as are all functions. The organism's distinctive directional process is one of tension-increase for the sake of expansion and development.

## AUTONOMY

The actualizing tendency is a tendency toward autonomy of the person and away from heteronomy (Rogers, 1963). The person moves inherently toward self-regulation and self-determination, and away from being controlled. To avoid misunderstandings, it should be understood that this tendency does not imply a tendency away from relationships, interdependence, connection or socialization.

## SELF-ACTUALIZATION

The concept "self-actualization" in Rogers' theory (1959) refers to the actualizing tendency that is manifested in the "self," a human subsystem that becomes differentiated within the whole person through early life social interactions. The concept of "self" is essential to Rogers' (1951, 1959) theories of the development of normal personality and development of psychological disturbances. His theory of the self-system (Rogers, 1959), including the effects of detrimental socialization on the self, accounts for many outcomes of the actualization tendency which appear to contradict its constructive directionality.

## HUMAN PRO-SOCIAL NATURE

Human beings have a social nature with pro-social characteristics. Consequently, a basic direction of the actualizing tendency, in human functioning, is toward constructive social behavior (Rogers, 1982). The following pro-social tendencies are probably universal. They include the capacity for identification leading to feelings of sympathy for other persons, capacity for empathy, affiliative tendencies, tendencies toward attachment, communication, social cooperation and collaboration, capacities for forming moral or ethical rules, and tendencies to engage in struggles to live according to moral or ethical rules.

Human social nature is as fundamental as are human tendencies toward self-preservation and sexuality. Social nature involves innate capacities tempered or enhanced by life experiences. Like other inborn tendencies, there are great individual differences in the strength and in the forms that social tendencies may take. They can be enhanced or diminished in the person by circumstances. They can be distorted, exaggerated, suppressed or develop in balance with the whole person, according to circumstances. Human social nature is complex, and its expression is inevitably influenced by social contexts. It may become unrecognizable in some individuals through their struggle to maintain viable integration, or it may flower in ways that are socially valued.

## REFLECTIVE CONSCIOUSNESS

Reflective consciousness – specifically the capacity for self-awareness – is a salient channel of the actualizing tendency in humans (Rogers, 1963, 1980). This kind of consciousness involves a relatively high degree of precision and clarity. It involves knowing the things that appear to it – things in the world or self-experiences – but it also "knows that it knows them" (James, 1890/ 1981, p. 263). Self-awareness permits a great range of choices for self-regulation and for expansion of functions. It permits the development of potentials that do not exist in other organisms.

## IMPERFECT OUTCOMES OF A CONSTRUCTIVE DRIVE

It is a fact of life that defective or poorly realized organisms, as well as persons impaired in various ways, are born and live their lives. Obviously many inborn and environmental causes are involved in the creation and development of a normal, whole, well-functioning organism. The actualizing tendency principle describes the phenomena of organisms, including persons, persisting, developing and functioning as best they can, *given their capacities and their circumstances.* The processes involved in survival, development and realization of the potentialities of any given person or organism are vulnerable to circumstances (Rogers, 1980; Rogers & Sanford, 1984), and circumstances may be favorable or unfavorable. They may be physical, social/cultural or interpersonal. Circumstances affecting organisms may be optimal; they may be merely adequate. Circumstances may be totally inadequate or destructive to individuals.

Although the actualizing tendency is inherently constructive and aims the organism towards perfection, a living person's condition and behavior at any moment is also a result of other causes – innate characteristics, learned characteristics and circumstances. The dynamic interaction of the actualizing tendency with the other causes of behavior may or may not result in what is organismically constructive or what the person's society considers constructive outcomes. Optimal actualization of a person's nature requires many different, highly favorable and ongoing circumstances, and it is a rare phenomenon. Most circumstances affecting humans and other organisms range from the utterly deprived or destructive to a relatively adequate range. Human lives are lived in complex circumstances, sometimes including the whole range of qualities of circumstances in one general situation. The circumstances lived by many persons, probably most persons, are not appropriate for full development of many of their potentialities.

The concept of potentialities is complex. Potentials are characteristics or capabilities that are not yet developed and sometimes not even apparent, like the acorn that may become the oak tree. The realization of potentials into full capabilities depends upon biogenic ontogeny and upon circumstances. For example, humans usually crawl before they walk but unusual circumstances can produce a different sequence. The emergence of different potentials into capacities fulfills various roles in the whole person. It is desirable for some potentials – for example, language ability – to be realized under all circumstances. The development of other potentials may be desirable only for special goals – for example, the ability to behave without feeling certain emotional reactions as in performing surgery. The timing of expression of a potential may be important for survival or restoring well-being, but would be destructive under normal circumstances – vomiting, for example. The development of certain potentials often precludes the highest development of others within the temporal limits of a lifetime. For example a woman's choice to bear many children and to personally raise them may involve a sacrifice of her potential as a classical dancer or singer. The valid generalization that the actualizing tendency is directed towards fulfillment of potentialities covers a great variety of situations with many qualifying factors and variable results.

The actualizing tendency itself persists and is not less strong, less present, or less functional, under unfavorable circumstances. The tendency's *expression* in the person's *processes*, or in the *results of processes*, however, may be more or less distorted or stunted depending upon the unfavorable circumstances. Rogers uses the metaphor of the potato sprout in the dark cellar growing toward a spot of light to describe the actualizing tendency's persistence as well as its organismic vulnerability. Rogers (1980) wrote:

> These sad spindly sprouts would grow 2 or 3 feet in length as they reached toward the distant light of the window. The sprouts were, in their bizarre, futile growth, a sort of desperate expression of the directional tendency … They would never become plants, never mature, never fulfill their real potential. But under the most adverse circumstances, they were striving to become. (p. 118)

### THE ACTUALIZING TENDENCY IN THE CONSCIOUS PERSON

Human organisms have evolved the capacity for self-reflective awareness or reflective consciousness. This capacity makes actualizing tendency theory seem more complicated in humans because self-reflective awareness implies the capacity for conscious and deliberate choice. If humans are organismically constructive, and inherently pro-social, and if they are able to make conscious choices, one may ask the actualizing tendency theory why humans engage in so much personal and social destructivity. How can the constructively directed actualizing tendency, with the human organism's pro-social tendencies, and the human capacity for conscious choice, be reconciled with the obvious and frequent antisocial and self-destructive choices made by humans? The point made above addresses this question in a general way; the processes and results of the actualizing tendency involve other causes than the actualizing tendency itself.

Although it may seem contradictory to the idea of a basic constructive motivation, the unhealthy or the poorly realized person, or the person engaging in bad behavior is motivated as much by the constructive actualizing tendency as the healthy, highly realized or socially good person. The actualizing tendency is *a tendency; it is not a guarantee* of full health or full realization or good behavior. There are many causes, in addition to the actualizing tendency, involved in health and development and constructive social behavior. Poor personal early life circumstances may severely limit or distort the development of potentialities resulting in personal and social tragedies. A striking example that recently has become better understood is the role of child abuse in the etiology of war and other violence (Karr-Morse & Wiley, 1997; Miller, 1998).

Poor circumstances in more mature persons may also dramatically affect *outcomes* at the personal and social levels – for example, the incidence of suicide rates among elderly men.

According to actualizing tendency theory, a person is always doing the best he or she can under their circumstances. Behavior that is destructive in the social sense is in some way *organismically, or in its phenomenological meanings,* constructive as much as socially constructive behavior. Evil behavior, according to actualizing tendency theory, is as much the result of the actualizing tendency as socially good behavior. The first factor to keep in mind when examining why a person's behavior is evil or bad rather than good is that the judgment is one being made from one's own cultural or personal perspective. The second and related factor is to examine the person's cultural context and to relate the "bad" behavior to the beliefs and practices considered normal in the culture, subculture, or society. Scrutiny of contextual cultural values may reveal that the evil or bad behavior is encouraged and valued in the society and thus the person is expressing their pro-social nature very well, within that framework.

It is necessary, for understanding from the actualizing tendency framework, to examine a person's *individual* historical or current conditions when their bad behavior cannot be explained by expectations of their cultural context. It may in some cases require understanding of inborn characteristics, but it will more likely require understanding of exceptional personal experiences, or characteristics inculcated through personal relationships, or understanding the external conditions within which the person is existing. Some persons have been so deprived, punished or abused that their social identity and sense of connection is distorted, or their inherent pro-social potentialities largely undeveloped. Consequently some of their behavior may be considered bad or evil by the larger society. Theoretically, such persons, nevertheless, are motivated by a constructively directed actualizing tendency as much as good persons. How this is so in the particular case requires close scrutiny of the exceptional personal experiences.

Many of the contents and patterns of a person's reflective consciousness, as well as their unconscious reaction tendencies, are learned through important personal socializing relationships in early childhood. Personal socialization is a major part of what shapes psychological actualization processes in individuals. Rogers' (1959) self-theory describes the development of psychological contents that inhibit accurate awareness of organismic experiences, create anxiety, and limit personal realization. According to his theory, depending upon the attitudes and reactions of significant adults when relating to a child, the basic need for positive regard in early childhood may result in "conditions of worth." These become part of a self-concept structured to protect the individual from full and accurate awareness of organismic experiences that contradict the "conditions of worth." Having such a self-concept overrides the functioning of the person's basic *organismic valuing process* and limits the capacity for accuracy of awareness that favors a more complete personal development. The "honor killings" of girls and women in some contemporary cultures appear to be the result of a combination of cultural values and of learned conditions of worth. A man's sense of what he must do to maintain a "good self," a self that is worthy of standing and dignity in the community, requires he kill female relatives who violate local moral codes of male–female behavior. The example illustrates how a particular social value probably inculcated as a condition of worth, may override powerful feelings of affectionate connection and socially valued feelings of protection towards female family members. Many people are unlikely to recognize the constructive drive and pro-social tendencies in "honor killings." Nevertheless, wrong as the practice seems to many of us, the behavior in part expresses the actualizing tendency and pro-social human nature. Rogers (1982) wrote:

> I find … no … innate tendency toward destructiveness, toward evil … If the elements making for growth are present, the actualizing tendency develops in positive ways … Every person has the capacity for evil behavior … Whether I or anyone will translate these impulses into behavior depends … on two elements: social conditioning and voluntary choice. (p. 88)

Humans have the potential, through their capacity to reflect upon themselves and to make choices, to correct for at least some of the unfavorable or difficult forces that act within them and upon them. Many factors are at play. Personal, social, and contextual factors may determine any human choice. The more favorable the factors, given the constructive direction of the actualizing tendency and pro-social tendencies, the more likely it is that choices will have constructive intent and constructive consequences, at least from the framework of their culture.

Rogers observed that clients tend to develop in growthful and socially constructive ways and make constructive choices as they proceed in client-centered therapy. Granted the common general cultural context Rogers shared with his clients, and granted the culture-bound values of Rogers' judgment, his observation suggests that client-centered therapy is psychologically a very favorable interpersonal situation for personal actualization.

## THE ACTUALIZING TENDENCY IN CLIENT-CENTERED THERAPY

Client-centered therapy is nondirective (Rogers, in Evans, 1975, p. 26); the therapist strives in all of the ways he or she relates to clients to be constant in promoting clients' freedom of choice. Clients in this therapy, as it progresses, tend to make constructive choices *without* external direction from the therapist. Rogers (1986a) wrote:

> In client-centered therapy, the person is free to choose any directions, but actually selects positive and constructive pathways. I can only explain this in terms of a directional tendency inherent in the human organism – a tendency to grow, to develop, to realize its full potential. (p. 127)

The therapist's provision of the client-centered therapeutic attitudes in relationship facilitates the client's psychological healing and development. When clients perceive and experience these attitudes, distortions diminish in the psychological expression of the actualizing tendency and the person's untapped capabilities are revealed. In effect, client-centered therapy facilitates constructive results of actualizing tendency processes. Rogers (1980) wrote:

> The central hypothesis of this [client-centered] approach [is that] individuals have within themselves vast resources for self-understanding and for altering their self-concepts, basic attitudes, and self-directed behavior; these resources can be tapped if a definable climate of facilitative psychological attitudes can be provided. (p. 115)

These attitudes include respect for the client, trust in the client's inherent capabilities for growth, a nondirective attitude (Rogers, in Evans, 1975) and the therapeutic attitudes – congruence, unconditional positive regard and empathic understanding of the client's internal frame of reference (Rogers, 1957). Clients change therapeutically when a therapist consistently provides the totality of these attitudes at a high level. When clients perceive these attitudes they engage in self-correcting processes or "pathways" (Rogers, 1986a, p. 127). Ongoing therapeutic effects within the client facilitate constructive choices. Some of these effects are clients' decreased defensiveness, increased openness to experience, greater awareness, improved ability to create or find solutions to problems, and increased flexibility in behavior (Rogers, 1961). All of these therapeutic effects contribute to the processes of making constructive choices.

Anthropological, sociological and psychological observations across cultures support the idea of a human pro-social innate nature. It is also a rational inference given the positive and constructive choices made by clients in client-centered therapy. The likelihood that socially valued choices are different when made by persons in different cultures under the conditions of client-centered therapy does not negate the inference. It merely takes into account the role of culture in the specific learned meanings of "pro-social" to individuals. Emergence or development of clients' innate universal pro-social potentialities (for sympathy, empathy, care-taking, social affiliation, communication, cooperation and sense of morality or ethics) are involved in therapeutic choices. If humans did not possess a pro-social nature, the freeing effects of client-centered therapy would tend to result in self-centered and self-seeking solutions and behaviors. We would observe more selfish tendencies, tendencies towards making selfish choices at the expense of others. This is not, however, what happens. Instead, clients tend more to take others into account, and tend to choose "greater socialization, improved relationships with others" (Rogers, 1981/1989, p. 238) and greater social consciousness than they manifested before therapy. Rogers wrote:

> [I]f we can provide a growth-promoting climate ... choices prove to be, quite freely and spontaneously, in a socially constructive direction. (p. 238)

## THE ACTUALIZING TENDENCY: A BIOLOGICAL, NATURAL SCIENCE CONCEPT

Students often confuse Rogers' constructive actualizing tendency concept with a moral or ethical concept. The meaning of "constructive" at the organismic level, however, refers to a motivational direction towards maintenance, wholeness and realization of potentialities, not to the ethical or moral goodness of actualization solutions in response to circumstances. Rogers has been misunderstood. May (1982), for example, criticized Rogers, imputing to him a "good" and naive view of human nature. Rogers' view of the positive actualizing tendency did not mean he believed humanity is good. Rogers (1987) wrote:

> I have found that if you get to the core of the individual, you discover something constructive, not destructive. People say to me, "Oh, then you believe man is good." I do not like the term *good*. That is a moral judgment ... We look at a plant. We do not decide that it is [good or] evil by nature. We just take it for granted that, given the right conditions, it will grow, it will blossom, it will produce its normal life. We do not think that way about humans ... I have certainly dealt with plenty of people who are doing evil things, who are doing things that are socially

destructive. But … if you can get to know the person inside, you will find that the person would like to live in harmony and is constructive by nature. And that is the essential basis of the whole theory. (p. 41)

In other words, the actualizing tendency is a biological, natural science concept, not a moral or ethical idea. The misunderstanding that the actualizing tendency is an ethical concept expressing his optimism was a source of distress to Rogers. He (1956/1958) wrote:

> It disturbs me to be thought of as an optimist. My whole professional experience has been with the dark and often sordid side of life, and I know the incredibly destructive behavior of which man is capable. (p. 27)

Clients' constructive choices in the context of nondirective client-centered therapy reveal their pro-social capabilities. These innate potentialities are brought out by the facilitative therapeutic conditions. Rogers (1956/1958) wrote:

> [M]an, when you know him deeply, in his worst and most troubled states, is not evil or demonic … We do not need to ask who will socialize him, for one of his deepest needs is for affiliation and communication with others. When we are able to free the individual from defensiveness, so that he is open to the wide range of his own needs, as well as the wide range of environmental and social demands, his reactions may be trusted to be positive, forward-moving, constructive. (p. 28)

Without contradicting the natural science arena of client-centered therapy and actualization theory, there is an ethical meaning attributed to constructive choice in therapy that should be included in the picture. From a societal perspective, therapy is partly concerned with the moral or ethical aspects of client change. Granted, this is from our own cultural evaluative framework. A therapy that typically resulted in antisocial and self-destructive outcomes for clients, assuming our culture-bound definitions of these things, would not be acceptable to clients, therapists or society. This ethical or moral concern about therapeutic efficacy, however, does not imply that the actualizing tendency concept is itself an ethical or moral concept.

Human innate pro-social characteristics brought out by client-centered therapy are a biological reality. We value those characteristics in ethical terms. But they are biological characteristics. They are potentialities that may develop, more or less, depending upon many factors. The interpersonal conditions provided by client-centered therapy appear to be psychologically favorable to humans because they are free of elements of moral guidance and nevertheless lead to results many persons consider constructive. Thus innate pro-social tendencies appear to be revealed. Although we perceive these good consequences and consequently make positive ethical evaluations of these results of the actualizing tendency, nevertheless, *it is a biological, natural science concept.*

THE VALUE OF THE ACTUALIZING CONCEPT

What is the value of the actualizing tendency concept? What does actualizing tendency theory explain? The actualizing tendency is a constructively directional motivation, but it does not necessarily result in constructive outcomes. The outcomes of the actualizing tendency represent the whole range of biological results and moral possibilities. In truth, actualization theory does not specifically predict or explain anything. It is a very general heuristic concept. It may be used as a guide to inquiry and it may influence interpersonal attitudes. As a guide to understanding behavior the actualizing tendency focuses attention on finding out what it is about the person's perceptions or his situation that gives constructive meaning to his activity. This goal promotes a phenomenological approach, one that reaches into the world of the subject and looks at the subject's perceptions of his context. It requires listening to the person in order to understand his goals and feelings, the personal meanings that are involved in his behavior.

A person engages in some form of unconstructive or destructive behavior. Inquiry starts with the hypothesis or assumption of the actualizing tendency, the assumption that a person is necessarily actualizing her nature as best she can under her circumstances. She is doing the best she can and it is apparently not very good from a mental health or a moral perspective. The general question is – how is the person's actualization motivation expressed in this destructive behavior? What are the internal, subjective realities or external circumstances that are distorting the outcomes of this person's inherently constructive and pro-social directions? How is the destructive behavior serving the personal maintenance, the integration, or the fulfillment of the person? Answers following from inquiry based on the actualizing tendency assumption tend to make sense of destructive behavior in humane terms. Such understandings tend to promote compassion and rational considerations – fruitful conditions for creative and humane solutions to human problems.

Actualization theory views people as functioning as well as they can, given their circumstances at a particular time. They may be able to function better if certain conditions are changed – if unfavorable internal or external circumstances can be determined and removed and if favorable circumstances can be created. But, according to actualizing tendency theory, at a given moment, persons are doing the best they can. The actualizing tendency theory may function in a person's mind as a belief, a faith, an assumption or as an hypothesis. Adopted in any form, it is likely to influence a person's attitudes towards other persons. The assumption of a basic constructive motivation tends to dissipate critical judgments. It precludes invoking ideas of inherent badness or of *evil* as an explanation of destructive behavior. Evil may be a valid moral description of certain human behavior, but it is a dead end as a guide to understanding it. Instead, the actualizing tendency assumption leads to a particularly open intellectual approach and a compassionate or at least neutral attitudinal approach in understanding those actions.

The helping attitudes that are likely to emerge from holding the actualizing tendency as a belief or assumption are *trust* and *respect*. The trust is in persons' capacities and abilities to find constructive solutions to their problems and for their ability to change their behavior. Respect for persons is regardless of their flaws, mistakes or crimes. The person who adopts the actualizing tendency as an operative principle in his or her view of human functioning is likely to hold a compassionate attitude towards people and their shortcomings. Humans are profoundly vulnerable to circumstances beyond their control – especially in early developmental life. Destructive feelings and actions are thought to be the result of historical or immediate unfavorable circumstances acting in or on the person. Circumstances are, by definition in the theory, beyond the person's choice or control at that time. An implication of the actualizing tendency concept is that persons are fundamentally innocent even when they are obviously guilty of bad behavior.

The view that people are inherently innocent promotes understanding and sympathy. It does not, however, preclude moral, ethical or legal judgments about bad behavior. It does not preclude feeling responsible for one's behavior nor preclude holding other persons responsible for their actions. It does not prevent individuals or social groups from acting rationally to protect themselves or others from persons who commit bad actions. It does not preclude the creation of legal punishments for behavior that causes injury to others. It does affect the manner of judgments and the kinds of consequences imposed for bad actions. The view that people are basically innocent imbues moral, ethical and legal responses to them with compassion, empathy and the intention to be fair.

The actualizing tendency principle fosters an attitude of respect for persons and for persons' innate capacities for self-determination, for finding solutions and for therapeutic change. Therapists and other helpers who adopt actualizing tendency theory are likely to be motivated to protect the self-determination and autonomy of the person being helped and to be careful to not try to control or in any way disempower the person being helped. A nondirective facilitative attitude results in a humane non-authoritarian approach in helping relationships and in other human-relations situations.

CONCLUSION

Client-centered therapy was created and evolved pragmatically. As Rogers' therapy developed, he formulated theory (Rogers, 1942, 1951, 1959, 1963, 1977, 1980, 1986b) and the actualizing tendency concept became more salient. Actualization theory elaborates an idea of an inherent constructive motivation. This motivation is a kind of wisdom of the organism, to persist, to maintain its organization, to heal if needed and to develop its capacities. Favorable circumstances promote specific survival, integrative and developmental processes and socially valued outcomes in behavior. Unfavorable circumstances limit the processes and limit the results of the actualizing tendency in organismic and personal life. Sometimes the results of unfavorable circumstances involve behavior that is considered wrong. The actualizing tendency principle is biological, but it has consequences that we evaluate from an ethical or moral perspective.

The actualizing tendency is a first principle in client-centered therapy, and belief in the actualizing tendency leads such therapists to hold two fundamental beliefs. (1) The therapist can trust the client's tendency to grow, develop and heal. (2) All of the therapist's actions must express respect for the client – viewing the client as a person who is capable of self-determination with capacities for self-understanding and constructive change. These beliefs function as the therapist's fundamental attitudes towards clients. Actualizing tendency theory provides the intellectual grounding for these two functional beliefs. In this way the actualizing tendency has a functional role in client-centered therapy practice (Bozarth & Brodley, 1991). In reciprocation, client-centered therapy is an endeavor that tests the actualizing tendency premise with each client.

REFERENCES

Angyal, A. (1941). *Foundations for a science of personality.* New York: Commonwealth Fund.

Barrett-Lennard, G. T. (1998) *Carl Rogers' helping system.* London: Sage.

Bertalanffy, L. (1960). *Problems of life.* New York: Harper Torchbooks. (Original work published 1952)

Biermann-Ratjen, E. (1998). On the development of the person in relationships. In B. Thorne & E. Lambers (Eds.), *Person-centred therapy: A European perspective* (pp. 106–118). London: Sage.

Bohart, A. C., & Tallman, K. (1999). *How clients make therapy work.* Washington, DC: American Psychological Association.

Bozarth, J. D. (1998). *Person-centered therapy: A revolutionary paradigm.* Ross-on-Wye: PCCS Books.

Bozarth, J. D., & Brodley, B. T. (1991). Actualization: A functional concept in client-centered therapy. In A. Jones & R. Crandall (Eds.), Handbook of self-actualization. [Special Issue] *Journal of Social Behavior and Personality, 6*(5), 45–59.

Evans, R. I. (1975). *Carl Rogers, the man and his ideas.* New York: EP Dutton, Inc.

Goldstein, K. (1939). *The organism.* New York: American Book Co. (Republished (1963) Boston: Beacon Press)

Goldstein, K. (1940). *Human nature in the light of psychopathology.* Cambridge, MA: Harvard University Press.

Hawtin, S., & Moore, J. (1998). Empowerment or collusion? The social context of person-centred therapy. In B. Thorne & E. Lambers (Eds.), *Person-centred therapy: A European perspective* (pp. 91–105). London: Sage.

James, W. (1981). *The principles of psychology.* Cambridge, MA: Harvard University Press. (Original work published 1890)

Karr-Morse, R., & Wiley, M. S. (1997). *Ghosts from the nursery: Tracing the roots of violence.* New York: Atlantic Monthly Press.

May, R. (1982). The problem of evil: An open letter to Carl Rogers. *Journal of Humanistic Psychology, 22*(3), 10–21.

Merry, T., & Lusty, B. (1993). *What is person-centred therapy?* Loughton, Essex: Gale Centre Publications.

Miller, A. (1998). The political consequences of child abuse. *Journal of Psychohistory, 26*(2), 572–585.

Rogers, C. R. (1942). *Counseling and psychotherapy.* Boston: Houghton Mifflin.

Rogers, C. R. (1951). *Client-centered therapy.* Boston: Houghton Mifflin.

Rogers, C. R. (1957). The necessary and sufficient conditions of therapeutic personality change. *Journal of Consulting Psychology, 21,* 95–103.

Rogers, C. R. (1958). Reinhold Niebuhr's the self and the dramas of history: A criticism [with discussion by critics and Rogers' concluding comment]. *Pastoral Psychology, 9*(85), 15–28. (Original work published 1956)

Rogers, C. R. (1959). A theory of therapy, personality, and interpersonal relationships as developed in the client-centered framework. In S. Koch (Ed.), *Psychology: A study of a science. Vol. III: Formulations of the person and the social context* (pp. 184–256). New York: McGraw-Hill.

Rogers, C. R. (1961). *On becoming a person.* Boston: Houghton Mifflin.

Rogers, C. R. (1963). The actualizing tendency in relation to "motive" and to consciousness. In M. Jones (Ed.), *Nebraska symposium on motivation* (pp. 1–24). Lincoln, NE: University of Nebraska Press.

Rogers, C. R. (1977). *Carl Rogers on personal power.* New York: Delacorte Press.

Rogers, C. R. (1980). *A way of being.* Boston: Houghton Mifflin.

Rogers, C. R. (1982). Reply to Rollo May's letter. *Journal of Humanistic Psychology, 22,* 85–89.

Rogers, C. R. (1986a). Rogers, Kohut, and Erickson. *Person-Centered Review, 1*(2), 125–140.

Rogers, C. R. (1986b). Client-centered approach to therapy. In I. L. Kutash & A. Wolf (Eds.), *Psychotherapist's casebook: Theory and technique in practice* (pp. 197–208). San Francisco: Jossey-Bass.

Rogers, C. R. (1987). The underlying theory: Drawn from experience with individuals and groups. [In Carl Rogers and the person-centered approach to peace (Special issue)] *Counseling and Values, 32*(1), 38–46.

Rogers, C. R. (1989). Notes on Rollo May. In H. Kirschenbaum & V. L. Henderson (Eds.). *Carl Rogers: Dialogues* (pp. 237–239). Boston: Houghton Mifflin. (Originally published 1981, *Perspective, 2*(1), Special Issue; Rollo May: Man and philosopher)

Rogers, C. R., & Sanford, R. (1984). Client-centered psychotherapy. In H. I. Kaplan & B. J. Sadock (Eds.), *Comprehensive textbook of psychiatry IV* (pp. 1374–1388). Baltimore, MD: Williams & Wilkins.

Schmid, P. F. (1996). "Intimacy, tenderness and lust" – A person-centered approach to sexuality. In R. Hutterer, G. Pawlowsky, P. F. Schmid, & R. Stipsits (Eds.), *Client-centered and experiential psychotherapy: A paradigm in motion* (pp. 85–99). Frankfurt am Main: Peter Lang.

Schmid, P. F. (1998). "On becoming a *person*-centred approach": A person-centred understanding of the person. In B. Thorne & E. Lambers (Eds.), *Person-centred therapy: A European perspective* (pp. 38–52). London: Sage.

Thorne, B. (1992). *Carl Rogers.* London: Sage.

Van Kalmthout, M. (1998). Person-centred theory as a system of meaning. In B. Thorne & E. Lambers (Eds.), *Person-centred therapy: A European perspective* (pp. 11–22). London: Sage.

White, R. W. (1959) Motivation reconsidered: The concept of competence. *Psychological Review, 66,* 297–333.

# IMPLEMENTATION OF THE VALUES AND ATTITUDES IN AN EXPRESSIVE CLIENT-CENTERED THERAPY

# Chapter 12

# The empathic understanding response process

The empathic understanding response process is a term I have coined to refer to a major form of therapeutic experience that has developed out of the theory and practice of Carl R. Rogers and his colleagues. The empathic understanding response process refers to a complex phenomenon. It is the total therapeutic situation, persisting over time, created by a therapist using ideas and skills developed by Rogers and his colleagues, with a client who feels a need for help, and it exists when the therapist is able to make empathic understanding responses most of the time, thereby developing a distinctive relationship that results in constructive change in the experience of the client. The empathic understanding response process is defined primarily in terms of the frequent use of empathic understanding responses and by the application of Rogers' ideas embodied in the attitudes and behavior of the therapist.

In this presentation, first, I am going to describe the major principles or beliefs that define and inform the Rogerian, client-centered, therapist's behavior in a personal growth context. Second, I shall describe the specific psychotherapeutic theory that is the basis for practice. Third, I shall discuss the major technique employed, the empathic understanding response.

## THE MAJOR PRINCIPLES OR BELIEFS

*1. The self-determination and self-regulation of individual life is most constructive and beneficial for the individual and society.*
An assumption underlying this belief is that each person has the capacity for making his own decisions and determining which resources in the world are the ones he wants for development, personal satisfaction and for finding his own way of integrating himself into relationships with other persons.

---

An earlier version of this paper was presented March 6, 1977 to Changes, a "listening" community founded by Eugene Gendlin at the University of Chicago.

*2. Reality as perceived by the individual is the primary reality to be understood in constructive human interactions.*

Life is lived only through individual organisms, and human life is lived only through individual persons, through their experiencing process. Supra-individual phenomena (e.g., families, groups, communities, cultures) exist, and hypothetical constructs (e.g., "personality structure," "character," "personality dynamics," "drives") may be useful when thinking about individuals. But, from the point of view of influencing personal growth, these phenomena and constructs are aspects of the experience of the individual, and they may or may not be relevant to the individual.

*3. The unit of experience necessary for constructive human interaction is the experience of the whole person.*

The experience of the whole person is an abstraction in the sense that a person encountered at any particular moment is only an aspect of the whole person. In the first encounter, before we know a person, if we experience the whole person we do so in a limited way using our imaginations and by giving the person "the benefit of the doubt." We assume there is more to the person than what we can see at the time. This is highlighted by situations when people are "off" in some way when we first meet them. If they are grieving, drugged, upset, or doing something extraordinary that is open to various interpretations (e.g., a policeman shoots a dog), we often recognize that we have a very unrepresentative view of the person and withhold judgment about him. When we attempt to relate to the whole person we are assuming that they have feeling, attitudes, behavioral capabilities that are not represented at the moment. As we engage in some kind of relationship with the person we learn more about him under differing circumstances, learn "who the person is," specifically; we accumulate a picture of the person beyond the moment. As we become acquainted with a person the experience of the whole person becomes more grounded in accumulated facts about the person; but the experience of the whole person in any particular interaction remains an abstraction, including much that is beyond what is present or past.

*4. People always do the best they can under the circumstances they perceive and those which are acting upon them.*

People's experience and behavior, no matter how ugly or limited or destructive, is thought to be understandable and basically and commonly human if it is adequately understood from the point of view of the person. This belief is derived from the concept of the *actualizing tendency* in Rogers' personality theory (Rogers, 1959) and from the *drive for self-actualization* or *drive for self-realization* in Kurt Goldstein's organismic theory (Goldstein, 1939/1963). All human behavior is some more or less successful attempt at self-realization. Destructive behavior is the result of circumstances that constrict or distort the manner of self-realization. All human beings are deeply the same. Under similar circumstances phenomenally and objectively, we all tend to behave the same way. From this point of view it is always appropriate to say, no matter what the other person is doing, "There but for the grace of God go I."

These four principles or beliefs underlie the Rogerian, client-centered, therapeutic approach. They inform the therapist, influence his behavior in the therapy situation. Next I shall summarize Rogers' theory of creativity applied to the therapeutic situation and then describe the specific theory about psychotherapy, Carl Rogers' conditions for constructive personality change.

## THE CREATIVE THEORY

We can view the client's work in the client-centered therapeutic endeavor as a specific kind of creative activity. The client's work in therapy is the expression of individual creativity applied to problematic or painful personal experiences or to problems of living. In Rogers' theory of creativity (Rogers, 1961, pp. 347–359) there are two main features of the individual's psychological environment which are considered crucial for fostering creativity – *freedom* and *safety*. Freedom refers to allowing the person to discover his own way, try things unconstricted by rules and without imposed prohibitions or prescriptions. Safety refers to a condition under which a person knows he is not going to be hurt or punished for what he does in the situation. The entire enterprise of the client-centered therapist can be looked at as an attempt to create the conditions of freedom and safety in order to promote the client's creativity in self-exploration and personal problem solving. The creative theory helps one to understand the aims of the therapist from a slightly different vantage point than the therapeutic theory.

## THE PSYCHOTHERAPEUTIC THEORY

Carl Rogers' psychotherapeutic theory (Rogers, 1957) is based on the assumption that the personal growth process is intrinsic to the individual. The therapist creates a setting which promotes the realization of the individual's intrinsic capacity for growth. The therapeutic setting is an attempt at an optimal interpersonal environment.

The psychotherapeutic theory states the necessary and sufficient conditions for constructive personality change. The conditions posited by

Rogers are called *congruence, unconditional positive regard,* and *empathic understanding of the client's frame of reference.* In addition, *communication of these three things is to some extent received by the client.*

*Congruence* refers to the genuineness, wholeness, naturalness, honesty and transparency of the therapist in the situation. *Unconditional positive regard* refers to the therapist's acceptance, liking, nonjudgmental attitude, or love (in a sense of caring and appreciation) toward the client. *Empathic understanding of the client's frame of reference* refers to an effortful extension of the therapist's mind into the world of the client and an attempt to understand that world as it is presented by the client. In addition, it implies a degree of *feeling with* and *feeling for* the client as part of understanding the client's world. In Rogers' presentation of his theory, he argues that these conditions must be met, must be present *to some extent* – they do not have to be completely or absolutely true – for constructive personal change to occur. It is important to realize that the first three conditions – congruence, positive regard, and empathic understanding – are all *inner experiences* on the part of the therapist. These inner experiences must be communicated to the client, however, in order for the client to receive them and for change to consequently occur. How is that communication done? The major technique is the *empathic understanding response.*

### THE EMPATHIC UNDERSTANDING RESPONSE

The empathic understanding response is a discrete response in the form of an assertion that states the therapist's understanding of what the client has been expressing or attempting to express. The assertion is made in a manner that conveys it is from the client's point of view, or it implicitly conveys that understanding in the context of its utterance. Examples of empathic understanding responses are as follows: "You're feeling overpowered by that news and even though most of the feelings are good ones they are so strong they get in the way of doing your homework." "The worst is over and now you're exhausted." "You want to marry him, but the way he's been abusing you scares you and you feel like running away." "You can understand how what he says means growth for him, but it still leaves you abandoned and miserable."

The empathic understanding response is fundamentally a transformation of the client's communication inside the mind and experience of the therapist. A transformation involves a change of form without altering value or meaning. In this context a transformation involves the therapist in taking the meaning of his client's expression into himself and understanding it in the terms of his own covert symbols. On the basis of the transformation the therapist may communicate outwardly, usually with language, in a way that seems likely to communicate to the client.

There are a number of different forms of the empathic understanding response depending upon what comes to the therapist and what he senses will communicate accurately to the client. An empathic understanding response can be a restatement, a rephrasing, a summary or a response which involves elaboration that was not explicitly in the communication of the client. All of these forms of response are intended to convey the meaning that was expressed by the client and understood in the experience of the therapist.

There are a number of other important things about the empathic understanding response that I shall not discuss here. Some of these are features of the therapist's instructions to himself, for example, (a) What units of client communication are being understood? (b) What kinds of client communication permit or allow the empathic understanding response? (c) What are the criteria for making an overt response as distinguished from the therapist understanding the client empathically inside himself without making an overt response?

## THE EMPATHIC UNDERSTANDING RESPONSE PROCESS

I stated earlier that the empathic understanding response process occurs when it is possible for a therapist to make empathic understanding responses most of the time with a client, and for an extended period of time, usually through many therapy sessions. The empathic understanding response process is a process that takes time to come into being and evolves or develops over time. Trust in the therapist is an important component in this genesis and evolution. Trust permits the client to think and feel more deeply, fully and productively than in previous life situations. The therapist's behavior that represents fidelity to the client-centered task is the basis of the client's trust and, therefore, of the client's enriched experiencing. At this point it may be useful to recapitulate the conception of the task that is so crucial to the empathic understanding response process.

The therapist's task is to provide the conditions of congruence, unconditional regard, and empathic understanding, and to do so in ways that are guided or informed by the four major principles or beliefs presented earlier – the belief in self-determination, the belief in the salience of individual phenomenal reality, the belief in relating to the whole person, and the belief that people do the best they can. The behavior that often can best accomplish this complex task in the therapeutic situation is the empathic understanding response.

The empathic understanding response, when faithfully and appropriately used, is capable of conveying (a) the meanings understood from the client, (b) the acceptance felt toward the client, and (c) the genuineness, naturalness and authenticity of the therapist in the situation. In other words, if the therapist is understanding the client, accepting the client, and is genuine in the situation, these things will tend to be communicated to the client by means of empathic understanding responses. If all these things are adequately communicated by means of empathic understanding responses, then empathic understanding responses may predominate in the therapeutic interaction and the sole resulting process may be described as an instance of the empathic understanding response process. If the understanding, acceptance and genuineness of the therapist are not adequately communicated by empathic understanding responses, other forms of response may be necessary and the resulting therapeutic process will be different than the empathic understanding response process. Empathic understanding responses should not be forced upon clients as the sole form of response to their participation if empathic understanding responses are perceived as inadequate by the client. In my own experience as a therapist, most clients do accept the empathic understanding response and it is possible to appropriately employ it most of the time in interaction with them.

When the therapist is consistent and faithful to the Rogerian client-centered method I have been describing, the client gradually learns (a) that the intention of the therapist is simply to understand the client from the client's point of view, (b) that the therapist is accepting, not judgmental or manipulative, and (c) that the therapist is a genuine person, is *real* and not playing a role or hiding behind his therapeutic work. The client thus develops trust in the therapist about these things, and, as a consequence, his experiencing process – his inner life – is enriched and he is freer to symbolize and express his deepest thoughts and feelings. As this happens the empathic understanding response process is in process.

From the point of view of the therapist, as the empathic understanding response process comes into being the world of the client is gradually built into the mind of the therapist so that the therapist can more and more effectively enter into the experiential world of the client and lend his mind and feelings to the self-exploration and problem solving of the client. As this happens the empathic process is in process.

## REFERENCES

Goldstein, K. (1939). *The organism*. New York: American Book Company. (Republished (1963) Boston: Beacon Press)

Rogers, C. R. (1957). The necessary and sufficient conditions of therapeutic personality change. *Journal of Consulting Psychology, 21*, 95–103.

Rogers, C. R. (1959). A theory of therapy, personality, and interpersonal relationships, as developed in the client-centered framework. In S. Koch (Ed.), *Psychology: A study of a science. Vol. III: Formulations of the person and the social context* (pp. 184–256). New York: McGraw-Hill.

Rogers, C. R. (1961). *On becoming a person*. Boston: Houghton Mifflin.

# Chapter 13

# Client-centered: An expressive therapy

Many proponents of client-centered therapy recognize the nondirective attitude as an intrinsic feature of the approach (Bozarth, 1998; Brodley, 1986, 1987/1998, 1997/2011, 1999b; Prouty, 1999; Raskin, 1947/2005). Reflecting upon the deeper meanings and implications of this attitude, and upon my own work, it became apparent to me that therapeutic activity which involves the therapist in maintaining a nondirective attitude results in an expressive rather than an instrumental practice.

The theory and the attitudes of nondirective client-centered therapy articulated by Carl Rogers (1951, 1957, 1959), preclude the therapist from experiencing the mental set of using means to achieve ends while doing therapy. Instead, the client-centered therapist maintains an expressive attitude while engaging in the therapeutic relationship. Students of client-centered therapy who refer to "using empathic responses" or "using the self," or "using congruence" may not recognize the fundamentally expressive character of the work. Statements of "use" suggest it is possible to be authentically client-centered while experiencing and employing an instrumental attitude. Although there may be rare moments when a client-centered therapist does adopt an instrumental attitude and pursues a goal for the client that is conceived by the therapist, these instances are quite uncharacteristic of the approach (Bozarth, 1993).

## THE INSTRUMENTAL ATTITUDE

An instrumental attitude involves having immediate intentions to use means to achieve ends or goals outside the self. Instrumental communication is quite different from personal expression. The word "instrumental" means to choose and employ an action or other means in order to bring about a goal

This is a revised version of the article of the same title that appeared (2002) in *The Person-Centered Journal, 9*(1), 59–70. The version that appeared in *The Person-Centered Journal* was itself a slightly revised version of the paper published (2000) in J. E. Marques-Teixeira & S. Antunes (Eds.), *Client-centered and experiential psychotherapy* (pp. 133–147) Linda a Velha, Lisboa, Portugal: Vale & Vale. Reproduced with permission from *PCJ* and Vale and Vale Publishers, Portugal.

that is outside of, or other than, immediate expressive benefit to oneself. In the context of therapy, an instrumental attitude involves immediate intentions to achieve ends or goals in or about the client. For example, a (non-client-centered) therapist may intend to influence a client to recognize his hostility towards his boss as a factor in his frequent tardiness for work. Or such a therapist may intend to influence a client to feel compassion and sympathy for his wife's hurt. Or the therapist may intend to influence a client to recognize her own innocence and helplessness when she was sexually abused as a child. These are goals conceived by some therapists for their clients. They represent an instrumental therapeutic attitude.

## THE EXPRESSIVE ATTITUDE

The expressive attitude refers to client-centered therapists' intentions while interacting with clients. In general, an expressive attitude involves immediate intentions to express meanings, feelings, desires, values or attitudes primarily for oneself. Behavior expressed out of an expressive attitude, of course, may have effects outside the self. For example, a person screams expressively out of terror, but the scream may bring help. Expression refers to both *putting into words*, and *showing a feeling*. It involves looks, gestures, intonations, or language that exhibit meanings or feelings. It is an externalizing of what is internal primarily for the sake of the expresser. An expressive attitude often, although not necessarily, occurs in the context of communication or in a relationship. Thus expressive behavior may be, overall, for the sake of the communication or the relationship. The immediate expressive intentions, however, are for the purpose of the expression itself. This is the case even if they are serving communicative impulses or intentions. Expression transforms what is within one's mind or feelings into language or other expressive means. The purposes of actions flowing from an expressive attitude are immediate, self-expressive, self-relieving or self-releasing, even while they occur in the context of a relationship.

## OBJECTIVELY INSTRUMENTAL WHILE SUBJECTIVELY EXPRESSIVE

There appears to be a paradox in viewing client-centered therapy as expressive and not instrumental. It is immediately expressive; at the same time it is a practice intended to help other persons. As a therapy, it is designed to effect change in other persons. Consequently, in an objectively descriptive sense client-centered therapy is instrumental. The whole therapy is a means to an end. Its purpose, its most general goal, is the same as other therapies – to enhance the well-being and improve the mental health of clients, promote personal development, and to do these things without causing harm to clients.

Rogers' (1957) necessary and sufficient conditions for therapeutic personality change – specifically the therapeutic attitudes of congruence, unconditional positive regard and empathic understanding – are conceptualized as the means to these general therapeutic ends. This is a generally accurate descriptive statement about the cause–effect aspect of the therapy from an objective perspective. Nevertheless, it does not accurately characterize the immediate intentions or the actual behaviors of the client-centered therapist in therapy as they may be described from the perspective of the therapist.

The practical means of client-centered therapy are the implementations the therapist creates from moment to moment in the relationship – words and expressive gestures in interaction with the client. The expressive attitude concerns the phenomenological reason for these implementations. The client-centered principles of respect for the client and trust in the client's constructive capabilities are manifested in a ubiquitous nondirective attitude. This attitude shapes implementations. These implementations are distinctly intended to express the therapist's subjective therapeutic attitudes. Subjectively and in the immediate moments of interaction the therapist is *not intending* to produce effects in the client. Thus, the reason for the implementations is the therapist's nondirective expressive attitude intertwined with the nondirective therapeutic attitudes. The therapist wants to understand the client, acceptantly and empathically. The therapeutic attitudes and the expressive attitude are incorporated within the therapist's personality and brought out, or implemented, particularly in the therapeutic setting through the therapist's expressive verbal communications and nonverbal expressive behavior. The following [edited] excerpt from a demonstration therapy session (Brodley, 1999a) illustrates client-centered behavior which is the result of expressive intentions:

Client: I was thinking about my mother the other day ... She and I had a very competitive relationship ... (Pause) Three days ago in Budapest I saw a lady in the street who reminded me of my mother. But not at the age she has right now, but twenty years from now. I don't know why I was so struck by that. I saw my mother being old and, and weak. So she was not this powerful, domineering person she used to be at home, which I was so much afraid of.

Therapist: But old, and weakened and diminished.

Client: Diminished. That's the word. (T: Uhm Hmm) That's the word. (Begins to cry)

Therapist: It moved you to think of that, that she (C: Yeah) would be so weak and diminished.

Client: Um hum. I think there was something in that lady's eyes that reminded me of my mother (Voice breaks, crying) which I was not aware of when I was at home. (Pause) And it was fear. (T: Uhm hmm) I saw fear in the woman's eyes.

Therapist: Fear.

Client: Yeah. I was not aware of that.

Therapist: When you saw this woman, who resembled your mother, but twenty years from now, you saw in this woman's eyes something you had not realized was in fact in the eyes of your mother. (C: Yeah) And that was the quality of fear. And that had some great impact on (C: Yeah) you.

Client: I felt that … That this woman needed me. (Pause) It feels good that I am crying now (T: Uhm Hmm) I am feeling very well that I am crying.

Therapist: Uhm Hmm. It was a sense of your mother in the future, and that your mother will need you.

Client: That's it. In the future, not in the present. (Pause) It feels right here. (Places her hand over her abdomen)

Therapist: The feeling is that your mother will have fear and will have great need for you (C: Yeah) later on.

Client: And as I am going back home, I don't know if I'm ready to, be ready to take care of her. I don't know if I'm ready to see that need expressed by her. (Continuing to cry as she speaks)

Therapist: Uhm hmm, uhm hmm, uhm hmm. (Pause) You're afraid that when you get there, that will be more present in her. Or you will see it more than you did before, now that you've seen this woman, and that that will be a kind of demand on you and you're afraid you're not ready to meet that.

Client: That's it, yeah, and it's gotten too much for me. Or I, right now in Hungary, I perceive it as being too much. (Crying continues and session continues)

As the therapist in the interaction, my intentions were purely communicative and expressive. I was not intending to produce any effects on the client. I wanted to understand empathically and I spoke to the client in order to express what I thought I understood. I also felt emotionally present, untroubled and accepting. The client's, and observers', remarks afterwards confirmed that my face, my tone and bodily gestures conveyed that I was emotionally present during the session.

The client-centered therapist's immediate intentions are to experience the therapeutic attitudes and to communicate in order to find out from the client whether subjective understandings are accurate. The therapist checks (Rogers, 1986) to find out if he or she has accurately understood the client. Checking expresses a desire to receive a corrective or confirming response from the client. In checking, the therapist is seeking communicative interaction with the client as a means to further experience accurate empathic understanding.

Instead of being for the sake of goals for the client, Rogers' therapeutic attitudes – congruence, unconditional positive regard and empathic understanding – are primarily expressed in the relationship for the sake of the therapist's own expressive need to understand. They are also expressed for the sake of the therapist having further subjective experience of the attitudes in relation to the particular client. As the therapist expresses his or her understandings and receives confirmations or corrections from the client, the therapist's empathic attitude and feelings of acceptance are further enhanced and carried forward. In this way, authentic communication occurs between therapist and client because the therapist deeply wants to remain congruent, wants to be acceptant and wants to empathically understand. Reciprocally, the client wants to be accepted and understood.

Acceptant, empathic responses, intended to express the therapist's own desire to understand, do produce effects in the client and on the relationship. Many of these effects are therapeutic. They include a sense of being understood, a sense of safety with the therapist and concomitant feelings of greater freedom of self-expression, a sense of all of one's feelings being accepted, the experience of more immediate and real feelings, and the experience of insights and new self-understandings. Desirable as they are from an objective perspective, the effects are nevertheless incidental in respect to the therapist's immediate intentions. The therapeutic attitudes are not communicated or expressed in the immediate moments of the interaction to promote the therapeutic effects they often evoke.

## PROTECTION OF CLIENTS' SELF-DETERMINATION

From a theoretical and objective perspective the therapeutic attitudes – the therapist's congruence, unconditional positive regard and empathic understanding in the relationship – are expected to create interpersonal and intrapsychic conditions which foster the growth and therapeutic change capabilities of the client. But this conceptualization does not represent either the theoretical, phenomenological, intention or the actual, experienced, intention of the therapist in the relationship.

It may seem strange, but the therapeutic benefits of client-centered work are serendipitous in the sense that they are not the result of the therapist's concrete intentions when he or she is present with and expressively communicating with the client. The absence of intentional goals being pursued as goals for clients seems to be essential for some of the distinctive therapeutic benefits of the approach. Specifically, the nondirectivity inherent in the therapist's expressive attitude helps protect the client's autonomy and self-determination. The expressive character of the therapy contributes to the effect that the client is the architect of the therapy (Raskin, 1988). Thus the approach empowers the client and strengthens inherent growthful capabilities.

Many therapies help clients. Through various forms of directivity, however, they may simultaneously tend to disempower the client. In that way directive therapies tend to undermine clients while helping them in other ways. Client-centeredness, in being nondirective and expressive, and because it is nondiagnostic and concretely not a means to any ends in the usual meaning of being means to achieve ends – has an exceptional power to help without harming.

OBJECTIVE AND PHENOMENOLOGICAL DESCRIPTION

The means to ends issue is confused in discussions concerning client-centered therapy when a distinction is not made between objective description of the therapy and its description from within the phenomenology of the therapist. From the viewpoint of the therapist the activity (both subjective and behavioral) of being client-centered springs from fundamental attitudes and intentions. To avoid confusion, these must be distinguished from external or objective descriptions of client-centered therapy which imply instrumentality.

It is important to be conscious of the difference between phenomenological and objective descriptions of therapy because objective descriptions of therapeutic procedures tend to be interpreted as prescriptions or instructions for procedures. Prescriptions and instructions engender instrumental attitudes and intentions. Such confusion involves mis-understandings of client-centered therapy, a therapeutic approach that is already misunderstood, undervalued and underemployed in the psycho-therapeutic field. Confusion and misunderstandings are promoted, or not, partly depending upon the way descriptive statements are worded in respect to the therapist's frame of reference.

For example, a description of an important aspect of client-centered work may be stated, "empathic responses tend to communicate the empathic attitude to clients." The statement becomes misleading if it is slightly changed to "client-centered therapists often use empathic responses to communicate their empathic attitude." This latter statement implies that from the frame of reference of the therapist, empathic responses are deliberately used to produce an effect in or on the client. Such a statement is likely to be taken to mean what is usually meant in describing therapies. That a certain technique is employed by the therapist to pursue certain goals he has for the client. Further, the statement "… therapists often *use* empathic responses …" suggests a prescription or instruction to therapists. As such it is misleading.

Another example. Describing the effects of client-centered therapy, it is accurate to say "the client often becomes more focused on his inner feelings and his inner experiences and speaks from more depth in himself." This is a description of something that often happens in client-centered therapy. In contrast, the statement "the therapist *uses* client-centered therapy to focus the client on his experiences and feelings" would not be accurate. Client-centered therapists characteristically do not have any such specific goals for clients. Some therapies that are related to client-centered therapy do have such goals. An example of this is focusing-oriented experiential psychotherapy (Gendlin, 1996). It is in this sense – of not having goals for clients – that in the existential activity of doing therapy, client-centered therapists do not employ means to ends at all.

## CONTRASTING CLIENT-CENTERED WITH THE INTERSUBJECTIVE PSYCHOANALYTIC METHOD

The intersubjective approach that has some theoretical and behavioral similarities to client-centered therapy (Kahn, 1996, 1997) may be useful to clarify this essential expressive, nondirective characteristic of client-centered therapy. In the intersubjective approach as described by Stolorow and Atwood (1992), the therapist's attitude is an instrumental one, and the therapist's actions, such as empathic understanding communications, are employed as means to facilitate the therapist-determined goals or ends.

According to the intersubjective approach, the therapist's behavior is based on a conceptualization of three types of unconsciousness: (1) The pre-reflective unconscious that refers to organizing principles which were engendered early in a person's life that shape and thematize a person's experiences. (2) The dynamic unconscious that refers to experiences that have been kept from articulation because they were perceived to threaten needed connections to others. And (3) the unvalidated unconscious that refers to experiences which the person could not articulate because they were not validated by significant others. Although these forms of unconsciousness are interrelated, each is conceived as having a different and specific etiology.

What Stolorow and Atwood refer to as "sustained empathic inquiry," which appears to be similar to empathic understanding interaction in client-centered therapy, is a method employed by the analyst for investigating the patient's unconsciously organized experiences.

In intersubjective psychoanalytic work, in addition to empathic inquiry, different modes of therapeutic action are initiated by the analyst depending upon which of the three forms of unconsciousness are being examined in the analysis. Various modes of analytic treatment (empathic inquiry, analysis of the transference, analysis of the resistance) are means employed to effect certain specific, therapist-conceived goals in respect to uncovering and transforming the patient's experiences. The means selected for the therapeutic strategy of the moment depend upon the analyst's conception of the correct ends to pursue for the patient's good.

Rogers' (1959) personality theory – including his theories of congruence, incongruence, theory of the generation of psychological disturbance, and the theoretical conceptualization of the personality in therapeutic change – is similar to the intersubjective theory, although not as detailed. The empathic interaction process which is characteristic of much of client-centered work is similar to the empathic inquiry method of the intersubjective approach. In actual therapeutic work, however, there are profound differences that can be partly characterized in terms of the instrumental-expressive distinction.

The client-centered therapist usually makes no diagnostic or other classificatory decisions concerning the etiology of the client's problems. (Exceptions may occur when the therapist perceives the client might benefit from other professional services such as neurology or psychiatry.) Nor are decisions made about what process should be optimal for the client. Classificatory decisions are not necessary in the practice of client-centered therapy because the approach accommodates to the individual as a unique person and because the therapist's intentions are not mean–ends intentions. The client-centered therapist attunes him- or herself to the client as a unique individual, not to the client as representative of a class or category. Consequently diagnostic and other classifications of clients or their behavior are usually ignored as irrelevant to the way the therapist relates to the client.

The therapist attempts to empathically understand the client, consistently experience acceptance towards the client and maintain personal integration and an accurate self-awareness while in relation to the client. When it is perceived by the client, acceptant empathy is thought to free or increase the client's potential for self-healing. Thus personal growth occurs in each client's own way. Classificatory considerations are thought to be an obstacle to therapists' openness to their clients. They risk the appearance (if not the reality) to the client of not accepting or not understanding the unique person and may undermine the therapeutic relationship as it exists within the client-centered approach.

If the Stolorow and Atwood trichotomy of the unconsciousness of clients and etiology were considered to be correct and incorporated into Rogers' personality change theory, it would not affect the expressive nature of client-centered therapeutics. The intersubjective theoretical insert would remain irrelevant to the practice in the same way that Rogers' (1959) conception of personality and personality change does not influence the way the therapist proceeds. Client-centered therapy is based on the assumption of the actualization tendency and its implication for a nondirective attitude; it is not based on client-centered personality theory. The therapy is also based on ethical values concerning persons that logically and practically lead to the nondirective principle in the practice. The therapy from the top down is not designed according to a means-to-effect-ends model. The assumption underpinning the therapy is that the therapist's acceptant, empathic way of being – accommodative in its particulars to the individual client – is necessary and sufficient to free the developmental and self-healing capacities of clients (Rogers, 1957).

### WHY THERE IS NO CONFRONTATION IN CLIENT-CENTERED THERAPY

According to the theory, the therapist's behavior, the implementations, must truly express the attitudes and be consistent with the values of the approach that inform the therapeutic attitudes. Certain means–ends constructions and strategies that are common in other therapies have no place in client-centered work because they would conflict with the therapist's nondirective and expressive attitudes.

We cannot *confront* a client in order to influence him to recognize a connection in his experiences in order to make him better. This would employ a means that challenges the reality of the client, presumably to improve his accuracy of perception about something, which would (presumably) lead to his improved mental health. There are several client-centered principles or values that would be violated by confrontation. One is the principle of the therapist's respect for the client and trust in the power of the actualization tendency. Another is the view that the client is the best expert about himself. Another is the view that the client's own process of coming to self-understanding is the most effective process for personal change. Also, the empathic attitude that involves accepting the client's perceived world is violated by confrontation. In addition, an attitude of confrontation contradicts the important and ubiquitous client-centered attitude of humility in respect to the perceptual worlds of others.

The term "confrontation" means *to challenge another person's ideas or perceptions* usually from a posture assuming superior knowledge. The therapist doing the confronting thinks he or she knows the client's truth better than the client does. In contrast, if the genuine purpose of a therapist's "confrontation" is to understand something that seems unclear or internally inconsistent in what the client has been communicating, then it is not a confrontation at all. Responses aimed to understand confusing material are empathic understanding responses or they are questions for clarification, both of which express the empathic attitude. The attitude of confrontation is a different attitude. The wording and expressiveness of the statements communicating the two attitudes are different. Thus the messages and feelings perceived by the client and the client's reactions would very likely be different because the therapist's attitudes – expressing different concrete intentions – are different. The following interactions each contain an interpretive element but illustrate the difference between a confrontative and an empathic attitude.

Client: I was such a rebellious and hostile and disobedient kid. They couldn't tell me anything that I wouldn't go against it. (Pause) I always wanted to be a good boy, to please Mom and Dad and make them proud of me. It was my deepest wish, my deepest need.

Therapist (Confronting): You wanted the reward of them feeling good about you, but what you wanted more was to have your own way.

Therapist (Alternatively, expressing the empathic attitude): You wanted your parents' love and acceptance. But all the time you felt angry and resentful and rebellious; defeating what you wanted and needed from them.

An empathic response may include elements that are not explicit in the client's communication, but are inferred to be within the client's intended communication, as in the example when the therapist remarks "defeating what you wanted …." Unlike the confrontative response of the example, the empathic intention involves no goal to interpret the client's motives. Nor does it involve any goal to explain the client to his self, and it does not do so unless the client's communication appears to have intended some element of interpretation.

## THE IMPORTANCE OF EMPATHIC UNDERSTANDING RESPONSES

The view that client-centered therapists do not employ means to ends, however, does not imply that the behavioral methods of the therapy, or as Rogers (1951) expressed it, the "implementations" (pp. 24–26) of client-centered therapy, are unimportant. John Shlien (1995, personal communication) has expressed the view that the empathic understanding form of response is one of Rogers' major contributions to client-centered therapy. He remarks that we cannot adequately think of the approach in terms only of attitudes. Empathic understanding response process (Temaner, 1977/2011) is intrinsic to client-centered work. In other words, there is a form of interaction Rogers and his colleagues developed that is fundamental to client-centered therapy. Raskin (1947/2005) expressed this form of interaction:

> There is a process of counselor response which ... represents the nondirective attitude ... [It] becomes an active experiencing with the client of the feelings to which he gives expression ... the counselor makes a maximum effort to get under the skin of the person with whom he is communicating, he tries to get within and to live the attitudes expressed instead of observing them to catch every nuance of their changing nature; in a word, to absorb himself completely in the attitudes of the other. And in struggling to do this, there is simply no room for any other type of counselor activity or attitude; if he is attempting to live the attitudes of the other, he cannot be diagnosing them, he cannot be thinking of making the process go faster. Because he is an other, and not the client, the understanding is not spontaneous but must be acquired, and this through the most intense, continuous and active attention to the feelings of the other, to the exclusion of any other type of attention. (pp. 2–4)

Although necessary to the therapy, this does not mean empathic responses are employed as a means to effect some goal in the client from the perspective of the subjective intentions of the therapist who is engaging in the interaction.

The therapist's engagement is expressive and communicative, but the goal is one for the therapist's self. Although such a goal may bring to mind selfishness or coldness this is not at all the reality. When working well, according to the ideas of the theory, the therapist is primarily trying to understand the client's immediate phenomenology. Along with trying to understand, the therapist usually experiences feelings of warmth, caring and generosity in relation to the client. These feelings are intrinsic to acceptant empathy. In addition, the therapist's maintenance of a self-oriented goal protects the client's autonomy while the therapist externalizes these positive interpersonal feelings.

The therapist desires to understand, and explicitly communicates to find out whether or not his or her subjective empathic understanding is accurate. Empathic understanding interaction between therapist and client springs from the therapist's intentions to acceptantly and empathically experience understanding of the client. Interactively, it also springs from the client's intentions to represent himself and be understood.

## EMPATHIC UNDERSTANDING IS AN INTERACTIVE PHENOMENON

Empathic understanding itself is necessarily an interactive phenomenon. We only have our impressions of accurate empathic understanding of clients as the result of listening to the client and subjectively translating the client's words and expressiveness into our own meanings, into our own understandings. To truly empathically understand a client it is absolutely necessary to engage in a process of checking our understandings. We rely on the client's communications in response to our checking. We rely on the client's verifications, corrections or denials concerning our understandings, our further checking, and so forth.

Empathic understanding as both attitude and behavior, correctly understood, is a nondirective process of interaction. It is a nondirective process partly because it is in accord with the implied wishes and intentions of the client in the situation. The therapist assumes the client is communicating in order to be listened to and accurately understood. It is highly likely that anyone engaging in a self-disclosing narrative, while talking to another person, is seeking accurate understanding and, probably, acceptance. This seems even more likely in the context of therapy where the client has arrived because he has experiences that are painful or unsatisfying that he hopes to change. It seems logical to assume that clients' self-representing, communicative behavior is naturally intended to be listened to and acceptantly understood. Thus the client-centered therapist has reason to believe he or she is following the "voice" (Grant, 1990), or will of the client when empathically understanding.

The therapist is guided by the general theory that the attitudes of congruence, etc., create therapeutic conditions. But in the actual situation the therapist is engaging in a reciprocal interaction. The therapist is attempting to follow the will of the client, as well as following what the client is expressing, by experientially and behaviorally responding empathically.

Rogers stated that he does not have goals for his clients when he is effective (Baldwin, 1987/2004). His goals are for himself, "with the way I am" (p. 47) being present, congruent, acceptant, and empathic. This is a significant statement about Rogers' own form of client-centered therapy practice. In his personal statement, Rogers is communicating something fundamental in respect to the basic theory and attitudes of client-centered therapy. Although Rogers was not prone to suggest what other therapists should do, many nondirective client-centered therapists take from his personal statement an implication that the therapist's goals should not be goals for the client.

If we do therapy intending goals for clients we are not functioning consistently with Rogers' conception of client-centered practice – certainly a choice we can make or not. In addition, if we are thinking in terms of means to ends, we may appear to be trying to understand, we may appear to be acceptant, we may appear to be whole – of a single mind – in what we are doing. If we are doing what we are doing for some other purpose, however, – such as to produce an effect in the client whether to alter the client's process or content – we are *up to something* other than what we appear to be doing. Being *up to something* is not consistent with the totality of client-centered values including the idea that we are not engaged in pursuing goals for the client. It is not consistent with the attitude expressed in the concept of congruence. We aim to not deceive the client as to ourselves (Rogers, 1957).

## CONCLUSION

A fundamental stance of the client-centered therapist is to act spontaneously (although it is a disciplined spontaneity) and authentically in our relationships with clients. All client-centered therapeutic behavior is intended to be responsive to the unique client and springs otherwise primarily from the therapist's immediately experienced attitudes and values.

## REFERENCES

Baldwin, M. (1987). Interview with Carl Rogers on the use of the self in therapy. In M. Baldwin & V. Satir (Eds.), *The use of the self in therapy* (pp. 45–52). New York: Haworth Press. [Reprinted (2004) in R. Moodley, C. Lago, & A. Talahite (Eds.), *Carl Rogers counsels a Black client: Race and culture in person-centred counseling* (pp. 253–260). Ross-on-Wye: PCCS Books]

Bozarth, J. (1993). Not necessarily necessary but always sufficient. In D. Brazier (Ed.), *Beyond Carl Rogers* (pp. 92–108). London: Constable.

Bozarth, J. (1998). *Person-centered therapy: A revolutionary paradigm.* Ross-on-Wye: PCCS Books.

Brodley, B. T. (1986, September). *Client-centered therapy: What is it? What is it not?* Paper presented at the first annual meeting of the Association for the Development of the Person-Centered Approach, Chicago, IL.

Brodley, B. T. (1987). A client-centered psychotherapy practice. [Published (1998) in C. Wolter-Gustafson (Ed.), *A person-centered reader: Personal selections by our members* (pp. 59–87). Boston: Association for the Development of the Person-Centered Approach]

Brodley, B. T. (1997). The nondirective attitude in client-centered therapy. *The Person-Centered Journal, 4*(1), 18–30. [This volume, Chapter 5]

Brodley, B. T. (1999a). A client-centered demonstration in Hungary. In I. Fairhurst (Ed.), *Women writing in the person-centred approach* (pp. 85–92). Ross-on-Wye: PCCS Books.

Brodley, B. T. (1999b). About the nondirective attitude. *Person-Centred Practice, 7*(2), 79–82.

Gendlin, E. T. (1996). *Focusing-oriented psychotherapy: A manual of the experiential method.* New York: Guilford Press.

Grant, B. (1990). Principled and instrumental nondirectiveness in person-centered and client-centered therapy. *Person-Centered Review, 5*, 77–88.

Kahn, E. (1996). The intersubjective and the client-centered approach: Are they one at their core? *Psychotherapy, 33*, 30–42.

Kahn, E. (1997). Empathic understanding. Email message, Cctpca network, June 19.

Prouty, G. (1999). Carl Rogers and experiential therapies: A dissonance? *Person-Centred Practice, 7*(1), 4–11.

Raskin, N. J. (1947). The nondirective attitude. Unpublished manuscript. [Published (2005) in *The Person-Centered Journal 12*(1–2) and (2005) in B. E. Levitt (Ed.), *Embracing non-directivity* (pp. 327–347). Ross-on-Wye: PCCS Books]

Raskin, N. J. (1988). Responses to person-centered vs. client-centered? *Renaissance, 5*(3&4), 2–3.

Rogers, C. R. (1951). *Client-centered therapy.* Boston: Houghton Mifflin.

Rogers, C. R. (1957). The necessary and sufficient conditions of therapeutic personality change. *Journal of Consulting Psychology, 21*, 95–103.

Rogers, C. R. (1959). A theory of therapy, personality and interpersonal relationships, as developed in the client-centered framework. In S. Koch (Ed.), *Psychology: A study of a science. Vol. III: Formulations of the person and the social context* (pp. 184–256). New York: McGraw-Hill.

Rogers, C. R. (1986). Reflection of feelings. *Person-Centered Review, 1*(4), 375–377.

Stolorow, R. D., & Atwood, G. E. (1992). *Contexts of being: The intersubjective foundations of psychological life.* Hillsdale, NJ: The Analytic Press.

Temaner, B. [Brodley] (1977). The empathic understanding response process. Chicago Counseling and Psychotherapy Center. *Chicago Counseling Center Discussion Paper.* [This volume, Chapter 12]

# Chapter 14

# Criteria for making empathic responses
in client-centered therapy

The criteria for communicating empathic understanding described in this paper are based on my work as a client-centered therapist. As my therapy evolved, I only gradually identified these criteria and recognized that they express the nondirective attitude that informs my practice. An early version of the paper was prepared for the First International Forum on the Person-Centered Approach in Mexico in 1982. An excerpt was published in the Association for Development of the Person-Centered Approach newsletter, *Renaissance*, in 1984 [see Brodley, 1985]. In 1986 Carl Rogers published his article on "reflection of feelings" which gave support to my thesis that the client-centered therapist's intention in responding empathically is to verify understanding, not to manipulate the client's process nor to foster any therapist goal for the client. The fundamental nondirectiveness in client-centered work seems to be difficult for some students to understand or, perhaps, to believe. I hope that this paper will help to clarify the meaning of the nondirective attitude in empathic interaction process as well as clarify the criteria for overt empathic responding in client-centered therapy.

Client-centered therapy is a therapeutic approach theoretically based on the idea that all persons possess an inherent actualizing tendency. The actualizing concept involves an assumption that the motivation and capacities for personal growth, and the particular directions that evolve for such growth, arise from within the individual person (Rogers, 1951, 1980). Given this assumption of the client's inherent potential for growth and change, the therapist's function is to experience and express the therapeutic attitudes – congruence, unconditional positive regard and empathic understanding of the client's internal frame of reference – in relation to the client. Successful therapy also requires that the client perceive the therapist's empathic understanding and unconditional positive regard.

In the client-centered approach, the client is viewed as the best expert about the client (Bozarth, 1985; Bozarth & Brodley, 1986) and the "architect"

This paper was published (1998) in *The Person-Centered Journal*, 5(1), 20–28. Reproduced with permission from *PCJ*.

of the process (Raskin, 1988). The therapist's nondirective attitude (Raskin, 1947/2005) expresses trust in and respect for the client and a value to protect the client's autonomy and self-determination. It is an aspect of the therapist's personal philosophy of persons (Rogers, 1951, Chapter 2). In therapy, the nondirective attitude functions importantly to enhance the client's personal power and sense of self-value.

The client-centered therapist's overall goal is to facilitate a therapeutic climate in the client's experience. It does this through an interpersonal relationship wherein the therapist experiences particular psychological attitudes that may be perceived by the client. These attitudes, when perceived, promote therapeutic change and personal growth while they function to protect and enhance the client's autonomy and self-regulation. This general conception of the therapist's goal emphasizes the nondirective aspect of the client-centered philosophy.

As a consequence of holding this general notion of the therapist's goal and its emphasis on nondirectiveness, when doing client-centered psychotherapy, I implicitly give myself the following instructions:

1. To experience and personally embody, as much as I can, the therapeutic attitudes of congruence, unconditional positive regard and empathic understanding in relation to the client.

2. To express acceptant empathic understanding to the client,[1] often through explicit empathic responses, in order to check my inner understandings (Temaner, 1982/2011; Rogers, 1986).

3. To be willing to address the client's questions and requests as a person to a person without making assumptions (and without selectively responding according to such assumptions) about the possible benefits or harm to the client in getting honest answers.

These rather simple sounding instructions result in a very complex, variable and sometimes difficult sequence of events and experiences for both therapist and client. Nevertheless, over many years I have continued to find these

---

1. A major category of empathic responses are often termed "empathic understanding responses." Empathic understanding responses refer to a broad category of responses, all of which are an attempt to accurately articulate the experience the client has expressed or has been striving to express. They range from very literal restatements or summaries of what the client has expressed, to more fragmental responses, to forms of response which involve more inference or guessing about what the client has been expressing. But in all instances of empathic understanding responses, they represent the therapist's attempt to articulate the client's point of view and are an attempt at an empathic following of the client. They are not based on an attempt to interpret the client or get ahead of the client's awareness of his or her experiences.

instructions useful, and the resulting experiences to be therapeutic – to be helpful to clients in fostering their growth and healing.

The question addressed by this paper arises out of one of Rogers' (1957) conditions for therapeutic change. He expressed this essential therapeutic condition in two different ways. In 1957 his theory stated:

> The communication to the client of the therapist's empathic understanding and unconditional positive regard is to a minimal degree achieved. (p. 96)

In a slightly different theoretical statement, Rogers (1959) wrote:

> That the client perceives, at least to a minimal degree ... the unconditional positive regard of the therapist for him, and the empathic understanding of the therapist (p. 213)

On the basis of either statement, obviously, if the therapist is to communicate acceptant empathic understanding (not only experience these attitudes) then the therapist must behave in a manner that allows the client an opportunity to perceive these attitudes. It seems reasonable to assume that the therapist must at times make explicit empathic responses, along with nonverbal and expressive behaviors, that may communicate acceptance and empathy. The question logically following from this assumption is: When, or under what particular circumstances, or according to what criteria, should the therapist deliberately speak his or her understanding?

It may be helpful to clarify certain features of client-centered theory before articulating the specific criteria which answer the question of when, or under what circumstances, the therapist should deliberately speak his or her empathic understanding. To elucidate by contrast, I will first discuss a theoretical interpretation of the purpose of responses which is inconsistent with the basic theory.

Some client-centered theorists have developed the idea that explicit responses should evoke or stimulate the client's experiencing process (e.g., Rice, 1974). The unproved assumption behind this idea is that the fundamental cause of the change process is a particular experiencing process in the client (Leijssen, 1996). The problem with this idea is that it may produce therapist attitudes which undermine the essential therapeutic attitudes and essential character of the client-centered therapeutic relationship.

Specifically, the idea that therapists' responses must affect clients' experiencing process in a particular manner in order to promote therapeutic change requires the therapist to assume responsibility, at least at times, for the client having the "correct," or the truly therapeutic, experiencing process. This is likely to imply one of two things in respect to the therapist's behavior. One possibility is that the therapist must constantly be attempting to enhance, intensify or amplify the client's experiencing process. This is an unlikely meaning, given the general clinical observation that there are times when individuals appear to need to soften, or distance themselves from, the intensity of their experience in order to maintain their integration.

The alternative behavioral implication that the therapist should take responsibility for the client's experiencing process is that the therapist should be producing different effects (e.g., sometimes amplifying, sometimes softening the client's experience) for the client's benefit. Different experiences in the client are deemed the appropriate ones at different times or under different circumstances. This form of the inference, if put into practice, would require the therapist to engage in a diagnostic process and to engage in process directiveness (Greenberg, Rice, & Elliot, 1993) in relation to the client. In either case, the therapist has taken on the task and responsibility of doing something to the client to produce an effect on the client. In both cases, the therapist is presuming to know what the client needs and, in the second case, presuming to know when he or she needs it. Both require the therapist to make ongoing decisions about what is to be done to affect the client repeatedly through the therapy session.

When a therapist moves into the realm of deciding what is best for the client in the context of the specific therapy relationship, or moves into the realm of decisions concerning what is best for the client at particular points in the therapy interaction, he or she is no longer functioning within the basic values of the client-centered position. This view of client-centered therapy has been eloquently argued on the basis of research, clinical experience and study of Rogers' writings and therapy behavior by Bozarth (1992). Bozarth states:

> The essence of client-centered/person-centered therapy is the therapist's dedication to going with the client's direction, at the client's pace, and in the client's unique way of being (p. 13)

Certain values are thought to be, and seem to many of us who practice it to be, essential to the therapy's effectiveness. They are:

1. That the client is an autonomous person with growth and healing potentials within him- or herself which the person is in the best position to utilize.

2. That the therapist is committed to respecting and protecting that self-direction and autonomy.

3. That the responsibilities of the client-centered therapist rest in the therapist maintaining and living out the fundamental values and attitudes that are believed to be the basis for constructive personality change and healing.

Any form of paternalism[2] is inconsistent with client-centered therapy and undermines the distinctive client-centered relationship.

The actual general purpose of explicit responses in client-centered therapy is for the therapist to be a participant in an interaction between persons. Explicit responses, as well as the therapist's manner and tone – his or her presence, permit the client to perceive and understand the therapist. Within the interaction the therapist is trying to accurately and acceptantly empathically understand the client and the client has an opportunity to perceive the therapist's attitudes and the therapist's concrete accuracy of understandings. Explicit responses, along with a great variety of nonverbal behaviors that are also shaped by the therapist's therapeutic attitudes, are a major vehicle of communication to the client of the therapist's inner empathy and acceptance.

Setting the stage for presentation of the criteria for empathic responses in client-centered therapy also requires addressing the confusion that exists concerning the role of technique in client-centered therapy (see Bozarth & Brodley, 1986; Brodley & Brody, 1996/2011). Some teachers and practitioners have misunderstood Rogers' theory of therapy and mistakenly identify client-centered therapy with the use of the technique of "making reflections" (Rogers, 1986) or the technique of "active listening" (Gordon, 1970). In both of these techniques, the therapist makes a kind of restatement of the client's expression. Techniques of restatement are often employed subsequent to each unit of completed communication (roughly each spoken paragraph, or coherent idea or feeling) by the client. These techniques may, in fact, be helpful to clients and may produce a therapeutic change process, but they are not appreciative of Rogers' conception of therapeutic empathic understanding. Rogers' theory emphatically emphasizes the therapist's attitudes and feelings, not techniques, in the therapy relationship (Rogers, 1957).

Rogers' theory also asserts that the client must to some extent perceive and experience the therapist's attitudes. Such reception requires the therapist to have transmitted attitudinal information to the client. Spoken communication is highly likely to be at least part of the vehicle of transmission. It is, therefore, reasonable to refer to a means-to-an-end technique element in doing client-centered therapy or in teaching it. It may, for example, be

2. Paternalism is generally defined as doing something for, or to (or withholding from), another person, with the intention of doing the person some good, without the person's consent.

developmentally useful to students of therapy to practice reflecting the utterances of a practice client, or practice "active listening" as a technique to help students become comfortable with responsiveness and interaction in the therapeutic relation, or to become confident in their ability to represent the communications of another person from that person's point of view. But practice responding for these and other didactic purposes should not be confused by the student or teacher with client-centered therapeutic responding in which the therapist's attitudes determine his or her behavior (Brodley, 1995, 1997 [see 2000/2011]).

In Rogers' theory of therapy the attitudes and feelings of the therapist which become successfully communicated to the client are among the causes of client therapeutic change. Successful communication may have been achieved, however, through some different means than by making empathic understanding responses (Bozarth, 1984).

There is no dogma of technique in Rogers' theory. There is, actually, no technique in the real therapeutic process, if technique means deliberately employing means towards desired ends (Brodley, 1995; Brodley & Brody, 1996/2011). It does not matter, from the perspective of efficacy, how the therapist gets the therapeutic attitudes across to the client, as long as the particular client experiences acceptant empathic understanding (without experiencing contradictory experiences, or at least a minimum of other experiences which contradict those attitudes) from a therapist who comes across as authentic. Empathic understanding responses are only given emphasis in explaining the therapy because in most situations, with most clients, they are a form of overt responsiveness that can express the therapeutic attitudes and that have a likelihood of being perceived as acceptant empathic understandings.

Practices of speaking reflections, speaking empathic understanding responses, doing active listening, or doing any practices that are done as technique produce a different quality of relationship and interaction process, and one that is less therapeutic, than the relationship Rogers had in mind when expressing his theory.

Nevertheless, if a therapist does not make specific decisions about what is best for a client while interacting and responding, and does not engage in a routine or ritual application of technique, the therapist still needs a criterion, or criteria, for explicit expression of empathic experience of the client. The basis for explicit or overt expression should be (1) consistent with the growth premise of the theory, (2) consistent with the client-centered conception of causality as resting in a combination of the attitudes of the therapist and the basic nature of the person, and (3) consistent with the value placed on promoting and protecting the client's autonomy, self-regulation and self-determination. In addition, the basis for overt responses should be (4) consistent with what Rogers' considered the primary therapeutic attitude (Baldwin, 1987/2004) – the therapist's congruence. Congruence refers, specifically, to the therapist's wholeness and integration. When he or she is congruent, the therapist's responses are authentic, and thus will probably feel authentic to the client.

## THE EMPATHIC INTERACTION

Explicit empathic responses occur in the context of an empathic understanding response process (Temaner, 1977/2011) within the client-centered relationship. The typical events of empathic interaction are as follows:

1. The client talks to the therapist and expresses or describes some of his or her feelings, concerns, thoughts or life events. The client articulates something from personal experience and from his or her own viewpoint that he wishes to communicate at that time to the therapist (and may wish, also to say out loud to hear for himself).

2. While the client is expressing his or her experience the therapist is giving a full and undistracted attention to the client. The therapist is attempting to receive, to absorb and grasp the meanings and feelings the client is saying or trying to say from his or her own point of view, taking it in until the therapist has it in his own experiencing process such that he feels he understands to some extent (or does not have that feeling of understanding and recognizes the fact).

3. Next, the therapist may or may not make an explicit response that communicates his or her inner understanding (or acknowledges lack of understanding) to the client. If the therapist does not make an explicit verbal-oral response, he may nod, make a vocal gesture such as "Uhm-hm," or simply remain attentive and silent in a way that implies understanding to the client.

4. Finally, in this "empathic cycle" (Barrett-Lennard, 1981), in response to the presence, the attention, or the explicit responses of the therapist, the client may have the feeling of being understood and accepted. These experiences tend to stimulate the client to further self-reflection and expression.[3]

---

3. In the client-centered therapeutic situation, wherein the therapist experiences and embodies the therapeutic attitudinal conditions and when the "empathic cycle" occurs and reoccurs, a distinctive therapeutic process is taking place which I have termed "the empathic understanding response process" (Temaner, 1977/2011).

Over the years I have practiced, trying to develop my capability as a therapist from a client-centered theoretical perspective, I gradually realized I was spontaneously using criteria for making empathic responses which met theoretical conditions. These criteria are based on the wants or feelings of the therapist (given the general therapeutic intention and commitment to the therapeutic attitudes), or based on the request for response by the client. I distinguish five different criteria for making empathic responses on these particular bases. Each of the five is compatible with the nondirective attitude intrinsic to the theory. I shall describe these criteria in terms of circumstances that may occur in the first and second steps of the empathic interaction cycle (when the client is self-expressing and the therapist is attending and absorbing). Any one of these criteria is a sufficient reason for making an explicit response.

### The criteria for making empathic responses

*1. When the therapist feels some understanding but also experiences some uncertainty because of an ambiguity or imprecision or confusion perceived to be located in the client's communication.*

In this case the client's statements have been experienced as somewhat unclear by the therapist, but clear enough or coherent enough for the therapist to attempt an explicit response. (If the client's statements have been experienced as so unclear that the therapist does not feel any understanding, the therapist would usually ask the client for a restatement or new expression of what the client was trying to communicate.) If the client has not been fully understood because of coming across as unclear to the therapist, the client may or may not realize this when the therapist makes the response to check inner understanding. The therapist's aim is not to point out the client's imprecision. The empathic response, rather, is aimed to elicit the client's validation, correction or elaboration concerning what he or she is trying to communicate.

*2. When the therapist feels uncertain about his or her understanding of the client's communication.*

The therapist perceives the feeling of uncertainty to be located in the therapist's reception or absorption of the client's communication. The uncertainty about understanding coexists with the feeling that the client's communication was clear and coherent enough to be understood. The therapist feels unsure of his or her own grasp of the client's meanings or feelings.

*3. When the therapist feels an impulse or desire to express and communicate his or her self while immersed in the attempt to empathically understand.*[4]

This impulse or desire to express oneself which is resolved through expression of understandings probably originates in the interpersonal and interactional nature of the psychotherapeutic relation. Inherent in an interpersonal relation is an expectation of an exchange – a back and forth characteristic of the interaction. The deeply empathically engaged therapist, however, seldom will experience any specific content from his or her own frame of reference that could serve as a vehicle for self-expression. Thus when the interaction involves almost exclusive focus and attention on the client member of the dyad, the therapist may feel the desire to be responsive and expressive through the vehicle of tentative empathic understandings.

*4. When the therapist feels the need to establish the client's communication in experience or memory.*

The therapist may feel a need to make an explicit empathic response, possibly even a relatively literal one, in order to help him- or herself get the client's meanings incorporated into his own experience and memory. This form of empathic response sometimes may be prefaced with a brief explanation such as "I just need to be sure I have that clear in my own mind. What you were just saying is …"

*5. When the client asks the therapist if the therapist has been able to follow or understand, or asks the therapist whether the client has been clear in communication.*

In some instances the client may not ask explicitly, but conveys by a behavioral cue (e.g., the client looks searchingly at the therapist along with an incomplete expression of his or her idea), or an indirect expression (e.g., says "I don't know if I'm making sense") indicating he or she is wondering if the therapist understands. In these somewhat ambiguous instances the therapist may directly make an empathic response (or may first ask the client if he or she is concerned right then about being understood).

The above criteria for making explicit empathic responses, except for the fifth which is directly responsive to the client's wishes, have to do with the feelings of the therapist. None of the five are based on any therapist

---

4. This impulse or felt desire is not anxiety and should be consciously discriminated from anxiety feelings. A feeling of anxiety to make a response to the client may be stimulated in therapists (especially new therapists) when they or the client have been silent for awhile. The feeling of anxiety-to-respond is best taken as a cue to regain congruence, to relax, give oneself a chance to reflect on the impulse and dispel the anxiety.

speculation, judgment or assessment of the client's needs for a response. They all express the therapist's intention to experience accurate, acceptant, empathic understanding and the therapist's respect for the client as the determinant of what is or is not accurate. The criteria are nondirective and nonmanipulative in relation to the client. The therapist's specific and concrete intention in making empathic responses is simply to participate in empathic understanding of the client as a process of absorbing tentative understandings that become validated or corrected by the client.

The criteria are meant to be implicit guides to promote the achievement of the therapeutic attitudes in relationship with the client. I do not mean that the therapist in the midst of therapy should mentally run down the list of criteria, then make sure one of them is met, identify it, and then and only then make an explicit response to the client.

A main purpose in clarifying these criteria is to emphasize that the client-centered therapist relates to his client in a spontaneous and conversational manner. The therapist has a specific purpose, to be an effective therapist, but the manner of achieving effective therapy emerges from the sincerity of therapeutic attitudes, not through rational matching of means to ends. The client-centered manner does not involve making or acting upon speculations or inferences concerning the specific client. Nor does it involve speculations or inferences concerning the client's specific needs, nor judgments about how to foster the client's well-being in specific instances. Obviously, the entire theory involves inferential general judgments about what is therapeutic and what is not. Having a general position – a theory – is quite different from making moment-to-moment decisions concerning clients.

Adopting the criteria I've described for making responses, before the concrete occasion of doing therapy with clients, will likely influence the therapist through an implicit subjective process when he or she is doing therapy. Knowing the criteria should not lead to a conscious decision process added to the therapist's task while doing therapy. Often, when listening to recordings of empathic interactions, the therapist can identify which one of the criteria was operative when making specific responses. But even when so listening, it is not always possible to recognize or remember the operative criterion – and that is of no matter. The important thing is that the therapist has been genuinely trying to understand, not trying to exercise some conceived power to produce therapeutic effects on or in the client.

The criteria described are those which undeliberately influence the specific and concrete intention of the therapist in the empathic interaction. It should be understood – very emphatically – the client-centered therapist is, in principle and in the heart, not intending to produce effects on or in the client when doing therapy. The therapist is simply, but profoundly, being him- or herself in a person-to-person interaction. In this way the therapist is giving him- or herself to empathic reception and to following of the client and wanting, from time to time, to communicate about his or her empathic experience of the client to the client.[5]

The mechanisms of change in client-centered therapy are thought generally to be in the transmission of the therapeutic attitudes of the therapist from the therapist to the client. Consequently, the client becomes more integrated, more self-accepting and more empathically understanding towards him- or herself (Rogers, 1984). I believe this view points to the truth about therapeutic change and that, additionally, more specific processes can be described for individual clients within this general process framework. I do not believe there is only one therapeutic change process for all clients in the context of client-centered therapy. Rather, that the integrity of the relationship – one containing, consistently and without contradiction, the living out of the therapeutic attitudes by the therapist – allows whatever specific change processes are at work within particular clients. It is obvious to me, based on my work with many people, that therapeutic effects are produced when the therapist is free of specific intentions to produce effects on or in the client. Many different therapeutic processes and effects[6] do occur in the client-centered therapist's clients as the therapist works purely from the theory and empathically with clients. These effects seem to contribute in sometimes unexpected ways to accomplishing the general purpose and goal in the situation – the healing and growth of the client.

------------

5. The assumptions behind this extreme nondirective, nonmanipulative position are that (1) the autonomy and self-regulation of the client need protection in a therapeutic relationship even when the therapeutic conditions which are believed to cause constructive change are being provided; (2) the growth potential of the person is assumed to be the effective force that moves the individual towards growth and health; (3) the therapist provides an optimal psychological environment conducive to the client's potential for constructive change and health but the therapist also needs to be highly sensitive to the potency of his personality, status and role in the relationship. Note that all these are assumptions prior to the specific therapeutic relation, and apply in relation to all clients.

6. I have observed a number of different effects of empathic interaction which seem to be aspects of change processes in particular clients. Some examples: The client becomes reassured that he is understandable. The client feels himself becoming less confused or more coherent to himself. The client feels more understanding of his motivations, values and feelings. The client feels cared about and valued, less alone, less alienated, less different from other people, or less strange. The client feels more understanding of others, their motivations and feelings. The client feels he or she is being more realistic and open to the way things are. The client feels more aware of subtle processes of feeling and meanings within himself. Clients have reported that they feel these and many other effects and processes to have been stimulated by interaction with an acceptant and empathic therapist.

Indeed, there are many immediate and prevailing effects and impacts on clients as the consequence of the empathic relationship and interaction. But – while functioning in the spirit of the client-centered philosophy and embodying its values – the therapist is not intending to produce these or other beneficial effects. The therapist's specific and concrete intention is to be as present as possible in the relationship and to acceptantly and empathically experience and understand the client.

## REFERENCES

Baldwin, M. (1987). Interview with Carl Rogers on the use of the self in therapy. In M. Baldwin & V. Satir (Eds.), *The use of the self in therapy* (pp. 45–54). New York: Haworth Press. [Reprinted (2004) in R. Moodley, C. Lago, & A. Talahite (Eds.), *Carl Rogers counsels a Black client: Race and culture in person-centred counseling* (pp. 253–60). Ross-on-Wye: PCCS Books]

Barrett-Lennard, G. T. (1981). The empathy cycle: Refinement of a nuclear concept. *Journal of Counseling Psychology, 28*, 91–100.

Bozarth, J. D. (1984). Beyond reflection: Emergent modes of empathy. In R. F. Levant & J. M. Shlien (Eds.), *Client-centered therapy and the person-centered approach: New directions in theory, research, and practice* (pp. 59–75). New York: Praeger.

Bozarth, J. D. (1985). Quantum theory and the person-centered approach. *Journal of Counseling and Development, 64*, 179–182.

Bozarth, J. D. (1992). Coterminous intermingling of doing and being in person-centered therapy. *The Person-Centered Journal, 1*(1), 12–20.

Bozarth J. D., & Brodley, B. T. (1986). Client-centered psychotherapy: A statement. *Person-Centered Review, 1*(3), 262–271.

Brodley, B. T. (1985). Criteria for making empathic understanding responses in client-centered therapy. *Renaissance, 2*(1), 1–3.

Brodley, B. T. (1995). *Client-centered therapy: Not a means to an end.* Unpublished manuscript.

Brodley, B. T. (1997, July). *Client-centered therapy: An expressive therapy.* Paper presented at the Fourth International Conference on Client-Centered and Experiential Psychotherapy (ICCCEP) in Lisbon, Portugal. [See Brodley, 2000]

[Brodley, B. T. (2000) Client-centered: An expressive therapy. In J. E. Marques Teixeira & S. Antunes (Eds.), *Client-centered and experiential psychotherapy* (pp. 133–147). Linda a Velha, Lisboa, Portugal: Vale & Vale. Reprinted (2002) in *The Person-Centered Journal, 9*(1), 59–70; this volume Chapter 13]

Brodley, B. T., & Brody, A. F. (1996). Can one use techniques and still be client-centered? In R. Hutterer, G. Pawlowsky, P. F. Schmid, & R. Stipsits (Eds.), *Client-centered and experiential psychotherapy: A paradigm in motion* (pp. 369–374). Frankfurt am Main: Peter Lang. [This volume, Chapter 18]

Gordon, T. (1970). A theory of healthy relationships and a program of parent effectiveness training. In J. T. Hart & T. M. Tomlinson (Eds.), *New directions in client-centered therapy* (pp. 407–426). Boston: Houghton Mifflin.

Greenberg, L. S., Rice, L. N., & Elliott, R. (1993). *Facilitating emotional change.* New York: Guilford Press.

Leijssen, M. (1996). Focusing processes. In L. S. Greenberg, G. Lietaer, & J. Watson (Eds.), *Experiential psychotherapy: Differential intervention* (pp. 121–154). New York: Guilford Press.

Raskin, N. J. (1947). The nondirective attitude. Unpublished manuscript. [Published (2005) in *The Person-Centered Journal 12*(1–2) and (2005) B. E. Levitt (Ed.), *Embracing non-directivity* (pp. 327–347). Ross-on-Wye: PCCS Books]

Raskin, N. (1988). Responses to person-centered vs. client-centered? *Renaissance, 5*(3&4), 2–3.

Rice, L. N. (1974). The evocative function of the therapist. In D. A. Wexler & L. N. Rice (Eds.), *Innovations in client-centered therapy* (pp. 289–311). New York: Wiley.

Rogers, C. R. (1951). *Client-centered therapy*. Boston: Houghton Mifflin.

Rogers, C. R. (1957). The necessary and sufficient conditions of therapeutic personality change. *Journal of Consulting Psychology, 21*, 95–103.

Rogers, C. R. (1959). A theory of therapy, personality and interpersonal relationships, as developed in the client-centered framework. In S. Koch (Ed.), *Psychology: A study of a science. Vol. III: Formulations of the person and the social context* (pp. 184–256). New York: McGraw-Hill.

Rogers, C. R. (1980). The foundations of a person-centered approach. In *A way of being* (pp. 113–136). Boston: Houghton Mifflin.

Rogers, C. R. (1984, July). *Dialogue with Carl Rogers*. Tape of a dialogue between Carl Rogers and participants in the Second International Forum on the Person-Centered Approach, Norwich, England.

Rogers, C. R. (1986). Reflection of feelings. *Person-Centered Review, 1*(4), 375–377.

Temaner, B. [Brodley] (1977). The empathic understanding response process. Chicago Counseling and Psychotherapy Center. *Chicago Counseling Center Discussion Papers*. [This volume, Chapter 12]

Temaner, B. [Brodley] (1982). Criteria for making empathic responses. Prepared for the First International Forum on the Person-Centered Approach, Oaxtepec, Mexico, (June–July). [Revised version published in this volume, this chapter]

# Chapter 15

# Reasons for responses expressing the therapist's frame of reference in client-centered therapy

The nondirective attitude is fundamental in client-centered therapy (Brodley, 1997/2011). This principle is integrated into the client-centered therapist's intention to experience congruence, unconditional positive regard and empathic understanding in relation to clients (Rogers, 1957; Brodley, 1996/2011). Experiencing the totality of these attitudes with voluntary, self-representing, narrating clients tends to result in responses that represent or express the client's frame of reference. These responses, termed "empathic understanding responses,"[1] are usually expressed for the purpose of checking with the client as to the accuracy of the therapist's understandings (Rogers, 1986a; Brodley, 1998a/2011). Most other responses express the therapist's frame of reference, even when their content is about the client.

Tomlinson and Whitney (1970) have discussed the reasons client-centered therapists usually respond to clients with empathic responses. Little has been written, however, concerning the reasons client-centered therapists occasionally do respond to their clients from their own frame of reference (Rogers, 1957, 1961a; Baldwin, 1987/2004; Brodley, 1998b/2011). This paper will discuss reasons client-centered therapists may make responses that

---

1. True empathic understanding responses reveal some facet of the person or self of the client. They express, at least in part, the relation of the self to what the person is talking about. They include some element of the client as an agent. They reveal the client's dynamic – his feelings, his reactions. Or they reveal his adience to or avoidance of something or someone. Informational responses are also part of empathic following behavior. These responses attempt to check with the client about the accuracy of the therapist's understanding of the information that the client is narrating. Informational responses do not include the element of the client's self in relation to the information. Questions for clarification are also part of empathic following behavior. They are similar to empathic responses but they give explicit emphasis to the element of questioning. Questions for clarification are easily distinguished from leading or probing questions.

---

Slight revision of a paper published (1999) in *The Person-Centered Journal, 6*(1), 4–27. The 1999 publication was itself a revision of a paper presented at the annual meeting of the Association for the Development of the Person-Centered Approach, May 21–25, 1998, Wheaton College, Norton, MA. Reproduced with permission from *PCJ*.

represent their own frame. The reasons will be embedded in caution, warnings and some guidelines for therapists about this practice. My aim is to help students of client-centered therapy develop a differentiated awareness concerning the possibilities and the limitations of therapist-frame responses.

I think it is inevitable that client-centered therapists will make responses representing their own frame of reference from time to time – sometimes for very good reasons. Nevertheless, I do not wish to encourage this practice. Clients and the therapy relationship may suffer harmful effects when the therapist temporarily abandons acceptant empathic understanding. My aim is to encourage therapists' sense of freedom by clarifying reasons for therapist-frame responses, while I also advocate a conservative, self-aware and disciplined approach.

It is a fact that client-centered therapists sometimes make responses from their own frame of reference to their clients. In a sample of 31 of Carl Rogers' recorded sessions (Brodley, 1994/2011), a mean of 10% of his responses (range of 0 to 14%) were therapist-frame remarks that had not been elicited by questions from his clients.[2] In a 1998 sample of 14 other client/person-centered therapists, the self-estimated mean of responses from the therapist's frame of reference was 8.0% (with range of means of 3% to 25%).[3]

The written theory has not offered much rationale for therapist-frame responses to self-exploring clients. For the sake of responsible practice it is important to have theory for making therapist-frame responses. It is also important to realize the possible risks to clients as the result of even temporary loss of the acceptant, empathic relation to the client, which may occur when the therapist self-represents.

THEORETICAL CONTEXT

Recall that client-centered therapy is a therapy of values and attitudes (Rogers, 1951, 1957, 1959, 1980; Patterson, 1989, 1990; Bozarth, 1992). It is not a diagnostic type of therapy, which would require the therapist to conceptualize or diagnose the client's problems, conceptualize goals for the client and employ techniques to meet those goals. Client-centered, in contrast to most if not all other therapies, is an expressive kind of therapy (Brodley, 2000b/2011). The therapist's behavior flows from attitudes not strategies. The behavior expresses

2. Rogers also spoke from his own frame of reference in responding to questions asked by his clients. He answered their questions or in other ways responded respectfully from his own frame. Spontaneous responses from the therapist's frame are, by definition, unsolicited by the client.

3. A mean of over 10 or 12% of therapist-frame responses (other than those in response to clients' questions) probably casts doubt on the therapist's consistency in being client-centered.

attitudes and values. In accord with this expressive character of the therapy, the type of responses employed by the therapist and the therapist's manner with the client are primarily determined by generic, theoretically grounded intentions. These generic intentions – acceptantly, accurately, empathically to understand – apply to all clients.

Client-centered responses are determined, as well, by characteristics of the client as they are experienced uniquely in the relationship. Thus, the content of responses (both information and affective features), the therapist's frequency of response, rate of response, complexity of the structure of responses, vocabulary level, etc. are adjusted to the particular client. These adjustments are made on the grounds that (a) the therapist is attempting to understand the client and (b) when the therapist responds, the client must be given an opportunity to understand the therapist. Attunement to the client's language and his cognitive-affective complexity in the relationship also protects the client's sense of safety and comfort in the relationship. Adjustments to the client, however, are not made on the basis of classificatory considerations about the client such as diagnoses.

### The role of the nondirective attitude

A nondirective attitude (Raskin, 1947/2005) guides and constrains the client-centered therapist (Brodley, 1997/2011). It is intrinsic to the totality of congruence, unconditional positive regard and empathic understanding. This attitude shapes and molds essentially all of the therapist's behavior and responses with clients. The theoretical basis for the nondirective attitude rests in implications of the actualizing tendency construct.

The actualizing tendency – the client-centered basic assumption, or axiom – implies a fundamental respect for, and trust in persons' capacities for socially constructive self-determination. It is a tendency that has its most constructive effects under favorable circumstances (Bozarth & Brodley, 1991/2008; Brodley, 1998c/2000, 1999a/2011). The actualization tendency is believed to promote the development, social capabilities and healing of persons most powerfully when they are exposed to and experience empathic understanding and especially when they experience acceptance (Bozarth, 1996, 1998). The nondirective attitude is cultivated and maintained by therapists because of the primacy of their respect for, and trust in, the client as they provide the therapeutic conditions. The idea of the actualizing tendency concept tends to motivate the therapist to place a high value on protecting the client's sense of self and protecting the client's autonomy and self-determination. The therapist respects the client as the primary director – the *architect* (Raskin, 1988) – of the therapy process. The principle of trusting the client as the best expert about himself overrides the therapist's inclination to communicate his or her *wisdom* in all but very rare situations. Trust in the client includes willingness to accommodate to the client's wishes within the therapist's personal and ethical limitations. These accommodations will be discussed later in the paper. There is a caveat concerning them however, which is relevant to understanding the nondirective attitude.

Concretely, in specific instances, the client's wishes or inclinations *may or may not* promote the best direction of the moment for him. Nevertheless, the client is treated as the best expert about himself. Even if that assumption may be revealed to not be valid in the particular case, the client-centered approach still emphasizes the therapeutic wisdom and potency of the client. An important factor in this issue of following the client's direction is that the approach is conceptualized in terms of process. The client tries something, then observes and feels the consequences of it. He then tries something else, or makes corrections. If the client's original direction is unproductive or unsatisfying, the therapist's acceptance, nondirectiveness, and empathy promote the client's discovery of this outcome and promote self-corrective processes.

Therapists who maintain an acceptant and empathic attitude in relation to their clients and who seldom comment, interpret or otherwise intervene from their own frame (unless that is requested by the client) tend to promote a safe and consistent climate. This climate stimulates the client's trust in the therapist and in his or her self. Consistent empathic following promotes clients' clear discrimination of the rare occasions when the therapist is representing his or her own frame of reference. Clear discrimination permits the client to evaluate his or her own responses in relation to the therapist. This facilitates clients' realistic assignment of responsibility to their own psychological characteristics.

### Acceptant empathic understanding

The empathic understanding attitude together with acceptance and congruence are the core therapist attitudinal conditions in client-centered work. Empathic understanding in practice involves a subjective process of close following of the client's explications, disclosures and immediate feelings with the intention to understand from the client's perspective. This subjective, close following is imbued with acceptance and responsiveness towards the client as well as the effort to understand and *be present*.[4]

---

4. Presence refers to the totality or amalgam of the therapist's personal features and behaviors, along with their emotional/affective qualities, that are perceptible to the client. Presence as a personal self in client-centered therapy is thought to be crucial for therapeutic efficacy (Brodley, 1999b; Rogers, 1980). [Also published in Brodley (2000a/2011). See also (a different version) Brodley, 2003]

The most frequent pattern of interaction in client-centered work is the "empathic interaction response process" (Temaner, 1977/2011). This interaction process expresses the therapist's acceptant empathic attitude very well with most self-expressing, narrating clients. It fosters a self-directed process of introspection and personal exploration in clients. The therapist's role of communicating her empathic attitude in the process is embodied in acceptant, empathic understanding responses and other following responses.

The empathic understanding form of response is prevalent in client-centered therapy work. It is probably an inevitable form of response given the theory. Nevertheless, it is not required.[5] Empathic responses express the therapeutic attitudes and communicate effectively with most self-exploring clients. But in principle it is not a necessary form of communication in the therapy. Empathic responses are prevalent therapist utterances in client-centered work because they express the empathic understanding attitude, concomitantly express unconditional positive regard, and are nondirective in their intent. Clients can easily understand them, and they can be an authentic expression of the therapist's attitudes towards clients. They are also responsive to the client's intention and drive to disclose, express and explicate self.

Other forms of response, however, may express the empathic attitude (Rogers, 1957). There are examples in Rogers' therapy transcripts of responses that are not empathic understanding responses, but which nevertheless have empathic intent. In one of his interviews, the client, Jim, has been silent for over two minutes. Then Jim yawns and Rogers (1967) makes an empathic guess, saying, "Sounds discouraged or tired" (p. 404). A little later in the same interview, after a silence of 48 seconds, Rogers makes another empathic guess followed by an empathic question for clarification. Rogers says, "Just kind of feel sunk way down deep in these lousy, lousy feelings, Jim? – Is that something like it?" (p. 404).

Another example of a therapist-frame response from Rogers' own interviews occurs when his client begins to manifest abrupt involuntary jerking motions of her body. Rogers asks a leading question – one that he intends to permit him further empathic understanding, but a rare type of response for

---

5. Client-centered work with self-expressive, narrating clients involves a dominance of empathic understanding responses – usually 90% to 100% apart from responses to questions. Certain clients do not provide communications to therapists that permit informed empathic responses. Clients who appear to be out of contact, or those who are completely silent, or young children in play therapy often require empathic guesses. These responses are based on the therapist's observations of the environment or situation, previous understandings shared by the client, or the client's nonverbal behavior. Work employing empathic guesses may be no less client-centered than more typical empathic following work, depending upon the circumstances.

him. Rogers says, "Can you say what those jerks mean to you?" [Brodley & Lietaer, 2006, Vol. 17, Lydia, 1st Interview, p. 95].*

Another example of an empathic communication that is not an empathic understanding response occurs in Rogers' interview with Philip. Philip remarks concerning his own courage, "And it felt good at the moment, and I feel proud of that." Rogers' response is an observational comment. Rogers says, "I can see it in your face" [Brodley & Lietaer, 2006, Vol. 13, Philip Interview, p. 25]. Although it represents the therapist's frame, it has empathic intent and expresses the therapist's effort to closely follow the client's experiences.

Rogers (1986a) discussed his nondirective reason for uttering empathic responses. He explained that empathic responses are aimed to check his accuracy in understanding the client. For Rogers, the client is the expert about the therapist's accuracy in understanding. Thus, the therapist needs to let the client know his inner understanding in order to get feedback from the client. I have proposed five nondirective criteria for making empathic responses (see Temaner, 1982). Three of them are checking criteria. They are deduced from the basic theory of therapy (Rogers, 1956, 1957, 1959) and from introspection about my personal therapy behavior. Reasons the client-centered therapist might respond from his or her own frame of reference, however, do not stem as directly from the theory.

When the therapist's standard behavior involves a mixture of empathic understanding and interpretive, didactic, guiding or self-disclosing responses, there are a multitude of counter-therapeutic meanings and effects this behavior may have for clients. Clients often do not consciously identify the problems affecting them that arise from frequent instances of therapist-frame responses. The problematic impacts are submerged in the client's occupation with understanding the therapist's intentions or meanings or submerged in self-protective strategies. Other confused or self-protective counter-therapeutic effects may involve clients' self-denial or their surrender to the therapist's power.

Basic client-centered therapy theory – provision of unconditional positive regard and empathic understanding by a congruent therapist – combined with the therapist's salient nondirective attitude reveals no obvious reasons for therapist-frame communications. Rogers' (1957) discussion of his theory, however, suggests some reasons for such responses.

---

* Editors' note: In the course of many years, Barbara transcribed and supervised others in transcribing Rogers' therapy and demonstration sessions. In this paper she refers to transcripts that were in the process of being "polished" through multiple listenings to the tapes. It is uncertain at which point of evolution she quoted from the various transcripts. The transcript work culminated in a joint effort with Germain Lietaer resulting in a journal article (Lietaer & Brodley, 2003) and an informal email publication (Brodley & Lietaer, 2006).

## Guidance from Rogers concerning therapist-frame responses

Recordings and transcripts of Rogers' therapy work reveal that he usually expressed only a very small percentage of responses (such as comments, agreements, leading questions, explanations, interpretations or self-disclosures) from his own frame of reference (Brody, 1991; Brodley, 1994/2011; Merry, 1996). In some interviews there are no such responses at all. The transcripts and tapes of therapy sessions in themselves, of course, do not reveal what criteria or reasons are at work in Rogers' mind when he does make therapist-frame responses.

In his discussion of congruence in therapy, Rogers (1957) gives a lead to two reasons the therapist might respond to a client from the therapist's frame. He describes congruence as a state of "integration and wholeness" (p. 93). He defines an integrated state in terms of an accurate relation between experience and symbolization, or an accurate relation between experience and the self. He writes:

> [Congruence] means that within the relationship he is freely and deeply himself, with his actual experience accurately represented by his awareness of himself … It would take us too far afield to consider the puzzling matter as to the degree to which the therapist overtly communicates this reality [referring to counter-therapeutic feelings] in himself. Certainly the aim is not for the therapist to express or talk out his own feelings, but primarily that he should not be deceiving the client as to himself. At times he may need to talk out some of his own feelings (either to the client or to a colleague or supervisor) if they are standing in the way of the two following conditions [referring to unconditional positive regard and empathic understanding]. (pp. 97–98)

These reasons pertain when the therapist is not being empathic or the therapist is not experiencing acceptance, and this situation persists. The reasons for responding from the therapist's frame, and disclosing nontherapeutic experiences, are (a) in order that the therapist will not be deceiving the client and/or (b) to create a process, by talking out her feelings, that changes the therapist's nonacceptance or nonempathy to acceptance and empathy.

Rogers (1957) also referred to a third reason the therapist might make responses from his or her own frame:

> … the techniques of the various therapies are relatively unimportant except to the extent that they serve as channels for fulfilling one of the conditions … the theory I have presented would see no essential value to therapy of such techniques as interpretation of personality dynamics,

> free association, analysis of dreams, analysis of the transference ... these techniques, however, may be given in a way which communicates the essential conditions which have been formulated. (pp. 102–103)

Rogers' point is that certain responses from the therapist's frame of reference, "given in a way" that communicates the conditions, may contribute to the client's experience of the therapist's congruence, unconditional positive regard and empathic understanding. Rogers does not discuss the way this might be done. Most techniques from other therapies express purposes that are inconsistent with client-centered attitudes. He does not give examples to help us. Difficult as it may be in practice, Rogers' point *does* suggest a potential rationale for responses from the therapist-frame. They may contribute to the client's perceptions of the therapist as authentically providing acceptant empathy.

Rogers had stated the therapist might tell his client about *persistent* feelings that contradict the therapeutic attitudes. He reiterated this criterion for therapist-frame responses in his introduction to his interview with Gloria [Brodley & Lietaer, 2006, Vol. 12, Gloria, Introduction, p. 3]. Late in his life, Rogers revealed he had made some change in this earlier conservative position on this reason for self-disclosure. Rogers (Baldwin, 1987/2004) referred to an example from his work with a schizophrenic client in which he spoke directly to the client of his caring feelings. His example introduced a statement that contributes to the present discussion.

> I am inclined to think that in my writing perhaps I have stressed too much the three basic conditions (congruence, unconditional positive regard and empathic understanding). Perhaps it is something around the edges of those conditions that is really the most important element of therapy – when my self is very clearly, obviously present. (p. 45)

Rogers added:

> When I am with a client, I like to be aware of my feelings, and if there are feelings which run contrary to the conditions of therapy and occur persistently, *then I am sure I want to express them* [italics added]. (p. 46)

Rogers was not conducting therapy on a regular basis at the time he made these statements during his interview with Baldwin. His public demonstrations, during the final ten years or so of his life, that were intended to illustrate his personal version of client-centered therapy, included very few self-disclosures (Brody, 1991; Bradburn, 1996). It seems reasonable to infer from his therapy behavior that Rogers was not advocating a manner of conducting individual client-centered therapy in which presence is defined in terms of self-disclosures. Nor was he advocating self-disclosure as a frequent form of response although he was giving importance to *presence* (Brodley, 2000a/2011). His statement above does not provide a rationale for the self-disclosure type of response from the therapist's frame. It does suggest an effect of self-disclosure. Such responses may communicate the therapist's presence to the client.

ISSUES CONCERNING THERAPIST-FRAME RESPONSES

There are many possible kinds of therapist-frame responses. They include responses about the therapy, comments about something else other than the client, or comments about the client. They may be suggestions, explanations, interpretations, agreements and disagreements, instructions, descriptions, information, emotional exclamations, leading questions or self-disclosures. The reasons the client-centered therapist may have for expressing any of these kinds of response should conform to the general theory as much as possible and certainly should not contradict the basic principles of the approach. In other words, the therapist trusts the client's drive to realize his nature as best he can and trusts that the client has capacities that are adequate for realization and healing. Consequently, a very unlikely reason for a response from the therapist's frame is that the therapist believes it would be for the client's good. Client-centered therapists do not assume authority over their clients' experiences or well-being. Client-centered therapists do deliberately avoid behavior that might be damaging to clients' self-regard. At the same time, they eschew patronizing behavior that assumes what is best for the client.

## Normal inconsistency in practice

Responses from the therapist-frame risk directive impact on the client regardless of the therapist's nondirective intentions. Sometimes, as well, the therapist does experience and express a momentary directive intent. This may be surprising, given the strong nondirective principle in the theory. The efficacy of Rogers' theory (1957, 1959), however, does not depend upon an absolute therapist consistency in any of the therapist's attitudes. Rogers' (1957) wrote:

> Only condition 1 [psychological contact between therapist and client] is dichotomous (it either is present or is not) and the remaining five occur in varying degree, each on its continuum ... If all six conditions are present, then the greater degree to which conditions 2 to 6 exist, the more marked will be the constructive personality change in the client. (p. 100)

Rogers' theory does not involve the expectation that it is possible to maintain the therapeutic attitudes with absolute consistency. The therapist wants and *tries* to constantly experience the attitudes in relation to clients. The more consistently they are experienced (and the more they are perceived by the client), the more effective the therapy. The distinctly client-centered therapeutic relationship, however, does not suddenly disappear if the therapist briefly loses congruence, acceptance or the empathic attitude.

The client's sense of safety and freedom *may* be unaffected, or only momentarily affected by minor inconsistencies in the therapist's attitudes. Client-centered therapy's efficacy depends upon the client's perception of the therapeutic attitudes. A brief lapse in the therapist's inner experience of the therapeutic attitudes may not be perceived at all by a client, especially not by clients who are concentrating intently on their own thoughts and feelings.

Paradoxically, over-consistency in the manner the attitudes are implemented may be detrimental to the relationship. Consistency and over-consistency in this context are perceptions, not objective facts. Absolutely consistent empathic responding that closely follows the client may not result in the perception of over-consistency. It is likely to be perceived, however, if the therapist is reluctant to address questions or engage in minimal social interactions. The perception also may result from empathic responses that are cognitively accurate but emotionally inadequate. It may be the consequence of a lack in the therapist's spontaneity and therapeutic presence. Consistent but shallow empathic understandings also may stimulate the client's perception of over-consistency. He may perceive the therapist as expressing a false self. Over-consistency may be perceived as a disguise that covers nonacceptance.

In rapport with Rogers' (1980, 1986b; Baldwin, 1987/2004) late-in-life writings and talks, Raskin (1988) has asserted that the client-centered therapist may respond occasionally from his or her own frame of reference in various ways. Raskin's view is that doing so is an expression of a desirable therapist freedom. That it is valid in client-centered work as long as such communications are not systematic.

Empathic understanding is literally contradicted when the therapist represents her frame of reference. Limited literal contradiction of empathic understanding, however, may not undermine the therapeutic relationship especially if the therapist-frame remarks have empathic content. An occasional moment of therapist self-representation need not be experienced as a contradiction to the therapist's basic subjective context – intent to maintain the *therapeutic attitudes.*

It should be obvious, given the definition of congruence; it is not contradicted when the therapist communicates from his or her own frame of reference, as long as the therapist remains integrated and whole. Although, in effective therapy, they usually function together as a totality, congruence is not inextricably tied to acceptance or empathic understanding. Thus the therapist may remain congruent when experiencing the loss of acceptance or empathy.

The therapist's experience of acceptance of the client also need not waver when he or she expresses therapist-frame communications. There are, however, many more opportunities for clients to perceive or misinterpret therapists' remarks as implying nonacceptance when they communicate from their own frame. Whatever the momentary deviation from acceptant empathy, clients are most likely to continue to continuously perceive the therapeutic attitudes if therapists immediately resume attention to clients' phenomenology.

Another normal contradiction, infrequent as it is in good client-centered work, occurs when the therapist's remarks have a rare momentary directive intention. The therapist thinks the client needs, for his therapeutic good, to hear something from the therapist. Or the therapist has the desire to influence the client toward some particular idea, action or value. Or the therapist wants to change the manner in which the client is engaged in the relationship. An occasional, albeit rare, moment of directive intention need not undermine the client's experience of the nondirective attitude as a constant in the relationship. This assumes the directivity is not systematic and not frequent. This means that it is only a momentary directive intention, and the therapist experiences his or her investment in the directive intention as tentative. Or it may be only a brief impulsive reaction, or there are special circumstances. For example, the therapist urges the client to make an appointment with a neurologist to medically evaluate sudden symptoms of severe headache.

Human motivations, states and attitudes are inherently complex and full of contradictory feelings and experiences. Although therapeutic work is disciplined, it must also be spontaneous. Thus inherent experiential complexity may occasionally result in impulsive reactions within the disciplined context. Momentary fluctuations in the three therapeutic and the nondirective attitudes need not contradict the therapist's commitment to the attitudes. Nor do fluctuations necessarily undermine the client's experience of them. Therapeutic work is a process. In assessing meaningful therapeutic consistency, we look at sequences of interaction, not just single acts. On the other hand, some clients may feel misunderstood, unaccepted or betrayed by even momentary directive communications.

### Counter-therapeutic consequences of therapist-frame responses
There are many possible counter-therapeutic consequences of therapist-frame statements to clients. Time is taken from clients' use of the limited therapy time. Clients may become distracted from their own focus and introspective

process. Clients may feel they are being evaluated or judged. They may lose their sense of self-determination and empowerment in the therapy process. In theoretical terms, a client's *locus of evaluation* (Rogers, 1959) may be influenced away from within himself towards the therapist. Clients may become confused or defensive about the therapist's intentions, perceiving the therapist as having his own agenda for them. In addition, comments from the therapist's frame are inherently more difficult for clients to understand than empathic understanding responses.

Many forms of *process disruption* (Diss, 1996) may result from therapist-frame communications. These may occur either when the therapist does not have directive intentions or when her responses express directive attitudes. Even when they are infrequent and in the context of highly consistent empathic understanding they may be disturbing to some clients. The general impact of any of these effects is to jeopardize clients' self-determination and their sense of safety and freedom in the relationship. These negative effects can happen along with appealing client reactions, such as expressions of appreciation for the therapist's helpful intentions or thanks for the help of specific interjections.

The fact that a client expresses liking for a therapist's response does not guarantee it was harmless to the client. A broader perspective about what may be damaging to clients, in general, should qualify the therapist's personal reception to clients' praise. Such perspective may also protect the therapist from false ideas about what is a good thing to do with clients. Therapists need to distinguish (a) their respect for and accommodation to the particular client's wants or directions from (b) generic therapeutic instructions.

After sessions, therapists are wise to reflect upon their work during the session. Introspection should be even more conscientious when the therapist has made responses from his or her own frame of reference. Whether there are observable detrimental effects or not, the therapist should question herself as to whether her comments to clients justify the risks – some of which may not be easy to detect.

### Guidelines for responses from the therapist's frame of reference
There are three particular guidelines to keep in mind in a discussion of reasons client-centered therapists may make therapist-frame responses. First, reasons given for therapist-frame responses should not contradict the idea that the client knows or has the potentiality to know what is best for him- or herself. Unlike most other therapies, the reasons for therapists' responses, including therapist-frame responses, are not based on a belief that the therapist knows what is best for the client. There is a pervasive attitude of humility towards the client that is the context for the client-centered therapist's totality of subjective attitudes.

Second, responses volunteered from the therapist's frame of reference should be rare. The exception is in responding to clients' questions. These responses may be relatively frequent because their frequency largely depends upon the client. The therapist nevertheless maintains a mental set of restraint in respect to voluntary and elicited explicit therapist-frame utterances. Frequent responses, other than the various forms of acceptant empathic understanding, undermine the distinctive therapeutic processes within the client in client-centered work. Consistent empathic following fosters clients' self-determination and autonomy.

Third, therapist-frame responses are ideally never systematic. They should not be based on paternalistic, directive, uplifting, religious, conventional or other systematic attitudes that contradict client-centered theory and attitudes. This subjective context of client-centered practice is a motivation to sustain the therapeutic attitudes regardless of the demands being placed on the therapist and regardless of momentary fluctuations in the therapist's inner experiences or impulses.

THE REASONS

There are a number of reasons client-centered therapists may speak to their clients from their own frame of reference. Keep in mind that these reasons do not necessarily justify the behavior in any particular instance. Protection of the client's self-determination, among other values, may outweigh these reasons.

*1. Arrangements and terms of the therapy*
The most obvious reason for a therapist to represent his or her own frame of reference to clients is in order to clarify the terms of the therapy. This may be about the fee, the time, the length of sessions, or about the extent and limits of the therapist's services. The basic professional structure of therapy – a client choosing to receive such services – requires clear terms concerning mutual expectations, at least to the extent circumstances permit such clarity.

In the context of explanations about the terms of the therapy the client-centered therapist intends to be as empathically responsive to the client as in the other contexts of the therapy. The therapist, for example, may pause after each statement and wait for, or ask for, the client's reactions, and empathically follow, before moving forward with the next point. The consistent therapist tries to maintain the basic attitudes of respect towards and trust in clients. These attitudes show up in, and influence, all aspects of interaction with clients. While discussing arrangements or terms, the therapist remains oriented to the client with the therapeutic attitudes.

## 2. Addressing questions and requests

The most basic reason for a client-centered therapist to speak from his or her frame of reference is to answer, or in some other way directly address, a client's question or request. Accommodation to a client's question or request may involve answers, explanations, instructions, descriptions or questions addressed to the client as well as empathic responses.

An implication of the actualizing tendency axiom, applied to psychotherapy, involves responsiveness to clients. The axiom logically leads to the fundamental client-centered value of respect for the client as self-determining and the value of trust in the client's self-healing and self-corrective capabilities – powers most fully realized under favorable psychological and physical conditions. These values, in turn, lead to respect for the client's expression of desire for some kind of therapist-frame communication.[6]

Client questions or requests require the therapist's respectful responsiveness. This is often through some form of straightforward and non-evaluative response to this kind of client direction – often an answer or accommodation (Brodley, 1997/2011). Whatever their kind, responses to client's questions and requests also involve empathic following responses. In addition to expressing the empathic attitude in this context, empathic responses help the therapist be certain of understanding what the client wants. They also help to understand the client's reactions to answers or other accommodations.

Therapists, of course, may always decline to literally answer or accommodate the client because of personal feelings, needs or standards, or because they do not have the required expertise.

A client's question or request may be specific to the moment (e.g., what did that look mean?) or it may be a general instruction to the therapist (e.g., please tell me any time, if you have suggestions). It may seek personal information (e.g., how old is the therapist?) or other information (e.g., what different kinds of professionals do psychotherapy?). A question or request may be about the client (e.g., his diagnosis). It may be about what the client should do (e.g., should I take the medication?), about how to do something (e.g., how can I make myself relax before I go to sleep?), about psychological explanations or interpretations of behavior (e.g., why do people get angry when their feelings are hurt?). It may be about the therapy (e.g., what is the theory of this therapy?), and so forth.

---

6. There may be, of course, situations when the therapist chooses to not answer a client's question or not accommodate to a request. Refusals to honor the client's direction in these ways are not based on judgments of what is good or bad for the client except in special circumstances, such as occasionally with children. The therapist's reasons for refusal tend to be personal preferences or his or her limitations. The therapist always has the right to refuse to answer a question or not cooperate with a client's special wishes.

Addressing clients' questions and requests is a complex experience and demands much of the therapist. It optimally requires that the therapist is congruent, intellectually clear and that he or she emotionally accepts his or her own limits. It also requires the therapist to be able to maintain the therapeutic attitudes of acceptance and empathic understanding while being responsive and accommodating to the client.

The therapist's response to a question or request may be a direct answer or it may be one of many other possible responses depending upon the question and upon the therapist's capabilities and personal characteristics. Whatever the factors that are involved in the specifics of responsiveness, the basis for answering questions and attempting to accommodate clients' requests remains embedded in the therapist's nondirective attitude. While responding to questions or requests, the therapist avoids attachment to his or her ideas. The therapist strives to avoid developing expectations about how the client should respond. It is necessary to maintain respect for, and trust in, the client as self-determining of the therapy and in respect to personal choices.

## 3. Possibility of a question

The client's narrative or nonverbal behavior may suggest to the therapist that the client desires to ask a question. For example, the client looks up several times expectantly at the therapist. Or he remarks that he'd really like someone to tell him what to do in his situation. Rather than wait for the client to explicitly ask a question or make a request, the therapist chooses to inquire about the client's wishes. This may lead to further responses based on the client's clarification of what he feels he wants at that point in the interaction.

Regularly or rigidly waiting until a client explicitly voices a question may suggest to the client that the therapist is unwilling to answer questions. Choosing to inquire instead of waiting expresses the therapist's desire to promote the client's freedom and spontaneity in the relationship. It expresses the therapist's commitment to the client as leader. It expresses responsiveness to the client.

Some clients feel inhibited about asking questions or requests. The literature and media of our therapy-culture may have given the impression that the client must solve problems on his own. That he should not ask questions of his therapist. Or the client may have felt punished by a previous therapist when asking a question. Interpreting clients' questions, or challenging their motivations for asking them, frequently results in clients feeling punished or criticized. The client-centered therapist does not wish to reinforce such inhibiting experiences. Instead, she or he wishes to communicate respect and to support the client's freedom of self-expression and self-determination.

## 4. Empathic observations

The therapist may vocalize perceptions of aspects of the client's communication or emotional expression. These therapist-frame responses are similar to empathic responses because they attend to the client's inner world and are also tentative. As therapist-frame responses about the client, however, they may bring to the client the sense of the therapist as an observer. To the extent they have this effect, they break the usual experience of understanding that is characteristic of the empathic process. Although not intended to do so, they may also have a directive impact.

Empathic understanding is an attitude that involves the therapist's intention to understand a client's *intended* meanings and feelings, although the client may not be aware of his or her intentions until after the therapist's checking response. The client's intended communication may not be fully explicit, consequently empathic responses often involve inference. The therapist's intention, expressed in empathic responses, is to understand what the client is intending to express, especially personal meanings and feelings, whether they are explicit or not. An example of an empathic response interaction:

Client: I go over it and over it but I can't find a way.

Therapist: So much fruitless effort feels very discouraging.

Client: Very discouraging.

The client had not said she is discouraged although she subsequently verifies it. The emotion in her words had been ambiguous. She could have been feeling frustration, fatigue or annoyance instead of discouragement. The basis for the element of "discouraging" in the response may be something in the client's tone or some element in the client's immediately preceding remarks. The crucial factor is that the therapist is intending only to understand the client's intended message. The therapist is not intending to point out or emphasize feelings. The therapist may be correct or incorrect about the inferred element. Whether the client confirms the therapist's understanding or not, the therapist has intended to express a tentative understanding of the client's *intended* communication. She or he has no directive intention when responding.

Empathically relevant therapist-frame comments run the risk that the client will perceive them as intending to expand the client's awareness, or they may come across as telling the client something about herself. In either case they risk being perceived as the therapist assuming a posture of expert about the client's experience. The client's agreement to the therapist's comment is not necessarily proof that the element was part of the client's intended communication. The therapist may have succeeded in enlarging the client's awareness, whether or not that effect was intended. This may actually be beneficial to the client in the particular instance. However, frequent instances may produce a directive therapeutic process and usurp control of the therapy from the client.

In the first moments of the interview with Gloria (Shostrum, 1965; [Brodley & Lietaer, 2006]), Rogers responds with an empathically intended observational comment.

Gloria: Right now I'm nervous but I feel more comfortable the way you are talking in a low voice and I don't feel like you'll be so harsh with me.

Rogers: I hear the tremor in your voice …

[Brodley & Lietaer, 2006, Vol. 12, Gloria Interview, p. 5]

The response conveys a strong empathic element although tells of Rogers' perception about the client. Later in the same interview, in response to Gloria's assertion that she wants to be "so perfect," Rogers makes another, less empathic therapist-frame observation.

Rogers: Or, I guess I hear it a little differently – that what you want is to *seem* perfect.

[p. 8]

Gloria does not confirm this response. The first type of therapist-frame comment, illustrated by Rogers in response to Gloria, is the most benign type. If infrequent, and if they are very close to what the client intended to communicate, they may blend into empathic process such that clients perceive them as empathic understanding responses, not as observations. An observation such as the one in the second example, that emphasizes the therapist's frame of reference and opposes the client's assertion about self, risks jeopardizing the client's sense of safety in the relationship.

Frequent therapist-frame observational comments stimulate a different relationship with the client. This difference results from the *likely* impression on the client that the therapist is functioning as an observer of the client. A therapist who *observes* and who communicates an observing attitude creates a less intimate and less empowering climate. He or she risks being experienced as emotionally distant or as asserting authority over the client's experience.

Observational responses risk directing the interaction although the client may not be fully aware of the directivity. Nevertheless, they are likely to diminish the client's sense of potency and position in the relationship. Occasional empathically relevant therapist-frame observational comments, however, may contribute to the client's experience of his therapist's empathy and not stimulate a sense of being objectified or directed.

### 5. Corrections for loss of acceptance or loss of empathy or incongruence

The therapist does not intend nor wish to deceive her client. There may be instances, however, when her behavior does not expose experiences that are inconsistent with the therapeutic attitudes. Becoming distracted, or a judgmental reaction to something the client says, or to the client's manner, or a disruption in the therapist's congruence, may be only momentary reactions. The therapist may not explicitly disclose these experiences to the client because they seem unimportant to the therapist. Or the therapist may not disclose them because revealing them would take up the client's focus and time, or distract the therapist from empathic engagement. Or disclosure might risk a disturbance in the relationship that the therapist does not feel confident he can handle therapeutically.

If inconsistencies in attitude persist, however, the therapist may feel insincere or inauthentic and fear the inconsistencies may be obvious. Obviously, persistent inconsistencies, more than momentary slips, are likely to become apparent to the client. The therapist's behavior may come across to the client at least as ambiguous. Consequently, it may undermine the client's focus on his narrative or it may jeopardize the client's sense of safety in the relationship. Signs of disturbance in the client's attention or in the client's feelings, in the context of deviations in the therapist's attitude, are strong reasons for the therapist to inquire whether the client feels something is wrong. The subsequent interaction may lead the therapist to address the difficulty he or she is experiencing in maintaining the therapeutic attitudes.

Assuming the client does not ask the therapist what is going on, and there is no sign that the client is aware of the therapist's deviation, the therapist may decide to discuss the problem with a supervisor or colleague. Alternatively, the therapist may choose to disclose his or her actual experience to the client.

There are two reasons the therapist might choose to disclose a judgmental reaction or disclose a loss of empathic understanding to the client or reveal incongruence. First, the therapist cannot be sure the client does not detect the deviation, even when there is no sign the client is aware of a problem. The therapist wishes to remain entirely trustworthy to the client and not deceive or confuse about his or her attitudes at any time. This appears to have been Rogers' own view late in his life revealed in a comment to Baldwin (1987/2004).

> When I am with a client, I like to be aware of my feelings, and if there are feelings which run contrary to the conditions of therapy and occur persistently, then I am sure I want to express them. (p. 46)

A second reason for a self-disclosure when the therapist has deviated from the therapeutic attitudes is *to talk out the problem* with the client. The hope is that doing so will restore the therapist's experience of the therapeutic attitudes. If the problem has been one of the therapist being distracted from the client, the interaction acknowledging the distraction may immediately restore the therapist's empathy. If the problem has been a judgmental reaction – a loss of acceptance – concerning some aspect of the client or his communication, the interaction may lead to new understandings and dispel the judgment. Or, the therapist's confession and the subsequent interaction may give the client perspective on the therapist's feelings. Perspective on the therapist's judgments or distractions may allow the client to better trust the therapist's authenticity. At the same time, of course, it may jeopardize the client's sense of safety in the relationship.

The therapist's manner of self-disclosure to correct for slips in the experience of the therapeutic attitudes makes a great difference for its impact on clients. This is true especially if the disclosure involves a disagreement with the client or feelings of disapproval concerning something about the client. The therapist's approach to the issue is crucial. Rogers' corollary to congruence (1961a) offers partial guidance concerning the manner of communication. Self-disclosure should be congruent communication. He proposes that congruent communications should be only expressed as personal perceptions, not assertions of fact. (See the discussion in Brodley, 1998b/2011.) The therapist's sensitive empathic understanding of all of the client's reactions to the disclosure helps to prevent serious disturbance in the relationship.

### 6. Insights and ideas

Client-centered therapists occasionally may speak from their own frame of reference when they have an insight or idea that fits into what the client is exploring or trying to understand about his experience. This is least threatening to the client's autonomy and self-determination when the client has earlier mentioned he wants to hear the therapist's perspectives from time to time. The contents of the particular moment appear to fit the client's expressed interest in hearing the therapist's ideas or perspectives. Because the client's wishes at the moment are unclear, it is wise to ask the client if this is a time when he would be interested in the therapist's thoughts. This kind of action shifts the control back to the client even as the therapist has intervened and temporarily usurped control.

Or, the therapist may *feel inspired* to say something from his or her own frame, imagining it might be helpful to the client. In this case there has been no prior request from the client for such material. The therapist does not know at all whether or not the client would wish to hear from the therapist's frame. The therapist might ameliorate the directive impact of the intervention by acknowledging she would like to share her idea or perspective. She might ask if the client wishes to hear what the therapist is thinking. These steps of inquiry temper the impact of impulsive directivity. They tend to shift control back to the client. Consequently, the client is more likely to continue to feel self-determining in the therapy process. Therapists should not delude themselves that there is no detrimental effect on the therapy because the client expressed interest in, or made constructive use of, therapist-frame comments.

A particular problem in the two situations has to do with whether the client can understand the therapist. The therapist's remarks should be succinct. It is helpful to pause to allow the client to ask a question or make his own remarks, as the therapist unfolds the idea. If there are explanations or interpretations underpinning the idea whose source is not obvious, the therapist should spell out that data and the logical steps leading to the idea. In being clear about the underpinnings of ideas, therapists are sharing power with the client even while introducing their own material.

## 7. Emotionally compelling circumstances

Spontaneous therapist-frame responses may emerge from the therapist's feelings and emotions. The therapist expresses them without having prior rationalization for them, and without the intention to appear authentic or make any other impression on the client. They are impulsively emitted.

One category of spontaneous therapist-frame emotional response is that of emotional utterances that are reactions to emotionally compelling circumstances reported by the client. Some events have relatively compelling social meaning which leads to common socially patterned emotional responses. For example, the therapist says: "Oh, I'm so sorry!" when told that the client's child has been hurt in an accident. This kind of response reveals that the therapist is engaged in the relationship in a personal manner. That she is emotionally present and responsive to basic human situations.

Such responses have hazards. An emotional reaction almost always implies a value and it might well be that the particular client's feelings or values are quite different than those implied by the therapist's emotional reaction. The therapist reacts with "Oh, no!" to the information that the client's brother was beaten up. It turns out that the client feels his brother deserved the punishment. The therapist's emotional utterance may immediately place the client at odds with the therapist or stimulate the client to feel the therapist may judge him critically.

## 8. Prior information

Other special circumstances leading to spontaneous emotional responses from the therapist's frame are ones which are based on something the client previously has said is specifically important to him in a positive or negative way. For example, the client reports that he has finally telephoned a girl to whom he is attracted. This occurs in the context of having spoken at length in the past about being unable to take that initiative. The therapist spontaneously responds "great!" The hazards are less in this category, because the client has previously shared the feelings and value. On the other hand the client's feelings may have changed and the therapist's reaction may contradict the client's present *emotional direction*.

## 9. Spontaneous agreements

Another form of spontaneous response is an agreement with the client based on compelling or very common knowledge. For example, the therapist says "that's true" when the client says it is too late to change the legal contract he has signed. Rogers' demonstration interview with Peterann includes an agreement response. The client wants to have a baby after losing her twins.

C1: I suppose all I can do is keep working at it.

T1: Mhm, hm.

C2: 'Course then there's a biological time clock. And so not everything is in my corner.

T2: That's right.

[See Brodley & Lietaer, 2006, Vol. 16, Peterann, Interview, pp. 66–67]

These common knowledge type agreements are usually benign – their grounds are obvious to clients.

## 10. Evaluative reactions

Another form of spontaneous response from the therapist's frame may be a comment that voices an opinion, judgment or evaluation. The risk of harm to the therapy relation is somewhat higher in this case, than those described above. Expressions of opinion, or approval etc., may damage the safety of the therapy relation by raising the specter of evaluations about the client. Among evaluative possibilities, evaluative reactions to something or someone other than the client are least likely to damage the therapy relationship although they too involve the risk. For example, the therapist remarks "How rude!" in response to a client's description of how someone at the client's workplace acted towards another person. Although intended sympathetically, the client may feel he has done worse on other occasions and feel the therapist would disapprove of him if she knew.

Whether they are spontaneous or considered, emotional reactions, opinions, judgments or evaluative remarks all entail risks to clients' sense of safety with their therapists. In addition to breaking the empathic process of interaction, they tend to raise or reinforce the client's expectations that the therapist is evaluative, especially that the therapist may be judgmental about the client. This impact occurs even if the particular remarks are not about the client. Frequent evaluative remarks are detrimental to the client's perception of the therapeutic conditions.

Occasional spontaneous responses are natural to client-centered work as a consequence of the therapist's relaxed and responsive presence. They are also naturally limited in frequency because of the strong influence of the therapist's nondirective attitude and the therapist's discipline in maintaining the therapeutic attitudes. Spontaneous therapist-frame responses may have a good impact on the client's sense that the therapist is personally present. They take place, nevertheless, in the context of and are qualified by the therapist's nondirective attitude, commitment to unconditional positive regard and to empathic understanding. These basic features of client-centered work produce a natural restraint and reserve. They do not, however, rigidly prohibit the therapist's emotional or spontaneous expression. Occasional therapist emotional reactions reveal the therapist's involvement and spontaneous presence. The therapist wishes to be spontaneous while not getting in the client's way.

### 11. Impulses to exteriorize

There is another category of therapist-frame responses that is similar to the emotional, spontaneous types. These responses are also not reasoned out beforehand. Nor are they intended to produce an effect. They do suggest to the client that the therapist is willing to be transparent. They are of two types. The first type is a disclosure expressing a therapist's interior thought that would usually not be disclosed. Rogers' demonstration interview with Ms. G (Merry, 1995; [Brodley & Lietaer, 2006]) includes an example (italics in T4) where Rogers speaks out loud to himself.

C1: I always feel guilty when I'm crying. And I always feel as though I'm not allowed to cry.

T1: Mhm, mhm. Mhm mhm. Um ... "Don't cry. Be a big girl."

C2: Yeah.

T2: But when the tears were dropping, it was the four-year-old, feeling very hurt.

C3: [Pause 25 seconds] And angry, very angry.

T4: And angry at them. *Can you say that? Then I thought maybe not.* Angry too, um hm. "Damn you. Why don't you consider me?"

C5: [Nods agreement].

[See Brodley & Lietaer, 2006, Vol. 15, Ms. G, Interview, pp. 30–31]

The second type may be what Rogers was referring to as "intuitive" responses. Rogers (1986b) describes them as follows: "I may behave in strange and impulsive ways in the relationship, ways which I cannot justify rationally, which have nothing to do with my thought processes" (p. 199).

Exteriorizing responses of this type may consist of speculations, interpretations, metaphors, visual images, associations, or fantasies that come to the therapist's mind. They may be obviously related to the client's remarks or not – but they occur in the context of the therapist's empathic immersion in the client's presented world of experiences, ideas and feelings. Some "idiosyncratic responses," described by Bozarth (1984), appear to include this category.

The therapist, who is likely to be surprised by her own exteriorizing utterances, may couch these responses in an almost apologetic manner. They are certainly tentative in respect to their relevance to the client. Rogers (1986b), for instance, prefaced one such response with the remark, "… this may seem like a silly idea …" (p. 206).

Sometimes these exteriorizing types of therapist-frame responses stimulate the client towards new awareness. The client also may express appreciation to the therapist for the remark. The fact that they are appreciated and that they seem to promote some good productivity in the client does not validate such responses in general. The therapist should realize that the constructive use clients may make of exteriorizing responses (or any other therapist-frame responses) may not be the result of the therapist's genius or sensitivity. Clients may accept, use and appreciate such responses because they are inclined to accommodate or are compliant with therapists.

The client's constructive use or follow-through in reaction to the therapist-frame response has probably changed the direction of the dialogue. Productive as it may be for the client in the moment, it at least briefly undermines the client's self-directive potency in the interaction. Frequent therapist-frame responses that constructively stimulate the client result in a therapist directed therapy – a different kind of therapy.

## 12. Correcting misunderstandings

Another reason for making therapist-frame responses is when the therapist experiences the need to correct a client's misunderstandings about the therapist. The therapist may initiate a correction if the client has wrong ideas that could affect the client's perception of the attitudes, or influence his expectations about the therapy. A common occasion for this type of response is that the therapist needs to clarify his or her limitations in respect to the services being offered. For example, the therapist cannot be available for between-session long telephone calls. But, the client has made a remark that suggests he believes he has unlimited telephone access to the therapist.

A problem for the therapy in making corrections is its risk to the client's feelings of safety in the relationship. The client may perceive the therapist as criticizing him for his mistake. Another problem is that the correction may involve disappointment for the client. The client may not be able to voice his reactions to either of these problems. The client sustains a negative emotional experience that the therapist may not perceive. It is probably wise to ask the client for their reactions to any corrections if the client does not volunteer them. This inquiry may provide an opportunity to correct for any unfavorable impact of the corrections.

## 13. The therapist is a source of information

Clients have a reasonable expectation that therapists will provide them with any important information that appears to be relevant to their problems. This information might be about outside resources that may be appropriate and helpful to the client in pursuing his emotional well-being or other self-defined personal goals. The therapist legitimately functions as source of information for the client in respect to help for his pain or other concerns that may not be fully resolved by psychotherapy. For example, the therapist may introduce the idea of the use of psychotropic drugs for alleviating certain symptoms. Or the therapist might know of community services that address the client's particular rehabilitation needs.

Providing information (especially when a client has not specifically requested it), however, involves the same risks of misunderstanding and counter-therapeutic impact as other therapist-frame responses. Suggesting the possibility of medication, or suggesting a behavioral technique for allaying anxiety when performing, for example, may have counter-therapeutic implications for a client. The medication implies psychotherapy is hopeless for the client. Or techniques may be thought of as additional burdens and the therapist consequently appears insensitive to the client's burdens. Information, also, may be perceived as representing the therapist's expectation. The client must follow through or disappoint the therapist. The multitude of counter-therapeutic misunderstandings that may arise from therapist-frame responses, without the therapist's immediate knowledge, should not be minimized.

## DISCUSSION

Something that may stand out to readers familiar with other kinds of therapy is the absence of *generating information from clients* as a reason for responding from the therapist's frame of reference. Client-centered therapists almost never ask leading questions. Empathic understanding interactions serendipitously generate a great amount of information about clients but client-centered therapists are not therapeutically interested in information about their clients except as the clients are inclined to disclose it. Pursuit of information through leading questions is one of the major methods other kinds of therapists may employ to exercise control of the therapy, but client-centered therapists do not wish to control the client or the therapy. This kind of therapist sincerely wishes to avoid directing the therapy.

Readers also may have noticed that altering the manner of the client's self-disclosing process has not been given as a reason for responses from the therapist's frame. Empathic understanding interactions tend to influence clients towards a more immediate and experiential manner of self-disclosure (Rogers, 1961b) but this is not part of the client-centered therapist's intentions in responding empathically. Vocalizing responses to direct clients to a more immediate and felt process is part of experiential and process-directive type therapies (Gendlin, 1974; Brodley, 1990/2011) that are related to client-centered, but it is not part of client-centered therapy. The client-centered therapist believes such methods are unnecessary for therapeutic results as well as involving the same risks as other directivities – they may undermine the client's safety, autonomy and self-determination.

Readers also may have noticed that confrontation to provoke insight is not given as a reason for therapist-frame responses. The basic meaning of confrontation involves opposition, an adversarial stance. It is intrinsically contradictory to client-centered attitudes. In the context of therapy it also expresses an attitude of therapist expertise over the experience of the client. In contrast, a client-centered therapist may feel puzzled by a client's reasoning or motivations. The puzzlement might lead to a question for clarification. The attitude that brings forth a question for clarification is not an adversarial one nor is it based on the therapist's authority. Questions for clarification express, instead, an empathic attitude – wanting to understand from the client's frame of reference. Intentions to provoke insight are also absent from the list of reasons because insight is not viewed as necessary for therapeutic change in client-centered therapy, although it often occurs in the change process.

Congruence also is not included in the list of reasons for therapist-frame responses although it is cited as a reason by some person-centered therapists. It is invoked most frequently when the therapist has made self-disclosures to her client. In fact, congruence cannot be employed logically or legitimately as a reason, justification or rationale for therapist-frame communications. To do so represents a misunderstanding of client-centered theory.

Congruence, in Rogers' (1957, 1959) theory of therapy, refers to the therapist's state of integration and wholeness. Integration is a state that occurs, by Rogers' definition, when a person is capable of accurate symbolization of experiences in awareness. Rogers (1961a) also refers to congruence as the accurate relation between inner symbols and communication, (assuming an accurate inner symbolization of experience). Congruence in Rogers' theories (1957, 1959, 1961a) is basically a *relation*. It is an *accurate relation* between experiences and their inner symbols or between inner symbols and communications. Communications may be congruent and ideally all the therapist's communications are congruent. It is an important qualifier of the character of therapist-frame communications, but there must be some other basis for making the utterances. (See Brodley 1998b/2011 for further discussion of this issue.)

Several of the reasons a client-centered therapist may make responses from her own frame of reference (reasons numbered 7, 8, 9 and 10) are based on the fact that the therapist is foremost a person in a social situation. Great deviations from the common norms of participation in an interpersonal relationship may be perceived as artificial, insincere or manipulative. Avoidance of minimal social interactions may make the therapist appear distant or rigid. These qualities may seem ambiguous and stimulate a client to interpret the therapist as judgmental or unempathic. Answering "I'm very well thank you" to the client's "how are you?" shows in part a respect for the social nature of the therapy situation. It is civil behavior and responsive to a client's reasonable expectations of courteous treatment. Such responsiveness takes up very little space in the therapy setting and normalizes the situation.

In normal social intercourse people usually respond to others from their own frame of reference. Their responses involve or assume some degree of intake of the other person's remarks and feelings. Social conversational responses typically include agreements, disagreements, emotional reactions or elaboration of the other person's remarks. Also, responses in social situations are often non sequiturs. Explicit empathic understanding following responses are not part of typical social communication behavior.

Certain kinds of statements, although they are tempered by restraint, from the therapist's frame of reference may give a quality of naturalness and authenticity (as contrasted with role playing or mouthing a technique) to the highly specialized therapeutic situation. Valid as this point may be, it requires careful qualification given that client-centered is an expressive, not instrumental, therapy (Brodley, 2000b/2011).

The expressive character of client-centered therapy affects the intentions that underpin responses from the therapist's frame of reference. A light sprinkling of remarks from the therapist's frame probably increases the appearance of a naturalistic conversation. This idea, however, does not imply that the therapist deliberately should make such remarks in order to produce the appearance of a more natural social situation. Such a deliberate and systematic intention is in conflict with the spontaneous and expressive character of client-centered work.

The rationale for allowing a sprinkling of remarks from the therapist's frame is similar to the basis for adjustments to individual clients (such as to the client's vocabulary) for the sake of comprehensible communication. It is an element in the therapist's back-of-the-mind understandings of the complex role of client perception in the therapeutic situation. Many such understandings influence therapists' adjustments to their individual clients. It is a facet of the personal and psychological complexity of the therapy relationship.

Recall that Rogers' theory (1957, 1959) asserts that therapeutic efficacy requires the client's *perception* of the therapist's empathy and acceptance. It is an implicit feature of this point in the theory that the client's perceptions of the therapist as sincere and transparent are necessary for the client to experience the greatest benefit from his perceptions of being empathically understood and accepted. Certain kinds of therapist-frame nonsystematic communications may contribute to the client's perception of the therapist's authentic and sincere presence.

Without deliberate or manipulative intentions, the client-centered therapist must project his or her presence as an authentic person in the relationship in order to be most effective. This is in contrast to projecting a role-playing presence. What are the behaviors that contribute to an authentic or sincere presence in the therapy? The basic way client-centered therapists communicate their authenticity is through their sincere empathic and accepting attitudes. These shape tone, manner, and gestures as well as words. A therapist's presence of realness or of naturalness also may be enhanced by occasional spontaneous utterances from her own frame.

Responses from the therapist's frame involve putting aside, at least momentarily, the empathic focus that is part of the essence of the therapy. It should be understood to involve risks of being misinterpreted, and risks of undermining the client's sense of safety, autonomy or self-determination in the therapy relation.

CONCLUSION

Thirteen reasons for therapist-frame responses have been discussed. They are:

1.  Arrangements and terms of the therapy
2.  Addressing questions and requests
3.  Possibility of a question
4.  Empathic observations
5.  Corrections for loss of acceptance or loss of empathy or incongruence
6.  Insights and ideas
7.  Emotionally compelling circumstances
8.  Prior information
9.  Spontaneous agreements
10. Evaluative reactions
11. Impulses to exteriorize
12. Correcting misunderstandings
13. The therapist is a source of information

Listing or describing these reasons is not identical to asserting that the responses are good for a client or for the therapy process. Reasons are not necessarily justifications or adequate rationales for the behavior. Mindfulness about the essential therapeutic features of client-centered work and awareness of the complexity of client's perceptions, and their probable vulnerabilities, should override the therapist's temptations to easily represent his or her own frame.

All of the reasons client-centered therapists may occasionally communicate from their own frame of reference with clients assume that the therapist tries to remain congruent – integrated – in the relationship. The reasons given also assume that the therapist continues to acceptantly and empathically understand the client and communicate empathy throughout the ensuing conversations. Therapist-frame responses explaining the arrangements and terms of the therapy are necessary. The frequency of responses to client's questions or requests partly depends upon the frequency of these things coming from the client. Other therapist-frame responses should be infrequent. If they become frequent, they are probably systematic – the therapist has a persistent directive intention. The therapist has some agenda or goal for the client or an inappropriate goal for herself. The therapist then has stepped outside the parameters of client-centered work.

My effort has been to clarify some possible reasons for responses from the therapist's frame in client-centered work. I hope I shall *not* be misunderstood as intending to encourage them. Client-centered therapy is a nondirective therapy that protects a client's sense of self, autonomy and self-determination in the relationship. It succeeds when practitioners experience the therapeutic attitudes conceived by Rogers (1957), are capable of implementing them appropriately with the particular client, and are faithful to the basic premises and theory (Rogers, 1951). For the most part, this means the therapist (a) is trying to understand – his or her attention is focused on acceptant empathic following of the client – and (b) explicitly checks with the client to find out if the therapist's inner understandings are correct.

There is some latitude for various forms of verbal (as well as nonverbal) expression of the therapist as a person in social interaction with another person – representing his or her own point of view – or as an expert or informant in certain matters. But these functions are secondary and neither necessary nor sufficient for effective client-centered practice. As Patterson (1990) states about client-centered therapy: "There is some freedom. But there are limits. The freedom of the therapist stops when it infringes on the freedom of the client to be responsible for and direct his own life" (p. 431).

It is not easy to avoid infringement on the client's freedom. Appropriately protecting the client's freedom is a subtle and complex process. The therapist needs freedom to function spontaneously and naturally in the relationship. The therapist's freedom involves risks to the client's freedom as well as his sense of safety.

The reader may grant the general validity of the reasons I have described for client-centered therapists to respond occasionally from their own frame of reference. At the same time, it should be realized that the loss of the client's safety and loss of the client's freedom is much more likely, even in unexpected ways, when we respond from our own frames of reference.

REFERENCES

Baldwin, M. (1987). Interview with Carl Rogers on the use of the self in therapy. In M. Baldwin & V. Satir (Eds.), *The use of self in therapy* (pp. 45–52). London: Haworth Press. [Reprinted (2004) in R. Moodley, C. Lago, & A. Talahite (Eds.), *Carl Rogers counsels a Black client: Race and culture in person-centred counseling* (pp. 253–260). Ross-on-Wye: PCCS Books]
Bozarth, J. D. (1984). Beyond reflection: Emergent modes of empathy. In R. F. Levant & J. M. Shlien (Eds.), *Client-centered therapy and the person-centered approach* (pp. 59–75). New York: Praeger.
Bozarth, J. D. (1992). Coterminous intermingling of doing and being in person-centered therapy. *The Person-Centered Journal, 1*(1), 33–39.

Bozarth, J. D. (1996). A theoretical reconsideration of the necessary and sufficient conditions for therapeutic personality change. *The Person-Centered Journal, 3*(1), 44–51.

Bozarth, J. D. (1998). *Person-centered therapy: A revolutionary paradigm.* Ross-on-Wye: PCCS Books.

Bozarth, J. D., & Brodley, B. T. (1991). Actualization: A functional concept in client-centered therapy. In A. Jones & R. Crandall (Eds.), *Handbook of self-actualization* (pp. 45–60). Madera, CA: Select Press. [Reprinted (2008) in B. E. Levitt (Ed.), *Reflections on human potential* (pp. 33–45). Ross-on-Wye: PCCS Books]

Bradburn, W. M. (1996). *Did Carl Rogers' positive view of human nature bias his psychotherapy?* An empirical investigation. Unpublished doctoral clinical research project, Illinois School of Professional Psychology, Chicago (now Argosy University, Chicago).

Brodley, B. T. (1990). Client-centered and experiential: Two different therapies. In G. Lietaer, J. Rombauts, & R. Van Balen (Eds.), *Client-centered and experiential psychotherapy in the nineties* (pp. 87–107). Leuven, Belgium: Leuven University Press. [This volume, Chapter 23]

Brodley, B. T. (1994). Some observations of Carl Rogers' behavior in therapy interviews. *The Person-Centered Journal, 1*(2), 37–47. [This volume, Chapter 25]

Brodley, B. T. (1996). Empathic understanding and feelings in client-centered therapy. *The Person-Centered Journal, 3*(1), 22–30. [This volume, Chapter 8]

Brodley, B. T. (1997). The nondirective attitude in client-centered therapy. *The Person-Centered Journal, 4*(1), 18–30. [This volume, Chapter 5]

Brodley, B. T. (1998a). Criteria for making empathic responses in client-centered therapy. *The Person-Centered Journal, 5*(1), 20–28. [This volume, Chapter 14]

Brodley, B. T. (1998b) Congruence and its relation to communication in client-centered therapy. *The Person-Centered Journal, 5*(2), 83–116. [This volume, Chapter 7]

Brodley, B. T. (1998c). O conceito de tendencia actualizate na teoria centrada no cliente [The actualizing tendency concept in client-centered theory]. *A Pessoa Como Centro, 2*, 37–48. [English version reprinted (2000) in D. Bower (Ed.), *The person-centered approach: Applications for living* (pp. 81–106) San Jose, CA: The Writers Club Press. For a different version see 1999a]

Brodley, B. T. (1999a). The actualizing tendency concept in client-centered theory. *The Person-Centered Journal, 6*(2), 108–120. [This volume, Chapter 11]

Brodley, B. T. (1999b, April). *The concept of presence in client-centered therapy.* Paper presented in the Chicago Counseling and Psychotherapy Lecture Series, April 16.

Brodley, B. T. (2000a). Personal presence in client-centered therapy. *The Person-Centered Journal, 7*(2), 139–149. [This volume, Chapter 10]

Brodley, B. T. (2000b). Client-centered: An expressive therapy. In J. E. Marques-Teixeira & S. Antunes (Eds.), *Client-centered and experiential psychotherapy* (pp. 133–147). Linda a Velha, Lisboa, Portugal: Vale & Vale. [Also published (2002) in *The Person-Centered Journal 9*(1), 59–70; this volume, Chapter 13]

[Brodley, B. T. (2003). Presence in client-centered therapy. *A Pessoa Como Centro:*

*Revista de Estudos Rogerianos, 6,* 48–77. This is a slightly altered version of 2000a/2011]

[Brodley, B. T., & Lietaer, G. (Eds.). (2006). *Transcripts of Carl Rogers' therapy sessions, Vols. 1–17.* Available from germain.lietaer@psy.kuleuven.be and kmoon1@alumni.uchicago.edu]

Brody, A. F. (1991). *Understanding client-centered therapy through interviews conducted by Carl Rogers.* Unpublished doctoral clinical research project, Illinois School of Professional Psychology, Chicago (now Argosy University, Chicago).

Diss, J. W. (1996). *Facilitative responses leading to client process disruption in Carl Rogers' therapy behavior.* Unpublished doctoral clinical research project, Illinois School of Professional Psychology, Chicago (now Argosy University, Chicago).

Gendlin, E. T. (1974). Client-centered and experiential psychotherapy. In D. A. Wexler & L. N. Rice (Eds.), *Innovations in client-centered therapy* (pp. 211–246). New York: Wiley.

[Lietaer, G., & Brodley, B. T. (2003). Carl Rogers in the therapy room: A listing of session transcripts and a survey of publications referring to Rogers' sessions. *Person-Centered & Experiential Psychotherapies, 2,* 274–291.]

Merry, T. (1995). *Invitation to person-centred psychology.* London: Whurr. [Republished (2006) Ross-on-Wye: PCCS Books]

Merry, T. (1996). An analysis of ten demonstration interviews by Carl Rogers: Implications for the training of client-centered counselors. In R. Hutterer, G. Pawlowsky, P. F. Schmid, & R. Stipsits (Eds.), *Client-centered and experiential psychotherapy: A paradigm in motion* (pp. 273–284). Vienna: Peter Lang.

Patterson, C. H. (1989). Values in counseling and psychotherapy. *Counseling and Values, 33,* 164–176.

Patterson, C. H. (1990). On being client-centered. *Person-Centered Review, 5*(4), 425–432.

Raskin, N. J. (1947). The nondirective attitude. Unpublished manuscript. [Published (2005) in *The Person-Centered Journal 12*(1–2), and (2005) in B. E. Levitt (Ed.), *Embracing non-directivity* (pp. 327–347). Ross-on-Wye: PCCS Books]

Raskin, N. J. (1988). Responses to person-centered vs. client-centered. *Renaissance, 5*(3&4), 2–3.

Rogers, C. R. (1951). The attitude and orientation of the counselor. In *Client-centered therapy* (pp. 19–64). Boston: Houghton Mifflin.

Rogers, C. R. (1956). The necessary and sufficient conditions of therapeutic personality change. University of Chicago Counseling Center. *Discussion Papers, 2*(8).

Rogers, C. R. (1957). The necessary and sufficient conditions of therapeutic personality change. *Journal of Consulting Psychology, 21,* 95–103. [Also (1989) in H. Kirschenbaum & V. L. Henderson (Eds.), *The Carl Rogers reader* (pp. 219–235). Boston: Houghton Mifflin]

Rogers, C. R. (1959). A theory of therapy, personality, and interpersonal relationships, as developed in the client-centered framework. In S. Koch (Ed.), *Psychology: A study of a science. Vol. III: Formulations of the person and the social context* (pp. 184–256). New York: McGraw-Hill.

Rogers, C. R. (1961a). A tentative formulation of a general law of interpersonal relations. In *On becoming a person* (pp. 338–346). Boston: Houghton Mifflin.

Rogers, C. R. (1961b). A process conception of psychotherapy. In *On becoming a person* (pp. 125–159). Boston: Houghton Mifflin.

Rogers, C. R. (1967). A silent young man. In *The therapeutic relationship and its impact* (pp. 401–418). Westport, CT: Greenwood Press.

Rogers, C. R. (1980). The foundations of a person-centered approach. In *A way of being* (pp. 113–136). Boston: Houghton Mifflin.

Rogers, C. R. (1986a). Reflection of feelings. *Person-Centered Review, 1*(4), 375–377.

Rogers, C. R. (1986b). Client-centered therapy. In I. L. Kutash & A. Wolf (Eds.), *Psychotherapist's casebook* (pp. 197–208). San Francisco: Jossey-Bass.

Shostrom, E. L. (Producer). (1965). *Three Approaches to Psychotherapy Series* [Film]. Santa Ana, CA: Psychological Films.

Temaner, B. [Brodley] (1977). The empathic understanding response process. Chicago Counseling and Psychotherapy Center. *Chicago Counseling Center Discussion Paper.* [This volume, Chapter 12]

Temaner, B. [Brodley] (1982). Criteria for making empathic responses in client-centered therapy. Chicago Counseling and Psychotherapy Center. *Chicago Counseling Center Discussion Paper.* [Published (1984) under Brodley in A. S. Segrera (Ed.), *Proceedings of the 1st International Forum on the Person-Centered Approach.* México, Distrito Federal, Mexico: Universidad Iberoamericana. Excerpted in *Renaissance, 2*(1), 1–3 under altered title; revision published 1998 in *The Person-Centered Journal, 5*(1), 20–28; this volume, Chapter 14]

Tomlinson, T. M., & Whitney, R. E. (1970). Values and strategy in client-centered therapy. In J. T. Hart & T. M. Tomlinson (Eds.), *New directions in client-centered therapy* (pp. 453–467). Boston: Houghton Mifflin.

# Chapter 16

## Considerations when responding to questions and requests in client-centered therapy

There are a number of considerations that the client-centered therapist needs to take into account in the process of answering questions or responding to requests in a manner that respects the client and follows the client's lead. Some of these considerations are listed below in the form of questions the therapist may address to her/himself.

1. Do I understand the question or request? Do I need to ask the client a question for clarification, or make a statement summarizing what I understand in order to be sure I accurately understand the question or request?

2. Do I feel my commitment to protect the client's autonomy, self-regulation and self-direction as I attempt to address the client's question or request? Do I, at the same time, recognize the client's right to have his/her questions and requests addressed directly, to not be interpreted or avoided?

3. Do I feel at ease with the question or request? Am I comfortable enough with it to address the question or request without being distracted or defensive? Do I need to postpone a response to think about it further, or to regain my congruence (wholeness, integration, authenticity)?

4. Do I have the information, the competencies or the personal circumstances that are necessary to answer the question or to accommodate the request? If I am not able to answer or accommodate, can I be honest and direct in my explanation?

5. Am I continuing to maintain my empathic and acceptant attitudes and respond with acceptant empathy throughout the interaction concerning the client's question or request?

6. Am I maintaining my ethical standards throughout the interaction?

7. Do I feel free to not give the client the answer being asked for, or feel free

---

This unpublished paper seems to have been completed October 4, 1995.

to not participate in the client's request? If I do not wish to answer or participate, am I able to explain myself to my client undefensively and honestly, and without implying blame or criticism of my client?

8.  Are my values and my therapeutic attitudes (congruence, unconditional positive regard, and empathic understanding) firmly in place, within me, with this client? Can my values and my therapeutic attitudes influence each moment of the process of interacting with the client about his/her questions or requests? Am I authentic as I respond? Am I accepting and nonjudgmental? Am I remaining open and responsive to the client and his/her internal frame of reference? Am I free of directive intentions and goals for the client as I respond to the question or request?

9.  Am I truly being responsive to the client from the client's point of view? Do I need to ask the client, from time to time, if my responses from my own frame of reference are appropriate and relevant to the client's wishes? Am I adjusting myself and what I say to the client as I receive information from the client about his/her wishes, feelings and reactions?

10. Am I prepared, in the sense of remaining open to empathic understanding of the client, for surprising or unexpected reactions from the client concerning the way I have interacted with him/her in the questions and requests situation? Am I confident I can adequately respond to surprising or unexpected client reactions? Am I prepared in the sense of feeling I am able to respond while maintaining the therapeutic attitudes and with other appropriate responses to surprising or unexpected consequences of my answers or my accommodations to the client?

Answering questions and being responsive to clients' requests in client-centered therapy are significant elements in our communication to clients of the therapist's respect and trust, communication of a deeply held nondirective attitude, and communication of the therapeutic attitudes. At our best, the interactions about clients' questions and requests come from as deep a source in ourselves as pure empathic interactions.

# Chapter 17

# The therapeutic clinical interview: Guidelines for beginning practice

Clinical interviews can be distinguished into two general types – the therapeutic clinical interview and the diagnostic/assessment clinical interview. The guidelines that follow are an introduction to the practice of the therapeutic interview for the beginning clinical student. They are based on client-centered psychotherapy theory (Rogers, 1957, 1959, 1986a) and emphasize an empathic and nondirective way of conducting a therapeutic interview.

The empathic understanding interview is applied in the context of many contemporary therapeutic theoretical orientations. It is fundamental to client-centered work, but it is an essential process in Kohut's psychodynamic approach (Kohut, 1959, 1981) and it is an important aspect of psychoanalytic therapies (Josephs, 1988) as well as gestalt, cognitive, behavioral, hypnotherapy, relationship, and other therapies.

Psychotherapy is an art enlightened by wisdom, theory and research. As a practiced art, it cannot be done by consciously following rules. For effective practice most, if not all, therapeutic approaches require the therapist to have incorporated, or assimilated, their relevant philosophy of humankind and their conception of how and why therapeutic personality change occurs. The attitudes and inexplicit, or nonconscious, mental activities of experienced therapists are more frequently involved in determining their responses than their explicit, conscious cognitive activity. The beginning clinician must, however, *behave* with clients as much as possible as an experienced therapist, long before having had the hours and the years of practice required to become experienced and "intuitive." Guidelines are intended as a means to help students enter into therapeutic clinical interviews before they have committed themselves to any particular therapeutic approach and before development of the chosen theory's mental set and attitudes.

First published (1993) in *Person-Centred Practice, 1*(2), 15–21. Subsequently published (2000) in T. Merry (Ed.), *Person-centred practice: The BAPCA reader* (pp. 103–109). Ross-on-Wye: PCCS Books.

## THE SITUATION

The student will either (a) be taking turns as therapist and client with another student or (b) will have enlisted a volunteer from among acquaintances to function as a practice-client. A time frame for the interview should be established of, at least, one half-hour in length to as much as one hour. The setting should be private and comfortable and free from interruptions.

After each interview, clients should be asked for their feelings and reactions to the interview and in the case of co-counselors it is desirable for both persons to discuss their reactions to the interview.

Practice interviews should be tape-recorded, so they may be reviewed. Counselors should make sure that clients have given their permission (in writing if possible) for tapes and transcripts to be used in supervision.

Counselors, when functioning as clients and practice-clients, should be asked to talk about a personal concern, about something that has recently been upsetting or worrisome or a source of anxiety or other feelings. The client may be given a simple initial instruction such as the following: "Tell me anything that is of concern, or bothering you, these days." The practice-therapist might also say: "You can start anywhere you choose. I am going to be trying to understand what you tell me as best as I can." The therapist might want to add: "If any questions occur to you to ask me during our interview, would you try to postpone asking them until we have finished the interview?" If the therapist does not choose to defer questions, then answer them directly and honestly during the interview and follow the answer with a question to the client such as: "What is your reaction to what I said?" In beginning practice it is best to defer questions and this approach is recommended.

Practice interviews are confidential except for consultation and transcription that disguises identities.

## THE PROCEDURE

The procedure of the empathic therapeutic interview requires the student to inhibit, or put aside, any and all assumptions concerning their clients, and to attend to them as unique individuals with their own particular manner of expression, manner of relating interpersonally and their own personal situations, stories and concerns. A manner of respect and courtesy towards the client is fundamental to the procedure.

The therapist listens attentively to the client and *attempts to understand*, maintaining an acceptant attitude towards whatever the client is describing, explaining or expressing. The therapist *attempts to understand*, specifically, whatever the client is attempting to communicate, *from the client's internal frame of reference*, or perspective. The therapist, thus, is attempting empathically to understand the client in the immediate moments of the interaction.

Empathic understanding is a subjective experience, not an overt behavior. Empathic understanding is a sense, or feeling, of understanding that develops in the mind and feelings of the therapist. It is an experience of taking into oneself the ideas, meanings and feelings that clients have been expressing as their own in the immediate moments of the interaction.

This kind of understanding necessarily involves a therapist's mental processes that are associative, interpretive and emotive. There is no grasp of meanings or experiences of one person by another person without such processes. Nevertheless, in empathic understanding, the therapist is striving to achieve representation in her own mind, feelings and experience – into the therapist's own subjective verbal symbol system – an accurate grasp of whatever the client is expressing in the interaction. The therapist's subjective understandings should be as free as possible from her or his own assumptions, beliefs and evaluative attitudes.

Empathic understanding is fundamentally a subjective experience on the part of the therapist. However, the only way in which the accuracy of such understanding of the client can be verified is by its coherent communication to the client. Thus, in the therapeutic interaction, it is necessary, from time to time, for the therapist to speak, to verbalize, and expressively communicate, what he or she has immediately understood from the client. This permits the client an opportunity to verify its accuracy or correct it (Rogers, 1986b). The client is the only expert about what it is she was attempting to communicate in the immediate moments or minutes before the therapist speaks to check her subjective empathic understandings.

In addition to the quality of acceptance and the checking to determine the accuracy of empathic understanding, another crucial feature is the neutrality of the therapist in respect to the realities, values, feelings and attitudes that are expressed by the client. The overall impact of the therapist's communicated empathic understandings is usually experienced by clients as supportive of them. Nevertheless, empathic understandings and the responses that express those understandings are always neutral in respect to the frame of reference of the therapist. The evaluative neutrality of responses in an empathic and nondirective interview is intrinsic to this type of therapeutic interview. The therapist tries acceptantly, noncritically and nonjudgmentally to understand the point of view, and specific feelings and meanings expressed by the client. A therapist's response is not a true empathic understanding response if it conveys or signals an evaluative stance of the therapist, regardless of whether the evaluative stance is positive or negative.

The most general point about the empathic therapeutic clinical interview that the student needs to keep in mind is that it is a form of *following*. Both the concept and the practice of empathically understanding a client's internal frame of reference, as well as communicating specific understandings, is a form of *following* the client. True empathic understanding, however, *is not a technique* of restating or mirroring the client's intended communications and is almost never experienced as a technique by clients. Instead, it is perceived as *being understood*, as having one's personal meanings grasped by the other person. This usually feels like an authentic interaction wherein the listener has genuinely paid attention and tried to understand. And it feels good to clients and stimulates further exploration and disclosure.

Empathic understanding is a form of following the client and does not involve trying to get ahead of the client. Occasionally, however, when a therapist has been closely attuned to a client, and closely following the client's expression, the client may experience the therapist's empathic response as accurate to the client's inner experience, but also as a new idea or new realization. This occurrence of seeming to be somewhat ahead of the client is a therapeutic and valued experience, but it is not something for the therapist to *try* to achieve. It arises out of the understanding and trusting relationship created by the means of the therapist closely, respectfully and accurately following the client.

In summary, the therapist feels empathic understanding as she follows the client's narrative. This empathic understanding is a subjective experience on the therapist's part. From time to time, the therapist feels the need to articulate empathic understanding responses (based on subjectively felt understandings) in order to find out from the client whether or not those understandings are accurate or in need of correction. The empathic understanding responses are usually articulated in the form of statements that imply the question, "Am I understanding you?" Their tentativeness is communicated by intonation and by the therapist's acceptance of corrections. Empathic understanding responses are always offered for the client to confirm, reject or qualify (Rogers, 1986b).

Most of the guidelines that follow indicate what the therapist student should avoid or *not* do. If all the "do nots" are adhered to, and the student's efforts have been focused upon empathically understanding as well as she or he is able, it is quite possible that the process that ensues will be productive for the client. It may result in the client's increased emotional openness and willingness to disclose further. It may show a development in the client's themes of concerns, and some movement towards new self-understanding. It may result in more positive feelings as well as other signs of therapeutic change.

THE GUIDELINES

When you are attending and listening to your client, try to do the following:

1.  Absorb the meanings which the client is expressing to you. What is the client succeeding at "getting at," or what is he or she trying to "get at"?

2.  When you express your tentative understanding, think of yourself as trying to check whether or not you have, in fact, understood. You may express this tentativeness simply by your intonation, or you might preface your empathic response with an introductory statement that communicates your tentativeness and your interest in the client's assessment of the accuracy of your understanding. Examples of such introductory statements are: "Is this right?" or "Are you saying …?" or "Is this a correct understanding right now?" or "I think I understand. Is this what you mean?" You might use a declarative form of introduction to your empathic response, although it should be in a tentative spirit, such as "You are feeling …"; "You want to …"; or "You are telling me that …."

3.  Avoid introductions to your empathic responses which suggest you are trying to interpret the client or that your task is to discover or elicit "deeper" meanings buried in what the client is expressing. Introductions which sometimes create such misunderstanding are "I sense you are really feeling …"; "I sense you are feeling …"; or "You sound like you …." Try to avoid these introductions to your empathic responses.

4.  While making responses which are intended to express the client's point of view, frame of reference, perspective, perceptions and feelings, *stay completely within the client's frame of reference*. As you are listening, try to grasp the client's viewpoint together with the meanings and feelings that are the client's at that time. Try to absorb those things into yourself – without the reservations and interferences of skepticism or criticism – in order to reach a feeling of understanding. Put aside any doubts or critical feelings about the client's statements and *try to understand the client's point of view and feelings*.

5.  If you don't understand what the client has been expressing to you – perhaps your thoughts were distracting you, or perhaps the client's communication was eluding you at the time – simply say you haven't understood yet, and then ask the client to repeat or state in a different way what was being expressed.

6.  After you make an empathic understanding response, allow your client to initiate the next response. Allow silence. Relax and give yourself and your

client a chance to think and feel further – to reflect upon the experiences that are being expressed between you.

7.    Do not ask leading or probing questions. Examples of typical leading or probing questions are: "How do you feel about that?" "Tell me more about ..." "What do you think he would feel about that?" "Can you tell me more about your relationship to ...?"

8.    Do not ask your client questions that involve assumptions or theories that are not part of those directly expressed or clearly implied in what your client has been saying. Examples of such interpretive-probing questions are: "Do you find yourself waking up early and not being able to go back to sleep?" "Do you remember how you felt about things when your brother was born?" "How do you feel when someone has authority over you?" etc. Of course, many empathic understanding responses may be literally in the form of a question because you are wanting to find out if your subjective empathic understanding is correct or not. And sometimes you will find you need to ask a question for simple factual clarification. For example, "Did you say that was your sister or your cousin?" or "Did you say you got home late or that he got home late?" or "Did you mean 'now' in the sense of 'these days' or in the sense of 'right now' here with me?" These types of questions are called "questions for clarification" and are a form of empathic following.

9.    Do not volunteer interpretations of any kind.

10. Do not volunteer comments upon what the client has expressed.

11. Do not volunteer agreement with what the client is saying.

12. Do not abstract feelings or emotions from the content or situation that the client is expressing, unless the client's point is the feelings or emotions.

13. Do not volunteer suggestions or guidance of any kind.

14. Do not volunteer praise or criticism of the client or of the client's behavior.

15. Do not turn a specific statement into a generality or a generality into a specific – unless that is what the client seems to be intending that you understand.

16. If your client indicates feeling "stopped" and doesn't know how to proceed and asks for your help, a relatively nondirective response that is often helpful is to say something such as "Sometimes, if one gives oneself a bit more time, some thoughts or direction will come to mind." Or "I feel there's no hurry, so if you can, try to let yourself relax to give yourself a chance to see if something comes to you."

17. If your clients say they don't have anything more to say about a topic and don't know what to do now (and you have already tried the approach above), and they ask for more help – then you may suggest they give themselves time to consider if there is some other topic they feel concern or worry about. Or say "Sometimes it helps to think back over the concerns that brought you in." We do not intend to avoid giving guidance or help in proceeding in the interaction when the client requests it, but the best guidance is usually the encouragement to take time and search the client's own experience and thoughts.

18. If clients lose their train of thought or forget what they were saying, do not prompt or remind them – unless they ask for help. Scattered thoughts and discontinuity of theme should be accepted in the same manner as developed and coherent thought.

19. Do not integrate for the client, e.g., "That sounds like it may be related to the problem you have with your mother." Empathic interviews often result in integrations, but it is not the therapist's responsibility to find or direct such connections.

20. Do not volunteer comments about the client's apparent feelings, state or other experiences, e.g., "You seem to have a lot of emotions about that topic," or "It seems you have an issue with abandonment or loss," or "You are feeling pretty angry at me right now." Of course, these examples may be similar to empathic responses, if the client has been expressing any of these ideas.

21. If your client asks you a question, (a) give yourself a chance to absorb the question, (b) ask for further clarification of the question if you need it, (c) respond to the question in a direct, person-to-person manner. This can mean different things, depending upon the nature of the question, your own knowledge and expertise in the arena being inquired about, your own personal feelings about self-disclosure and your personal feelings about expressing opinions. In any case, to respond to a question in a direct, person-to-person manner means one does not avoid the question or treat the client as the issue for asking a question. Depending on factors such as those mentioned above, you may literally answer the question, you may say you don't know the answer to that question, you may say you don't feel comfortable revealing such personal things, or you may say something that is a general answer to the question but also demur because you do not know if the general answer applies in the present situation. After responding in some direct way to the client's question, you may want to check the client's satisfaction or dissatisfaction with your response.

It is also possible to respond to questions directly and, in addition, express an empathic response with respect to the feelings, concerns or perspectives that seemed to have sparked the question. Responding to the feelings behind a question, however, should not be a means of avoiding the question.

In general, try to remember that the therapist's interest is in the client as a whole person. The whole person is primarily represented in the therapy relationship by the client expressing a personal point of view, personal meanings and reactions to things. Respect for and trust in clients is communicated by the therapist's interest in the clients' representations of their inner worlds and inner perspectives and reactions to their worlds. Speaking to check the accuracy of empathic understandings is the therapist's basic medium for communication of empathy and acceptance towards the client. Empathic following responses, embodying the therapeutic *attitudes* of empathy and acceptance, stimulate constructive processes in the client.

### REFERENCES

Josephs, L. (1988). A comparison of archeological and empathic modes of listening. *Contemporary Psychoanalysis, 24*, 282–300.

Kohut, H. (1959). Introspection, empathy and psychoanalysis. *Journal of the American Psychoanalytic Association, 7*, 459–483.

Kohut, H. (Producer). (1981, October 4). *Remarks on empathy* [Film]. Filmed at Conference on Self Psychology, Los Angeles.

Rogers, C. R. (1957). The necessary and sufficient conditions of therapeutic personality change. *Journal of Consulting Psychology, 21*, 95–103.

Rogers, C. R. (1959). A theory of therapy, personality and interpersonal relationships as developed in the client-centered framework. In S. Koch (Ed.), *Psychology: A study of a science. Vol. III: Formulations of the person and the social context* (pp. 184–256). New York: McGraw-Hill.

Rogers, C. R. (1986a). Client-centered therapy. In I. L. Kutash & A. Wolf (Eds.), *Psychotherapist's casebook* (pp. 197–208). San Francisco: Jossey-Bass.

Rogers, C. R. (1986b). Reflection of feelings. *Person-Centered Review, 1*(4), 375–377.

# Chapter 18

# Can one use techniques and still be client-centered?

Barbara Temaner Brodley
and
Anne F. Brody

*Abstract*

Can a therapist who uses techniques still be client-centered? The specific meaning given to this question implies several different answers. Therapists whose client-centered values influence the *application* of goal-oriented treatments and techniques might describe themselves as client-centered behavioral therapists or client-centered relationship trainers, etc. However, this should not, be confused with the practice of actual client-centered psychotherapy. The question might be rephrased to say, "Does client-centered therapy use techniques?" In this case, the answer is YES. Technique of some sort is intrinsic to all therapy practice. Another meaning of the question might be, "Can specific techniques that have specific goals and effects be applied in the context of true client-centered therapy?" Here, the answer is YES, if they are the result of the client's questions or requests, and NO if they are the result of the therapist's having a diagnostic mindset that determines which goals and techniques are indicated.

CAN ONE USE TECHNIQUES AND STILL BE CLIENT-CENTERED?

Depending upon the specific meanings given to the panel question, there are several different answers. We shall first try to put aside one meaning of the question with a quick, but hopefully clear, answer in order to pursue some meanings of the question that are of greater interest to us.

"Client-centered" can refer to a general framework of theory, a philosophy that attributes high value to the individual person, values an egalitarian and democratic approach to the relations among persons, and also views Rogers' (1957) attitudinal conditions of congruence, unconditional positive regard and empathic understanding as necessary therapist attributes in helping

---

This chapter was previously published (1996) in R. Hutterer, G. Pawlowsky, P. F. Schmid, & R. Stipsits (Eds.), *Client-centered and experiential psychotherapy: A paradigm in motion* (pp. 369–374). Frankfurt am Main, Berlin, Bern, New York, Paris, Wien: Peter Lang. Reproduced with permission.

relationships. The term "person-centered" is also used to refer to this general framework.

Some therapists who work from this general framework provide services that involve having specific goals for clients and/or involve specific goal-directed techniques. Examples are teaching relaxation for alleviating pain, teaching behavioral techniques to cope with anxiety or obsession, teaching relationship or parenting skills, psychodrama, gestalt therapy, artistic or expressive procedures, and teaching meditation or focusing techniques. When the general client-centered framework is combined with other therapies or specific goal-directed techniques, the answer to the panel question is a very qualified YES. One can use techniques and still be client-centered – at least sort of.

The meaning of being "client-centered" in this regard is that the therapist is basically not a client-centered therapist but is, for example, a relaxation therapist, a cognitive therapist, a relationship trainer, or a focusing trainer approaching his or her work with client-centered values. Such therapists employ the theory and techniques of their specific therapies *in ways that are as faithful as possible to client-centered values and attitudes*, given the contradictory and limiting features of their basic approach.

Such therapists and trainers might describe themselves as client-centered whatever – client-centered behavioral therapists, client-centered gestalt therapists, client-centered relationship trainers, etc. These kinds of applications of the general client-centered theoretical framework to specific treatment goals, using specific goal-directed techniques for the benefit of clients, are not, however, client-centered therapy.

In our opinion, infusing specific goal-oriented treatments and techniques with client-centered values in ways that influence the actual application of the treatments and techniques might well tend to greatly humanize and improve the efficacy of the treatments and the techniques. But they should not be confused with client-centered therapy.

A different meaning to the panel question might be phrased: "Are techniques employed in client-centered therapy?" In addressing this question we first wish to clarify the meaning of "technique." A technique is a method or procedure that exists in practical or formal *details*. It involves actions that are usually employed to carry out an artistic work or scientific operation (Webster, 1979, p. 1972). This definition does not obviously fit into our topic of psychotherapy (or at least it raises questions about the nature of therapeutic theories). But basically, putting aside those complexities, a technique is doing something according to some principle or following some steps in order to promote or effect an end or a goal.

Adapting this definition to our topic of psychotherapy, we can say techniques refer to procedures, steps, actions, specific behaviors that implement ideas (that is, our theories) about how to help persons psychologically in order to enhance their well-being and functioning as persons. In terms of this definition, techniques are intrinsic to client-centered therapy. There is no therapy, of any kind, without techniques. And although client-centered therapy is correctly described as a theory of values and attitudes (Rogers, 1951, 1957, 1959, 1986), it cannot be practiced without techniques.

To express this point we quote John Shlien (1993) about client-centered therapy:

> Attitudes are not enough. Techniques are extremely important, because they are what express the attitudes. The theory is not expressed in the grand design; it is expressed in the method. The principles are in the practice. The attitudes are in the technique.

Corroboration of Shlien's statements can be found in Rogers' theory of therapy (1957), which requires that the client perceive the therapist's offering of the therapeutic attitudes for change to occur. This theoretical element mandates that the therapist be present and act towards the client in ways that communicate the therapeutic attitudes, thus giving the client an opportunity to perceive them. The therapist's actions that express the therapeutic attitudes are, in effect, techniques. Thus, the panel question, rephrased as "Does client-centered therapy use techniques?" must be answered YES. Without techniques there would be no therapy because there would be no communication to the client and, consequently, no perception of the therapeutic attitudes by the client.

Another meaning of the panel question can be stated: "Can specific techniques that have specific goals and effects be applied in the context of true client-centered psychotherapy?" This question might mean, more specifically, "Can a client-centered therapist teach relaxation, teach focusing, apply a gestalt or a psychodrama technique, etc., in the context of client-centered therapy and still genuinely be doing client-centered therapy?" In order to address this question we need to refer to the conclusion, above, that techniques are necessarily employed in client-centered therapy, and then attempt to answer the question: "Towards what goals are techniques employed in client-centered therapy?"

If it is true, that implementation of the therapeutic attitudes is an application of techniques, then towards what goal or end are these techniques employed in client-centered therapy? Simply put, the answer in Rogers' theory is that the therapeutic attitudes provide a highly favorable interpersonal and intrapsychic environment for the client. This climate promotes the client's own capabilities for self-understanding, problem solving, more effective functioning in the client's interpersonal world and realization of untapped potentialities. Thus the goal of the techniques of client-centered therapy is only the successful provision of the attitudes in ways that communicate to the individual client. If the client perceives the attitudes, the consequent effects on the client are the result of the client's inherent capabilities for growth and healing. The consequences of the client's perception of the attitudes are not the therapist's goals for the client. In fact, the client-centered therapist has no goals for his or her clients other than providing his or her presence and communicating in such a way that the client is able to perceive the therapeutic attitudes.

Rogers was very clear – he had no goals for his clients. He said, "the goal has to be within myself, with the way I am" (Baldwin, 1987/2004, p. 47). He also said that therapy is most effective "when the therapist's goals are limited to the process of therapy and not the outcome" (p. 47). But even these process goals are not goals for the *client's* process. They are goals for the therapist's inner experience and for the therapist's implementation of inner experience in ways that can accurately communicate to the client.

Rogers elaborated on what he meant about his goals being limited to the process of therapy and not the outcome. He said, "I want to be as present to this person as possible. I want to really listen to what is going on. I want to be real in this relationship ..." (Baldwin, 1987/2004, p. 47). He said he asked himself, "Am I really with this person in this moment?" (p. 48), and concluded that these are "suitable goals for the therapist" (p. 48). In other words, the goals of the client-centered therapist are goals for him- or herself in the relationship – how he or she feels toward the client and relates to the client. They are goals in respect to the therapist's subjective states and his or her clarity of communication of those states to the client.

In client-centered work the therapist is not occupied with evaluating the client in respect to any expectations about, or goals conceived for, the client. It is not a client-centered concern to be evaluating how well the client's process of self-expression is attuned to his or her experiencing. It is not a client-centered concern to be evaluating how coherently or how deeply or how realistically the client is proceeding in his or her interaction with the therapist. Client-centeredness involves a profoundly nondiagnostic mindset. The therapist is neither reflecting upon the client's clinical diagnosis nor reflecting upon any other scheme for deciding what the therapist should or should not do in relation to the client at that particular time. The mindset of client-centeredness involves the therapist in giving total attention to the client and towards understanding the client's frame of reference and what it is the client is attempting to have understood in the moment.

A client-centered therapist's behavior in relation to the client is affected by the client's behavior and communications but not in any diagnostic sense.

The client-centered therapist is in a relationship with the client, in a dialogue with the client, in order to try to understand the client from the client's frame of reference. In the relationship and in attempting to empathically understand, the therapist is responsive to the client. The therapist needs to be understood by the client in respect to the therapist's intentions to understand, accept and be authentic with the client. Thus, if the client responds to the therapist in ways that communicate that there are misunderstandings, the therapist attempts to adjust his or her behavior so his or her intentions can be accurately perceived by the client.

The therapist wants to accurately understand the client, and to this end makes empathic responses to find out from the client whether or not he or she does accurately understand. And the therapist wants to be accurately understood by the client, at least as far as that is perceptible. The therapist does make adjustments in his or her manner of communication and in his or her expressive behavior on the basis of feedback from the client for the sake of accurate intercommunication and clarity of communication between therapist and client. But even taking into account this adjustive responsiveness on the part of the therapist, it should be evident that client-centered attitudes and their implementation are profoundly nondirective. This fact is crucial in addressing the question of whether one is being client-centered if one is employing techniques that have goals other than the goals the therapist has for him- or herself.

Rogers expressed the nondirective character of client-centered therapy in many ways in his writings and in his therapy demonstrations. In the context of his recognition of the political aspect of client-centeredness, Rogers (1977) stated:

> The politics of the client-centered approach is a conscious renunciation and avoidance by the therapist of all control over, or decision making for, the client. It is the facilitation of self-ownership by the client and the strategies by which this can be achieved; the placing of the locus of decision making and the responsibility for the effects of these decisions. It is politically centered in the client. (p. 14)

The client-centered therapist's techniques when interacting with a self-expressing client are subjective procedures for maintaining total attention to the client, understanding empathically, and correcting experiences of momentary incongruence. The techniques are also behavioral forms that communicate acceptant empathic understanding. In this context of trying to understand, the therapist has no reason to think about specific goals for the client or about techniques to apply in relation to the client. It is not consistent with being an authentic client-centered therapist to apply specific techniques to effect changes in the client's experience, content of focus or process of communication.

Clients usually have specific therapy goals, such as alleviating anxiety or depression, recovering from trauma, getting along better with a partner, deciding what kind of a job to get, as well as having a general goal of improving their overall well-being or of being happier. Client-centered therapists interact with their clients through a process of understanding these specific goals as well as trying to understand any other focus that is occupying the client. The fact of the client's having specific goals does not set the client-centered therapist on a track of trying to figure out how to help the client with those goals in ways other than providing the therapeutic conditions. It is assumed, and it is our experience, that clients' specific goals are reached in a great variety of ways and that the ways are designed or discovered by the clients themselves. Occasionally a client-centered therapist will be called upon by the client to contribute ideas or procedures to help the client towards one of his or her specific goals.

It is consistent with, and actually an implication of, client-centered theory for the therapist to address client's questions and accommodate his or her requests, if doing so is within the therapist's capabilities. Answering questions and honoring client's requests for information, ideas, guidance, or techniques follows from the nondirective attitude (Brodley, 1994) and the client-centered values of respect for and trust in clients. Often, participation in a client's request for help towards reaching specific goals that is other than acceptant empathic understanding involves discussion with the client about treatments or techniques available outside of the client-centered therapy relationship. These treatments or techniques may be available through self-help literature or from therapists, physicians or trainers who are sought as a concomitant or adjunctive form of help by the client.

Sometimes, when requests are made, the client-centered therapist has knowledge and/or expertise in other specific therapies or specific psychotechnologies. For example, we know some cognitive and behavioral techniques for alleviating depression, getting through panics, controlling one's focus of attention and for relaxation. In the context of authentic client-centered therapy, while being responsive and accommodating to the client's direction, some such techniques occasionally may be practiced with a client. When the therapist participates in this manner the procedure is conceptualized as an experiment in the service of the client. It is directed as much as possible by the client. And it is under the client's control throughout the time of the experiment. Its value and benefit is assessed by the client.

Client-centered therapy does not pretend or presume to provide all of the personal and psychological resources a client might need, or believes that he or she may need, in the process of therapeutic personal change. It does show its valuing of clients' autonomy, self-direction and self-responsibility by providing the therapeutic attitudes. It also shows respect for, and trust in, clients by responding to their questions and honoring their requests when it is possible for the therapist to do so. Any specific goal-aimed techniques that the client-centered therapist might provide, however, are not sourced in any kind of diagnostic mindset towards the client.

One cannot employ techniques based on any kind of diagnostic mindset and still be functioning as a client-centered therapist. Thus, in the sense of the panel question expressed, "Can specific techniques, that have specific goals and effects, be applied in the context of true client-centered psychotherapy?" the answer is NO if they are the result of the therapist's having a diagnostic mindset, and YES if they are the result of the client's questions or requests, and if the therapist is able to participate in applying a technique while integrating such participation into his or her maintaining the therapeutic attitudes.

### REFERENCES

Baldwin, M. (1987). Interview with Carl Rogers on the use of the self in therapy. In M. Baldwin & V. Satir (Eds.), *The use of self in therapy* (pp. 45–52). New York: Haworth Press. [Reprinted (2004) in R. Moodley, C. Lago, & A. Talahite (Eds.), *Carl Rogers counsels a Black client: Race and culture in person-centred counseling* (pp. 253–60). Ross-on-Wye: PCCS Books]

Brodley, B. T. (1994, May). *Meanings and implications of the nondirective attitude in client-centered therapy.* Revision of paper presented at the annual meeting of the Association for the Development of the Person-Centered Approach, Kendall College, Evanston, IL.

Rogers, C. R. (1951). *Client-centered psychotherapy.* Boston: Houghton Mifflin.

Rogers, C. R. (1957). The necessary and sufficient conditions of therapeutic personality change. *Journal of Consulting Psychology, 21,* 95–103.

Rogers, C. R. (1959). A theory of therapy, personality, and interpersonal relationships, as developed in the client-centered framework. In S. Koch (Ed.), *Psychology: A study of a science. Vol. III: Formulations of the person and the social context* (pp. 184–256). New York: McGraw-Hill.

Rogers C. R. (1977). *Carl Rogers on personal power.* New York: Delacorte Press.

Rogers, C. R. (1986). Client-centered therapy. In I. L. Kutash & A. Wolf (Eds.), *Psychotherapist's casebook: Therapy and technique in practice* (pp. 197–208). San Francisco: Jossey-Bass.

Shlien, J. (1993, November) *God is in the details* [Videotape]. Lecture presented to Portuguese Society of Client-Centered Therapy and Person-Centered Approach, Lisbon.

Webster, N. (1979). *Webster's new twentieth century dictionary* (2nd ed.). New York: Simon & Shuster.

## Chapter 19

# An introduction to the application of client-centered theory to therapy with two persons together

The basic theory of client-centered therapy applies to helping relationships with two persons coming to therapy together. As in individual work, the therapist offers a deep and constant respect for the individual persons and trust in their capacities for self-understanding, self-direction and personal therapeutic change. The therapist also offers the attitudinal conditions of congruence, unconditional positive regard and empathic understanding of the client's (in this case, each client's) internal frame of reference and, overall, maintains a nondirective attitude (Raskin, 1947/2005; Brodley, 1987/1998) toward each client. These attitudes create a psychological atmosphere or climate, which can be experienced as personally safe and as fostering of personal freedom of thought and emotion. This climate is conducive to and enables the actualizing tendency and brings about therapeutic change. The change process has been described by Rogers and is applicable to therapy with two persons together.

## CLIENT-CENTERED CHANGE THEORY APPLIED TO TWO PERSONS TOGETHER IN THERAPY

The theory of the change process in client-centered individual therapy has been expressed by Rogers in two ways and pertains to two different levels of analysis of the process. At the more microscopic level Rogers (1956) described the "moments of change" which occur frequently in successful psychotherapy. Such a moment has four characteristics: (1) It is "something which occurs in this existential moment … it is an experience of something at this instant in (the context of) the relationship" (p. 3). (2) "It is an experiencing which is without barrier or inhibition, or holding back" (p. 4). It is fully experienced. (3) It is freely present in awareness. (4) It "has the experience of being

We believe that this unfinished paper was written about 1989. We include it here as the first of three papers about multiple person therapy that show different perspectives at different times.

acceptable" (p. 4). Thus, in the procedure of self-disclosure, the client comes to experience moments having these four characteristics, and they are the change moments that accrue to the overall therapeutic change.

Rogers' (1984) second theory of change in client-centered therapy takes the view that therapeutic change occurs through the process of the client taking into himself, adopting, the therapeutic attitudes towards and about himself (and, secondarily, towards others) (Stock, 1948; Sheerer, 1949). The client becomes more self-accepting (i.e., adopting the attitude of unconditional positive regard towards self), more empathically, nonjudgmentally and deeply understanding towards self, and more authentic, real, and genuine (i.e., congruent) in himself. The client, in incorporating these attitudes towards self, is thereby providing himself intrapsychically with the therapeutic conditions which enable his inherent actualizing tendency to function more fruitfully toward healing and self-development than it was able to function under the previous-to-therapy attitudes towards self.

The implications of these two levels of change theory when applied to the two-persons-together-in-therapy situation are mostly straightforward. The therapist provides the therapeutic attitudes in relation to the two persons, and they each respond with the expected benefits. The two-persons-together situation is, however, different from the individual therapy situation in that the two persons have come to the therapy together specifically because one or both of them feel there are problems in the relation between them, and those problems are discussed between them and manifest between them in the therapy situation. This characteristic of the two-persons-together situation has some implications for description of the change process in terms of the second change theory pertaining to the client taking on the therapeutic attitudes towards himself and others.

Each (or one) person of the two may experience the presence of the other person as antagonistic, intimidating, threatening or provocative. And the level of trust between the two persons may be very low. If any of these possibilities are the case, and one or more often are, then the total climate of the therapy situation is mixed with anti-therapeutic features of psychological danger and constriction. The purer climate of safety and freedom which the therapist might be able to provide in relation to each of the clients separately is not entirely present and so is unlikely to be experienced.

The processes of the two clients together taking on the therapeutic attitudes as their own, towards self and in relation to others, depends primarily upon each client discriminating the sources of the therapeutic and the anti-therapeutic attitudes that are present in the situation. This discrimination is usually made without difficulty. The amelioration of therapeutic climate-confounding factors then evolves, through sessions, towards the purer climate as the therapist's attitudes consistently provide each client with sufficient safety for relatively nondefensive self-expression and self-representation to which the other client is the witness or the recipient. Even if one client remains somewhat, or sometimes, attacking toward the other, the clients' increasing abilities to respond authentically in the situation decrease the anti-therapeutic components in the climate. It may be recalled that Rogers' (1957) theory asserts that therapeutic change occurs to the extent the therapeutic attitudes are present, but the theory does not require a totally consistent climate for some change to occur.

The goals of the two-together situation are defined by one or both of the persons who have come to therapy. Usually the purpose conceived by at least one of the two is some change in one or both persons in relation to each other or in relation to others (e.g., children, a lover) or in relation to a situation (e.g., a divorce, a move). Successful therapy for twos involves results that satisfy the person, or both persons in the two, in respect to the relationship issue that brought the two persons to therapy. The goal of a two is often, perhaps usually, felt to be reached in one of three ways: (1) one or both persons modify their behaviors or their attitudes toward the other and/or towards the outsiders or situation; (2) understandings develop on the part of one or both persons which obviate changes; (3) the resolution is the withdrawal from the before-therapy relationship. The personal changes that occur, through the therapy work, in one or both persons may also be weighed in by the fact of clients feeling that the work has been successful concerning self from each client's point of view concerning himself.

The change process described in a way that takes into account the two-persons-together situation with relationship goals is as follows. The therapist provides the therapeutic attitudinal conditions towards each client (as each client speaks to the therapist, and as the therapist responds when one client speaks to the other client). Consequently each client becomes less defensive in self-disclosing and becomes more self-accepting, self-understanding and genuine (as the individual theory of change indicates). As this change is occurring in one client, the other client perceives these changes and experiences better conditions towards himself as well as specific understandings of the internal frame of reference of the other client. The new specific understandings of each person provide a truer perspective for each person in respect to previously disturbing events that have occurred between the two persons. As broader and more empathic understandings develop, each person accepts the other person more than he or she has before, and, thus, each person begins to provide better, more therapeutic, conditions towards the other. The two persons become relatively therapeutic for each other, and the total climate of the therapy situation is more consistently a safe and freeing one.

Previous differences are seen in a new light, with some degree of empathic understanding, and processes of interaction that are needed in working out solutions to the perceived problems are better processes with more productive outcomes than the previous interpersonal situation provided.

## SIMILARITIES AND DIFFERENCES BETWEEN INDIVIDUAL CLIENT-CENTERED THERAPY AND TWO-PERSONS-TOGETHER THERAPY

Client-centered therapy is based on the belief or hypothesis that each person has "the capacity ... to deal with his psychological situation and with himself" (Rogers, 1951, p. 23). This faith in and respect for others is the fundamental premise of client-centered work. The therapist attempts to live out the therapeutic attitudinal conditions which express respect for persons and provide the interpersonal and psychological environment which frees and augments the client's inherent capabilities for growth, change, healing and self-understanding. The basic ideas of client-centered therapy were developed primarily through work with individuals, but, from early in the work with and research on nondirective therapy, couples were also seen. The basic premises of client-centered work apply equally to work with couples.

Client-centered couple work emerged out of two basic therapy situations: (1) individual clients chose to have sessions with their partners; and (2) the parents of children who were brought for therapy worked on their own relationship in the context of coming in to discuss their child's problems, or child/parent couples had sessions together as adjunct to the work with the child.

Couple work, with client-centered therapists, has traditionally involved no conceptions on the therapist's part about the desirability of the couple persisting as an entity. It has had no prejudices concerning the composition of the couple, that is, about whether the pair were married, living together, friends, lovers, related by blood (such as mother/daughter couples) or partners in romantic/sexual relations who are of the same sex.

Additional theories such as those about specific relationships (e.g., spouses) are not practically relevant to the approach and do not influence the way the client-centered therapist proceeds in being of help. Rogers has provided the student of his therapy with a theory of interpersonal relationships (Rogers, 1959, pp. 235–240) to enhance intellectual perspective, but this theory does not function to direct the aims of the therapist any more than Rogers' theory of personality (1959, pp. 221–233) directs the therapist's efforts in individual therapy.

Couple work has been client-centered as purely as individual work. The only difference brought about by the presence of two clients in a relationship and interested in working on the relationship between them is that the client-centered therapist takes on the additional responsibility of facilitating communication between the partners – helping them to understand each other and express themselves to each other.

As in individual work, therapy with two persons together engages the therapist with the uniqueness of the persons rather than the features that they share with other persons with whom they may be classified. It is a value which is corollary to the theory in client-centered work for the therapist to relate to individuals as persons (Bozarth & Brodley, 1986/1993) and not to abstract concepts that may describe them (e.g., status, race), to concepts of their groupings (e.g., spousal dynamics or family dynamics) nor to concepts about their psyches (e.g., ego, persona). Client-centered work with two persons, as with individuals, families and groups, does not proceed by applying theories about the way the persons are in abstract units (e.g., "the individual," "the family," "the group," etc.). Instead, the feelings, perceptions, responsibilities, and expectations that each person in the two has about himself, about the other person, and also about their mutual situation, their relationship, or their two-ness are to be understood from each person's own frame of reference, empathically, by the therapist.

Client-centered therapy developed primarily through work with individual clients. Client-centered literature about theory, practice and research is primarily and almost exclusively about individual work. Consequently, the nature of the therapeutic task and the implementations of the theory are most familiar in work with individual clients alone. But couples and families have been seen by client-centered therapists [Raskin & van der Veen, 1970] since shortly after the founding of the Counseling Center at the University of Chicago in 1945. It may be that because the differences that exist in working with two persons together or in various family groupings compared to individual work do not require adjustments in the theory of therapy, so little writing about client-centered twos and families has been done.

Work with two persons together, however, modifies the therapist's task somewhat and occasionally requires some adjustments from the implementations with individuals. These adjustments are responses to the fact that the therapist is interacting with two persons, and the two persons are, at times, interacting with each other in the presence of the therapist. The adjustments result from the therapist's perceptions when working with two persons at the same time and in the same place.

There are three categories of factors which may occur in the two-persons-together therapy situation which lead to modifying the therapist's behavior or additional implementations of client-centered theory. These are: (1) the complexity of perceptual focal points present in the situation; (2) factors diminishing the level of therapist attitudinal conditions provided to the clients; (3) the clients' differences in respect to their personal power in the therapy situation. Each factor will be discussed with its implications for the therapist attempting to provide the Rogerian therapeutic conditions for both clients in the two-persons-together therapy situation.

## The complexity of perceptual focal points

The client-centered therapist attempts to empathically understand the client from the client's internal frame of reference as manifestation of an empathic understanding attitude toward the client. This aim, on the therapist's part, to empathically understand and, from time to time (as the therapist has the need), to check the adequacy of his or her understanding, remains the same as in individual therapy when the situation is therapy with two persons together. There is, superficially, simply a second person/client present to be empathically understood by the therapist.

The two clients together, however, create a different perceptual situation which is much more complex than that of one client alone. In the individual situation the one client, while in the company of the therapist and having perceptions of the therapist, expresses and represents him- or herself. The client's perceptions of the therapist crucially influence the experiences of the client and, consequently, what the client expresses and represents. In the situation of two persons together there are more perceptual focal points and more sources of influence than in the single client/therapist interface. The perceptual focal points are as follows:

Client one expresses his internal frame of reference
Client two expresses his internal frame of reference
Client one's expression is perceived by client two
Client two's expression is perceived by client one
Client one perceives the therapist's empathic understanding and acceptance and specific understandings expressed to client two
Client two perceives the therapist's empathic understanding and acceptance and specific understandings expressed to client one
Client one perceives client two's responses to the therapist when the therapist has expressed empathic understanding to two
Client two perceives client one's responses to the therapist when the therapist has expressed empathic understanding to one
Client one perceives client two's responses to client one's expression
Client two perceives client one's responses to client two's expression

These multiple perceptual focal points have impact upon the therapist in several ways. First, the therapist has more facts, personal meanings and feelings to take in, to process and, to some extent, to remember. Second, the therapist has to keep track of and keep sorted out the responses of each client to the other as they develop in the interaction. In the two-persons-together therapy situation there is not only the self-presentation of each person to attend to, but, through the interaction that occurs between them in the situation, there are new elements – feelings and content and themes – stimulated. Third, the therapist has to be mindful of the impact, including misunderstandings, generated in one client as that client listens to the therapist respond to the other client.

The therapeutic task, from the therapist's point of view, is significantly more complex and demanding when working with two clients together because of the increased number and complexity of perceptual focal points to be taken into account. The therapist's main adaptation to be made on account of this factor is finding a way to remain relaxed and receptive to both clients while having to keep track of and process much more complex material.

In individual work it is sometimes difficult to identify the salient points or the theme in a client's presentation. With two persons it becomes more difficult because the therapist has to sort out garrulous or aside elements from two persons and from the interaction events as well. There is more chance of error and, as a consequence, inadvertent therapist-caused confusion or therapist directivity.

An example of a relatively simple interaction (from the therapist's point of view) is the section from an interview with Jean, a single mother, and Bill, her live-in boyfriend, that follows:[1]

1. Bill: (to therapist, referring to Jean) She comes on complaining and running me down. If she was just reminding me of something, I wouldn't start shouting. But she's very angry, and she attacks me.

2. Jean: (to Bill) I don't attack you! (to therapist) I try very hard to just say "please do it" without any attitude. I am *feeling* pissed because it's always something he promised he'd do, and it's way past the time I needed it done.

3. Bill: (to therapist, sarcastically) It doesn't come across like there's been any effort.

---

1. This session excerpt is based on memory. The names and the situation here and in the subsequent vignette have been disguised.

4. Therapist: (to Jean) So you feel you're taking pains not to be provoking towards Bill, but you're doing that having to override how angry you feel about how he hasn't followed through the way he promised you. (Jean: Yeah.) (to Bill) You feel she's attacking you, and it comes across like that's what she's wanting to do right then.

5. Bill: Yeah … She gets too angry. She wants these things done when she wants them done, and I'm not dancing to her tune.

6. Therapist: (to Bill) You're supposed to function according to her timing because she's got a big stake in when these things get done. (Bill: Yeah.)

7. Jean: (to therapist) That's not true. (to Bill) You don't care about my feelings; that's the problem. I can tell you over and over why something is important to me. (to therapist) For example, if he goes to bed after I do and leaves some dishes, then, when I'm in a hurry in the morning, I have to take the time to clear away his stuff before I can fix breakfast for the kids. (to Bill) It's inconsiderate of you to leave stuff like that! So, of course, I'm pissed off the 15th time you've done the same thing.

8. Bill: (to Jean) You're pissed the first time!

9. Therapist: (to Jean) He seems to be willfully disregarding your feelings and your inconvenience, not just forgetting. (Jean: Yeah, that's how I feel.)

10. Bill: (to therapist) But I'm not! (to Jean) You don't understand. (to therapist) I can see how it looks that way. But the problem is that I just don't care about some things the way Jean does. I'm not bothered if I have to do some cooking, and there's a mess in the way. I just take care of it, and it doesn't take that long. Jean reacts like it's a big deal.

11. Jean: (to therapist) He *is* much more easygoing than I am. I get pissed if Toni (her child) leaves a mess in my way too (Bill: But not as pissed …), but not as pissed as I feel toward Bill. She hasn't learned yet, she's a kid, she means well, she says, "I'm sorry" when I remind her (Bill: You're not hostile to her.). But, (to Bill) why can't you remember for *me*? Don't I matter enough to you so you'd want to make things easier for me (starts to weep)?

12. Bill: (to Jean, tenderly) I'm sorry … I don't know why it's so hard for me to think about what you want. But it isn't what it seems to you. I'd like to make things easier for you; honestly I would.

13. Jean: (weeping) I wish I believed that.

14. Bill: (to therapist) This is new for me; I haven't ever lived with a woman before. And right away Jean started getting on my case when I wouldn't do things that seemed natural to her. She hasn't been giving me a chance to get used to the responsibilities or the situation.

15. Jean: (to therapist) I can see that. Right away it felt like he didn't care how I felt about things ... He seemed so self-centered. But it's true: I wasn't thinking about how much adjustment there was from his point of view.

The complexity of working with two people together can be seen, from the therapist's perspective of trying to empathically follow both persons and their interaction, in the sequence above. Things happen fast. There is no chance, for example, for the therapist to respond to Bill between responses 1 and 2. And Bill intercepts before the therapist can respond to Jean (2). In 4 the therapist lays out Jean's feelings, gets affirmation, and follows with an empathic understanding response to Bill. Bill doesn't get a chance to respond to therapist (6) because Jean (7) comes in to deny the interpretation of Jean that therapist (6) has expressed in response to Bill (5). Then Jean (7) directly addresses Bill with an accusation and then, almost in the same breath, explains herself to the therapist, giving an example of the kind of thing that leads to her complaining to Bill about his behavior. Then Bill (8) quickly responds by undercutting Jean's view that her anger is justified by Bill's repetitive inconsiderations. And so forth. Despite the complexity here, which includes accusations and angry and hurt responses, the clients appear to be moving towards a more understanding attitude about each other in the problem they are working on.

## Factors which may diminish the level of therapist attitudinal conditions

Misunderstanding of the therapist by the client may disturb or preclude the client's perception of the therapist *conditions* being offered from the therapist's point of view. The therapist, in individual work, has considerable control over the possibility that the client will perceive his attitudes of empathic understanding and unconditional positive regard. The relative simplicity of the situation of direct, one-on-one interaction between therapist and client allows the therapist to have a steady focused attention on the client, and it is correspondingly relatively easy to identify a misunderstanding on the client's part about the therapist's attitudes and relatively easy to address such a misunderstanding. For example:

Client: All these problems crowd in on me so much that I can't think so well. I can't concentrate. I forget things. Then I make a lot of mistakes, and the next thing is – I'm worried that I'm not going to be able to get the grades I need to get into medical school, and then I get more anxious and distractible.

Therapist: A downward spiral ...

Client: (interrupting) But I don't know for sure I won't be able to get into medical school.

Therapist: I didn't mean that ... I just meant there is a downward spiral you were describing in bad feelings and worry. (Client: Yeah.)

Correction of misunderstanding of the therapist by the client is swift in this example and probably so in part because it is a one-to-one interaction without distraction of input from others.

There are two main realities of therapy with two persons together that may diminish the level of therapeutic conditions perceived by the client. In the two-persons-together therapy situation the therapist may not develop the awareness that one client has misunderstood the therapist's responses to the other person. The one client may interpret the therapist as sympathetic, supportive or in agreement with the other client. Such an interpretation by the client may occur when the therapist, from his point of view, is feeling quite neutral and only checking his empathic understanding. In the interaction between Bill, Jean and the therapist it is not clear whether Jean (7) speaks to the therapist because she understands the therapist was expressing Bill's viewpoint (which Jean doesn't accept as true) or because she thinks the therapist was (in 6) telling Bill what she believes about Jean. It is likely, given the progress that occurs in the interaction, that Jean does perceive the therapist's intention correctly (that the therapist is expressing an understanding not an agreement). If that is not the case, it might be many interactions further along before the therapist is given a clear sense that Jean feels the therapist has a bias in favor of Bill. When such a misunderstanding is lingering, unperceived and unattended by the therapist, the therapist conditions are lessened for that client.

The second main factor which may diminish the level of therapeutic attitudinal conditions provided by the therapist is the effect on the therapist of behavior that the therapist experiences as hurtful or abusive directed from one of the two persons towards the other. The therapist's ability to accept and understand the perpetrator may be taxed or undermined. Hostile, critical or mean statements expressed by one client towards the other in the therapist's presence are, generally, more intense and provocative than the report by a client of such experiences with another person. But, even if the therapist responds to a report about an absent person with anger at the perpetrator, that person is outside the therapy situation and is not there to be responded to in any way, while the presence of the hurtful interaction requires the therapist to, somehow, deal with his own reaction to the perpetrator who is present. While the psychological safety of the outsider is not jeopardized by the therapist's feelings, in the two-person-together therapy situation, the therapist having difficulty with hurtful behavior on the part of one client toward the other may undermine the therapist's capacity for unconditional positive regard toward and empathic understanding of the perpetrator.

An example of a therapist becoming momentarily aggressive toward one of his clients in reaction to the client's critical (and hurtful) remarks to the other client follows:

Luke (1): She's doing a lot of things she says are part of some process of really developing herself. (to therapist, sarcastically) But I don't know if anybody is going to want what gets developed!

Blyth (2): Yeah (looking hurt), you said that before.

Therapist (3): (to Luke) You mean Blyth is changing in ways you find *you* don't like?

Luke (4): (to therapist) It's not just that I have a problem with what she's doing … Everybody we know is saying, "What's happening to Blyth? … She used to be such a caring type of person …" (to Blyth) You're really hurting people, and I think you're going to find out that nobody will be around for you one of these days!

Therapist (5): (to Luke, interpreting him) It sounds like you've been lobbying for support against Blyth and getting what you want …

Blyth (6): (breaking in on therapist and speaking to Luke) I don't see why you say that. I think I'm bothering you, and then you build up a picture that everybody else is upset at me, and I don't believe I'm coming across to our friends as such a bad person. But it hurts me a lot that you think I'm being so bad, and that you're trying to make me feel insecure with other people.

The therapist in response 3 attempts a neutral-sounding response although the interpretational form betrays some tension. Then, in response 5, the therapist loses his neutrality and makes an accusational response. Blyth interrupts the therapist from continuing and expresses her own interpretation and feeling. The therapist has ceased experiencing understanding and acceptance of Luke in this interaction, and it is likely that Luke will have felt that diminishment of the therapeutic conditions and, also, will perceive the therapist as biased towards Blyth.

### Personal power differences of the two persons in therapy together
The two persons coming into therapy together usually show differences in respect to their personal power or dominance in the situation. These differences that appear in the therapy situation may or may not reveal or

relate to the whole balance and fluctuations or areas of relative power in the relationship outside of therapy. The weight of relative power does become a factor, nevertheless, in the therapist's experience and in the implementation of the therapeutic attitudes.

There are three general ways in which disparities in power or dominance show up in the situation of two persons together in therapy. (1) One of the two persons is more articulate, clearer about his or her experiences and/or speaks up more aggressively than does the other. This person's dominance manifests in having or taking more opportunity to express self and point of view. (2) One of the two is more expressive of anger, criticism, accusation, and/or blameful interpretation of the other, and this has the effect of upsetting the other, stimulating defensiveness, and/or hurt feelings in the other person. (3) One of the two is given more authority about their mutual situation by the other than the other asserts in the situation.

One of the main values in client-centered work is the belief in the equality of persons regardless of differences in their talents, social status or condition in respect to mental or physical health. The therapist/client relationship, when it is optimal, is experienced by the therapist and client as a person-to-person relation (Rogers, 1984; Brink, 1987). The therapeutic attitude of congruence, particularly, promotes a sense of equality between therapist and client. This person-to-person relating in the two-together situation that occurs between the therapist and each of the two clients causes a divergence from that equality in the client-to-client relation to stand out in the therapist's perceptions. The therapist's fundamental task, of course, in response to such perceptions is to maintain congruence, unconditional positive regard and empathic understanding regardless of the inequality of the clients in relation to each other.

The problem for the therapist in unequal client situations when there are two clients together is that the nondominant client may be insufficiently self-representing, and, consequently, the therapist is unable to respond empathically. This suggests that the therapist may need to act towards the two clients in some manner that results in sufficient self-expression and self-representation on the part of the nondominant client – sufficient to permit the therapist to experience empathic understanding. The attempt to elicit sufficient self-representation for empathic understanding cannot, however, be grounded in the therapist having the goal of greater equality in the relation between the two clients. The client-centered therapist in principle and in action does not conceive of goals for client.

The client-centered therapist does have, however, the license to adjust implementations to an extent that permits or fosters his or her own capability to offer the therapeutic conditions. On this basis the therapist may produce responses which bring forth the expression of the nondominant client.

## REFERENCES

Bozarth, J. D., & Brodley, B. T. (1986, September). *The core values and theory of the person-centered approach*. A paper presented at the first annual meeting of the Association for the Development of the Person-Centered Approach, University of Chicago, International House. [Les valeurs essentieles de l'approche centrée sur la personne. The core values of the person-centered approach. Published (1993) in French and English in *Le Journal du PCAII*, France (Person-Centered Approach Institute International – France)]

Brink, D. C. (1987). The issues of equality and control in the client or person-centered approach. *Journal of Humanistic Psychology 27*, 27–37.

Brodley, B. T. (1987). *A client-centered psychotherapy practice.* Paper prepared for the Third International Forum on the Person-Centered Approach. La Jolla, CA. [Published (1998) in C. Wolter-Gustafson (Ed.), *A person-centered reader: Personal selections by our members* (pp. 59–87). Boston: Association for the Development of the Person-Centered Approach]

Raskin, N. J. (1947). The nondirective attitude. Unpublished manuscript. [Published (2005) in *The Person-Centered Journal 12*(1–2) and (2005) in B. E. Levitt (Ed.), *Embracing non-directivity* (pp. 327–347). Ross-on-Wye: PCCS Books]

[Raskin, N. J., & van der Veen, F. (1970). Client-centered family therapy: Some clinical and research perspectives. In J. T. Hart & T. M. Tomlinson (Eds.), *New directions in client-centered therapy* (pp. 387–406). Boston: Houghton Mifflin.]

Rogers, C. R. (1951). *Client-centered therapy.* Boston: Houghton Mifflin.

Rogers, C. R. (1956). *The essence of psychotherapy: Moments of movement.* Presentation [Symposium] at the 1st Annual Meeting of the American Academy of Psychotherapists, New York.

Rogers, C. R. (1957). The necessary and sufficient conditions of therapeutic personality change. *Journal of Consulting Psychology, 21*, 95–103.

Rogers, C. R. (1959). A theory of therapy, personality, and interpersonal relationships, as developed in the client-centered framework. In S. Koch (Ed.), *Psychology: A study of a science. Vol. III: Formulations of the person and the social context* (pp. 184–256). New York: McGraw-Hill.

Rogers, C. R. (1984). A discussion group titled "A conversation with Carl Rogers" at the Second International Forum on the Person-Centered Approach in Norwich, England [Cassette Recording].

Sheerer, E. T. (1949). An analysis of the relationship between acceptance of and respect for self and acceptance of and respect for others in ten counseling cases. *Journal of Consulting Psychology, 13*(3), 69–175.

Stock, D. (1948). *An investigation into the inter-relations between the self-concept and feelings directed toward other persons and groups.* Unpublished master's thesis. University of Chicago.

# Chapter 20

# Client-centered couple therapy

My approach to couple therapy has evolved since I began doing couple work in 1960 or 1961. My most recent shift in view relates to my reservations about the term "therapy" for couple and family work. I am now thinking that the couple and family situation is primarily an educational one that has therapeutic benefits. All through the years, my position has been that only individuals can be the units of therapy because there is no organism or personality of a duo or family. This point of view has not changed. A couple or family is not a system in my view, and the use of the system metaphor is problematic and unhelpful as well. Clinicians may say a family presents dysfunction, but in my view that presupposes a system that has a natural function, and I don't agree with that notion concerning any aggregate of individuals.

ASSUMPTIONS

A. The organism/person is the unit of therapy, regardless of the setting (couple, family, group, community)

B. The unit of therapy involves a whole with an integrated purpose, and when a whole is conflicted it still must conform to a single identity and choose directions in the moment. Conflicts between individuals in a group can be acted on independently, without any effect on other individuals in some circumstances.

C. I define therapy as unequivocally nondirective, permitting the individual to be self-directive and function as an integrated person or regulate his own disintegrated aspects. Couples often have opposing goals and wishes. Couple therapy often needs to create a substitute for lack of wholeness by means of a

---

This paper was presented at the annual meeting of the Association for Development of the Person-Centered Approach in Kutztown, PA, May 23–27, 1996. We include it not as a finished paper but as possibly helpful or thought provoking to therapists who work within the more complex situation of dyadic (or group and family) work. We have made minor edits to make it easier to read.

cooperative and democratic procedure. This is a directivity, and I see this as a goal I have as the therapist/educator in couple or family work, the educational goal of promoting a cooperative, relatively equal power situation and a democratic procedure.

In respect to the mutual goals of the couple and the individual goals of the individuals, and in terms of the topics discussed, the order of discussion, the continuity or discontinuity, and my understandings of each individual, I remain faithful to the nondirective attitude.

D. Consequently, couple work is almost always educative and directive in order to be therapeutic for both individuals. By therapeutic I mean promoting the well-being, integration and self-direction of the individual. To the extent persons in a couple have shared purposes, actually or potentially, the therapeutic activity fosters the relationship. But, therapeutic couple work may not foster the relationship. With individuals it is always assumed and wanted that the individual's integrity and self-direction is primary (within limits of not violating the rights of others).

Although people usually come to couple therapy because of dissatisfactions with the relationship, this is represented in many different ways. I make no assumptions about the goodness or viability of the relationship as a social unit.

THE DIRECTIVITY: THE THERAPIST'S EDUCATIVE GOALS FOR CLIENTS IN THE COUPLE OR FAMILY SITUATION

1. Ability to accurately hear and understand each other. Empathic understanding

2. Ability to self-represent adequately to each other (individual choice about extent)

3. Ability to accept equality of power in respect to the process and issues (may not be equality outside the therapy)

4. Help clients adopt the therapist's procedure for interaction and learn the therapist's procedure. Promote equality of attention and understanding and curtail interpersonal violence (based on therapist preference, not on assumption that curtailing violence is good for clients). Basically the therapist orchestrates the interaction as needed (what to talk about, who goes first, is one understood, what is reaction of other, etc.)

THERAPIST ASSUMPTIONS:

1. No system overview – no system metaphor

2. No idea of outcome in terms of decisions or existence of couple

3. No ideas about values of individuals

4. No siding with one person in couple. Protective of both regarding being understood

5. Empathic understanding of both parties. Attunement to incomplete communications in order to promote responsiveness to each from other. Both understanding of each by the other and bringing out reactions of each to other when understood

## CAROL TOPPING'S DISSERTATION RESEARCH

In the course of research for her 1993 doctoral dissertation at the University of Georgia, Carol made transcripts of 10 sessions with 10 different duos from my work. Session tapes were randomly selected but required to be audible at the beginning.

Carol took my own writing about theory and my response to her questionnaire and developed a set of response types. She came up with a response typology that would cover all my therapeutic behavior with the couples in the sample.

1. Agenda responses
2. Empathic understanding responses
3. Empathic facilitative responses
4. Congruency responses
5. Equalizing responses
6. Goal clarification responses
7. Spontaneous responses

### Responses to Topping questionnaire

Client-centered couple therapy is an application of Rogers' therapeutic theory to work with duos – any pairing – family, non-family relationships, work colleagues, etc. The actualizing tendency assumption applies to each person in the duo. It does not apply to the duo as an entity.

There is in client-centered theory an additional assumption of a basic affiliative tendency, and this is viewed as the underlying motivation in couple work. The manifest motivation is expressed in the duo where one or both persons perceive a problem/problems in the relationship.

The general goal is to deal with differences between the persons in a nondestructive-to-either-person manner that results in both persons feeling their personal realization has been enhanced or developed, whether the relation improves or continues or not.

As in individual work, the therapist attempts to experience the therapeutic attitudes, but towards both persons in the duo. Empathic understanding is communicated largely via empathic understanding responses – following responses – to each person. In couple therapy, an additional response occurs, in the manner of checking understanding of person A by person B when the therapist has empathically checked with person A, and A confirms being understood by the therapist, [and B consequently hears the therapist's empathic understanding of A]. This promotes empathic understanding of each client by the other.

The differences in empathic understanding in couple work: (1) The goal is not only that each person feels empathically understood, but each feels the other person empathically understands as well. (2) Each person can witness empathic understanding by the therapist to the other and must be able to tolerate this. (Note: accurate empathic understanding is purified when doing couple work because the therapist should not agree in empathic understanding so the manner of experiencing pure empathic understanding is honed.)

Another difference is that rarely are the two persons equal in power (one loves more, one is more aggressive, one is more intelligent, one is more wealthy or has more access to resources, etc.). The differences in power may or may not be relevant to the interaction. If they are, the therapist needs to equalize the situation. This means behavioral directivity/facilitation to equalize use of time and opportunities for self-representation. I may direct attention to one of the persons, stop one or both from communicating, or ask for responses from one.

Therapist behavior is not only to acceptantly empathically understand each person, but to facilitate empathic understanding between the two. The therapist has a role in bringing out the more complete, nondefensive, expressions of each person. This gives the other person a chance of being empathically understood, an experience of his cohort that he would not produce alone (because of interference by the other, or violent reactions or loss of control).

Additional therapist behavior is to provide perspectives when requested. If it is requested, the therapist's effort is to honestly state whatever is appropriate to the question. Sometimes I also offer perspectives. Unrequested perspectives are observations about the nature of communication, about society as it bears on the couple, about tendencies I've observed in men and/or women, or observed patterns of behavior, sexual or domestic, or with children or whatever. These may be direct assertion of my beliefs, or my ideas. Or they may be indirect communication of ideas by telling something personal about me or my life.

I classify volunteered perspectives as "spontaneous" responses that often are stimulated by my interpretation that the problem is an example of a common or natural one in couple or family life. Or my perspective illustrates the normalcy of differences even when they are causing pain and conflict. The perspective is intended to soften the clients' judgmental attitudes toward the issue or conflict. At least they inform the couple of my nonjudgmental perspective and compassion. Or the perspective illustrates variability and thus the normality of the problem.

Aside from the directivity in regard to education for communication and my nonsystematic directivities I do not have goals for the clients. I facilitate the clarification of the clients' goals, whether they are shared goals or different ones.

## Procedure

At the start of therapy and at each session, I usually ask for the agenda and spend the first minutes facilitating the clarification of the topics for focus. Both people must agree to discuss a topic, or it won't be discussed at that time. This is a principle throughout the therapy – that both people must be willing to hear the other at any moment. If one doesn't want to hear something, it won't be said at that time.

After the agenda is stated I ask "who goes first?" and facilitate that decision. As one person speaks, I make empathic responses as I need to and ask the second person if they are following and understanding. After that I ask the second person if they have any response from their point of view. I emphasize the distinction between understanding and responding. Sometimes the clients speak only through me. They tell me, I check understandings, and I turn to find out if the other has understood, and if he has a response. Then I empathically respond to the second person, if needed, and check with the first for his understanding of the second, and so forth.

If the duo are able to speak directly to each other, I only interfere if I think the communication is being misunderstood, or one person is not getting his full opportunity. I will say "Stop, let her finish," or "Wait, you'll get your turn."

I do not interpret unless directly asked.

I do not advise unless asked, with rare exceptions.

I suggest individual sessions to get a one-to-one empathic connection with both persons.

I keep secrets of one partner. I impose no requirement to be honest between partners.

**Carol Topping's findings**

1. Therapy behavior consistent with my writings and ideas.

2. Therapy behavior mostly consistent with the theory of Carl Rogers, except for lack of purity of nondirective attitude.

3. Some types of response, such as equalizing and goal clarification responses and perspectives, are based on my beliefs, traits and idiosyncrasies more than on client-centered therapy. The equalizing and goal clarification responses point to the fact that I do not trust the clients to be their own best resources. It is true: I do not trust duos or families to maintain equal power among the members. I do not trust they will restrain themselves from emotional violence. Also, spontaneous responses of suggestions, observations, and personal opinions at least imply I am not relying on the inherent direction of the clients.

## Chapter 21

# Summary of an interview with Barbara Temaner Brodley: Views of the nondirective attitude in couple and family therapy

### Noriko Motomasa

Barbara Brodley self-describes as a nondirective, client-centered therapist when working with couples and families. Her experience and expression of Rogers' attitudes is basically the same as in individual work. She attempts to maintain the attitudes of congruence, unconditional positive regard, and empathic understanding toward all the persons in the session. Barbara does not think there is any difference in experiencing the attitudes from individual work, although it seems to be a little more challenging to maintain the attitudes, given the complexity of the interaction among multiple persons. However, she does not think that this difficulty means that the basic theory is incomplete; it is just harder to implement with more than one client.

When the therapy involves more than one client at the same time, Barbara perceives the manifestation of the attitudes as a little different than with single clients. That there are two qualifications for couple and family therapy – a facilitating function and an equalizing function. Barbara feels that it is necessary to provide an opportunity for all the clients in a session to have sufficient voice so that they may feel they are adequately representing themselves. Also, she thinks, again, in terms of opportunity, that it is important that the clients have a feeling that they are equally respected and valued by the therapist. Here, equality is not an objective notion but exists in the perceptions of the clients. These therapist functions may be interpreted as contrary to Rogers' therapeutic attitudes by some client-centered therapists; Barbara, however, views them as a situational expression of the attitudes.

This chapter is taken from Motomasa, N. (2004). *Client-centered couple and family therapy: Experienced therapists' views of theory and practice.* Unpublished doctoral clinical research project, Illinois School of Professional Psychology, (now Argosy University, Chicago) (pp. 129–134).

In her clinical research project, Noriko "… sought to discover how a sample of experienced client-centered therapists adapts Rogers' theory of therapy to their work with couples and families, giving special attention to the therapists' views of the nondirective attitude in couples and family work" (Motomasa, 2004, p. 44). Reproduced with permission from Noriko Motomasa.

Because there is more than one client, for example, Barbara checks whether one person feels he or she understands what another person has said; Barbara asks if it is all right for one person to go on or whether another one wants to get in some of his or her thoughts. Also, when Barbara is empathically responding and giving attention to one person, she then might acknowledge to the other person(s) that she is aware of this situation. Barbara might ask them if they feel the concentration on one of the clients is a problem to the others, and attempt to find out how they are reacting to the situation. Barbara thinks that the therapist's attentiveness to this situation helps all the clients, although one person is given more attention at the moment. The acknowledgments are not for the purpose of controlling or dominating the situation, but for providing an opportunity for clearer communication among the clients. The "orchestrating" behavior is attuned to trying to be equally sensitive to the different parties in the situation. In addition to those functions, there are other things; for example, the therapist has to be very aware of his or her own feelings, and be very mindful and careful in the language she or he uses in the situation, taking each person into account.

Barbara thinks that there is a difference in the rhythm of empathic responding when she is working with more than one person. More judgment and awareness of the other clients are necessary concerning when to empathically check, whereas if the client were speaking alone to her, then Barbara can rely only on her own feeling of a need to check. With multiple clients, the therapist can become very dominant if the therapist chooses to be constantly responding according to his or her own need to check for accuracy of understanding. Depending on the situation, even though the therapist is failing to fully or accurately understand, he or she allows this in order to avoid dominating the situation. Focusing on empathic understanding as behavior, there is a risk that one will engage in too much behavior and take up too much time, space, and sound in the situation. The therapist needs more tolerance to let things happen and allow clients to express themselves. However, in a small family group, if one person is speaking, and everybody seems attentive, and Barbara finds something in what the person is saying ambiguous, instead of making an empathic response, she might say, "Does everyone feel like you understand pretty clearly what so-and-so said?" This is a different kind of checking. In effect, a facilitating goal manifests itself.

Also, after Person One's speech, Person Two and Three sometimes start to make comments from their own frames of reference that seem to indicate that they did not quite understand what One was saying. Barbara might then say to Two and Three, "There is something in what you said that made me unsure about what One said." Additionally, she might ask One, "Did you mean this and that?" This might, in effect, function as a correction for Two and Three, helping them to more accurately understand Person One.

Sometimes in couple and family therapy, the interaction resembles sequential individual sessions with Person One, Two, and Three, with Barbara responding at some length with each, afterwards going from one to another. To help this become more participative by all the clients, for example, she may have an interaction with One, making empathic following responses. The therapist then might say, "Do the rest of you feel you were following this? Does anybody have any reaction to …?" The therapist's empathic understanding in that interaction with One probably helps Two and Three to have a clearer understanding of One, even though they were not interacting. Although it is not facilitating between them, it has a facilitative effect.

Barbara thinks that if the therapist keeps the basic therapeutic attitudes while allowing the additional goals (facilitating and equalizing), the couple or family therapy will be effective. The very therapy setting (i.e., a room with privacy, less external distraction, a certain slot of time) can be therapeutic as well. She thinks the therapist's genuine, empathic and acceptant presence in this structure creates a powerful set of conditions.

It is rare that Barbara would make a kind of response she calls an "empathic comment" – a comment from the therapist's own frame of reference – about what is happening. She does not think of group dynamics at all while interacting with couples or families. She does not presume any particular organization or dynamic pattern to be understood working with a family or couple. This is because she does not think there are standard dynamic forms and considers those ideas to be interpretive and directive. Making comments about the situation or the interpersonal dynamics emphasizes the authority of the therapist and the subordination of the clients, which is not consistent with the client-centered viewpoint.

Barbara, however, considers clients' questions to require responses from the therapist's frame on the grounds of the theory of the nondirective attitude. She answers clients' questions as best she can with some tentativeness and humility, while taking into consideration the risk of highlighting herself as an observer. She has made spontaneous comments to clients, which are not intended to be directive. However, they are rare and not systematic.

According to Barbara, the units of therapy are always the individuals. Couples and families are aggregates of individuals and not to be treated as analogous to organisms. She does not think the sociological discipline – focusing on social organization – is relevant to the therapist's job. The therapist is always trying to be attuned to each individual and to each individual as they perceive themselves in relation to other person(s).

Barbara sees the merits in couple and family therapy, in comparison to individual therapy, as depending on the individuals. People often need to talk to each other about the problems they have between them. Some can do that outside of therapy. If clients personally change through their individual therapy, it is very likely that their behavior will change outside the therapy situation. Other clients are more successful at making constructive relationship changes if they come in together.

Regarding disadvantages for the clients to be in couple and family therapy, Barbara thinks that sometimes what gets disclosed to other participants may be more than they would choose to know or have disclosed. Each individual does not have control in this respect. There's a greater chance of a participant in multiple situations experiencing some kind of emotional blow that they are not prepared for.

Barbara is uncertain about how to describe differences between couple therapy and family therapy. Power seems to be more likely to be distributed unequally in a family because of generational differences; however, she thinks it is a matter of degree because nobody is equal to anybody else in any relationship. Family-based inequalities do not affect the way the therapist works with the clients.

Regarding differences in couple and family therapy from group therapy, Barbara emphasizes that group therapy consists of people who are not related or familiar with each other. The group has an aggregate of individuals who come into the situation usually without knowledge or issues about each other. Through the interactions that occur in the group, they develop issues among themselves. Another difference is that group therapy has an educational feature because of differences in the therapist's roles. The therapist in a group not only understands each individual in the situation, but also is aware of functioning as a model for the attitudes and the expression of the attitudes. Additionally, depending upon how the group members develop as facilitating agents, she at times functions as a participant in the group, while keeping the therapist mindset. In contrast, in couple and family therapy, the therapist remains the therapist.

Barbara does not have any agenda, goals, or hope for certain outcomes of therapy for the clients. She does want to function in a way that feels to the couple and family clients the same as to individual clients – that she is acceptant, empathic and authentic and that the relationship is constructive for the clients. Attitudinally, she always attempts to maintain a nondirective *attitude*. This is qualified only by Barbara being mindful to provide clients with the opportunity to adequately represent themselves and to not feel she is biased towards any one of the participants. The most general reason for any "orchestration" is to provide opportunities for each member to feel as safe and free as possible in the situation.

However, since the therapist is not controlling what people do by using authority, it is difficult to maintain a safe and free situation when working with more than one client. People can and do hurt each other in couple and family therapy. Thus, for the therapist, it is a matter of engaging with both parties in such a way that there is an empathic process, which ameliorates the hurt or felt injuries, as the consequence of a non-empathic interaction among them. When Barbara realizes that what one client is saying is abusively felt by the other, the reason she may not just let it happen, and for "orchestrating," is to provide a chance not for the therapist but for the client parties to have more control over what happens.

Barbara, however, is likely to just let difficult situations between clients happen, and then, at a point when one person has pretty much got anger or rampage out of his or her system, Barbara may attempt to find out how the other person is reacting about that. If it was all right from their viewpoint, Barbara does not try to curtail it in any way. If clients express their preference that Barbara should intervene in an emotionally abusive situation, she might say, "would you like if I say, 'could you stop for a minute to see what so-and-so has to say?'" However, she does not make assumptions about what the clients want in the situation.

Regarding suggestions or referral behavior, Barbara has occasionally mentioned to clients, who initially came for individual work, the possibility of couple and/or family therapy as an option that might be helpful for the relationship issues that the person is talking about and the way they are talking about them. However, she would not automatically do that just because someone is talking about relationships. It is most likely initiated by the client. Barbara views offering options as consistent with the client-centered theory although not a systematic feature of the therapy. She considers the therapist to have responsibilities beyond his or her therapy, including to be a resource for the client's more general well-being. It is not part of the therapy, nor does it follow from the theory; it is part of the larger role of the therapist as Barbara ethically defines that role.

Determinations of the clients' participation (e.g., frequency of meetings, number of sessions, variations in which members have sessions with the therapist, timing of the end of therapy) are up to the clients within Barbara's limits of availability. She would not introduce a decision about what is best for the clients. In terms of the length of a therapy session, she prefers to have one and a half or two hours because it often takes more time in couple and family therapy for all the clients to bring out their issues. Although she suggests the longer time, in the end it is up to the clients. Regarding phone contact for therapeutic discussions, recently, Barbara would rather not do them if it is avoidable. Still, she thinks it is the therapist's choice; the crucial thing is how the therapist can comfortably give the best service.

Barbara starts an initial session with a new couple or family by asking if they have any questions in the beginning. Generally, there is telephone contact beforehand, and if she has additional information to give them, she volunteers it on the basis of what has been said in the past. Then, after checking if all the questions are asked and answered, Barbara asks questions such as, "What are the things you want to focus on today? Could everybody take turns to say what they would like to talk about?" Depending on the situation, she might ask, "Who would like to begin?" or ask the clients to negotiate, "There are three topics here. Which one should we start with?" The beginning of the following sessions is pretty much the same. Barbara facilitates the topic being decided upon, but she does not try to influence the decision. Generally, after the first session, people will have decided the topic before they come in. They learn that they have a choice about what to talk about and take initiative.

Barbara tries to answer clients' questions, as well as responding empathically to them. She believes that addressing questions is compatible with the idea of respecting the client and also the nondirective attitude when the client has interest in Barbara's frame of reference at a particular point of time. She is very open to addressing questions as questions, including attempts to answer some questions tentatively with an empathic emphasis on the clients' reactions. For the same reason, Barbara has, on rare occasions, given advice, guidance, and comments on clients' behavior or problems, in response to requests, because she wants to consistently show respect for the client and their questions as questions. She has volunteered ideas to clients. However, this is rare; she is nonsystematic and tentative when making comments and avoids conveying an attitude of expertise.

Barbara has asked participants to respond with empathic understanding toward other members of the couple or family without offering any systematic instructions. When there is evidence that a client has felt difficulty about being understood by the other(s), Barbara thinks facilitation of empathic interactions may be called for by the situation. Then, she might ask a question for clarification, asking whether the client thinks it might be helpful for the other client(s) to make an empathic type of response. If the client answers yes, she would ask the other client(s) to attempt to express what the first client said, for the sake of clarity of communication. Although all of those are not intended to exercise control, Barbara believes they risk directive impact on the clients.

Barbara is open to receive from an individual client some information as secret – to be kept from the other client(s). She believes that unless the therapist sets it up initially that anything any of the clients tell the therapist may be brought out to the others, the information is confidential between the therapist and the individual client.

When the time allotted for sessions is up, either one of the clients notices or Barbara says that the time is up. When clients are in the middle of something toward the end of the session, she gives some minutes advance notice. When she occasionally goes over time, Barbara lets people know in the next occasion that she needs to stop on time, if that is the truth. The ending of therapeutic contact is very simple in her practice and is initiated by clients, never the therapist. At the end of the final session, Barbara might acknowledge the end of the therapeutic contact and tell them to feel free to contact her if they want to have any more sessions.

Over the years, Barbara has received some very strong appreciation from couple and family clients. Besides, she feels successful in avoiding mistakes that clients have reported about their previous therapists from other approaches, such as biases about the nature of personal relationships, being unfair to one or another of the clients, and imposing advice.

**REFERENCE**

Motomasa, N. (2004). *Client-centered couple and family therapy: Experienced therapists' views of theory and practice.* Unpublished doctoral dissertation, Illinois School of Professional Psychology, (now Argosy University, Chicago).

# Chapter 22

# Email to Maureen O'Hara on brief therapy

**June 26, 1998**

Dear Maureen,

I think you are heroic to take on the article on CC/PCE/ET [client-centered/person-centered experiential/experiential therapy] brief therapy. Thank you for doing it for all of us.

There are a couple of things you should know for perspective about me. I have been a client-centered therapist for over 40 years. The first five years were in a mental hospital where I mostly did short-term therapy (1 to 20 sessions) with psychotic clients. Always client-centered. I also did short-term therapy for several years in an inpatient male alcoholic treatment center (patients had a six-week limit on their stay) and had hospital privileges in a general hospital and I was called in to see patients (emergency panic attacks, fear of leaving hospital, etc.). Also brief or short-term work in several other settings.

Client-centered therapy to me means providing the therapeutic attitudes (Rogers') including the nondirective attitude. I think my client-centered presence with clients is very strong because I am convinced it is effective and respectful, so I am totally comfortable and I am very experienced and disciplined. I have no goals whatsoever for my clients other than not to harm them, to be a helper in some way, and try to be understood by the client so they can perceive I am trying to understand and nothing else. Behaviorally I respond empathically (make empathic understanding responses) as I need to ascertain my accuracy of understanding. My acceptance is high and constant. I interpret the nondirective attitude and the mandate to respect the person to imply that clients' questions should never be avoided – although in some instances I cannot give them exactly what they want – it is always a process.

I am responsive to clients' "experiments" and – if asked, for example, – I

---

Dr. Maureen O'Hara is a former colleague of Carl Rogers and has served as President of Saybrook Institute, a graduate school for humanistic psychological studies in California. On the CCTPCA email network Maureen had asked for input on the subject of client-centered brief therapy and received a response from Barbara. We have edited this excerpt from that email.

will give a behavior instruction (e.g., explain a relaxation technique), without losing the nondirective attitude. (I don't get caught up or invested in experiments working.) I have no goals for my clients other than to provide the therapeutic attitudes and communicate effectively and accurately according to the client.

I also allow myself a modicum of chaos in expression. Aside from responding to questions which, of course, constitute responses from my frame of reference, I volunteer a very small percentage of responses (approximately 1% or less) from my frame. They are unsystematic, having no directive goal. These are sometimes compelling social responses such as "I'm so sorry" if the client is telling me of a sick relative they care about, etc. (I've written a paper recently on the kind of responses these may be.) Anyway, Maureen, this is just to give you a very sketchy idea of my interpretation of client-centered therapy as context for the data.

### In respect to brief client-centered therapy:
If it is known by the client (and therefore by me) that the therapy will be brief (for insurance limits, leaving town, whatever) I have never that I can recall adjusted my behavior according to that limit. I behave exactly the same way as with an open-ended therapy. My impression is that clients who perceive the limit select what they can accomplish or in some way accelerate their process. There is a research report by Shlien and Jenney (I believe) on brief client-centered therapy which you probably already know that points up the clients' perceptions of the limit as a factor in the way they function.

My impression is that among my pre-known-to-be brief therapy clients there are fewer questions asked of me, and more directly getting to personal narrative. In other words, I think that sequences of questions by clients leading me to explain or suggest or instruct or self-disclose are more likely in clients who have settled in for a longer haul. This is the opposite of what many people would expect, I think.

One category of brief clients was at the University of Chicago Counseling Center (circa 1963–1964) when several of us were bothered by the long wait some clients had and we offered single sessions while the person stayed on the waiting list. One session!!! And some of the most exciting and productive sessions I have had were among that group. The crucial thing, I think, was the client's perception that he or she had the one hour. People solved problems, eased anxiety and depressions, made decisions, came up with insights, etc., and usually felt much better after the one session and felt they had "food for thought" or "a plan" or just felt "less tense," etc.

I am somewhat concerned with your article title, Maureen,* because only a 25% or so proportion of all the clients I have seen (approximately 50,000 hours) have changed with obvious moments of eternity (if I know what that means). The title implies a specific change process, which I do not think is the major one. I have always thought of my therapy as similar to Carl's (as I see him on the videos and some demonstrations I observed) which is to me a very straightforward, a plain style. Trying to understand, accept, be present. No covert intentions to get the client to focus or figure anything out or any goal at all. They are conversations that empathically focus on the client and the clients use them in many different ways with many different voices and tones and kinds of narrative. Change occurs often without any obvious signs of depth or experiencing or insights.

I know Carl wrote and talked about "moments of movement" and they exist. But most change I have seen (and I have seen a hell of a lot) does not involve any obvious or at least not dramatic moments of movement, even in brief therapy. Your title concerns me as somewhat misrepresenting client-centered therapy (although it is a great title from a literary perspective).

Here are some statistics.

First: A sample of 100 individual clients from my private practice (rough sampling, no intentional bias, went alphabetically through old accounts, picked every third or fourth case until I reached 100 cases).

50% 1–10 sessions
10% 11–30 sessions
23% 31–75 sessions
17% 101–507 sessions

$N$ = 100 clients. Range = 1–507 sessions. Mean = 54.45 sessions. Also note: 25% of the sample used 1–3 sessions.

All clients self-selected the end of therapy (or it was forced on them by something other than me). I never determined when a client stop therapy, and I never urged a client to take more sessions. I always tell clients they were free to return if they wish and if I am available. Some of the longer-term clients were not continuous, but came and went. Among 1–10 sessions clients, probably 75% of those clients determined at beginning of therapy that they would have only 1, 2, 3 or whatever number of sessions. Sometimes because of money limits, prior agreements with spouses, plans to move out of town, or simply wishing

---

* Editors' note: Maureen published a paper (O'Hara, 1999), Moments of Eternity: Carl Rogers and the contemporary demand for brief therapy.

to limit therapy, or other circumstances. Three or four clients in my practice had only a few sessions because they did not want to stay with me because of my gender or because I was practicing from my home or because they wanted a psychoanalytic therapist. The client's awareness of the number of sessions available is important because I think the client's perception of the short term is important for the way the client used the therapy.

Second: A subsample of 20 clients who were hospitalized for physical illnesses. I had hospital privileges to be called in for emergency therapy – always short term/brief therapy.

> Range = 1–13 sessions. Mean = 3.15 sessions.

> Note: 90% of these clients were in 1–5 sessions of therapy with me. All clients (including clients in the larger hospital sample) reported benefits, and nurses and doctors reported sessions made obvious differences in patients' adjustment and reduced anxiety and in some symptoms. Note, all these clients knew that sessions were limited and they self-determined limit because they anticipated when they would leave the hospital.

Third: 25 couples (heterosexual and gay/lesbian).

> Range 1–65 sessions. Mean = 14.76 sessions.

As with individual clients, the sessions are client-determined for limit. Usually with couple sessions it is not decided beforehand how many will be used, although money factors are frequently limiting.

You can tell from my remarks that I do not think there needs to be or should be any adjustment in the therapist's behavior for brief therapy – that there is no special need other than knowing that it is going to be 1, 2, 5, 10 or whatever the number (or approximate number). I have done brief therapy in many settings and with many clients and there is no doubt in my mind that client-centered therapy is an effective brief therapy when the client knows the limit. It is effective even if the client does not know, of course [because my therapy is basically always effective]. But I think the issue of "brief therapy" is when the client knows the insurance will pay for 10 sessions, or for 1000 dollars' worth each year, or will be leaving town in a month, or something is going on that makes it known.

I don't think people ever do everything they can accomplish in therapy whether it is short or long. There is always more growth, development, even healing – depending upon the damage. The question is – does the time and effort result in significant benefit to the client, do they reach some of their own goals? Some typical effects I've observed: diminished anxiety, greater clarity about a problem or better ways to work with a problem, attitudinal or behavior changes that improve their relationships, and of course, personal strengthening, increased self-respect, less self-hatred, etc. All these things and more result from client-centered brief therapy.

...

I am not aware of client-centered brief therapy research going on, or even in the past, other than the Shlien and Jenney studies. Have you seen Cartwright's published listing of research at the University of Chicago under Rogers around 1956? It might have some leads.

Good luck with the paper. I hope what I have given you is some help.

Best wishes,
Barbara

REFERENCE

[O'Hara, M. (1999). Moments of eternity: Carl Rogers and the contemporary demand for brief therapy. In I. Fairhurst (Ed.), *Women writing in the person-centred approach* (pp. 63–78). Ross-on-Wye: PCCS Books.]

# DISTINGUISHING
# CLIENT-CENTERED THERAPY

# Chapter 23

## Client-centered and experiential: Two different therapies

Experiential psychotherapy (conceptualized by Gendlin, e.g., 1964, 1966) developed, in part, out of client-centered therapy in the 1960s. Through the ensuing years it has been viewed by its proponents as theoretically consistent with and an improvement upon client-centered therapy (e.g., Gendlin, 1974).

One of the arguments supporting the notion that experiential therapy is an improvement upon client-centered therapy rests on the empirical generalization that early-in-therapy experiencing level predicts outcome (e.g., Gendlin, 1969, p. 13). In a recent paper the research that had been considered supportive of the generalization was reviewed (Brodley, 1988/2011). The review showed that the research had been, in fact, inconclusive and cannot be used as a reason for substituting experiential for client-centered therapy. The task remains, however, to clarify the differences in the theories and the differences in the practices of the two therapies in order to show that they are actually two quite different kinds of therapy. This task is the aim in what follows.

The two theories will, first, be described. Second, two fundamental and unique features of client-centered therapy will be explained. Third, the two therapies will be compared to show some major theoretical differences between them. Finally, there will be discussion of the difference between the salient forms of response in the two therapies. The two therapies will not be compared in respect to their effectiveness.

### CLIENT-CENTERED THEORY

The primary construct in Rogers' client-centered theory is the "actualizing tendency" (Rogers, 1980, pp. 114–123). This axiom or first principle refers to the inherent and immutable tendency of organisms, including human beings, to grow, develop, expand, differentiate, maintain themselves, restore themselves and to realize their natures as best they can under their circumstances. The actualizing tendency is the basic characteristic of organic,

Published (1990) in G. Lietaer, J. Rombauts, & R. Van Balen (Eds.), *Client-centered and experiential psychotherapy in the nineties* (pp. 87–108). Leuven, Belgium: Leuven University Press. Reproduced with permission.

including human, life. Quotations from Rogers (1980) which express these ideas are:

> The actualizing tendency can ... be thwarted or warped, but it cannot be destroyed without destroying the organism. (p. 119)

> There is one central source of energy in the human organism. This source is a trustworthy function of the whole system ... it is ... a tendency toward fulfillment, toward actualization, involving not only the maintenance, but also the enhancement of the organism. (p. 123)

Rogers' theory of therapy is logically consistent with the actualizing principle. The therapist does not cause change but, rather, enables change by providing conditions that foster the optimal functioning of the inherent growth tendencies in the person. In Rogers' theory, therapeutic personality change is within the nature of the person. The client-centered therapist, therefore, does not apply treatments but, instead, provides salutary psychological conditions by forming a particular interpersonal environment with the client.

Client-centered therapy theory (Rogers, 1957, 1959) states that a vulnerable or anxious client must be in psychological contact with a therapist who experiences the attitudes of congruence, unconditional positive regard and empathic understanding of the client's internal frame of reference. The theory also states that the conditions of positive regard and empathic understanding must be perceived, at least to a minimum degree, by the client. If these conditions are met, then therapeutic personality change will occur (Rogers, 1959, p. 213). Rogers (1957, p. 100) predicts that the higher the level of the attitudinal conditions that are offered by the therapist in the relationship, and perceived by the client, then the greater the constructive personality change in the client.

This is the theory which was elucidated by Carl Rogers in articles (e.g., Rogers, 1975, 1980) and in demonstrations, films and recordings. From the many illuminating sources it is apparent that the behavior of the client-centered therapist is imbued with and consistently influenced by a nondirective attitude (Raskin, 1947/2005) toward the client and the therapy process.

The nondirective attitude results in the therapist's surrender of control – of the therapy process and content – over to the client. This surrender is in vivid contrast to the standard clinical mandate – that the therapist should maintain control over the therapy and, to the extent it is possible, over the experiences of the client in therapy. The consequence of the therapist's surrender of the usual control is an equalizing of the two persons in the relationship and their partnership in the events of the therapy situation.

## EXPERIENTIAL PSYCHOTHERAPY THEORY

Gendlin (1964, 1973, 1974, 1984) and Iberg (1988) have stated that Rogers' therapeutic attitudinal conditions are part of experiential therapy theory. The therapeutic attitudes are viewed as conducive to freeing the actualizing tendency of the individual. Also, the encounter between therapist and client occurring when the conditions are provided is "more a person-to-person than a person-to-professional authority" relationship (Iberg, 1988, p. 1). The explanation of therapeutic change in experiential theory is, however, attributed to a specific process of experiencing which can occur in the client, called "focusing" or "focused experiencing."

The theory as written and illustrated by Gendlin (e.g., 1982, 1984) makes it clear that the therapist's primary and active responsibility – that is, what the therapist should do in working with the client – is to *direct* the client toward the focused experiencing process (Gendlin, 1966, p. 9, 1974, p. 222) and help the client to maintain a "high experiencing level" (Gendlin, Beebe, Cassens, Klein, & Oberlander, 1968).

Theoretically, this view – that there is a particular and necessary client-located process which must occur for therapy to happen, and the corollary view of the therapist's crucial role to influence that process – subordinates the therapeutic attitudes into a supportive role in experiential theory.

The primary role of the therapist in experiential therapy appears to be in his evaluative and directive function in relation to the client's experiencing process, not in his providing the therapeutic attitudes. Gendlin expresses this difference in the two therapies in the following quotes:

> This felt experience is not what people say but what they talk from. And only as they work with this experiencing, and as its felt meanings evolve, does change happen. (Gendlin, 1966, p. 9)

> A therapist must strive ... to help the person allow directly felt referents to form, to attend to a bodily felt sense, and to let that live further in words and interactions. (Gendlin, 1974, p. 222)

> We must ... reformulate Rogers' view that personality change depends on the client's *perception* of the therapist's attitude. The present theory implies that the client may perceive the therapist's attitudes correctly, or he may not. He may be convinced that the therapist must dislike him and cannot possibly understand him. Not these *perceptions*, but *the manner of process which is actually occurring*, will determine whether personality change results. (Gendlin, 1964, pp. 135–136)

## TWO CONTRIBUTIONS OF ROGERS' THEORY OF THERAPY

We return now to Rogers' theory in order to examine two fundamental characteristics of the theory which are unique and important contributions to therapy practice.

The first is *the principle of trust in the client.* The high degree of trust in the client is a unique characteristic of Rogers' therapy. This trust is not a matter of following a rule to be nondirective. But, rather, trust results from the fact that in client-centered therapy the therapist is functioning from a philosophy of persons, which leads to certain values and feelings. These particular values and feelings melt into the ubiquitous nondirective attitude. This attitude, along with the specific therapeutic attitudes, creates the interpersonal conditions which enable change in the client. These attitudes express the trust that is felt by the therapist towards the client.

In his relationship with the client, the Rogerian therapist desires to function consistently and constantly from the hypothesis (or from the belief) that the client has the inherent capability to determine his own constructive directions in life and in the therapy. This hypothesis is represented in an attitude of trust in the client's capabilities, which is not qualified by preconceptions about the client's status as client or the nature or level of his disturbance. An attitude of paternalism is not justifiable in the context of client-centered theory. Although on rare occasions and under special circumstances the therapist may take responsibility for the client as an expression of congruence.

In practice, with rare exceptions, the client-centered therapist, guided by his nondirective attitude, has no *directive intentions* in relation to the client. The therapist's intentions are distinctly and only to experience and manifest the attitudinal conditions in such a way that unconditional positive regard and empathic understanding can be perceived by the client.

The second special contribution of client-centered theory is *the idea that therapeutic personality change can be the result of being understood.* In this context, "being understood" means, specifically, that the client perceives and experiences the therapist's empathic understanding and the therapist's acceptance of the client as a whole person. Empathic understanding – deeply experienced by the therapist, coexisting in the therapist along with unconditional positive regard of the client, and embedded in the therapist's wholeness and realness in the relationship – this understanding is the therapist's causal role in the client's change and healing. Nothing else is conceived, by the theory, as needed from the therapist.

To clarify further, Rogers' empathic understanding is a pure empathic *following* of the client. In this *following* the therapist is taken along on an emotive and intellectual journey with the client, under the lead of the client, into the client's world of memories, perceptions, feelings and perspectives. While following empathetically, the therapist is sincere, responsive and wholly present – a companion to the client.

An assumption underlying empathic understanding-following is that the processes and contents experienced and expressed by the client may be of many different kinds, or even unique to a particular client. In Rogers' client-centered therapy there is not an assumption of any specific process nor any particular class of contents being viewed as necessary for therapeutic change to occur.

It should be recognized that Rogers' description of a process development in the course of therapy (Rogers, 1958) – which has been given emphasis in Gendlin's interpretation of client-centered therapy – was meant as a description of the way clients who are experiencing the attitudinal conditions at a high level appeared, to Rogers, to change in their verbal expression as therapy progressed. Rogers interpreted this change in expression to reflect inner change, including change in the experience of self and change in experiencing itself. But *the process theory was not intended as an instruction concerning how the client or therapist should proceed in therapy.*

Rogers felt that his process conception is misunderstood whenever it is translated into goals for therapy that influence the therapist's attitudes and behavior towards the client. He is being particularly misunderstood when a change in attitudes is manifest in trying to influence the client towards goals conceived by the therapist (Rogers, 1982, personal communication).

## HOW THE TWO THEORIES ARE DIFFERENT

There are two important theoretical differences between Rogers' client-centered theory and Gendlin's experiential theory to be emphasized here. These differences show up when comparing the two theories in respect to the characteristics of Rogers' theory described above.

The first difference: *In client-centered therapy the therapist functions consistently with trust in the client as a whole person, while in experiential therapy the therapist's trust is in the client's experiencing process.*

In client-centered, the principle of trust manifests in the therapist's nondirective attitude. Consequently the client is free to function in the relationship in his own way as long as he does not violate the therapist's rights. The client's way of relating to the therapist and of expressing himself is accepted. The therapist, if necessary, extends himself to accept and to appreciate – to understand – the client's way (Bozarth, 1990). There is, for example, no client-centered judgment that the client is "just talking" (Gendlin, 1974, p. 221) as there is, sometimes, in experiential therapy.

In client-centered there is no theoretical directive to intervene to change the way the client is talking.[1] The salient client-centered attitude is nondirective and the therapist's trust in the client's capacities for self-direction, growth and self-restoration is, theoretically, consistent and constant.

In experiential theory, the therapist functions from an a priori assumption that he knows exactly which process of self-expression and interaction is therapeutic. Consequently the experiential therapist is supposed to adopt the attitude of expert in promoting this process.

The experiential therapy client is free to function in the therapy in his own way if he is spontaneously able to function with a high experiencing level or if he is able to choose to resist or refuse the therapist's focusing interventions.

The experiential therapist does not intend to be coercive or insensitive to the client in his directivity. He readily backs off (Gendlin, 1984, p. 92) if the client feels resistant or is disinclined to the therapist's instructions or promptings. But, even when the experiential therapist is not obviously influencing the client to focus he is, indeed, mindful of the client's experiencing level and is trying to increase or sustain the level by the ways he empathetically responds. The client may or may not be aware of this directive intention and behavior by the therapist.

This difference – that the client-centered therapist functions from a principle of trust in the person and that the experiential therapist does not – may seem incorrect to the student of experiential because it appears to contradict Gendlin's emphasis on and respect for the focusing process as the basis of personality growth and as the source of personal autonomy.

It should be apparent, however, that trust in the client's high-level focusing process, when it occurs spontaneously or is stimulated by the therapist, is not the same as trust in the whole person. In experiential therapy, this qualified trust is especially obvious when the client is functioning with a low experiencing level and the therapist sees it as his responsibility to influence the process to a higher level.

Friedman, an experiential therapist, expresses the difference between Rogers' therapy and experiential therapy in regard to trust and directivity in the following:

---

1. Rogers wrote of being selective in his listening and acknowledged he could be viewed as directive (Rogers, 1970, p. 47). Rogers' selectivity, however, has to do with the essence of empathic understanding and is not a directivity. In empathic understanding the listener is attempting to understand/follow not only what the client is talking about. In fact, the crucial understanding concerns the client's expressed relation of *himself to what he is talking about.* Understanding is not empathic until and unless the listener grasps these relations (e.g., reactions, feelings, attitudes, desires, wants, wishes, etc.) in the client's communication.

Rogers put too much faith in [the] self-actualizing tendency. He doesn't offer it enough help ... Clients have to do "felt sense talk" if therapy is to succeed ... Therapists need to be able to help clients learn how to do this ... When a person isn't talking from a felt sense my task is to help him/her do so. (Friedman, 1982, pp. 101–114)

It is important to emphasize for the sake of accuracy and fairness that the experiential therapist tries to do his job of being expert and directive in relation to the client's process in a very gentle, respectful and sensitive way. But this does not obviate the fact that the position of the therapist is theoretically determined to be that of an expert about the client. Gentleness and sensitivity does not obviate the fact that the experiential attitude is directive and is not based on trust in the person as is the client-centered.

The second difference: *In client-centered theory the therapist-attributed cause of therapeutic change is in the therapist's attitudinal condition while in experiential theory the therapist-attributed cause of change is in the* therapist's *functions as monitor, director and teacher* of *focused experiencing* (Gendlin, 1984, p. 82).

Gendlin and Iberg state that Rogers' therapeutic attitudes have a role in experiential therapy. That role, however, is secondary. The Rogerian therapeutic attitudes appear to operate in experiential therapy in two ways:

1. The attitudinal conditions contribute to therapeutic change when or if they have the direct effect of stimulating or sustaining a focused experiencing process at a high level in the client.

2. The attitudinal conditions may create a quality of relationship between therapist and client such that the client feels safe and trusting in relation to the therapist. The trust thus generated may have the result that the client is likely to respond cooperatively to the therapist's impact on focusing level as he makes his interventions.

In contrast, the trust, which is stimulated by the client-centered therapist when he provides the attitudinal conditions, is not exploited by any intentions to direct or specifically influence the client. The absence of directivity in client-centered therapy does not imply there is an absence of direction in the client's change. Nor does it imply the therapist has little impact.[2]

---

2. Rogers ventured to describe the process of change occurring in clients when the attitudinal conditions are present in two different ways. One approach was described as "the central or crucial element in change" (Rogers, 1956) and as "the moment of movement." Rogers described movement as having several qualities: immediate experiencing, without inhibition, with full awareness, and with the feeling of acceptability to the self (of whatever it is the client   ... contd.

In fact, the absence of directivity of the therapist along with the remarkable constructive directions of change in client-centered clients gives support to the theory of the actualization tendency and inherent therapeutic powers in the client and tends to justify the client-centered principle of trust in the client.

## COMPARISON OF RESPONSES IN CLIENT–CENTERED AND EXPERIENTIAL THERAPIES

The salient forms of therapist response in client-centered and experiential therapies express the difference in the theories and the attitudes of each type.

### Responses in client-centered therapy

The "reflection of feeling" (Rogers, 1986) or, as it has been called more recently, the "empathic understanding response" (Temaner, 1977/2011; Brodley, 1987/1998) is a form of response identified with client-centered therapy. In fact, however, there is no specific form of response that fully characterizes client-centered work.

Instead there *is a characteristic process, which may be called "empathic following" which includes the reflection of feeling but is not limited to that response form.* Reflections, questions for clarification, summarizing responses, figures of speech, vocal gestures and physical gestures and/or any other forms of response may function in empathic following. A therapist's response can be considered to be contributing to the whole experience of the empathic following process if the response has one or both of the following purposes from the therapist's point of view:

1. The response serves to check, in order to validate or correct, the therapist's subjective experience of empathic understanding of the client's present internal frame of reference (Rogers, 1986).

2. The response expresses the therapist's desire to overtly participate in the relationship. In both criteria the therapist's purpose is to follow the client's internal frame of reference insofar as that is being revealed by the client through words, intonations and gestures.

---

contd. ...   is talking about). Rogers thought these moments are the change moments which occur more or less frequently whenever there is an overall constructive change in the client. The second approach to change process in the client described by Rogers (1984) was his view that the client gradually adopts the three therapeutic attitudes – congruence, unconditional positive regard and empathic understanding – in himself, towards himself and towards others. In this view the sequence of events in the client's adoption of the therapeutic attitudes varies on the basis of individual differences in personality and problems. These two approaches to change are not contradictory but refer to different levels of analysis of change process.

The most articulate and precise form of empathic following response is the reflection of feeling or empathic understanding response. This response is usually present in an empathic following sequence. Empathic following, including some reflection responses, is illustrated in this client-centered therapy interaction that took place a few months ago between the writer (Barbara: B) and her client (Lall: L).

L: I'm just ... aching to feel more normal. I'm just aching to feel more integrated, you know ...

B: You want it so much (L: Yeah) and it's so painful the way it's always been ...

L: It's such a waste, you know?

B: Mm-hm. A waste of you.

L: Mhm, a waste of all the gifts I have, and a waste of the relationships that have gone astray (B: Mm-hm) ... (client begins to weep) I'm really sad about that.

B: Mm-hm ... All that's lost in the stifling of your own growth ... (L: Mm-hm) ... what's missed ... It's something to cry about ... (L: Yeah)

L: I cry about it a lot of the time, you know, in and out of therapy ... and wherever else ... I just feel like ... I've lost a lot of time ... (B: Mm-hm) I mean, life is so short ... (B: Hm-hm) and I feel like I've wasted a good chunk of it ...

B: Whatever you can do now ... (L: Yeah) you still have lost what you've lost. (L: Yeah) And life isn't long ... So you're just, you're not ... Whatever you do is not the same as what you could have done if you hadn't had all this ... blockage. (L: Yeah) Mm-hm, and that's a real loss, no matter what ... (L: Uh-huh) ... Mhm ... something to cry about.

L: I'm very afraid that ... it'll be like this for the rest of my life. (B: Mh-hm) ... And I'll die old and lonely like my dad, and be like my mother is ...

B: Unrealized ... so much.

L: Oh, Yeah! ... Never getting to the point where you look back and say, "I'm comfortable with who I was and the life I've lived." (B: Mm-hm) And if I just, if I didn't know that that should be one of the things that you should feel when you're old ... (B: Mm-hm) ... it would be easier but I'm not headed in the direction where I can say ...

B: Mm-hm ... that you'll be able to say that. (L: yeah) Mhm ... and when you're feeling like you're feeling right now, it's not only the past ... but later, when you're close to death and ... you fear

L: Yeah, yeah ...

In this example, the therapist's empathic following of the client includes communication of several elements of the client's expression. It includes responses which acknowledge situations (e.g., the past, the parents' situations, the imagined future), feelings (e.g., desire, pain, remorse, sadness, fear), perspectives (e.g., "whatever you can do now, you have still lost what you have lost"). It also includes responses which are vocal gestures (Mm-hm, Mhm) and physical gestures (e.g., nods and hand movements).

The therapist's intentions appear clear in the example – to empathetically follow and understand the client's complex of meanings and feelings as they unfold in the interaction. Empathic understanding implies the intention to follow in client-centered work. The therapist does not try to get ahead of the client or to bring particular aspects of the client's experiencing into awareness.

Fully immersed empathic following, however, does sometimes involve the therapist in verbalizing aspects of the client's feelings or meanings that he was not aware of up until the moment they were expressed by the therapist. This happens naturally, but not deliberately, as part of close following, it is an outcome of the therapist's attempt to check the adequacy of his empathic understanding, not because the therapist has intentions such as wanting to enlighten the client.

Another example of empathic following including articulate empathic understanding responses and, also, including what appears to be a verbalization of an element that the client was not aware of, is this excerpt from a demonstration interview by Rogers (Carl: C) with June (J) (Rogers, 1985).

J: I'm not really in touch with her ... and I think the sense of it is that it's like that person is not really any good ... no value ...

C: So you're not really well acquainted with that person behind the fence, but you do have a sense that she's no good, she's not worth anything much.

J: Yes, she's selfish, self-centered, arrogant, wants things for herself ... I guess she comes through sometimes, ... but not really, not often, ... it's rare.

C: You are sort of ashamed of that selfish arrogant and miserable person that's inside. (J: Yes) Even though sometimes she pokes her way out through the fence.

[See also Brodley & Lietaer, 2006, Vol. 16, June Interview, p. 48]*

---

*Editors' note: In the course of many years, Barbara transcribed and supervised others in transcribing Rogers' therapy and demonstration sessions. In this paper she refers to transcripts that were in the process of being "polished" through multiple listenings to the tapes. It is uncertain at which point of evolution she quoted from the various transcripts. The transcript work culminated in a joint effort with Germain Lietaer resulting in a journal article (Lietaer & Brodley, 2003) and an informal email publication (Brodley & Lietaer, 2006).

Apparently, based on the way June expressed her description of the hidden aspects of herself, Carl thought she was communicating a feeling of shame about these qualities of her inner self. Consequently he checked that out in his second empathic response. This illustrates that the point in empathic following is not to try to keep behind any more than to try to get ahead. It is, rather, to engage in trying to understand the other person, the client. The therapist is following because the source of the experiences to be understood is in what the client is expressing. The therapist may grasp some aspect of what the client is expressing and of which the client is less than fully aware, but what the therapist is doing is, nonetheless, following.

The examples, above, of client-centered interactions illustrate the way in which empathic understanding of the client's internal frame of reference is an attempt to attend to the whole person (not only the person's feelings) by trying to absorb and respond to the person's view of his world including his various reactions and feelings (Zimring, 1988).

Empathic understanding responses and other following responses communicate the client-centered therapist's empathic understanding, attention, interest in and acceptance of the client. The constancy of empathic following and the constant implicit communications of (1) asking the client to listen to what the therapist thinks he has understood, and (2) asking the client to let the therapist know if he has understood or not, and to correct him if he is wrong, along with the communications (3) that imply "I am here, attentive and interested and acceptant and truly trying to understand" – all together produce an effect of respectfulness, valuing and trust in the client and in the client's perceptions and feelings.

In experiential therapy there are two salient response forms. One is a form of responding called "listening" which includes "listening responses" sometimes called "client-centered responding" (Gendlin, 1974, p. 216) or "saying back" responses. The second form of response is a focusing prompt or focusing instruction.

Listening resembles empathic following and listening responses resemble reflections of feeling and other following responses in client-centered therapy. But listening is different from empathic following in having a different purpose.

Listening is empathic, insofar as it attempts to reflect the client's inner experience as the client tries to express it. But listening is more specifically directed toward making the client feel and be aware of his felt sense. Listening is intended by the therapist to help the client refer to his felt sense. And it helps the client learn to attend to his felt sense especially as a bodily felt sensation or a process of sensations from which meanings emerge when attention is given to the felt sense. It also helps the client learn that he can choose to attend to that process from which meanings are created, and heighten the intensity of that process. Some statements that express the experiential viewpoint are:

> … the experiential dimension in the psychotherapy process defines the core content of therapy and outlines the necessary sequence of tasks (for the client) … the concrete feeling, personal meaning and experiencing of the patient must be revealed and worked with … progressively more advanced levels of focusing are essential for progress … The approach also defines the therapist's work as independent of … the emotional climate of the relationship. In this light, the therapist is to help the patient expand his experience by supporting the process of focusing by responding to his (the client's) implicit referent … a step beyond the patient's experiential level, directing him toward the implicit meaning or aspect of his experience, so that the patient can experience it and refer to it more directly. (Klein, Mathieu, Gendlin & Kiesler, 1969, pp. 1–9)

> It is my claim that only in this physical way does real change occur … the problem must change in how it literally sets in the body. When that changes, one senses a stirring, a seeping, a physical shift … (Gendlin, 1982, pp. 4–6)

A special form of listening response described by Hendricks (1986, p. 155) is called a "focusing reflection." This form of response is consciously used by the experientially aware therapist to direct the client's attention toward the "implicit" by referring directly to the felt experience in the wording of the empathic understanding response. An example of the focusing reflection given by Hendricks is as follows:

C: Yeah. I think so. I think so because … this person feels inaccessible. Yet, not so inaccessible that it's a total impossibility. So it's like I keep trying out my worth … on him … and keep coming up against, "Yeah, I like you, but …"

T: OK. So, how about, "Yeah, I like you, but …." Does that fit? Is that exactly right to that whole feeling?

C: Yeah, it really is. Really is.

T: "I like you, but …"

It is evident, in the above, that the therapist is trying to focus the client's attention on the relation between her words and the felt sense (which is pointed to with "that whole feeling") and to heighten awareness of the felt sense. The therapist's responses draw the client's attention to the specific feeling in her body which is stimulated in response to the statement "I like you but ...."

The experiential therapist's responses in the example show how the client is helped to become aware of her bodily felt experience. They also may help the client discover meanings that arise from attention to the bodily experience. In addition, the focusing reflection helps to teach the client the method of referring to bodily feelings as a generally desirable and healthy procedure.

In contrast, client-centered empathic following might be expressed in response to the initial client statement in the example above in this way:

T: You have the sense that he might want you ... so you keep exposing yourself towards him ... then you get that ... "but" ... that reservation about you, and you feel devalued.

In the client-centered version of the interaction, the therapist is trying to express the complex of perceptions and personal meanings that seem to be conveyed by the client. That is, the response is an attempt to check the correctness of the therapist's empathic understanding of the client's internal frame of reference at the time of expression. This means trying to understand what she is talking about and, crucially for true empathic understanding, *what the client is expressing as her relation to what she is talking about.*

In the example the client is communicating the situation of her attempt to gain intimacy and acceptance from a person who might respond to her in those ways. In her attempt she feels she is risking her "worth." She reports she gets hit with a qualified rather than a wholehearted feeling from him.

There are three elements in the client-centered response that are intended to check accuracy of empathic understanding. First, the client's perception of the semi-accessibility of the man. Second, the client's attempt to draw him towards her. Finally, the semi-rejection she interprets from his "but ..." and her feeling of being devalued by that qualified response from him.

It is the whole meaning, or at least the most personal and dynamic elements of it, that the client-centered responses are expressing in reaction to the client. In contrast to the experiential therapy response the client-centered one is not deliberately trying to draw the client's attention to her felt sense in order to make her more aware of it or more attuned to it. Although, attention to felt sense is often one of the psychological effects of empathic understanding in client-centered therapy and it might be one of the effects of the client-centered response in this instance.

The second salient form of response in experiential therapy – the focusing prompt or focusing instruction – is illustrated in the following interaction from Gendlin (1982):

C: I have all these excuses about why I never do my best. Um …

T: You come right up to the line and then something holds back.

C: Yeah … Well. I think it's … ah … that I don't want to test myself. And I'm afraid, ah, the bad things will be confirmed.

T: Can you feel the pull back, if you imagine yourself going ahead?

The first experiential therapist response, above, translates the clients meaning (his "excuses") into a dynamic description intended to evoke the felt sense of trying to do something and then stopping or blocking. The second focusing response is a focusing instruction type of response. It ignores the client's explanation of why he does not do his best (the fear of bad things being confirmed) and, instead, asks the client to attend to the feel of the "pull back" in the context of imagining (with feeling) "going ahead." In both responses the therapist is pointing up the inner dynamic of the "go-then-stopped" experience in order to bring the client's attention to it and have the client feel the experience in his body, i.e., to have the felt sense of that situation.

A version of the above interaction showing a possible client-centered way of responding to the same client material is as follows:

C: I have all these excuses about why I never do my best, um …

T: Avoiding trying …

C: Yeah … Well, I think it's … ah … that I don't want to test myself. And I'm afraid, ah, the bad things will be confirmed.

T: Afraid you won't measure up, and … that some bad things about you will really show up …

The client-centered intention in this illustration is simply to understand the client's experiences as he brings them out in his communication. This intention is one without a concern for focusing level.

Experiential therapists acknowledge that they direct process. They truly have, however, no preconceptions about what the client should talk about or what issues need to be explored as is the case in many other therapies. The experiential therapist is committed to openness and receptivity concerning the client's choice of subject matter.

Nevertheless, it should be apparent even from the two short experiential examples above, that experiential work directly influences content as an effect of directing process. This is because content is embedded in process, or vice versa, depending upon one's perspective.

Content is influenced when experiential techniques are used, especially when the therapist explicitly directs the client's process with focusing prompts or focusing instructions. (See the example of experiential work below.) The influence on the content of client expression is, usually, that the client gives fewer descriptions and expressions coming from his whole self. Examples of the type of self-referring statements which uninfluenced clients make as they express and represent themselves are: "I have all these excuses." "I'm just aching to feel more normal." "I cry about it a lot of the time." "I'm very afraid that … it'll be like this for the rest of my life." "I'll die lonely." "I'm afraid the bad things will be confirmed." "I keep trying out my worth."

The type of client statement illustrated above becomes less frequent when the experiential therapist uses focusing prompting or instructing techniques. Instead there are statements of the following type: "It's like a heavy wall." "It wants to scream." "Some of me wants to find out …" "Running from the vague thing is sad." The client's subject often changes from "I" referring to the whole self to "they" or "it" referring to feelings, sensations or an aspect of the self. Under the influence of focusing techniques the client tends to describe something he observes in himself or about himself. The client's voice becomes an implicit, passive, novelistic voice rather than the more natural, or spontaneous, active, volitional, self-revealing and self-owning voice that occurs in client-centered interactions.

Another quality of experiential work that often results from the conception of the therapist's task and the techniques that implement the task is the disjunction in the communication situation between therapist and client.

Common purposes of communication are to express oneself and/or to transmit information and feelings. These are often the purposes of the client who has come to the therapist and who begins by discussing his problems, his feelings and situations. What is being said by the client is important to him. His reason for saying what he is saying is, usually, because it has importance to him. He expects, or more often hopes, it will be of interest to the therapist and be an expression of the therapist's interest in him. This expectation appears to be fulfilled by the experiential therapist who gives detailed responses that indicate attention is being given to what the client is saying.

The experiential therapist, however, is not doing what he appears to be doing as he listens to the client. He is not, despite appearance, sharing the client's aim to be understood and of interest. Instead, the experiential therapist is listening closely to what the client is saying primarily in order to monitor the level of experiencing and to help the person engage in the focused experiencing process at a high level. Consequently, unless the experiential client is educated about the therapy, and chooses to actively cooperate in the method, the therapist and the client will tend to be engaged in two different and nonreciprocal activities. They will only have the appearance of shared purpose. Specifically, the therapist will be trying to help the client focus, while the client will be trying to communicate about himself to the therapist and be seeking the therapist's interest in him.

Under the circumstances that the client is familiar with and chooses to cooperate with experiential procedures, the purposes of therapist and client are mutual and not disjunctive. In this kind of experiential partnership the content of the conversation becomes very different from usual conversation and from the conversation of client-centered therapy. The following example of interaction from an experiential therapy session presented by Gendlin (1982) illustrates the distinctiveness of the conversation in experiential therapy when the client is cooperating with the therapist's purpose.

T: So we have to go see where your good energy went to.

(long silence)

C: I have lots of energy there, but it's all tied up.

T: You can feel your energy there, but it's tied up.

C: Yes.

T: Can you sense what's tying it up?

(long silence)

C: It's like a heavy wall in front of it. It's behind that.

T: You can feel a heavy wall.

C: It's a whole part of me that I keep in. Like when I say it's OK when it's not. The way I hold everything in. (long silence) There's a part of me that's dead, and a part that isn't.

T: Two parts, one is dead, and one ... ah

C: Survived. (long silence) It wants to scream.

T: The dead parts wants to scream and to be let out.

C: To live. (long silence) And there's also something vague. I can't get what that is.

T: Make a space for that vague thing, you don't know what it is yet. There's something vague there, but it isn't clear what it is.

C: I feel a lot of tension.

T: OK, Take a break. Just step back a little bit. There's the vague thing, and then, also, there's the tension. Let's talk a little. You've come a lot of steps.

In the interaction above it seems that both therapist and client are in agreement that their task is to talk about the client's inner feelings and bodily experiences and to draw forth from the experiential source more feelings and meanings. At times this appears as if the client were trying to view a film or video showing events that are not entirely clear but trying to report them in as much detail as possible.

The example shows how the experiential therapist is in control of the procedure, directing the client towards the source of what is sensed and towards what is sensed. Directivity is also apparent in the instruction "Take a break" and "Let's talk a little." The therapist acts as though he knows what the client needs in this procedure pretty much moment to moment. The client seems to accept the therapist's authority and is cooperating in being directed.

Experiential listening and focusing prompts, and focusing instructions are different from client-centered empathic following. The purpose of deliberately focusing the client on the basis that the therapist decides it is desirable does not exist in client-centered therapy. Empathic following, in client-centered therapy, often has the effect of focusing the client. But this effect is secondary to its contribution to the client's perception that the therapist is engaged in empathic understanding. The focusing purpose does not exist in client-centered work because such a purpose presumes the therapist knows which kind of experience the client should have in order to change. Client-centered theory does not make that assumption.

CONCLUSION

Client-centered theory and experiential therapy theory are fundamentally different in their views of the therapist's role in constructive personality change. Also, client-centered therapy fundamentally involves the therapist in working with a nondirective attitude whereas experiential involves the therapist in working from a specific directive attitude. These differences, with their many consequences in practice, make it accurate and appropriate to view the two therapies as different kinds of therapy, not ones in an internally consistent continuum of development. Experiential is one of the directive therapies. Client-centered is unique in the arena of psychotherapies – it is distinctly not a directive therapy.

SUMMARY

Rogers' client-centered theory and Gendlin's experiential therapy theory have been described and compared. Differences in the salient forms of response used in the two therapies were discussed and illustrated.

The experiential position involves assumption of a particular therapeutic process – focusing – as necessary for therapeutic change, and posits the view that the therapist's role is to promote this process. These features are different from client-centered therapy and contradict the nondirective essence of client-centered work.

This presentation of the two therapies shows that they are different, and that experiential therapy is not an internally consistent development out of client-centered therapy.

Prior to this writing the real and significant differences between client-centered and experiential attitudes have not been addressed in the literature. Experiential therapy has been viewed simply as an advancement over client-centered therapy. Consequently, people who might be considering these approaches were being confused. Choice about how they might want to work with their clients was obfuscated.

The answer to the important question of which therapy is the most effective remains, at this point in time, a matter of opinion. But it is hoped that this presentation contributes to recognition of the differences between the therapies and, thereby, a clearer choice of approach and, potentially, a clearer comparison of therapies in respect to outcomes.

REFERENCES

Bozarth, J. D. (1990). The essence of client-centered/person-centered therapy. In G. Lietaer, J. Rombauts, & R. Van Balen (Eds.), *Client-centered and experiential psychotherapy in the nineties* (pp. 59–64). Leuven, Belgium: Leuven University Press.

Brodley, B. T. (1987). *A client-centered psychotherapy practice.* Paper prepared for the Third International Forum on the Person-Centered Approach. La Jolla, CA. [Published (1998) in C. Wolter-Gustafson (Ed.), *A person-centered reader: Personal selections by our members* (pp. 59–87). Boston: Association for the Development of the Person-Centered Approach]

Brodley, B. T. (1988). *Does early-in-therapy experiencing level predict outcome? A review of research.* Paper presented at the annual conference of the Association for the Development of the Person-Centered Approach, New York.

[Brodley, B. T., & Lietaer, G. (Eds.). (2006). *Transcripts of Carl Rogers' therapy sessions, Vols. 1–17.* Available from germain.lietaer@psy.kuleuven.be and kmoon1@alumni.uchicago.edu]

Friedman, N. (1982). *Experiential therapy and focusing.* New York: Half Court Press.

Gendlin, E. T. (1964). A theory of personality change. In P. Worchel & D. Byrne (Eds.), *Personality change* (pp. 100–148). New York: Wiley.

Gendlin, E. T. (1966). Research in psychotherapy with schizophrenic patients and the nature of that illness. *American Journal of Psychotherapy. 20,* 4–16.

Gendlin, E. T. (1969). Focusing. *Psychotherapy: Theory, Research and Practice, 6,* 4–15.

Gendlin, E. T. (1973). Experiential psychotherapy. In R. Corsini (Ed.), *Current psychotherapies* (pp. 317–352). Itasca, IL: Peacock Books.

Gendlin, E. T. (1974). Client-centered and experiential psychotherapy. In D. A. Wexler & L. N. Rice (Eds.), *Innovations in client-centered therapy* (pp. 211–246). New York: Wiley.

Gendlin, E. T. (1982). *Experiential psychotherapy.* Unpublished manuscript (371 pp.). (Available at The Focusing Institute).

Gendlin, E. T. (1984). The client's client: The edge of awareness. In R. F. Levant & J. M. Shlien (Eds.), *Client-centered therapy and the person-centered approach* (pp. 76–107). New York: Praeger.

Gendlin, E. T., Beebe, J., Cassens, J., Klein, M., & Oberlander, R. (1968). Focusing ability in psychotherapy, personality, and creativity. In J. M. Shlien (Ed.), *Research in psychotherapy, Vol. 3* (pp. 217–241). Washington, DC: American Psychological Association.

Hendricks, M. N. (1986). Experiencing level as a therapeutic variable. *Person-Centered Review, 1,* 142–161.

Iberg, J. (1988) *Experiential psychotherapy.* Unpublished manuscript.

Klein, M. H., Mathieu, P. L., Gendlin, E. T., & Kiesler, D. J. (1969). *The Experiencing Scale: A research and training manual, Vol. 1.* Madison, WI: University of Wisconsin.

[Lietaer, G., & Brodley, B. T. (2003). Carl Rogers in the therapy room: A listing of session transcripts and a survey of publications referring to Rogers' sessions. *Person-Centered & Experiential Psychotherapies, 2,* 274–291.]

Raskin, N. (1947). *The nondirective attitude.* Unpublished manuscript. [Published (2005) in *The Person-Centered Journal 12*(1–2) and (2005) in B. E. Levitt (Ed.), *Embracing non-directivity* (pp. 327–347). Ross-on-Wye: PCCS Books]

Rogers, C. R. (1956). *The essence of psychotherapy: Moments of movement.* Paper given at first meeting of the American Academy of Psychotherapists, New York.

Rogers, C. R. (1957). The necessary and sufficient conditions of therapeutic personality change. *Journal of Consulting Psychology. 21,* 95–103.

Rogers, C. R. (1958). A process conception of psychotherapy. *American Psychologist, 13,* 142–148.

Rogers, C. R. (1959). A theory of therapy, personality and interpersonal relationships as developed in the client-centered framework. In S. Koch (Ed.), *Psychology: A study of a science. Vol. III: Formulations of the person and the social context* (pp. 184–256). New York: McGraw-Hill.

Rogers, C. R. (1970). *Carl Rogers on encounter groups.* New York: Harper & Row.

Rogers, C. R. (1975). Empathic: An unappreciated way of being. *Counseling Psychologist, 5*(2), 2–10.

Rogers, C. R. (1980). *A way of being.* Boston: Houghton Mifflin.

Rogers, C. R. (1984). *A conversation with Carl Rogers.* A discussion recorded at the

Second International Forum on the Person-Centered Approach. Norwich, England [Cassette Recording].

Rogers, C. R. (1985). *Demonstration interview with June.* Recorded Dublin. [See Brodley & Lietaer, 2006]

Rogers, C. R. (1986). Reflection of feelings. *Person-Centered Review, 1,* 375–377.

Temaner, B. [Brodley] (1977). The empathic understanding response process. Chicago Counseling and Psychotherapy Center. *Chicago Counseling Center Discussion Paper.* [This volume, Chapter 12]

Zimring, F. (1988). *A unique characteristic of client-centered therapy.* Unpublished manuscript.

# Chapter 24

# Concerning "transference," "countertransference," and other psychoanalytically developed concepts from a client/person-centered perspective

Psychologists, as well as other therapists and students, often express themselves in clinical settings using psychoanalytically derived terminology. Questions are asked such as "what about the transference?" In discussion of a family there may be casual references to the "latency-child." Supervisors make statements to student therapists such as "your 'countertransference' is stimulating the patient to 'act out' on the unit."

The terms "transference," "countertransference" and other psychoanalytic terms such as "ego-defense," "resistance," "latency-child," "self-object," etc. are used in these clinical settings *as if* they refer to consensually validated phenomena instead of theoretical constructs. This confusion of theoretical concepts with observable phenomena is a common intellectual mistake made by clinicians in the helping professions. It is a mistake that ill serves clients, students, or the clinicians themselves.

It seems difficult to find a good argument against requiring of oneself intellectual clarity and precision of "communication" when discussing psychotherapy in general or when discussing work with particular clients. It also seems difficult to deny (1) that psychoanalytically developed terms refer not to behavior itself, but to complex interpretations of behavior, to inferred cause–effect relations among intrapsychic events and observable behaviors; (2) that these terms themselves refer to a variety of observable, sometimes contradictory, behaviors; (3) that there are many different versions of psychoanalytic theory as it has developed and therefore different definitions of many of the concepts (e.g., Epstein, 1983; Freud, 1974; Gelso & Carter, 1984; Greenson, 1974; Joseph, 1985; Kernberg 1981; Racker, 1982; Searles, 1979; Stevens, 1986; Sullivan, 1987; Winnicott, 1949); and (4) that

Revision of a lecture prepared for PP341, Client-Centered Therapy: Theory and practice, Illinois School of Professional Psychology, Chicago, 1988. Published (1992) in *Renaissance, 9*(2), 1–2. Reproduced with permission.

psychoanalytic theory is not the only accepted explanation of human behavior or the only theory of therapy (e.g., Rogers, 1959; Skinner, 1989). If these points are granted, it would seem to follow that intellectual clarity and precision in communication would be enhanced by specifying the theory and defining the concepts that are being used and by stating which observables are being referred to in discussions of any particular clients.

It would also be considerate to nonpsychoanalytic colleagues if analytically oriented people (and other clinicians) would acknowledge that some clinician (or student) participants in a discussion may not utilize any of the versions of analytic theory. When psychoanalytic terms are used without specifying the theory, the definitions or the behaviors, the nonpsychoanalytic participant (e.g., client-centered, person-centered, some humanistic psychologists) is placed in an awkward and unfair position. In order to function responsibly and authentically in the situation, he or she must explicitly or implicitly challenge the assumptions of the psychoanalytically speaking person by asking for clarification of theory, assumptions, definitions and behaviors in the specific (or generic) client. Or the person knuckles under and adopts the psychoanalytic terminology while suffering a sense of being a coward, or the sense of being complicit in careless thinking, or the sense of self-misrepresentation.

Statements and questions that use psychoanalytic terms *as if* they refer to a shared reality and a shared way of conceptualizing people perpetuate fuzzy clinical thought and stimulate irresponsible work. The casual or unexplicated use of psychoanalytic terms is also a form of intellectual bullying. This is especially the case when the terms are employed by clinicians in higher authority than those to whom they are speaking. A student, for example, is unlikely to feel safe in challenging a supervisor's theoretical assumptions in the context of a clinical case discussion.

Any instance of the usage of psychoanalytic terms in discussions about clients would be wisely countered with the questions: "What precisely is the theory you are employing?" "What are your assumptions?" "What exactly are the definitions of the terms you are using?" "What specific behaviors of the client are you referring to?" Unfortunately, this kind of questioning for clarification is rare.

The mistake of using terms such as "transference" and "counter-transference" as if they refer to consensually validated phenomena is not due entirely to the carelessness of clinicians and educators. It is due to carelessness at times. At other times it is due to ignorance and to poor intellectual education with respect to clinical psychology. But it is also, I suggest, the legacy of the high social status attributed to psychoanalysts and to the mystique of psychoanalysis promoted by its adherents.

For reasons that have much more to do with the social history of the theory and practice of psychoanalysis than with the truth of the theory or the efficacy of the practice, terminology developed by Freud and other psychoanalysts has become the insider language of clinical psychologists and other therapists. Using terms such as "transference," etc. communicates an "insider" position to many people in the therapeutic community as well as to "outsiders." As a sign of status, the terms are used either as if they designate reality or as if the theory from which they are derived is valid. Neither is true. Psychoanalytic theory has not been proved. Nor has any other theory.

The client/person-centered viewpoint concerning the concept of "transference," in particular, has been discussed by Rogers (1951, 1987/2002), by Shlien (1984, 1987/2002) and by Seeman (1987/2002). Many of us who work from a client/person-centered framework do not find psychoanalytically developed terms useful. We do not use them ourselves and when used by others we find them obfuscating. Some of us, also, experience these terms as offensive to our sensibilities and to our feelings of humility and respect towards our clients and towards persons in general.

Whether or not a therapist or instructor subscribes to a version of psychoanalytic theory or practice, it should be obvious that sincere efforts to truly understand and to work effectively with clients or patients would be enhanced by intellectual clarity and openness of communication with colleagues and students. Deliberately avoiding psychoanalytic terms (at least until after discussion has taken place to specify behaviors, to explain theory and to define terms) would be a practice likely to lead to better communication with colleagues, and to better understanding of clients.

## REFERENCES

Epstein, L. (1983). The therapeutic function of hate in the countertransference. In L. Epstein & A. H. Feiner (Eds.), *Countertransference: The therapist's contribution to the therapeutic situation* (pp. 213–234). New York: Jason Aronson.

Freud, S. (1974). Letter from Freud to Jung dated 1909. In W. McGuire (Ed.), *The Freud–Jung Letters,* (p. 231). Princeton, NJ: Princeton University Press.

Gelso, C. J., & Carter, J. A. (1984). The relationship in counseling and psychotherapy: Components, consequences, and theoretical antecedents. *Counseling Psychology, 1,* 155–237.

Greenson, R. (1974). Loving, hating and indifference towards the patient. *International Review of Psychoanalysis, 1,* 259–266.

Joseph, B. (1985). Transference: The total situation. *International Journal of Psychoanalysis, 66,* 447–454.

Kernberg, O. (1981). Countertransference. In R. Langs (Ed.), *Classics in psychoanalytic techniques* (pp. 207–216). New York: Jason Aronson.

Racker, H. (1982). *Transference and countertransference.* New York: International Universities Press, Inc.

Rogers, C. R. (1951). *Client-centered therapy*. Boston: Houghton Mifflin.

Rogers, C. R. (1959). A theory of therapy, personality and interpersonal relationships, as developed in the client-centered framework. In S. Koch (Ed.), *Psychology: A study of a science. Vol. III: Formulations of the person and the social context* (pp. 184–256). New York: McGraw-Hill.

Rogers, C. R. (1987). Comment on Shlien's article "A countertheory of transference." *Person-Centered Review, 2,* 182–188. [Republished (2002) in D. J. Cain (Ed.), *Classics in the person-centered approach* (pp. 453–456). Ross-on Wye: PCCS Books]

Searles, H. F. (1979). *Countertransference and related subjects: Selected papers.* New York: International Universities Press.

Seeman, J. (1987). Transference and psychotherapy. *Person-Centered Review, 2,* 185–195. [Republished (2002) in D. J. Cain (Ed.), *Classics in the person-centered approach* (pp. 457–460). Ross-on Wye: PCCS Books]

Shlien, J. M. (1984). A countertheory of transference. In R. E. Levant & J. M. Shlien (Eds.), *Client-centered therapy and the person-centered approach* (pp. 153–181). New York: Praeger.

Shlien, J. M. (1987). A countertheory of transference. *Person-Centered Review, 2,* 15–49. [Republished (2002) in D. J. Cain (Ed.), *Classics in the person-centered approach* (pp. 415–435). Ross-on Wye: PCCS Books, and (2003) in P. Sanders (Ed.), *To lead an honorable life* (pp. 93–119). Ross-on-Wye: PCCS Books]

Skinner, B. F. (1989). Dialogue with Carl Rogers. In H. Kirschenbaum & V. L. Henderson (Eds.), *Carl Rogers: Dialogues* (pp. 79–152). Boston: Houghton Mifflin.

Stevens, B. (1986). A Jungian perspective on transference and countertransference. *Contemporary Psychoanalysis, 22,* 185–201.

Sullivan, B. S. (1987). The disliked client. *Quadrant, 2,* 55–71.

Winnicott, D. W. (1949). Hate in the countertransference. *International Journal of Psychoanalysis, 1,* 69–74.

# Chapter 25

# Some observations of Carl Rogers' behavior in therapy interviews

Carl Rogers' psychotherapy behavior, recorded on film, video, audiotape and in verbatim transcripts, is a rich source for learning about psychotherapy in general and specifically about the client/person-centered approach that Rogers developed (Rogers, 1957, 1959, 1980, 1986a). My interest in Rogers' own therapy behavior – how it relates to his theory and development as a therapist – has led me to examine, thus far, 34 sessions, consisting of 1,930 responses Rogers made in reaction to his clients, conducted over a 46-year time span – from 1940 through 1986.[1]

This report is primarily based on a system for rating client/person-centered therapy sessions which I developed with Anne Brody (Brodley & Brody, 1990, 1993/2008; Brody, 1991).[2] I shall summarize the findings from the total sample of 1,930 responses, show comparisons between Rogers' behavior in the frames of three consecutive time spans over the 46-year period of the 34 sessions, and relate the findings to Rogers' theoretical writings.

## THE RATING SYSTEM

The rating system distinguishes Rogers' articulate verbal responses into two basic categories – "empathic following responses" and "responses from the therapist's frame of reference." *Empathic following responses* are responses that the therapist makes to check with the client about the accuracy of her or his *experience* of empathic understanding of the client's internal frame of reference (Rogers, 1986b). Or, they are responses spoken to communicate explicitly to the client that the therapist is trying to follow and understand the client's

---

1. Responses reported include all of Rogers' responses to his clients except his responses to the 97 questions addressed to him and except his vocal gestures of acknowledgment such as "Umhum," etc.

2. Ratings were made by Anne Brody or Judith Nelson and the writer.

---

This is a revision of a paper presented at the Second International Conference on Client-Centered and Experiential Therapy, University of Stirling, Scotland, July, 1991. Published (1994) *The Person-Centered Journal*, 1(2), 37–48. Reproduced with permission from *PCJ*.

communication and self-expression. Empathic following responses may be in the form of empathic understanding responses, restatements, metaphors, or they may be fragments – incomplete communications. All forms of responses thus rated are identifiable as responses which intended to follow the client. They are, whatever form they may take, always the therapist's expression of her or his *grasp of the client's point of view or frame of reference*, never of the therapist's frame of reference. The following is an example of an empathic following response:

Client: I want to be in touch with my feelings, but not in this way. Because here I am and I can't even do what I believe in, it's taking up all of me.

Rogers: You want to get in touch with your feelings but you don't want to drown in them.

Empathic following responses may also be in the form of a question for clarification. An example of this form is:

Client: I'm just feeling how afraid I am of talking to you.

Rogers: Mhm, mhm. Mhm, mhm. Frightened of me or frightened of the situation or both?

*Responses from the therapist's frame of reference* consist of four subcategories of response in which the therapist is speaking *for her- or himself to the client*.[3] These responses always express the therapist's point of view or frame of reference. The content may be about the client or about the therapist her- or himself, or about something else – but are always from the therapist's perspective. In addition, these responses are almost always in response to whatever the client has been immediately expressing.

The four subcategories of responses from the therapist's frame of reference consist of: (1) "therapist comment"; (2) "therapist explanation/interpretation"; (3) "therapist agreement";[4] and (4) "leading or probing question." Examples of the four subcategories are:

Client: I feel that you're waiting for me to say something else (small laugh). I have trouble with silences.

---

3. Rogers' comments introducing the sessions, about the environment, and those at the end of sessions addressed to the audience are not rated in the system.

4. Responses which express *disagreement* with the client (if they were to have occurred) would be classified as "therapist comment."

Rogers: Mmm ... I don't have that trouble, I'm perfectly willing to wait until you know what you wish to say. (Therapist comment)

and

Client: But how can I change from being directive and dominant, but not be completely submissive, just ... I don't, I can't find any keys, any ways to do it. I find I'm hemmed in with an internal struggle.

Rogers: Maybe, maybe that's the answer; that there is no way without an internal struggle. (Therapist explanation/interpretation)

and

Client: Usually I can work on things or put things in perspective and do things that I have some control ... and this is something I don't have control of.

Rogers: That's right. There are some things you can't manipulate ... you can't control. (Therapist agreement)

and

Client: I stop myself when I start treating her as badly as I treat myself.

Rogers: Mm, mhm ... (pause) ... Can you see what's going on in you? (Leading or probing question)

## RELIABILITY

The 34 sessions were rated independently by two different raters in most cases. Reliability, in percentage of agreement per session, ranged from 90% to 100%. Differences were resolved jointly by the two raters.

## RESULTS

The 1,930 responses in the sample will be discussed as classified into one of four possible categories: (1) "empathic following responses," (2) "therapist comment" or "therapist explanation/interpretation,"[5] (3) "therapist agreement," or (4) "therapist leading/probing question." (The results are summarized in Table 1.)

---

5. Responses rated into the categories "therapist comment" and "therapist explanation/ interpretation" were added together in this presentation because so few of Rogers' responses could be rated as "explanation/interpretation." Additionally, the two categories for response are only very subtly different in Rogers' work because he does not make interpretations or give explanations that derive from a theoretical framework.

**Table 1: Summary of ratings of Rogers' responses in 34 therapy interviews, 1940–1966**

| | 1 | 2 | 3 | 4 | 5 | 6 |
|---|---|---|---|---|---|---|
| Samples | Total responses | Empathic following responses | Responses from the therapist's frame of reference | Therapist's comments, explanations and interpretations | Therapist's agreements with clients | Therapist's leading or probing questions |
| A:<br>Mr. Bryan<br>1940–41<br>3 sessions | 157 | 73 (46%) | 84 (54%) | 47 (30%) | 17 (11%) | 20 (13%) |
| B:<br>1944–64<br>17 sessions<br>8 clients | 811 | 775 (96%) | 36 (4%) | 33 (4%) | 0 (0%) | 3 (<1%) |
| C:<br>1977–86<br>14 sessions<br>14 clients | 962 | 811 (84%) | 151 (16%) | 127 (14%) | 7 (<1%) | 17 (2%) |
| B+C:<br>1944–86,<br>31 sessions<br>22 clients | 1,773 | 1,586 (90%) | 187 (10%) | 160 (9%) | 7 (<1%) | 20 (1%) |
| A+B+C:<br>1940–1986,<br>34 sessions<br>23 clients | 1,930 | 1,659 (86%) | 271 (14%) | 207 (10%) | 24 (<2%) | 40 (<3%) |

Eighty-six percent of Rogers' responses were classified as falling into the "empathic following" category. Ten percent were classified as "therapist comment" or "therapist explanation/interpretation." Slightly more than 1% were classified as "therapist agreement," and slightly more than 2% were rated as "leading/probing questions."

These findings suggest that Rogers' verbal therapy behavior was largely empathic and nondirective through the 46-year time span of the sessions in the sample. However, looking more closely at the ratings and taking note of Rogers' behavior in the earliest group of three sessions which consists of 157 responses from the case of Mr. Bryan (Rogers, 1942), and comparing that earliest group with the later 31 sessions consisting of 962 responses, there are some interesting contrasts.

Rogers made 15.6 responses per session that were classified as "therapist comment" or "explanation/interpretation" in the Mr. Bryan sample. He made, however, only 5 such responses per session in the following 31 sessions. He made, with Mr. Bryan, 5.6 responses per session that classified as "therapist agreement," but made fewer than one such response per session in the later sessions. Also, he made, with Mr. Bryan, 6.6 responses per session that classify as "leading/probing question" while he made fewer than one such response per session in the later sessions.

These results demonstrate that Rogers' behavior with Mr. Bryan expressed much less empathic understanding and was less nondirective than his later therapeutic work, even though the Bryan case served to illustrate his new nondirective therapeutic approach described in *Counseling and Psychotherapy* (1942). Because of this difference in the characteristics of his work with Bryan contrasted with his work with later clients in the sample, and because the sample available at the time of this study had no sessions taking place between 1964 and 1977 – a 13-year blank – the total sample of 34 sessions was divided into three consecutive time-frame subsamples so comparisons could be made between them as a possible way of assessing Rogers' evolution as a therapist over approximately 46 years of his career. Sample A consists of 3 sessions with Mr. Bryan. Sample B consists of 17 sessions between 1944 and 1964. Sample C consists of 14 sessions from 1977 through December 1986.

RESULTS FROM THE TIME-FRAME SUBSAMPLES

*Sample A.* This sample consists of all 157 of Rogers' responses found in sessions one, five and seven of the eight-session therapy conducted by Rogers with Mr. Bryan circa 1940–1941.[6] The entire case, footnoted with Rogers' critical commentary, was published in Rogers' 1942 book, *Counseling and Psychotherapy*. Mr. Bryan's therapy is one of the first published verbatim texts of an entire therapy.

The published case of Mr. Bryan illustrated Rogers' new nondirective approach to therapy which he had been developing at Ohio State University. Rogers explained that he was presenting the full case to show the way the therapist could create "an atmosphere in which the client can develop insight and begin to re-direct his life in new directions" (Rogers, 1942, p. 262).

At that time Rogers described his therapy as a "permissive relationship which allows the client to gain an understanding of himself to a degree which

---

6. The year of the eight Mr. Bryan sessions is not known, but must have been within two or three years of their publication in 1942.

enables him to take positive steps … [and] … all the techniques used should aim toward developing this free and permissive relationship … and this [the client's] tendency toward positive, self-initiated action" (p. 18).

In regard to the manner of implementation of the idea of a permissive atmosphere which enables self-initiations on the part of the client, Rogers stated "the best techniques for interviewing are those which encourage the client to express himself as freely as possible, with the counselor consciously endeavoring to refrain from any activity or any response which would guide the direction of the interview or the content brought forth" (p. 132). Rogers was explicitly and clearly advocating a nondirective approach in therapy.

Rogers' therapy behavior with Mr. Bryan, however, was not entirely consistent with his *idea* of nondirectivity. Fewer than half – specifically 46% – of Rogers' responses were empathic following responses (see Table 1). Reciprocally, more than half of Rogers' responses were responses from Rogers' own frame of reference (see column 3 in Table 1) in reaction to Mr. Bryan. Thirty percent of Rogers' responses to Bryan were comments or explanations/ interpretations. Eleven percent of his responses expressed agreement with the client's statements, and 13% were leading/probing questions.

Rogers' commentary to the verbatim Bryan text (Rogers, 1942, pp. 265– 435) [Brodley & Lietaer, 2006, Vol. 2, Mr. Bryan]* shows that he recognized that his comments, interpretations, explanations and leading/probing questions were directive or empathically inadequate. In the commentary he consistently criticized the responses made from his own frame of reference. He viewed them as less effective than empathic understanding responses in fostering his goal of promoting the client's self-directed and self-motivated experience.

The evidence in the sessions with Mr. Bryan indicates that Rogers – at the time of conducting the therapy with Mr. Bryan – had reached a developed intellectual position in regard to trusting the client and creating a climate that allowed and promoted a client-directed therapy process. But he had not yet completely incorporated his ideas into *functional attitudes*, with their consistent implementations, of nondirectivity and acceptant empathic understanding that show up in the next time-frame subsample.

It should be noted and emphasized, however, that Rogers' behavior with Mr. Bryan is that of a very skilled and effective psychotherapist. It is obvious on the printed pages of the case that Rogers is very natural, very at ease and authentic as well as understanding, sympathetic, kind, responsive, participative

---

* Editors' note: In the course of many years, Barbara transcribed and supervised others in transcribing Rogers' therapy and demonstration sessions. In this paper she refers to transcripts that were in the process of being "polished" through multiple listenings to the tapes. It is uncertain at which point of evolution she quoted from the various transcripts. The transcript work culminated in a joint effort with Germain Lietaer resulting in a journal article (Lietaer & Brodley, 2003) and an informal email publication (Brodley & Lietaer, 2006).

and non-authoritarian. Rogers was an effective and admirable psychotherapist in his work with Mr. Bryan but he was not a very nondirective one, nor was he consistently empathic.

*Sample B.* This sample consists of 17 sessions with eight different clients, conducted by Rogers from 1944 or 1945 through 1964. Five of the clients represented in these Sample B sessions were Rogers' regular clients, and three were demonstration clients. One of the demonstration interviews in this time-frame group is that of Gloria, which was filmed in 1964 (Shostrum, 1965).

Sample B sessions show a very different picture in respect to the proportion of his responses that express the clients' frames of reference versus those expressing Rogers' frame of reference, compared with the sessions conducted with Mr. Bryan. In this sample 96% (of Rogers' total of 811 responses) are empathic following responses. In respect to the frequency of Rogers' nondirective and empathic behavior, there is a 50% difference between the Sample B sessions and those of the earlier Bryan case.

In Sample B only 4% of Rogers' responses are expressed from his frame of reference in contrast to the 54% in the Bryan interviews. Among the 36 responses made from Rogers' frame of reference in Sample B, fewer than 0.3% of Rogers' responses are leading or probing questions, whereas in the Bryan interviews, 13% of Rogers' responses are leading or probing questions. It is obvious from these simple statistics that a radical shift had taken place in Rogers' therapy behavior between the time he was conducting the Bryan sessions and the later period from 1944 through 1964.

Rogers' shift to functional nondirectivity and almost total reliance upon empathic understanding seems to have occurred immediately between the time of the Bryan therapy and before publication of *Client-Centered Therapy* (1951). The evidence for the timing of the shift is shown by the ratings of the group of 12 sessions from four cases in Sample B which were conducted between 1944 and 1946 or 1947. Ninety-eight percent of Rogers' responses in these 12 sessions are empathic following responses. This is compared to only 46% of empathic following responses in the Bryan sessions.

Among the types of response Rogers makes that are from his own frame of reference, leading/probing questions are the most obviously directive. In the Sample B subgroup of four cases conducted between 1944 and 1946/1947, only one response out of a total of 569 responses by Rogers was a leading/probing question. In the whole of Sample B (962 responses) there are only three – less than 1% – leading/probing questions. It appears that Rogers had deeply adopted the nondirective attitude he described in *Client-Centered Therapy* (1951). He quotes an eloquent statement by Raskin concerning this attitude:

> There is [another] level of nondirective counselor response ... which ... changes the nature of the counseling process in a radical way ... [such] counselor participation becomes an active experiencing with the client of the feelings to which he gives expression, the counselor makes a maximum effort to get under the skin of the person with whom he is communicating, he tries to get *within* and to live the attitudes expressed instead of observing them, to catch every nuance of their changing nature ... to absorb himself completely in the attitudes of the other. And in struggling to do this, there is simply no room for any other type of ... activity or attitude; if he is attempting to live the attitudes of the other, he cannot be diagnosing them, he cannot be thinking of making the process go faster. Because he [the counselor] is another, and not the client, the understanding is not spontaneous but must be acquired, and this through the most intense, continuous and active attention to the feelings of the other, to the exclusion of any other type of attention. (Raskin, 1947, p. 29/2005, pp. 330–331)

The nondirective attitude expresses the client-centered therapist's consistent trust in the client as having the inherent capability and the right to direct the process of her or his own therapy. The therapist expresses the nondirective attitude by offering deep and acceptant attention to the client's representations of her or his perceptions, attitudes and feelings *as the client is expressing her- or himself.* And by responding with responses that are an attempt to find out from the client whether or not the therapist's inner, subjective, understandings are accurate according to the client.

Although Rogers' therapy, after the Bryan case, is characterized by a very high frequency of empathic following responses, along with an almost complete absence of directive types of response, Rogers did not discuss or ever advocate in his writings or lectures any specific techniques or specific forms of response to implement his theory of therapy after (circa) 1942.

*Sample C.* This sample consists of 14 sessions with 14 different clients. The interviews took place between the years 1977 and late 1986. All these sessions are demonstration interviews. With these clients, Rogers maintains a salient nondirective attitude and the core therapeutic attitudes although there is an increase in the frequency of responses from Rogers' frame of reference in Sample C compared with his work with the clients in Sample B. (See column 3, rows 2 and 3 in Table 1). There is an increase in Rogers' responses, spoken from his own frame of reference, from 4% in Sample B to 16% in Sample C. Most of this increase appears in the categories of "therapist comment" or "explanation/interpretation" (see column 4, Table 1). There is also a slight increase in Rogers' statements of agreement with his clients from 0% to less than 1% (column 5, Table 1). And there is a slight increase in Rogers' leading/probing questions from less than 0.3% to approximately 2% (column 6, Table 1).

Close examination of the 14 Sample C transcripts, and listening to or viewing the interviews, shows Rogers to be functioning – with only rare exception within limited sequences of interaction in one or two interviews (see Brodley, 1996) – in a manner highly consistent with his basic client-centered therapeutic goals for himself – to be real, to be acceptant, to be empathic and to trust the client to be the source of the content and manner of movement in therapy.

Empathic following responses are the most frequent responses employed by Rogers. But they do not come across as techniques in his work. Rather, they seem to be genuine and natural attempts to be as sure as he can that his inner understandings are accurate *empathic* understandings. The rarity of his clients' disagreements with Rogers' empathic following responses, and the way in which his clients almost always proceed in productive and undefensive further self-disclosures, give a vivid impression that Rogers is experienced by his clients as unthreatening, genuine, acceptant and empathic.

## RESPONSES FROM ROGERS' FRAME OF REFERENCE AND A NEW ELEMENT IN THEORY

The session in this study's sample, that Rogers conducted after Mr. Bryan, as rated by the Brodley and Brody system, shows that Rogers functionally adopted and maintained his client-centered approach with great consistency from (circa) 1944 through 1986, shortly before his death. In this time frame, however, there are 187 responses (column 3, row 4, Table 1) from Rogers' frame of reference. Ten percent of all of his responses made in the 31 sessions with 22 clients (Samples B and C together) are from Rogers' frame of reference.

The frequency of these responses in individual interviews range from 0% in a (circa) 1955 session, to 25% in a 1977 session. In most of the sessions there are at least a few such responses. It appears that even after Rogers had deeply adopted the nondirective attitude and communication of the client-centered therapeutic attitudes of congruence, unconditional positive regard and empathic understanding primarily through expression of empathic following responses, he usually gives himself the leeway to make spontaneous and unsystematic responses from his own frame of reference. These responses from his own frame of reference, in reaction to his client's self-explorations, are interspersed throughout his interviews, their frequency varying with different clients.

Rogers refers to this fact of the existence of other than empathic following responses in his remarks which were filmed immediately after his demonstration session with Gloria (Shostrum, 1965). Rogers says:

> ... When I am able really to let myself enter into a relationship – and I feel that this was true in this instance – then I find myself not only being increasingly moved by my being in touch with the inner world of my client – but I find myself bringing out of my own inner experience, statements which seem to have no connection with what's going on, but which usually prove to be, or prove to have, a very significant relationship to what the client is experiencing.
> [Brodley & Lietaer, 2006, Vol. 12, Gloria Post-Session Commentary, p. 19]

Rogers appears to mean that the responses he brings out of his own inner experience are not empathic following responses and, by implication, that they cannot be theoretically explained or justified from within his previously stated theory.

Twenty-two years after the filming of the Gloria session, Rogers discussed the phenomenon of his "presence" (Rogers, 1986a, pp. 198–199). Rogers states that he sometimes behaves in "strange and impulsive" ways that he "cannot justify rationally" but which seem "right" in some way for the client. The responses to which he refers are necessarily ones expressed from his own frame of reference. *They cannot be empathic following responses* because empathic following responses always express the client's frame of reference and are always theoretically justified whenever a client is speaking self-expressively, (other than when addressing a question to the therapist).

In an interview that Rogers gave (to Baldwin, 1987/2004) in the last year or so of his life concerning his approach to therapy, he added another observation about his work which might have led to additional theoretical explanations of his approach, if he had lived longer. He said:

> Over time, ... I have become more aware of the fact that in therapy I do use myself. I recognize that when I am intensely focused on a client, just my presence seems to be healing ... I am inclined to think that in my writing perhaps I have stressed too much the three basic conditions (congruence, unconditional positive regard and empathic understanding). Perhaps it is something around the edges of those conditions that is really the most important element of therapy – when my self is very clearly, obviously present. (p. 45)

Rogers equates the behavior "use myself" with his concept of "presence," and his presence is connected with the responses he makes that come out of his "own inner experiences" which are not empathic following responses but, nevertheless, according to Rogers, "have a very significant relationship to what the client is expressing." That is, they are to some extent empathic.

There are several possible elements in Rogers' therapy behavior, besides his very expressive statements of empathic understanding, which may contribute to communication of his presence in the relationship. Some of these are his physical appearance, manner and gestures, his references to himself, and the statements he makes from his own frame of reference.

Rogers became less formal, more casual and freer in his physical presence over the years. His empathic following of Miss Mun (circa 1954), was verbally and vocally highly attuned and sensitive to his client who was exploring and feeling very deeply at places in the session. Without the sound, however, Rogers appears very formal and professional – although also very kindly. In the film, Rogers is seated next to a table which is to the side between him and his client. He is dressed in business attire, sits in an upright and relatively unmoving position, gestures little and does not lean toward or touch the client, even in the most emotional and closest moments of the session.

In contrast – although Rogers was also verbally and vocally highly attuned and sensitive in his empathic following of a young woman in a 1983 demonstration – his physical presence at this later time was informal, expressive and very personal. In the 1983 session, Rogers is seated directly in front of the young woman. He is dressed in slacks, an open shirt and sweater. He is leaning forward towards the client, and his face and gestures are emotionally communicative even seen only from the side. He wipes away a tear during moments when the client is weeping and talking about sad experiences. In testimony to Rogers' strong physical presence, after the session during group discussion the client says "I felt very *held*" [Brodley & Lietaer, 2006, Vol. 15, Ms. G., Discussion, p. 38]. Similarly, during a 1986 demonstration, Rogers takes his client's hands and holds them through part of that very emotional session [see Brodley & Lietaer, 2006, Vol. 17, Lydia, 1st and 2nd Interviews].

In his later work Rogers' face, body and movements express his emotional involvement, and he often shows signs of his emotional reactions that occur concomitant with his empathic following responses. This freer, expressive, behavior most certainly contributes more than his earlier therapy behavior to a perceivable personal presence in relationship with his clients.

Examination of Rogers' self-references, per se, (using as a measure the number of self-references Rogers makes in a session divided by the total number of words he speaks in a session) results in a mean of less than 2% of such self-references. And this mean is the same in early and later sessions.

Most of Rogers' self-references are involved in his introductions to empathic following responses, although some occur in statements from his own frame of reference. In either case, Rogers' focus on himself is very light and in a *passing* manner rather than emphasized. This measure does not show any evidence of change in the extent Rogers manifested presence in his therapy relationship, but it does suggest, along with the real change found in his – apparently spontaneous – physical behavior, that Rogers' use of *himself* in therapy was not via any obvious focus on himself.

Nonsystematic, spontaneous responses from Rogers' frame of reference may contribute to Rogers' presence in the therapeutic relationship. The 187 responses Rogers makes from his own frame of reference in Sample B plus Sample C (see column 3, row 4, in Table 1) seem to be mostly discrete and spontaneous statements. They represent Rogers, in the interaction, having a reaction, a wish, an observation, or a feeling of curiosity for a few moments within the flow of his empathic following of the client.

There is often, in fact, a distinctly empathic quality to Rogers' responses from his own frame of reference which can be observed more clearly when such responses are impressionistically segregated into several sub-types. Some responses are, for example, *empathically observational*. These are comments descriptive of what the client has been saying or has been manifesting in their body language. These comments are from Rogers' frame of reference and are *about the client*, and are sometimes very close to empathic understanding responses. The following are several examples of Rogers' responses to different clients:

> That sounds like a dilemma.
>
> There's something very emotional about this moment.
>
> That's a little too much.
>
> It almost brings tears to your eyes, doesn't it?
>
> One thing that comes through in almost everything you say is how much you dislike the abstract, the intellectual ... so distant from the realness of people.

A slightly different type of statement that Rogers makes from his own frame of reference, in some instances, is a comment about himself or about his feelings, or a comment that expresses a wish Rogers experiences in interaction with his client.

> Yeah, that helps to clarify it.
>
> I guess I'd appreciate it if you'd try me out.

I feel close to you in this moment.

I appreciate being with you.

Rogers also produces a few responses which are interpretations or explanations to the client about the client. These are not based on theoretical interpolations but, rather, are *like descriptions* even though they involve an interpretive element. Examples from Rogers' work with several different clients:

You quickly restrain those outbursts which seem both pain, and almost like laughter.

It strikes me you're so much harder on yourself than you would be on a client – much more judgmental.

You say "as if" she were one of your children; it seems to me she is your child.

Among Rogers' 20 responses that are categorized as "leading/probing questions" in Sample B plus Sample C, most of these obviously *leading* statements depend upon Rogers' empathic attunement to his clients. Examples are:

If you did cry, what would some of the themes of that crying be?

Can you say more about that sadness? I'm not quite clear what it is that feels sad.

Can you even begin to say what those tears are about?

Can you say more about that fear? What's the feeling of fear?

Something that has caused you pain? You mentioned guilt.

Dominant in what way?

When you first started, you said you wanted to talk about death.

Rogers' conception of empathic understanding of the client's internal frame of reference refers to an acceptant understanding of the client's own perspective, feelings, ideas and personal meanings. His conception does give emphasis to feelings and personal meanings – and personal meanings involve the attitudes, feelings and emotions that intersperse and qualitatively affect the cognitive elements. Rogers' responses *from his own frame of reference* also tend to emphasize feelings and personal meanings. In those types of response Rogers is *speaking from his own perceptions and impressions* that are, albeit, *very directly stimulated by the client's revelations and behavior.* Other than the client-centered emphasis given to feelings and personal meanings, however, Rogers' responses from his own frame of reference – whether they are comments or interpretations or explanations or even leading/probing questions – are atheoretical.

## IN CONCLUSION

This very limited culling from the rich data of Rogers' 34 sessions conducted over a 46-year time span permits several general observations. First, there is evidence of a radical shift from a theoretical to a functional nondirectivity and empathic understanding in Rogers' therapy between (circa) 1941 and (circa) 1945. Second, through the time frame since (circa) 1944 through 1986, and especially in the period after Rogers hypothesized the necessary and sufficient conditions for therapeutic change (Rogers, 1957), Rogers appears to typically make at least a few responses from his own frame of reference in his therapeutic interviews. Third, there is evidence of a development in Rogers, between the 1944–1964 phase and the 1977–1986 phase of his therapeutic work, towards a more personal expression of himself in his interaction with his clients. Fourth, there is evidence that Rogers expressed responses from his own frame of reference more frequently during the final, 1977–1986, phase of his work than in the earlier, 1944–1964 phase. They remained a minor proportion of his total responses, are usually spontaneous, nonsystematic and related to the client's immediate self-presentation. Even though spoken from the therapist's frame of reference they are usually empathic in the general sense of being lifted from the client's internal frame of reference and are spoken with a tentativeness indicating that the authority for their accuracy lies with the client. They are also, almost always, consistent with Rogers' theoretical and personal view that the only goals, when working with a client, are the goals for oneself – to be real, to be acceptant and to be empathic.

Finally, there is evidence in his writings and, subtly, in his therapy behavior, that Rogers – had he lived longer – may well have further clarified and enlightened us with new theoretical insights and guidelines about client/person-centered therapy.

## REFERENCES

Baldwin, M. (1987). Interview with Carl Rogers on the use of the self in therapy. In M. Baldwin & V. Satir (Eds.), *The use of self in therapy* (pp. 45–52). Haworth Press: London. [Reprinted (2004) in R. Moodley, C. Lago, & A. Talahite (Eds.), *Carl Rogers counsels a Black client: Race and culture in person-centred counseling* (pp. 253–260). Ross-on-Wye: PCCS Books]

Brodley, B. T. (1996). Uncharacteristic directiveness and the "anger and hurt" client. In B. A. Farber, D. C. Brink, & P. M. Raskin (Eds.), *The psychotherapy of Carl Rogers. Cases and commentary* (pp. 310–321). New York: Guilford.

Brodley, B. T., & Brody, A. F. (1990, August). Understanding client-centered therapy through interviews conducted by Carl Rogers. Paper presented on the panel *Fifty years of client-centered therapy: Recent research*, at the American Psychological Association annual conference in Boston.

Brodley, B. T., & Brody, A. F. (1993). A rating system for studying client/person-centered interviews. Unpublished paper. [See Wilczynski, J., Brodley, B. T., & Brody, A. F. (2008). A rating system for studying client/person-centered interviews. *The Person-Centered Journal, 15*(1–2), 34–57, for the most recent version of the rating system]

[Brodley, B. T., & Lietaer, G. (Eds.). (2006). *Transcripts of Carl Rogers' therapy sessions, Vols. 1–17.* Email publication available from Germain.Lietaer@psy.kuleuven.be and kmoon1@alumni.uchicago.edu]

Brody, A. F. (1991). *Understanding client-centered therapy through interviews conducted by Carl Rogers.* Unpublished doctoral clinical research project, Illinois School of Professional Psychology, Chicago (now Arogosy University, Chicago).

[Lietaer, G., & Brodley, B. T. (2003). Carl Rogers in the therapy room: A listing of session transcripts and a survey of publications referring to Rogers' sessions. *Person-Centered & Experiential Psychotherapies, 2,* 274–291.]

Raskin, N. J. (1947). *The nondirective attitude.* Unpublished manuscript. [Published (2005) in *The Person-Centered Journal 12*(1–2), and (2005) in B. E. Levitt (Ed.), *Embracing non-directivity* (pp. 327–347). Ross-on-Wye: PCCS Books]

Rogers, C. R. (1942). *Counseling and psychotherapy.* Boston: Houghton Mifflin.

Rogers, C. R. (1951). *Client-centered therapy.* Boston: Houghton Mifflin.

Rogers, C. R. (1957). The necessary and sufficient conditions of therapeutic personality change. *Journal of Consulting Psychology, 21,* 95–103.

Rogers, C. R. (1959). A theory of therapy, personality, and interpersonal relationships, as developed in the client-centered framework. In S. Koch (Ed.), *Psychology: A study of a science. Vol. III: Formulations of the person and the social context* (pp. 184–256). New York: McGraw-Hill.

Rogers, C. R. (1980). The foundations of a person-centered approach. In *A way of being* (pp. 113–136). Boston: Houghton Mifflin.

Rogers, C. R. (1986a). Client-centered therapy. In I. L. Kutash & A. Wolf (Eds.), *Psychotherapist's casebook* (pp. 197–208). San Francisco: Jossey-Bass.

Rogers, C. R. (1986b). Reflection of feelings. *Person-Centered Review, 1,* 375–7.

Shostrum, E. L. (Producer). (1965). *Three approachers to psychotherapy (Part I)* [Film]. Orange, CA: Psychological Films.

# Chapter 26

# Observations of empathic understanding
# in two client-centered therapists

## INTRODUCTION

This paper reports a study of empathic responses in 22 client-centered therapy sessions conducted by Carl Rogers and in 20 sessions by the writer. The basic question addressed by the study is "what specifically does empathic understanding, in client-centered therapy, appear to be understanding?" The study addresses this question by examining responses made by Rogers – the creator and a master of the approach – and by the writer who has had long experience as a client-centered therapist. The specific aim of the study was to identify certain elements in the therapists' empathic responses on the basis of theory about empathic understanding, to determine the frequency of the elements, and compare the empathic responses of the two therapists. The paper presents my view of empathic understanding in client-centered work and some of Rogers' elucidating views about it. I shall describe the study and its findings, and discuss the observations in the context of Zimring's (2000) theory of the *targets* of empathic understanding in client-centered therapy.

## ACCEPTANT EMPATHIC UNDERSTANDING

As a nondirective, client-centered therapist, a*cceptant empathic understanding* is my fundamental attitude in relation to clients. My immediate and constant goal in therapeutic interactions with clients is to experience and maintain this complex *attitude*. Logically, to have a therapeutic effect, I must behave such that the attitude is communicated to the client. According to Rogers' (1957, 1959) theory of therapy, the client must perceive or experience the therapist's acceptant empathic understanding in order to experience

Thanks to Charley Knapp, Julie Roe and Christine Badger, who made transcripts and reliability ratings for the study.

This chapter is a revision of a paper presented at the International Conference on Client-Centered and Experiential Psychotherapy, Chicago 2000. Published (2002) in J. C. Watson, R. N. Goldman, & M. S. Warner (Eds.), *Client-centered and experiential psychotherapy in the 21st century: Advances in theory, research and practice* (pp. 182–203). Ross-on-Wye: PCCS Books.

therapeutic benefits from the relationship. Therefore, with most clients, the therapist must deliberately communicate acceptant empathic understanding. Empathic responses are primarily *explicit* communications – expressed in words representing the therapist's understanding of the client's intended communications and expression. Acceptance, however, is communicated indirectly by the therapist's tone and manner, and by the absence of evaluative or judgmental elements (Brodley & Schneider, 2001/2011) in empathic responses.

Communication of the acceptant empathic attitude usually takes place through an interaction – the *empathic understanding response process* (Temaner, 1977/2011) – between the client and the therapist. The empathic understanding response process is also referred to as the *empathy cycle* by Barrett-Lennard (1981). The following segment from a session illustrates the empathic understanding response process in client-centered therapy.

Client 1: I expected to get a severe rejection. I expect this all the time. I don't know why this is, but even if I go up to somebody and ask for the time, the thing that I'm really bracing myself against is a severe rejection of me, even if it is realistically and completely unlikely. I really have to brace myself against something as strong as that just to ask for the time.

Therapist 1: Even in the most trivial kind of relationships the feeling is ... "Here comes rejection!"

Client 2: Here comes ... some tremendous danger. And physical violence doesn't even get the danger in it ... although I do fear physical violence a lot. That's the same kind of thing ... That if whatever the worst that can happen can be, that's what I feel most concerned about.

Therapist 2: That's almost a better phrase for it than rejection. That the point is, you're expecting the worst. Exactly what the definition of worst is, may not be too easy to know. But you just know ... "This will be catastrophe."

Client 3: Yeah. And the idea that it's not so, is very hard. But somehow I even feel it with you. Or at least this is what I kinda have ta' be ready for, and if I do something which seems like it might make it a little more possible, then I have to ... sorta compensate ... to make sure it's all right again.

Therapist 3: So it's in this relationship too. There is the feeling that ..."Look out if I do something a little out of line ... the world will fall in on me." Or something like that.

Client 4: (Very long pause, 35 seconds) It's hard to talk about it because I don't know quite ... or it's that I want to be so good with you somehow, you know ...?

Therapist 4: Uhm, hm.

Client 5: I want to be the best I can possibly be with you ... kinda like that ... But that somehow ties with this idea that you ... of feeling so good with ... you were my father. That I just try to do good for you.

Therapist 5: You want to be the best possible here in my terms. Is that the way you mean it?

Client 6: Yeah. It would feel good being that way. But it was somehow a past need that I had to be the best possible for you in your terms. (Pause) But there was some negative side to the idea I was picking up somehow ... (Pause)

Therapist 6: But anyway, that doesn't quite catch the present feeling.

Client 7: I kinda still have to work through that ... work through the feeling of being a little boy ... feeling good pleasing his father.

Therapist 7: Uhm, hm.

Client 8: That's sorta one of the stages I'm at somehow.

Therapist 8: That sorta, that has felt good. Is this the stage you're in or about to leave ... or something?

Client 9: I just don't know exactly what it is. (Long pause, 25 seconds) That this idea of needing to please ... of having to do it ... that's the same thing again. That's really been kinda (weeps) ... been a basic assumption of my life ... kinda the very unquestioned axiom that ... I have to please ... I have no choice; I just have to ... (Rogers, circa 1955)

[See also Brodley & Lietaer, 2006, Vol. 10, Mr. Necta, Session 58, pp. 115–116] *

All of the therapist's responses in the segment are empathic understandings (or acknowledgments, e.g., therapist responses 4 and 7). They are *following-the-client* responses. They are expressed tentatively and they are open to correction by the client. Therapist response number 8, that appears to be a question addressed to the client, is an empathic response expressing the therapist's sense of the question the client is considering.

As the segment suggests, in order for the empathic understanding response process to happen, the client must be minimally motivated to reveal, and capable of expressing, something of his or her inner world or

---

* Editors' note: In the course of many years, Barbara transcribed and supervised others in transcribing Rogers' therapy and demonstration sessions. In this paper she refers to transcripts that were in the process of being "polished" through multiple listenings to the tapes. It is uncertain at which point of evolution she quoted from the various transcripts. The transcript work culminated in a joint effort with Germain Lietaer resulting in a journal article (Lietaer & Brodley, 2003) and an informal email publication (Brodley & Lietaer, 2006).

life experiences to the therapist. In the empathic understanding response process, the therapist expresses (a) an intention to pay authentic attention to the client, (b) an intention to accurately understand the client's immediate experience as the client intends that it be communicated, (c) an intention to seek verification or correction of inner understandings by representing them to the client. Nondirective following also expresses the therapist's unconditional positive regard for the client. In this activity the client-centered therapist is not gathering information about the client's phenomenology in order to make effective interpretations, but engaging in understanding for its own value. The ultimate purpose of this empathic understanding is the therapeutic benefit that is found to be inherent in the understanding interaction and relationship.

The therapist's responses include simple acknowledgments of following – nodding or vocal gestures such as "uhm hm" – as well as articulate following responses that represent part of what the client has expressed or communicated to the therapist. Articulate following responses may consist only of *information* that the client communicates or they may be acceptant empathic understanding responses. True empathic responses contain expression of *the client's relation to what he or she is talking about* that often involve personal meanings or feelings. The therapist's reason for making an articulate empathic or other following-type response is to check his or her inner, subjective accuracy of understanding, to find out if it is correct according to the client (Rogers, 1986; Brodley, 1998/2011).

The therapist's verbal and expressive behavior that communicates the acceptant empathic understanding attitude typically has several additional qualities. It represents portions of a close following of the client's narrative and *related* vocal and nonverbal expressive behavior. It represents the client's *immediate* focus and communicative intentions. It communicates the therapist's *inner* acceptant empathic understanding of the client as accurately as possible. The client-centered therapist's behavior does not involve intentions to point the client towards any goal originating from the therapist regarding content or process. The therapist's intention in relation to the client is to understand what the client is getting at. The therapist maintains an acceptant attitude towards the client and usually experiences warm feelings towards him or her while listening and responding.

The client-centered therapist intends to remain integrated, relaxed, attentive and undistracted by irrelevant stimuli in order to accomplish acceptant empathic understanding. The therapist is open to awareness of his or her own associations and emotional reactions, as they are needed for the purpose of discriminating her personal reactions from the client's intended communications. The interaction consisting of the client's self-disclosures and expressive behavior and the therapist's acceptant, following behavior builds empathic understanding of the client in the therapist's mind and promotes the client's sense of being understood and accepted by the therapist – the components of an evolving client-centered therapeutic relationship. Through this interaction process therapeutic change occurs in the client (Patterson, 1985).

Acceptant empathic understanding in client-centered therapy is a particular kind of understanding. Unless informed otherwise, the therapist assumes it is the kind of understanding that the client is expecting or hoping to receive when entering the therapy situation – an uncritical understanding especially of the client's personal thoughts and feelings. Thus, if the assumption about the client's expectations is correct, acceptant empathic understanding is intrinsically a nondirective following. The client-centered therapist intends to remain nonjudgmental and acceptant towards all of the client's communication and expressive behavior. The therapist is listening to understand all of the client's communications. He or she, however, is especially interested in and responsive to certain aspects of it in order to understand *empathically*.

Zimring (2000) uses the term *targets* to refer to the particular aspects in clients' communications that client-centered therapists strive to grasp in listening to clients, in order to experience *accurate* empathic understanding. Rogers described targets of empathic understanding in his explanations, without referring to the term. Rogers (1959) wrote as follows:

> Being empathic, is to perceive the internal frame of reference of another with accuracy and with the emotional components and meanings which pertain thereto …. Thus it means to sense the hurt or the pleasure of another as he senses it and to perceive the causes thereof as he perceives them, but without ever losing the recognition that it is *as if* I were hurt or pleased. (pp. 210–211)

Rogers' targets of acceptant empathic understanding in this description involve (a) "emotional components" which would include basic feelings such as *fear* or *anger*, and also (b) more complex experiences having affective qualities, such as *conflicted* or *perplexed*. The targets also involve (c) personal "meanings," as they appear in one client's statement, "I feel *we're so isolated*," or in her statement, "There's *a big hollow of things* that aren't there," or in another client's statement "I developed obsession and then tension in the back of my head and then *it centralized in one spot like a hook*." Rogers also suggests that the targets include (d) the person's explanations and interpretations of his experience such as the statement "I'm doing something to push people away."

In a later formulation, Rogers (1980) emphasized that empathy is a process, not a state. Through *interaction* between client and therapist the therapist enters "the private perceptual world of the other and becomes thoroughly at home in it" (p. 142). According to Rogers, empathy involves "frequently *checking with the person* [my italics] as to the accuracy of your sensing, and being guided by the responses you receive" (p. 142).

Rogers' writings, as well as his own therapy behavior, reveal that the experience of empathic understanding involves inferential processes, as is true of understanding in any context. A mother of small children describes, in a tired tone of voice, a list of chores she accomplished today. The listener responds with the remark, "You must be worn out" or he says, "Would you like me to take the kids so you can get a break?" The woman's point has been inferred by the combination of words and expressive behavior. Similarly, the empathic therapist is not focused on understanding in the sense of knowing what a client said so the literal words may be reproduced. The therapist is trying to grasp the meanings and experiences that the client *seems to intend* to be understood by the listener. Rogers reveals this focus when he uses the phrases "sense the hurt or the pleasure of another" above, and when he describes the therapist's responses as ones "pointing to the *possible* [my italics] meanings in the flow of another person's experiencing" (p. 142).

The therapist expresses his acceptant empathic understanding in a manner that is likely to result in the client having the experience of *feeling understood*. This latter part of the goal is implied in Rogers (1959) sixth condition "that the client perceives … the empathic understanding of the therapist" (p. 213). In other words, the goal is accurate empathic understanding of the client, and the client determines what is accurate. The forms of the therapist's communication, consequently, depend in part upon a client's characteristics – the client's vocabulary, style of speech, and flow that become apparent as the therapist interacts with the client.

Previous analyses of Rogers' therapy behavior (Brodley & Brody, 1990; Brody, 1991; Brodley, 1994/2011; Nelson, 1994; Diss, 1996; Merry, 1996; Bradburn, 1996) have contributed to my formulation (Brodley, 1996/2011) concerning the elements the therapist especially attends to in the process of empathic understanding. Studies of transcripts of Rogers' therapy behavior, from the mid-1940s until his death in 1987, for example, reveal he produces (a mean of ) approximately 90% empathic responses in his therapy interviews. Most of these responses explicitly or implicitly communicate that Rogers is understanding the client as an *agent or actor*, as *an active and reactive person*, and as *a source of meanings, feelings, reactions and other experiences about self or about the external world*. Words for feelings, however, are only contained in approximately 25% of Rogers' empathic responses according to past studies. Thus clients' feelings that the therapist can express in single words have been observed to be only part of Rogers' focus.

The evidence from Rogers' sessions and impressions of other client-centered therapists suggests that client-confirmed empathic understanding responses usually emphasize the client as an *agent, actor* or *source of actions*. Rogers' clients show an almost ubiquitous explicit approval of his acceptant empathic understanding responses. These responses tend to show his understanding of their *agency*. It appears that clients feel well understood when he has grasped and communicated to them that their talk expresses their *intentions* and relates to their self as an *agent, an actor,* or *a source* of thoughts, feelings and actions. If one follows Rogers as a model, to empathically understand very accurately, the therapist should aim to recognize the client's *intentions* in his communications and relate the client's feelings, meanings, perspectives, explanations and reactions to those intentions. This conception of the aim in acceptant empathic understanding is similar to the recent formulation by Zimring (2000).

THE STUDY

The specific aim of the study is to determine the frequency of client-centered therapists' representations of certain elements of their clients' communications and expressive behavior in empathic responses. The study is based on two samples of therapists' responses – one sample of responses selected unsystematically from transcripts of 22 interviews conducted by Carl Rogers and another sample from 20 interviews I have conducted. Various ratings and counts were made on the selected responses in order to produce a summary picture of salient features of each therapist's empathic responses.

The following features of empathic responses were rated: words or phrases that express emotions or feelings; words or phrases with vivid or evocative qualities; phrases without feeling or evocative qualities; words for specific cognitive processes; words that point to subjective experiences; responses that speak for the client in the first person; dramatic-form responses that represent third persons' remarks to the client; references to the therapist; responses that represent the client as having a *want*; responses that represent the client as *trying*; and sentence units that represent the client as agent or actor. The reliability ratings of the features studied were either interrater or test-retest type, depending upon the availability of raters. All were in the 85%–98% range of agreement; I personally resolved all differences.

## The interviews

The two sets of interviews consist of client–therapist interactions in which 85% to 100% of all the therapists' responses are empathic following responses. All the sessions of both sets combined show a mean of 91% empathic following responses. Responses to clients' questions were omitted on theoretical grounds (see Brodley, 1999b/2011). The two sets of interviews are similar in the percentage of total words spoken by the therapists – 29% by Rogers and 27% by Brodley. Both sets include interviews with regular clients and with clients who volunteered for demonstrations. The clients are persons living in the community, with the exception of several of Rogers' clients who were hospitalized mentally ill persons.

### The Rogers sample

The Rogers sample of empathic responses is from 22 sessions conducted by Carl Rogers (the CR sample) – many of them not previously studied. Altogether, 131 responses were selected, culled from the beginning, middle and end of each session. In my reading of the empathic interactions and viewing of videotapes, Rogers is obviously attempting to represent his understanding of the clients' immediately previous communications and expressive behavior. Also, clients' immediate reactions to the responses selected for the sample showed that the clients accepted all Rogers' responses as representing their prior intended communications. There were no disagreements voiced by his clients to any of the selected responses.

### The BTB sample

The empathic responses from my 20 interviews were selected on the basis of clients' strong confirming responses. When clients perceive that a therapist's empathic understanding response is adequately accurate, they may make several types of response that confirm the therapist's accuracy. Often, client statements immediately following a therapist's empathic response imply confirmation by the way they continue or further develop what he or she has been expressing prior to the therapist's response. Or, clients nod their affirmation and then elaborate or expand on their point. At other times clients first make a vocal gesture, such as "ah haw," "uh huh" or "uhm hm" and then continue their narrative. Alternatively, clients will say "yes," or "right," or "yeah" before they continue their narrative. Sometimes they repeat the point the therapist expressed, using the therapist's words, in that way indicating their confirmation.

The BTB sample consists of responses eliciting the clients' *strongest* explicit confirmations in the 20 interviews. These strong confirmations included the following responses: "Yeah! Yeah!" "Absolutely, absolutely," "That's exactly right," "Yes I do. Right! Absolutely." The selection was based on the assumption that strong confirmations indicate that the therapist's preceding empathic responses were accurate and possibly especially meaningful to the clients. The BTB sample consists of 86 therapist empathic understanding responses that elicited the clients' strong confirmations.

## Observations and comments
### Words-for-feelings
Using single words-for-feelings in empathic responses is one way a therapist may communicate his or her understanding of clients' feelings. The first observation involves the frequency of words-for-feelings that the therapist expresses. (See Rosenberg, 1983 for lists of feeling-words.) The words rated exclusively represent the feelings of the client, not third persons. In the CR sample, Rogers expressed 53 feeling-words (1.1% of all therapist-words) including "rage," "afraid," "hurt," "desire." In the BTB sample there are 36 feeling-words (1.3% of all therapist words) including "tense," "joyful," "furious," "calm." The two samples are almost identical in frequency of feeling-words.

Feeling-words pertaining to the client sometimes occur more than once in an empathic response in a particular *natural unit of interaction* between client and therapist. A word is repeated, or different words-for-feeling may be expressed in the same response. When a client-centered therapist is closely following, the variation in the frequency of feeling-words in specific responses to clients is closely related to the individual client's complexity of expression of experiences that may be accurately represented by such words. In the CR sample, for example, the range is zero to seven occurrences of feeling-words within particular empathic responses. In the BTB sample, the range is zero to five occurrences.

A different approach to assess the frequency of words-for-feelings (as well as for assessing the incidence of other features of an interview), instead of counting the words to find the percentage of total words, is to count the natural interaction units in which at least one feeling-word occurs. Using this method, in the CR sample we find feeling-words occur in 30% of Rogers' responses; in the BTB sample, feeling-words occur in 31% of the responses. The two samples are almost identical in respect to frequency of occurrence of words-for-feelings (30% versus 31%; D = 1%); they appear in slightly less than one-third of all empathic responses.

The striking point of the observation is that the clients in both samples are responding with confirmations – always with strong confirmations in the BTB sample – to over two-thirds of the therapists' responses (70% in the CR sample and 69% in the BTB sample) that contain *no words-for-feelings*.

Although these two therapists perceive and respond to clients' communications that include such "hot feelings" (Zimring, personal communication), it appears that both therapists' clients seem able to feel empathically understood much of the time without hearing responses containing feeling-words. This observation supports the idea that the therapists are frequently empathically understanding and communicating *other experiences* that may involve more subtle or complex feelings or cognitive components.

### Words or phrases that allude-to-feelings

The second observation involves the frequency of words or phrases that express experiences that involve feelings (of the client, not third persons) that are not feeling-words. These words or phrases refer to experiences that involve a feeling quality, but are more subtle or complex than *hot* feelings, or that may involve cognitive elements. They are words or phrases that express dispositions, evaluations, volitional states and other experiences. Examples of words and phrases for these experiences include "ignored," "pleading," "resisting," "very careful," "subjective," "worried," "intimate aspect," "don't feel good," "not feeling safe," "care," "closeness," "merged," "dissatisfaction," "confusing." Words or phrases are included in the category if the rater *senses feelings in his or her self* while introspecting on the word or phrase. The high – 96% – inter-rater reliability for the rating of alluding-to-feeling is surprising, given the extremely subjective criterion for rating.

In the CR sample, approximately 1% of Rogers' total words are words or phrases alluding-to-feelings, whereas these elements occur in approximately 6% of total words in the BTB sample. The counts include single words and words in short phrases, consequently this method may make counts aimed to measure incidence artificially vary in the two samples. The alternative method used for assessing incidence of words-for-feelings counts empathic response units that include one or more words or phrases that allude-to-feelings (but are not words for feelings). This method gives a more accurate picture of the incidence and the difference in the two samples.

Forty-five percent of the empathic responses in the CR sample contain words or phrases alluding-to-feelings, 59% in the BTB sample (45% versus 59%; D = 14%). This 14% difference in percentage responses containing alluding-words between the two samples is a surprise given that the percentage of units containing feeling-words was almost identical in both samples (31% versus 30%). Although there is a difference in the two samples, Rogers is still verbalizing alluding-to-feeling words in almost 50% of his responses. I have no speculations to account for the difference.

Combining the samples, compared to the pure or *hot* feelings in the therapists' empathic responses, both therapists together express these complex feelings more frequently to represent their understandings of clients (30.5% words-for feelings versus 52% alluding-to-feelings words; D = 21.5%). Approximately half of all acceptant empathic understanding responses contain alluding-to-feelings words. This observation is consistent with the view that empathic understanding is an attempt to understand much more than clients' simple feelings.

### Combining words-for-feelings and words or phrases that allude-to-feelings

Empathic responses that include feeling-words and/or alluding-to-feeling-words were counted to obtain a picture of the therapists' responsiveness to feeling experiences that they perceived in their clients' communications. If a response had at least one feeling-word or at least one word or phrase that alludes to feelings it was counted. In some instances a response had only one feeling-word or one alluding-to-feelings word or phrase. In others it had more than one of the same kind of element or it had both feeling-words and words or phrases alluding-to-feelings. An example of an empathic response that combines a feeling-word and an alluding-to-feeling word is "You feel *sad* about *not feeling safe.*" The word "sad" was rated as a feeling-word, and "not feeling safe" is a phrase classed as alluding-to-feeling.

This method of counting occurrences reveals that 61% of the total acceptant empathic understanding responses in the CR sample and 73% in the BTB sample contain both, or either, words-for-feelings and words-alluding-to-feelings. There is a 12% difference in the two samples (61% versus 73%; D = 12%). Thus it appears that I perceive my clients as communicating their feeling experiences more frequently that Rogers.

Examining both samples together and putting aside the difference in them, a large majority (67%) of responses include reference to clients' feeling experiences using feeling-words or alluding-to-feelings words or phrases. Almost two-thirds (61%) of Rogers' empathic response units and almost three-fourths (73%) of my response units include one or more reference to clients' feeling experiences. The majority of the references in both samples are to states and experiences that are a mixture of cognitive and affective elements rather than to relatively pure or *hot* feelings such as "fear," "anger" or "joy."

This observation is consistent with the results of a study of 25 of Rogers' sessions by Bradburn (1996; Brodley, 1999a) that showed a substantial portion of his empathic responses *do not* reveal affective features. She found that 27% of a randomized sample of Rogers' clients' statements were *without* affective features and that Rogers' empathic responses tracked those absences. Twenty-four percent of his responses did not include affective features compared with the larger percentage (39%) without affective features in the present CR sample. In the current BTB sample, 27% of the responses were without affective features – close to the observation in the Bradburn sample. In the Bradburn study, the 76% of Rogers' responses *with affective features* did track the presence, quality and intensity of his client's affect.

## Figures of speech

Figures of speech are common, short metaphors that contribute to the vividness and liveliness of speech. They serve various expressive functions although they often refer to *what is happening to the person* or *what the person is doing* in their life. The figures of speech, "drain on your life," "take a lot out of you," "part of you is torn away," "that pulls you down," "you give weight," "lost your ground," "in a black hole," "clam up," "it's before your eyes," and so forth, illustrate this function. Figures of speech require variable numbers of words. Consequently, a count of empathic responses containing figures of speech is more informative than word frequencies.

The frequencies of responses containing figures of speech were high and similar in the two samples (Rogers: 61% and BTB: 66%; D =5). These therapists are frequently – in approximately two-thirds of their empathic responses – expressing their clients' experiences in an idiosyncratic and lively manner.

Almost all figures of speech are brief elements in the responses using only a few words. There are no similes and only a few semi-extended metaphors in the CR sample. One metaphor quotes the client's homily, "Poor man throws away and rich man puts in his pocket." In a response to another client Rogers creates the following metaphor: "You'll be glad to wash the dust of Madison off your feet." In response to another client he says, "It's so risky, coming from the lighted spot into the darkness, into the unknown."

Rogers' use of figures of speech is rich and varied. They include, "root it out," "touch the core," "you had an eye on him," "shut it out of mind," "bright world," "the dark side," "a little shaky," "wave a magic wand." The figures of speech in the BTB sample are similar to those of Rogers, such as "stand up and fight," "open the gate," "people jump in," "your spirits went up," "in a black hole," "clam up," "your impotence," "pull back," "doesn't hold water." In the BTB sample there are two similes – "like the ground were suddenly up there," and "like a camera that won't go into focus." There are no extended metaphors whatsoever in the BTB sample, only brief figures of speech. Neither therapist appears likely to coin an extended metaphor in an empathic response. Sometimes they do pick up on a client's own metaphor and carry it or an element in it forward, such as the use of the words "octopus" and "tentacles" in one of Rogers' client's metaphor for his mother. With only a few exceptions, in both therapists, their figures of speech are not picked up from their clients. They are spontaneous expressions of part of their empathic understanding of their clients.

The vividness of even common figures of speech, that often use visual images (e.g., "crossed the line," "let down a step"), may contribute to clients' perceptions of therapists' personal presence – to the perception that the therapist is emotionally alive in the relationship. Rice (1974) discusses figures of speech as evocative *technique*. My impression of Rogers is that his use of figures of speech in empathic responses is spontaneously expressive, and not a deliberate technique to stimulate the client. I am certain that in my own therapy I do not express figures of speech as technique. I do not intend them to evoke the client's feelings or emotions, but they may tend to have that evocative effect. Phrases such as "going too far," "wound your pride," "damned," "pulled out from under you," and "seeps into you" are stimulating and probably convey a liveliness in a therapist's understandings more than similar meanings not communicated with figures of speech.

### Combining feeling-words, words or phrases that allude-to-feelings and figures of speech

Three kinds of elements – feeling-words, the words or phrases that allude-to-feelings and the words or phrases that compose the figures of speech together express most of the emotional, feeling, and evocative or stimulating qualities in the therapist's responses. Using feeling-words plus using alluding-to-feeling words or phrases are the main ways the therapists capture their clients' feeling-experiences in empathic responses. Figures of speech sometimes express clients' feelings but they also capture what client-centered therapists understand is happening to or impacting their clients. To get a picture of the presence of all these emotion/feeling/evocative elements in acceptant empathic understanding responses, I employed the method of counting instances of empathic responses in which one or the other, or many, or all of these elements occur. A response was counted if any one or any combination of the elements was found in the response.

The following is an example of an empathic response that includes all three elements – feeling-words, an alluding-to-feeling phrase, and a figure of speech: "In expressing some of the *stress* of this and some of your *upset* feelings, people *jump in* with solutions that *don't feel good to you*." The words "stress" and "upset" are rated as feeling-words, the phrase "don't feel good to you" is rated as an alluding-to-feeling phrase, and "jump in" is a figure of speech. It is a complex empathic response; it tells what the client does (she reveals some feelings to others), it expresses her reactions (she feels imposed on by their solutions), and it states the client's feelings (she doesn't feel good). A lot of information is expressed in the response; but at the same time it has a vividness that suggests the therapist's close presence in the relationship.

The percentage of empathic responses containing any or all of the three elements were found to be equal in the two samples. In both the CR sample and the BTB sample 85% of the units contain at least one feeling-word and/ or at least one word or phrase that alludes to feelings and/or at least one figure of speech (CR: 85% and BTB: 85%; D = 0%).

*Responses that have no feeling-related words or phrases (no feeling-words, no words or phrases that allude-to-feeling, and no figures of speech) relating to, or about, the client*

In both samples, 15% of the therapists' responses are devoid of feeling-related or evocative words or phrases. These responses consist of three kinds of statements. One kind is about a third person's wants, feelings or reactions such as, "But he clearly wants you, he really wants you." A second is a statement about facts or information such as, "The ones that follow from earlier choices," or "Such a good thing after all, and natural, and it kills him." A third is a response that expresses conceptual, rational or cognitive experiences such as, "You knew that quite well," or "That decided it for you," or "Every calculation makes it less important." These responses that express no feeling or evocative experiences, nevertheless contribute to the empathic understanding response process. They elicited clients' confirmations – strong confirmations in the BTB sample. Consequently, I infer they are accurate understandings of the clients' immediate communicative intentions.

*Responses that include specific words for cognitive processes*

Words for cognitive processes such as "think," "interest," "consider," "means," "implies," or "aware" occur more frequently in the natural response units in the CR sample than in the BTB sample (35% versus 28%; D = 7%). Many empathic responses in both samples contain words or phrases that express feeling experiences or evocative experiences and also express cognitive experiences such as "a *desire* [feeling-word] to *wave a magic wand* [figure of speech] and have it be *true*" [cognitive word]. Some responses contain only cognitive words such as "You're coming to the only possible *conclusion*" [cognitive word]. Although representations of feeling experiences are most frequent, found in two-thirds of responses, the therapists also understand their clients' cognitive experiences in one-third of their empathic responses.

### Responses that include the words "feel," "feeling," "feels," "felt"

The words "feel," "feeling," "feels," "felt" occur in 37% of the responses in the CR sample and in 26% of the responses in the BTB sample (37% versus 26%; D = 11%). This 11% difference in the two therapists' use of these words is not surprising to me given the fact that I consciously tend to avoid the terms "you feel," "it feels" etc., if my response refers to what the client thinks, believes, imagines or to other cognitive activities. I prefer to use the words that explicitly describe the mental activity the client expressed, rather than employ "you feel" etc. to point to those mental activities. My preference shows up in our difference in respect to juxtaposing "feel," etc. with cognitive words.

The CR sample includes more responses combining "feel" etc. with cognitive words than the BTB sample (CR: 48% versus BTB: 4%; D = 44%). Only 4% of my responses that contain "feel" words also include specific words for cognitive experiences. This is a small portion of all empathic responses – only 1%. It contrasts with the 18% portion of all responses (containing "feel" etc., plus a cognitive word) in the CR sample (CR: 18% versus BTB: 1%; D = 17%). Examples of these responses from both samples include "You feel it's kind of *characteristic* of you," "You feel that it's just a *mystery* to you," "You feel as though you *can understand*," "That is the feeling," "If they really *knew* …," "You feel that's kind of the same *pattern*," "You're trying to feel out the *implications*," "It feels *overdone*," and "It just feels it was *clear*."

In pointing to cognitive experiences with the words "feel" etc., Rogers apparently uses these words as a pointer to clients' internal processes more frequently than I am inclined to do this. Nevertheless, Rogers uses "feel" etc. as a specific reference to feeling experiences in the majority of instances of using "feel" etc. words (CR: feeling-words 8%, alluding-words 31%, and figures of speech expressing feelings 13% = 52% words for feeling experiences versus 48% cognitive words).

In both samples, the words "feel" etc. occur in relation to feeling experiences expressed by words-for-feelings or words alluding-to-feelings. Examples are "you feel very *tense*," "*panicky* feeling," "a feeling of *despair*," "you feel you are being *disapproved of*," "you feel *hopeless*," and "you feel *persecuted*." As discussed in an earlier paper (Brodley, 1996/2011) Rogers' use of the words "feel" etc. often appears to signal that he is understanding clients' experiences that cannot be accurately communicated by words for feelings, but are ones that convey a quality of underlying or associated feelings. This observation is supported in the current CR samples by Rogers' use of words-for-feeling (such as "sad" or "afraid") as the object of "feel" etc. in only 8% of his empathic responses containing "feel" etc., thus in only 3% of all responses. This is in contrast to his use of words or phrases alluding-to-feelings in 31% of his responses containing "feel" etc., thus in 12% of all his empathic responses. He also uses figures of speech that characterize feeling states (for example, "the *hole* that you feel," or "you feel *tiny* and *shriveled*," or "you do feel a little *bitter*") in 13% of his responses containing "feel" etc., thus in 5% of all responses. The portions are small, but alluding-to-feeling words and figures of speech expressed as the objects of "feel" etc. appear more frequently in Rogers' total empathic responses than the purer words-for-feelings (CR: 3% words-for-feeling versus 17% other words or phrases referring to feeling experiences; D = 14%).

Some uses of the words "feel" etc. refer to an experience that may have been mentioned previously by the therapist or the client. The following examples are of this type: "A preoccupation with your feeling," "When you're feeling that way," or "You have some feelings on this side." Granted a variety of usages, with feeling experiences and with cognitive experiences, reference to "feel" etc. often signals to the client that the therapist's response pertains to clients' subjective experiences that are complex or subtle. When the words "feel" etc. are voiced in an empathic response, they sometimes have the effect of focusing the client inward, towards the *subjective experiences* that are the source of meanings and feelings that may be expressed in language. They may have the effect, in the terms of Gendlin's (1964, 1974) *experiencing* theory, of focusing the client's attention towards his or her *felt sense.*

### First-person empathic responses

An immediate or dramatic way to express an empathic response is to employ the first person and state the response exactly as one thinks the client would express it. This is a form of empathic understanding response observed in earlier studies of Rogers' therapy behavior (Brodley & Brody, 1990; Brody, 1991; Brodley, 1996/2011; Merry, 1996). Merry found a mean frequency of 10% (range of 5% to 14%) of first-person empathic responses in the 10 Rogers sessions he studied. The current Rogers sample includes the following responses: "How am I going to deal with it within myself?" "I need maturity to live with that fear within myself," "Where am I going? What is my purpose? What do I want to make of my life?" First-person empathic responses also appear in the BTB sample: "I must be empty," "I have to find something to bring him to me," "God damn it!" and "I don't think it's always been this way for me."

Twenty-nine percent of the empathic response units in the CR sample include a first-person statement compared with 14% of the response units in the BTB sample (29% versus 14%; D = 15%). This makes twice as many first-person responses in the CR sample as in the BTB sample and three times as many first-person responses in the current CR sample compared to the earlier sample of Rogers' responses studied by Merry.

The greater frequency of this form of response in the current Rogers sample compared to the Merry sample (29% versus 10%; D = 19%) is probably because the Merry sample consists solely of demonstration interviews conducted by Rogers. The present CR sample from 22 sessions, in contrast, consists of responses from 18 sessions with regular clients. A client-centered therapist is likely to feel more confident in the context of an ongoing relationship that his or her empathic responses will not be confusing to clients when expressed in the first-person form. The 15% difference in the two current samples may also be accounted for by the fact that the BTB sample of responses was taken from 20 interviews of which 11 (55%) were demonstration interviews. Nevertheless, the first-person form of empathic response conveys a sense of the therapist's close participation in the client's world. In the current samples, Rogers expresses this immediacy in approximately one-third of his empathic responses, while I do so only half as often, in only one-sixth of my responses.

Together, the greater frequency of "feel" etc. being related to cognitions, and the greater frequency of "I-form" responses in the CR sample suggests that Rogers is subtly orienting his clients towards their immediate subjective experiences or *felt sense.* Rogers is responding less frequently than I am to *feeling experiences,* consequently it appears he is not biased towards feeling experiences in particular. But the use of "feel" etc. about cognitive experiences may suggest to clients that there is more to know, or be revealed to them, if they attend more closely to their subjective processes. In contrast, I am consciously motivated to represent clients' experiences as *what they seem to be to them* rather than alluding, by voicing "you feel …," to the inner source of the experiences. In this difference, it appears that I am responding to my clients *slightly* more nondirectively than Rogers is responding to his clients.

### Third-person dramatic empathic responses

Another dramatic form of empathic response is a statement representing a third person – not the client or the therapist – presented as a quote of the person. These are rare in Rogers' behavior and rare in mine, but they do occur in both. In the CR sample, one speaks for the client's parent: "I don't like this, so you mustn't, because you're a part of me." Another speaks for the client's old acquaintances: "That reminds you of those days when they asked, 'What's new?' doesn't it?" There are two such responses in the BTB sample. The following example occurs in my Client E interview. Therapist: You get blamed – *"Well, if you hadn't."* The second example is in my client Q interview: Client: You know, "She'll have a career and have great children and all of that, but she'll be alone" (laughs). Therapist: *"And celebrate* (C: laughs) *for ten years* (C: laughs) ... *not five or six."* The response to client Q picks up on the client's third-person dramatic form. Third-person-form responses usually capture something happening in the client's personal relationships that are having an impact on the client.

Third-person dramatic-form responses may also speak for a client's invented persona or a *non-self-experience*. In the CR sample there are three of these. In one, the client has referred to an experience of himself as a "little boy" and Rogers speaks for the "little boy." "The little boy feels, 'this feels good to me, it's satisfying to me to me to do this.' " In a response to another client, Rogers speaks for the "deep thing" in the client. He speaks dramatically: "Look out, this might be another octopus." In the third instance, Rogers speaks for the client's hallucinatory voice, saying "If you are feeling desperate ...." The therapist usually makes up the piece of dialogue that captures the third person's attitude toward the client, although sometimes it is an elaboration on the client's use of dialogue. Like figures of speech and the first-person dramatic-form of response, these third-person statements give variety and vitality to the flow of empathic responses. The dramatic quality of these responses may help the client experience the therapist's engagement and presence (Brodley, 2000/2011) in the relationship.

### Therapist references to self

When client-centered therapists are following a client, making empathic understanding responses, and thus not representing their own frame of reference, they usually make no references to themselves. In the context of empathic following, therapist self-references are almost exclusively expressions of the therapist's tentativeness or uncertainty about the accuracy of his or her empathic responses. They usually preface the empathic response or follow it and they often form a question. The following statements from the two samples are explicit expressions of the therapists' tentativeness or uncertainty about their empathic understanding: "I guess the impression I get is ...," "What I hear you saying there is ...," "If I get it ...," "I guess you're saying there ...," "If I understand that ...," "If I sense some of your feeling there – let's see if I am ...," "Ah, it strikes me that what you're saying is ...," "But there too, I guess I get the feeling ...," "I don't know if this is right, but it seems ...," "You've been saying to me ...," "So, I guess ...." The following examples of uncertainty are in the form of questions: "Is this what you're saying ...?" "Am I getting this right?" "Would it be overstating it too much ...?" Therapists also make self-references as an acknowledgment response to the client, such as "I see" or "now I understand," followed by an empathic response.

The tentativeness- or uncertainty-type of self-reference is found in 20% of Rogers' empathic responses and in 9% of responses in the BTB sample (20% versus 9%; D = 11%). Rogers is explicitly communicating his tentativeness or uncertainty in one-fifth of his responses, twice as frequently as BTB.

Although I explicitly indicate my tentativeness to my clients when I am very unsure, Rogers has impressed me as especially scrupulous in indicating uncertainty when he feels it is beyond the basic tentativeness of all client-centered empathic responses. Care to be explicit about uncertainty expresses Rogers' sincere desire to accurately understand his clients and not impose his interpretations on their meanings. Rogers goes to lengths to make it clear he has a strongly felt uncertainty about his accuracy in the following empathic response: "*In the way I'm understanding that, though I'm not quite sure*, is ... you would want to be the best possible here in my terms. *Is that the way you mean it?*"

Rogers and I are both likely to be particularly careful to explicitly signal our uncertainty if the empathic response expresses the client's feelings *about us* or the client's perception of his or her *relation to us*. Explicit expressions of uncertainty, of course, are not a strategy. They are not aimed to produce an effect in clients. Nevertheless, there probably is a serendipitous effect on the client's sense of the therapist's presence as a personal participant when owning their imperfections as a listener.

### The client as agent or actor

Empathic understanding is a complex, ongoing process of listening to clients, of sensing clients' perceptions and experiences that they represent to the therapist, and of representing some of these to the client for their correction or confirmation. As mentioned earlier, I have speculated that the major focus for empathic understanding of clients' verbal and expressive communications is primarily clients' statements about themselves as an agent or actor, as an active force – as a *source* of intentions, experiences, actions and reactions.

The empathic therapist's particular focus of attention is on the client's reactions to, feelings about, thoughts about, and intentions in respect to, what the client is talking about. It follows that the therapist statements that should be productive to scrutinize in studying therapists' empathic understanding behavior are the words, expressions, phrases or sentences that communicate about the client's agency. These statements would be ones that represent the client's intentions, experiences (including feeling experiences), actions, reactions, or the client's role as a source of directed actions, as well as what is happening to the client. Examples of empathic responses whose structure and content (note italics) express the client's proactive or reactive agency are as follows: "*You want to find* some way of coming out of this hole, of really resolving a relationship, not just having it chopped off." "You were always *trying to find some way to win* him." "You're *worried about* the impact on your child." "It's *a preoccupation* with your feelings." "*What you want is a relationship* with someone *that will strengthen you* to fight what's in your mind." The following empathic response illustrates both the client's proactive and reactive agency: "There's one link *that you sense* [proactive]. That one time when you felt your internal *sexual organs were being hooked and manipulated*" [reactive].

### The words "want," "wanting," "wants," "wanted"

Remarking that "I want …" is a straightforward expression of the speaker as an agent or actor toward or away from something. Empathic responses that explicitly represent the client as *wanting* something are an obvious choice to examine in studying the frequency of agency elements. In the CR sample 9% of the therapist's acceptant empathic understanding responses contain the word "want" etc., and in the BTB sample 8% of the acceptant empathic understanding responses contain these words. The samples contain almost identical frequencies of "want" etc. (9% and 8%; D = 1%), although the less than 10% usage indicates these words obviously are not the only way the therapists represent their clients' expressions of their agency.

### The words "try," "trying," "tries," "tried"

A remark that "I am trying …" is another straightforward expression of the speaker as an agent or actor towards or away from something. In the CR sample "try" words appear in 4% of Rogers' empathic responses and in 2% of the responses in the BTB sample. The occurrence is small and similar in both samples (4% and 2%; D = 2%). Together, "want" and "try" words occur in 13% of Rogers' responses and 10% of mine (13% and 10%; D = 3%). In both samples they appear in only slightly more than one-tenth of all acceptant empathic understanding responses, thus there must be other ways the clients' agency gets expressed in empathic responses.

### The sentence units for observing agency

Empathic responses in natural interactions are often complex responses, containing more than one sentence or more than one complete statement in response to the client. The following example of an empathic response in a natural interaction, containing several sentence units, comes from one of Rogers' interviews:

Client: Another thing about the hook [in her head] is when I get too confused.
  When like I got up this morning and I felt so discouraged about the job

and so discouraged about B [husband]. And I also felt that something was oppressing me – the feeling of being dominated and oppressed. I went to have my coffee and I just sat and I thought really if I did what I feel like doing I'd just sit here and I wouldn't move. (T: Uhm, hm) And I think maybe I put the hook in, as an alternative to something worse. (T: Uhm, hm, uhm, hm) (Pause 5 seconds) The hook, the hook was once an organization.

Therapist: I don't think I get that. So the feeling was, "I'm discouraged – about various things. What I really feel like doing is just sinking into apathy." And you feel maybe that's when you put the hook in yourself. That the hook, really, in one sense, stands for ... I don't know, for making yourself be organized, something like that. (Rogers, circa 1954).

[See Brodley & Lietaer, 2006, Mrs. Roc, p. 50]

The therapist's response has four statements within it, as well as several indications of his uncertainty.

Taking the complexity of many empathic responses into account, the responses in the sample were divided up into their sentence units. There are 1.4 sentence-units per empathic response in the CR sample and 1.8 sentence units per empathic response in the BTB sample.

### Non-agency sentence units
Only 7% of the sentence units in the CR sample and 8% in the BTB sample contain *no expression of the client as an agent or actor* (CR: 7% and BTB: 8%; D = 1%). These non-agency sentence units are usually of two types. They are always part of the therapist's empathic responses, but one type consists of statements about someone other than the client such as, "He must have been very careless to get this," "He thought you had an eye on him." "She's got some outlet that doesn't criticize her," and "There's a point beyond which they disagree." Other non-agency sentence units are statements of fact, or information: "Everybody is low key in terms of approval responses," "Those are the qualities valued here," "The gifts are unevenly distributed in the world," "That's the way it is." The non-agency sentence units, like the agency units, either make up entire therapist natural response units or they are *sentence units* that are parts of whole complex empathic responses.

### The sentence units containing agency
The samples are almost identical in the percentage of sentence-units describing clients' agency features. Ninety-three percent of the sentence units in the CR

sample and 92% in the BTB sample (93% versus 92%; D = 1%) contain an expression of the client as an agent or actor – either proactive or reactive. Both therapists are making responses more than nine-tenths of the time that represent the client as an agent, actor or source of experiences, actions or reactions. This dominant feature of empathic responses encompasses representations of clients' feelings, meanings, perceptions, explanations, intentions and what is happening to them – all representing the clients as active personalities.

The observations indicate that most empathic responses wholly or in part represent clients as active personalities. The italicized elements in the following *clients' statements* emphasize this active quality that the therapists' attempt to represent in their empathic responses: "*It feels* oftentimes that *it's just too much for me.* Then *I build up* notions …," "*I mix it up* and *I can't separate* well enough what's in my head, what is an objective upset …," "*I resent* it because since I was 17 *I've been doing* everything for her," "*I can be attracted* to women and yet *I don't know.* It just *doesn't seem to be* the real thing. There's *no real attraction,*" "*I think about* buildings. *I try to picture* them but *I can't. I can't remember* them," "*I feel* like a broken record."

The therapists' representations of this important feature of clients' narratives – in their empathic understanding responses, or in parts of them, are illustrated by the following examples: "It [referring to the client's behavior] *feels overdone* [to the client] and it's even *boring to you* at a certain point"; "You were always *trying to find* some way to win him," "You *doubt,* because it *doesn't feel* like the right place; you *don't like* your job, you *don't like* your boss …," "You're somewhat *too quick* with it, even though you're *discriminating,*" "You definitely *expected* … and then all of a sudden that was pulled out from under you."

### Agency to the external, agency to the internal

I distinguished whether the therapist's agency-type sentence units expressed the client's *self* (a) in relation to something or someone external to him or her, or (b) in relation to subjective experiences of himself or herself. In both categories, the clients have revealed something about their subjective self-life (feelings, thoughts, wants, etc.). The difference is in the object of the self-life – whether it is about something outside the self, or within the person's subjective processes. Examples of responses that contain elements indicating (a) an external object of self are as follows: "You were feeling ignored *in relation to your father.*" "It's damned inconvenient *to have to stay here* all day" [an implied other]. "You wonder about *the authority.*" "You care *about her* and you want to be close *to her* …." "You want to influence *your husband* …." "As long as *he has that reaction* you can't turn to him." The following examples express the client's self about inner experiences: "*Deeply within you* there's a tremendous *sense of vulnerability*," "When *you try and think, it just doesn't come clear to you*," "This *sense of yourself* as not good enough," "It's *a felt need* to get more order," "Those *sensations* give you a whole other *level of stress*," "It's a *conflict of feelings*."

In the CR sample, 61%, in the BTB sample 65% of agency-type sentence units are expressions of clients' self *in relation to something or someone outside the self* – the (a) type (61% versus 65%; D = 4%). Accordingly, in the CR sample 39%, in the BTB sample 35% of the sentence-units *related clients' self towards subjective experiences* – the (b) type (39% versus 35%; D = 4%). The two samples are very similar. Given that all the therapists' clients confirmed accuracy of all the empathic understanding responses, the similarity of the samples in this observation is telling.

It appears that client-centered clients' engagement in therapy is *more* about their thoughts, feelings and reactions to persons and situations outside of themselves (two-thirds of the time) than to their intrapsychic world (one-third of the time). At least for the most part, it appears that these two client-centered therapists' clients are not focusing on their experiences in the sense of exploring their own inner feeling phenomenology. Instead they are mostly expressing their emotional and thoughtful actions towards, or reactions to, things going on in the external world that are having some impact on them or that are important to them. The similarity of the two samples in regard to their proportions is surprising and telling, because one would expect differences on the grounds of clients' individual differences and because the samples are small.

CONCLUDING DISCUSSION

**The interviews**
The sets of therapy interviews from which the samples of empathic responses were drawn are similar in a number of respects. This is not surprising, given the fact that I developed my approach to therapy on the basis of Rogers' writings and client-centered consultants.

Predominantly, Rogers and I closely follow our clients, making empathic responses from time to time. Both have written that the reason we verbalize our inner understandings to clients is in order to find out whether or not we understand correctly according to the clients (Rogers, 1986; Brodley, 1998/ 2011). Our tone, manner and expressive behavior, revealed in the interview transcripts, and in video or audiotapes of some of the sessions, appears to be consistent with our expressed rationale. Our clients indicate they disagree with our understandings in less than 1% of our responses. The sets of interviews are almost the same in the percentage of the words spoken by the therapist versus the percentage spoken by the client.

## Similarity of the therapists' empathic responses

The observations reveal that the two therapists' *empathic responses* are similar in a number of ways. Rogers and I are usually making empathic responses that represent clients' relatively complex experiences including feelings, thoughts, and personal meanings, including their explanations and interpretations, as well as memories, and their future hopes or expectations. We tend to express relatively complex feeling experiences – that are subtle or that involve cognitive elements – much more frequently than pure or *hot* feelings. We both represent clients' cognitive experiences in approximately one-third of all our empathic responses. Other evidence of our similarity is in the observation that most of our responses represent clients as agents or actors, acting or reacting in relation to their own subjective experiences, or towards or away from someone or something. In these responses we show the same proportions of self-agency relating to subjective experiences and relating to something outside the person. Several observations in the study show that both therapists are personally expressive in their empathic responses. Probably both, in this way, stimulate a strong sense of their presence (Brodley, 2000/2011) in their clients' perceptions.

## Some differences in the therapists

Rogers expressed fewer words or phrases that allude-to-feelings and more cognitive words than I do. This difference is carried out in the observation that Rogers expresses the words "feel" etc. more frequently than I in relation to cognitive experiences. Rogers also utilizes the first-person form in his empathic responses more frequently than I do.

There appears to be a subtle difference in the two therapists in the way their empathic responses orient to their clients' subjective experiences. Both therapists are profoundly nondirective. Rogers, however, tends more than I do to make responses that may stimulate the client to attend to the subjective source of feelings and meanings. I tend to aim towards a precise representation of the ways clients express what they are subjectively experiencing or doing. It is not apparent whether our slight behavioral difference reflects a somewhat different conception of the empathic task, or if it is a stylistic difference.

## Applying the Zimring theory to the study

The study is based on the idea that the contents of therapists' client-validated empathic responses reveal an answer to the question "what is being understood in empathic understanding?" Fred Zimring (2000) addressed this question in his explication of the *targets of empathic understanding*. Zimring's answers are based on an underlying theory of change that he developed from earlier formulations (Zimring, 1995, 1990a, 1990b).

His theoretical context for ideas about the targets includes the view that "it is the involved, acting self involved in a transaction that is central .... The person [*or self*] is not a separate object or entity, but rather is a part of an interacting system" (Zimring, 2000, p. 103). Consequently, "what we do or say is not determined by an inner state or entity, but rather is part of the transaction in which we are engaged" (p. 104). He further explains that a person's actions result from the *self* as part of transactional activity rather than from intrapsychic content. Actions involve *intentionality* or *purposiveness* and persons are constantly involved with and reacting to their world as they see it in order to fulfill intentions.

Zimring distinguishes two self-states; one is the "Me" state, when mental representations are about the objective world and transactions concern the objective world. In this state we perceive ourselves as objects. In the "I" transactional self-state, transactions are concerned with subjective representations. "We interact with representations of feelings and meanings; here one sees one's self as the initiating actor" (p. 106). Following from this theory, Zimring posits three targets for empathic understanding. One is "the speaker's self-sense and self-reactions." Second is "the speaker's intentions within the transactions in which he or she is engaged." Third is "the nature of the representations that are the context in which these intentional transactions are occurring" (p. 108). Zimring asserts that in general, the client-centered therapist primarily responds not to what the person may be feeling or experiencing, "but rather to the person's intention, to what the person is trying to convey to you about what is happening to him or her" (p. 110).

Although I did not analyze the two samples of empathic responses from the perspective of Zimring's conception of the targets of empathic understanding, the observations, nevertheless, lend support to his views. Clients' *self-sense* and *self-reactions* are found in part among the feeling-words, for example, "it hurts," "aloneness," "fear." They are also found among the alluding-to-feeling words or phrases, such as "dilemma," "shaky," "undigested lump," and among the agency sentence units in which the therapist represents the client relating directly to his or her own inner experiences, for example, "... it comes to you as sort of a hole," "you're getting calmer," "you just feel a kind of helpless rage."

Representations of clients' *intentions within their transactions* are found in the agency sentence units that make up most empathic responses. Clients' intentions are represented in the following sentence units: "You do *want to do something* about the problem." "You are *trying to help.*" "You *think its time* to go ahead." "You're *working to find* some way." "You're *determined* to keep apart from her." "You *have to* say things that this woman is not going to like to hear." *Intentions* in the agency sentences are also expressed by figures of speech such as "you want to *stand up and fight,*" "you want to keep your *battery charged,*" or "you want to *run away,*" and many others.

The therapists' responses expressing clients' representations that are *the context in which transactions are occurring* also are found among the agency sentence units. Words or phrases expressing context are in italics in these examples. "*After that* you realize ....*" "Even *in the most trivial kind of relationship* the feeling is rejection." "*He asked you questions* that would make you think of certain things that had happened, and you'd start to cry." "Your spirits went up, *thinking that brown is beautiful.*" "It has hurt you, even though *you haven't been the victim much compared to many people.*"

Many of the agency sentence units include *what is happening to the client.* For example, "you get support," "something happens in your gut," and "you are being disapproved of." Figures of speech that are prevalent in the agency units often express *what is happening to* the client, such as "that label really *destroys* you as a person," "you *lost your ground,*" "it's an *act of war,*" "you were in *a black hole,*" "that was *pulled out from under you,*" "you *explore various alleys* and they all have *stone walls* at the end of them."

Zimring's view that, in general, the client-centered therapist responds to the person's intentions and to what the person is trying to convey about what is happening to him or her, not pointedly to feelings, seems to be supported by the study. Judging by both therapists' responses, clients often talk about what is happening to them. What is happening to them may include their feelings or other experiences that have feeling components as in the response, "That's been hurting you and weakening you for years, but *now … you still suffer,* but *you resist her* and *stand up for yourself.*" Sometimes, however, *what is happening* to clients does not in itself involve feeling experiences. It may set the stage for their feeling experiences, as in the empathic response, "that's the tension you feel *when you're with people.*" References to feeling experiences are an important part of empathic understanding, but they usually appear in complex contexts of the clients' intentions and of experiences that are happening to them, as shown in the following complex empathic response: "You feel sad about not feeling safe to tell her what your intentions are because she might not accept them. And yet you care about her and you want to be close to her and keep that closeness. And yet you feel like you have to keep apart from her to protect your own direction – the direction that feels like the right one for you at this time."

Projects using different client-centered therapists' transcripts could contribute to understanding of the empathic understanding attitude and its verbal expression in client-centered therapy. I intend to do further analyses of such transcripts. Many of Rogers' preserved transcripts of sessions have not been studied, so there is more of that fascinating material to explore. None have been examined from the explicit perspective of Zimring's concept of the targets of empathic understanding – a provocative future project.

## REFERENCES

Barrett-Lennard, G. T. (1981). The empathy cycle: Refinement of a nuclear concept. *Journal of Counseling Psychology, 28*, 91–100.

Bradburn, W. M. (1996). *Did Carl Rogers' positive view of human nature bias his psychotherapy? An empirical investigation.* Unpublished doctoral clinical research project, Illinois School of Professional Psychology, Chicago (now Argosy University, Chicago).

Brodley, B. T. (1994). Some observations of Carl Rogers' behavior in therapy interviews. *The Person-Centered Journal, 1*(2), 37–48. [This volume, Chapter 25]

Brodley, B. T. (1996). Empathic understanding and feelings in client-centered therapy. *The Person-Centered Journal, 3*(1), 22–30. [This volume, Chapter 8]

Brodley, B. T. (1998). Criteria for making empathic responses in client-centered therapy. *The Person-Centered Journal, 5*(1), 20–28. [This volume, Chapter 14]

Brodley, B. T. (1999a, July). *Did Carl Rogers' positive view of human nature bias his psychotherapy?* (Based on the research doctoral dissertation (1996) by Wendy M. Bradburn.) Paper presented at the Second World Congress for Psychotherapy, Vienna, Austria. Also presented (2000, July) at the meeting of the Eastern Psychological Association, Baltimore, MD.

Brodley, B. T. (1999b). Reasons for responses expressing the therapist's frame of reference in client-centered therapy. *The Person-Centered Journal, 6*(1), 4–27. [This volume, Chapter 15]

Brodley, B. T. (2000). Personal presence in client-centered therapy. *The Person-Centered Journal, 7*(2), 139–149. [This volume, Chapter 10]

Brodley, B. T., & Brody, A. F. (1990, August). Understanding client-centered therapy through interviews conducted by Carl Rogers. Paper presented for the panel *Fifty years of client-centered therapy: Recent research* at the annual conference of the American Psychological Association, Boston.

[Brodley, B. T., & Lietaer, G. (Eds.). (2006). *Transcripts of Carl Rogers' therapy sessions, Vols. 1–17.* Email publication available from Germain.Lietaer@psy.kuleuven.be and kmoon1@alumni.uchicago.edu]

Brodley, B. T., & Schneider, C. (2001). Unconditional positive regard as communicated through verbal behavior in client-centered therapy. In J. D. Bozarth & P. Wilkins (Eds.), *Unconditional positive regard* (pp. 155–172). Ross-on-Wye: PCCS Books. [This volume, Chapter 9]

Brody, A. F. (1991). *Understanding client-centered therapy through interviews conducted by Carl Rogers.* Unpublished doctoral clinical research project, Illinois School of Professional Psychology, Chicago, (now Argosy University, Chicago).

Diss, J. W. (1996). *Facilitative responses leading to client process disruption in Carl Rogers' therapy behavior.* Unpublished doctoral clinical research project, Illinois School of Professional Psychology, Chicago, (now Argosy University, Chicago).

Gendlin, E. T. (1964). A theory of personality change. In P. Worchel & D. Byrne (Eds.), *Personality change* (pp. 100–148). New York: Wiley.

Gendlin, E. T. (1974). Client-centered and experiential psychotherapy. In D. A. Wexler & L. N. Rice (Eds.), *Innovations in client-centered therapy* (pp. 211–246). New York: Wiley.

[Lietaer, G., & Brodley, B. T. (2003). Carl Rogers in the therapy room: A listing of session transcripts and a survey of publications referring to Rogers' sessions. *Person-Centered & Experiential Psychotherapies, 2,* 274–291.]

Merry, T. (1996). An analysis of ten demonstration interviews by Carl Rogers: Implications for the training of client-centered counselors. In R. Hutterer, G. Pawlowsky, P. F. Schmid, & R. Stipsits (Eds.), *Client-centered and experiential therapy: A paradigm in motion* (pp. 273–284). Frankfurt am Main: Peter Lang.

Nelson, J. A. (1994). *Carl Rogers' verbal behavior in therapy: A comparison of theory and therapeutic practice.* Unpublished doctoral clinical research project, Illinois School of Professional Psychology, Chicago, (now Argosy University, Chicago).

Patterson, C. H. (1985). Some misconceptions of client-centered therapy. In *The therapeutic relationship* (pp. 213–217). Monterey, CA: Brooks/Cole.

Rice, L. N. (1974). The evocative function of the therapist. In D. A. Wexler & L. N. Rice (Eds.), *Innovations in client-centered therapy* (pp. 289–311). New York: Wiley.

Rogers, C. R. (circa 1954). Transcript of Carl Rogers' interview with Mrs. Roc. The Carl R. Rogers Archive, Library of Congress, Washington, DC. [See Brodley & Lietaer, 2006]

Rogers, C. R. (circa 1955). Transcript of Carl Rogers' interview with Mr. Necta. The Carl R. Rogers Archive, Library of Congress, Washington, DC. [See Brodley & Lietaer, 2006]

Rogers, C. R. (1957). The necessary and sufficient conditions for therapeutic personality change. *Journal of Consulting Psychology, 21,* 95–103.

Rogers, C. R. (1959). A theory of therapy, personality, and interpersonal relationships as developed in the client-centered framework. In S. Koch (Ed.), *Psychology: A study of a science. Vol. III: Formulations of the person and the social context* (pp. 184–256). New York: McGraw-Hill.

Rogers, C. R. (1980). Empathic: An unappreciated way of being. In *A way of being* (pp. 137–163). Boston: Houghton Mifflin.

Rogers, C. R. (1986). Reflection of feelings. *Person-Centered Review, 1*(4), 375–377.

Rosenberg, M. B. (1983). *A model for nonviolent communication.* Philadelphia, PA: New Society Publishers.

Temaner, B. [Brodley] (1977). The empathic understanding response process. Chicago Counseling and Psychotherapy Center. *Chicago Counseling Center Discussion Paper.* [This volume, Chapter 12]

Zimring, F. M. (1990a). Cognitive processes as a cause of psychotherapeutic change: Self-initiated processes. In G. Lietaer, J. Rombauts, & R. Van Balen (Eds.), *Client-centered and experiential psychotherapy in the nineties* (pp. 361–380). Leuven, Belgium: Leuven University Press.

Zimring, F. M. (1990b). A characteristic of Rogers' response to clients. *Person-Centered Review, 5*, 433–448.

Zimring, F. (1995). A new explanation for the beneficial results of client-centered therapy: The possibility of a new paradigm. *The Person-Centered Journal, 2*(2), 36–48.

Zimring, F. (2000). Empathic understanding grows the person. *The Person-Centered Journal, 7*(2), 101–113.

# SESSION TRANSCRIPTS

# Chapter 27

# Client-centered demonstration interview 2 with Alejandra

## Therapist: Barbara Temaner Brodley
### (Videotaped January 13, 1997)

C:   ... you want to say? Or shall I just go ahead and start?

T:   Why don't you go ahead.

C:   Go ahead?

T:   You know I'm interested and,

---

C1: OK. OK. Um, well, you know, I think today what I'd like to talk about is self-acceptance. Um, for the most part I feel good about myself. I'm not even self-conscious, day by day. And then there are times on a given day when I feel good about myself. If I am in a meeting and my contributions are well-received, (T: Mhm, hmm) then I feel good about myself.

T1: You find yourself noticing.

C2: Yes, yes. And then uh, (Sigh) and yet there are still pockets of self-rejection within me. That come up at times and uh, and that I would like to, well explore with you today. As I was driving here I was thinking of one thing that usually I don't think of, but I've noticed is there. At times I notice it's still there. It's not accepting the color of my skin or my Indian heritage. (T: Mhm, hmm) Something very strange happened to me one day. Very strange. I was thinking about it today as I was driving down here. There was a woman at the school where most of the time I don't experience racism, luckily. I go about my daily life and people accept me well, (T: Mhm, hmm) but there are times when I've known racism. And

This is the second in a series of four videotaped therapy demonstration sessions with Barbara Brodley as therapist and a volunteer client, Alejandra [code name]. The first session, not included here, occurred August 2, 1996.

These session transcripts were chosen specifically because they illustrate a client-centered therapist's responses to client questions. For a discussion of this subject see Chapter 16 in this volume.

I'm glad I've known it because a lot of people in my community, Columbian people in my church community, talk about racism. I'm glad to know what they're talking about.

T2: Directly.

C3: Yes, yes. And be able to relate to it. (T: Mhm, hmm) And I know how painful it is. So anyway, I was at the school that I went to, and there was a woman that looked very Scandinavian. She was, I'm gonna guess, six feet tall. And her hair was white, almost white it was so blonde. (T: Mhm, hmm) And she had blue eyes and she has this very um, just statuesque figure. (T: Mhm, hmm) Just like a model. She was really very, very, very beautiful. In my view, she appeared very self-aware of her beauty. (Laugh) (T: Mhm, hmm) She was also racist. And she did some things, while we were both at the school, that were just blatantly, blatantly racist. One day we were standing in line to talk to a teacher and then when I came she turned, I mean she was, I don't even recall. I mean I recall, but I don't want to get into it, the specifics of it. (T: Mhm, hmm) But she did things just openly and overtly rejecting me. (T: Mhm, hmm) For no other reason but the color of my skin. Because that's the other thing. Clearly you probably have never experienced it, (laugh) but there is a difference when people reject you because they don't like you. (T: Mhm, hmm) And when they reject you because of the color of your skin. You feel the difference, you know what it is. And I heard black people talk about it. (T: Mhm, hmm) They say "You know racism when it's there. You know it." And it's true. And it's true. So anyway I know this woman. She didn't know me, and I know what it was. I just know what it was. (T: Mhm, hmm) Anyway, she did some things that, there was a time when I couldn't take it anymore. It was just rejection to the 50th degree. It is just so much more painful than your average daily rejection. (T: Mhm, hmm) Anyway, there was a day when I just couldn't take it anymore and I went and talked to the Dean. I was in tears. And he was receptive and he was really really caring about it and so on. (T: Mhm, hmm) But anyway, what ended up happening was something very strange. Years later, a couple years later, I was in a workshop. And suddenly I see this woman. And I wanted to hide. That's the very strange thing that I'm telling you about (T: Mhm, hmm) that the reaction I had was just very odd.

T3: Very odd for you …

C4: Yes! Because

T4: You wanted to get away.

C5: Oh, I wanted to hide. (T: Mhm, hmm) It's not just that I wanted to avoid her. I wanted to hide.

T5: I see.

C6: It was just so weird. (T: Mhm, hmm)

T6: The feeling of hiding was, something very much, in yourself. Like, hiding within you, even within yourself. Or a shrinking ...

C7: Yeah. Shrinking is a good word for it. (T: A shrinking quality.) Shrinking is a good word. (Sigh)

T7: As opposed to simply avoiding someone, (C: Right) wanting to leave the room, (C: Exactly) or get out of the way (C: Right) much more physical, I ...

C8: More physical, and more, um ... Oh, let me think, um, well I like "shrinking." (T: Shrinking, mhm, hmm) Yes and it was as if I were this lesser person or that I didn't want to be seen. (T: Mhm, hmm) I just, like that.

T8: Almost ashamed?

C9: Yes! I guess. (T: Mhm, hmm) Yes, mhm, hmm, mhm, hmm.

T9: Well this is a very remarkable reaction, (C: Yeah) where you (C: Mhm, hmm) seeing this woman who exuded prejudice before (C: Yeah, right) brought that response.

C10: Yeah, right, exactly. I think it was shame. (T: Mhm, hmm) Yes. (Pause) So I thought "Oh my God, what is this?" Because I've never had this reaction before and I thought "Oh, this is so strange." But it let me know that, there is a part of me that I'm ashamed of. And I guess, and you know, this, this comes not just from here, the prejudice that exists here. But even in Columbia, people are very racist in our own way. People always favor fair skin and and when a child is born and the child has fair skin (T: Mhm, hmm) the mother is happier, the relatives are happier because here's this little blondie. (T: Mhm, hmm) And so, even in my own country I experience that. (T: Mhm, hmm) Pigmentism I call it. So (Sigh) it's much deeper than ... it goes way back. But, but I guess I want to, I want to be able to – I was talking about it recently with a co-worker. And she made me a card. Saturday she gave me a card. And she said something that is so simple and yet it was helpful. She drew a rainbow and she made a little poem and she said that the earth is brown. And I thought "Oh my God, this is, true!" (Laughing) (T: Mhm, hmm) The earth. And I was so, appreciative of soil. I like to touch it. I like to smell it. And I like the color of it. Then I thought "Oh my God, this is true. The earth is brown," (T: Mhm, hmm) "soil is brown." And I felt good. And I felt good. And then I, I was driving here and I thought "Brown is beautiful." (Laughs)

T10: Brown is beautiful.

C11: Yeah, I really felt that way.

T11: Mhm, hmm, mhm, hmm. A correction in yourself for that pigmentism. That you're a brown girl, a brown person.

C12: Yeah, I felt that ...

T12: But the thought that it,

C13: that it is beautiful.

T13: That it's beautiful, mhm, hmm.

C14: There's nothing to be, ashamed of. (Weak voice) Um, so, uh,

T14: That it has hurt you. Even though you haven't been the victim, a lot, compared to a lot of people.

C15: Yeah, oh my God, yeah.

T15: To the extent you have, (C: Yes) it's hurt you.

C16: Yeah, let me get a tissue. Oh yeah, I have some here.

T16: I have some right here. (C: Yes, yes) So your spirits went up, thinking that brown is beautiful.

C17: Yeah, yes.

T17: The earth and the rock.

C18: Mhm, hmm. Yeah.

T18: You love that color.

C19: Because I do. Mhm, hmm, and uh, is my mascara all running?

T19: On the side there's a little ... now it's gone.

C20: Oh good. And uh, so ...

T20: Like a healing uh, thought.

C21: It, it had, it had that effect on me, that card. It's amazing, you know little things like that, that can be, (Sigh) healing. Yes, um, so I think, I don't know, I mean, I, I hope this is lasting. I hope this stays. (T: Mhm, hmm) I hope, I hope I really don't ... even when I encounter racism. 'Cause it's easy when I'm accepted. And when I'm reminded that brown is fine. But, but I hope I can sustain that feeling about myself even in the presence of a racist person. (T: Mhm, hmm) Uh, (T: Mhm, hmm) but uh,

T21: The impact of thinking "the beauty of brown" and the good feeling it brought you that came out of that, is like filling one of those pockets that you referred to, as pockets of not self-esteem, right? (C: Yeah, right.) And you're hoping that it really is filled up. (C: Yeah) You don't know. (C:

Right) But you'd like to, like this to be filled up. (C: Yes) So that the wound is ...

C22: With self-acceptance. Yes, (T: Mhm, hmm) yeah. I guess another, another pocket is my lack of um, well, a couple really. My body. I have not accepted my body. Um, I want to be different, you know? I want to ... I guess,

T22: You want a different shape?

C23: Well, yes. I want (Laughs) I'm embarrassed to say this in the (T: In the filming) in the tape but, but I'll say it anyway. (Laughing) Um, I want to, to be more curvaceous.

T23: Curvaceous.

C24: Curvaceous, yes. Because I grew up knowing that that's what men like. (T: Mhm, hmm) And so I would like to be that way, um, and yet, Joseph, luckily, (T: Your husband really ...) Yes, likes me. (T: Likes the way you are.) The way I am. He's never made me feel less of a person because I'm not curvaceous. Or less attractive, rather. (T: Mhm, hmm) Not less of a person, that'd be too much, but even less attractive, (T: Mhm, hmm) so that's helpful. He tells me you know. (T: Sure) That he likes me when I'm attractive to him, because he knows. I tell him "Oh, Joseph," and he says "You're fine. And please believe me and trust me and so on." But I don't. I really, I mean,

T24: You don't believe it.

C25: I believe it. I believe it.

T25: You believe he's telling you the truth. (C: Yes, yes.) But you don't feel, completely reassured, by ...

C26: I still would like to be curvaceous. I still ...

T26: Would like to, be different.

C27: Yes, yes.

T27: More, more curves.

C28: (Laughs) Exactly! You know, I was talking about you yesterday, (Laughing) in the car. (T: Mhm, hmm) And I was describing you to Joseph. And everything about you, (T: Mhm, hmm) not just your physique, or your looks, but also your intelligence and, and your warmth and your caring and, and Joseph saying "Some people have it all. It's not fair." He said. (Laughing) I said, "No, it isn't. So we'll distribute it, so the gifts aren't ..."

T28: The gifts are unevenly distributed (C: Right) in the world. (C & T laugh)

C29: Right, right. And so uh, but not, but anyway, I guess uh, so,

T29: So that's another way you're not completely self-accepting. (C: No, no) That there's a criticism you have of your body, (C: Yeah) and about not being curved (C: Yes, yes) and voluptuous (C: Yes, yes, yes, right, right, and uh,) and that way not being as desirable.

C30: Right. And also I don't even want to go to the beach with my friends. I go to the beach with Joseph because I don't mind him seeing me in a swimming suit. But I don't want my friends to see me in a swimming suit. (T: Mhm, hmm) I don't want, I mean, there's shame in me (T: Oh) about my body, I mean it's just, shame, um,

T30: Mhm, hmm. That's the word for it, you feel ashamed. (C: Yeah, yeah) of the way you appear … (C: Yeah, yeah, that's just it) about your naked body, your exposed body.

C31: Yes, exactly, exactly. That's it. And my naked body, I just, don't want,

T31: Don't want it to be seen, (C: No) except perhaps (C: Mhm, hmm) your husband, who,

C32: Right, my husband. That's it.

T32: … has reassured you.

C33: Right. That accepts me. Um, and I guess the last, and I don't know how to exactly work on that, to become more self-accepting. But perhaps, and I want to explore that a little bit more with you, but before we do that I want to tell you that for the, I guess the last thing about, um, and that is, my intelligence. I, I just don't feel, um, intelligent enough, (Laughs) you know? It's just, I just wish I were, brighter. Um, I find it very interesting, very amazing really, that I do have friends who are brilliant. Not bright – brilliant. (T: Mhm, hmm) Um, a couple I know, I'm a lot, I consider my, my friends are bright. But I even have friends who are brilliant, who … one of them is T…, you know T… (T: Mhm, hmm) Um, he's brilliant, and, and we're friends, and um … And it's just amazing to me that uh, well I'm, I guess, interesting enough, you know, that I have,

T33: It amazes you that brilliant people, uh, are interested in you.

C34: In, in having a friendship, (T: Friendship) right, in convers- that my conversation is not so, that they wouldn't find me s- dull, (T: Mhm, hmm) or you know, that um,

T34: Mhm, hmm. Ahh, this reflects yourself somewhat. Having an adequate intelligence (C: Yeah) yourself, right? (C: Right) That, that if you look at some of the people you know, who are brilliant and that they, evidently, uh, enjoy conversation (C: Yeah) with you. You, you don't quite assimilate that. (C: Right) Mhm, hmm. (C Laughs) Not quite, you know it's true, but, (C: I scratched my head) you scratch – how can this be? How can that be true? (C: Puzzling. It's puzzling to me.) Mhm, hmm. Which really emphasizes that doubt about your ability, or dis, dissatisfaction about yourself.

C35: Yeah, yeah, well that's it. The bottom line. That's just it, you know? Because my intelligence is adequate (T: Mhm, hmm) for heaven sakes, you know? It's adequate to,

T35: Mhm, hmm. You have plenty of evidence that it's, adequate.

C36: Yeah, I mean, for the, for the things I want to do. (T: Mhm, hmm) If, it's fine. I want to do therapy and I understand people, fairly well and you know, rather well, really even. (T: Mhm, hmm) And uh, and, and so, (Sigh)

T36: Your, your objective appraisal is you have adequate intelligence, (C: Yeah) for the things that are important to you. (C: Yeah) So, (C: I do) so where does this (C: Yeah) dissatisfaction come from? (C: Right) A negative about yourself.

C37: Yeah, yeah, yeah. And I think that I, I was also thinking as I was driving here, that perhaps a, a lot of it comes from um, (sigh) from uh, my mother's rejection of me. Um, I'm an only child and I uh, grew up with my mother. Well, my, my parents divorced when I was little. A, a baby really. I never grew up with my father. I met him, but I never really get, briefly. I never got to know him, or, never spent time with him. Um ... but uh, for some reason, my mother was accepting of, of me when I was a child, but at some point around my, uh, puberty, she became, she turned. You know, or, she turned on me, I guess is the word. Um, and she became very, very overtly rejecting of me. And um, the word I like to use, although I don't even know if it's really accurate, but I like, I like the way – I say, "she's violently rejecting of me." To this day. To this day. (clears throat) And uh, and I've come to, I, I'm in the process of accepting that. I'm in the process of disconnecting from that. Not wanting to, (Sigh) to get her approval anymore, or to uh, feel affection from – or, or seek affection because she just won't give it, um, or ... anything, you know. Because for decades I've been um, I've been desperately trying to regain, that, that affection that I did, have, when I was (T: younger) mhm, hmm, mhm, hmm. Mhm, hmm and uh,

T37: Though more recently you've been experiencing yourself detaching from that concern.

C38: Detaching, detaching. (T: Mhm, hmm, mhm, hmm) That's just the word.

Detaching from her really. (T: Mhm, hmm) From her even. (T: Mhm, hmm) You know, just saying "OK, you know, that's the way you want it. That's the way it's gotta be." (T: Mhm, hmm) You know, so be it.

T38: Instead of longing for what was before.

C39: Yeah, right, right and um, and I guess that maybe, um maybe that is going to, hope, I'm hoping, that that is going to help me become more self-accepting. Joseph thinks that the two are, greatly connected. And, and he also thinks that, um, that um, if I become more self-accepting, then I've got it made. (T: Mhm, hmm) He says, you know that's just it, the bottom. You know, he's just – that's the, the key for you, the key. (T: Mhm, hmm) If you become more self-accepting, you'll feel so much better. You know, in general, about life, about, that guilt, that you have, he thinks it'll dissipate. I hope he's right. I don't see, quite see the connection he's making but, that's what he's (Phone rings) you know, his, assessment is. (Phone rings again) Anyway, um ... So I don't know. I don't, oh what, I, I guess what I want to ask is um, any, any reactions, any thoughts that you might have, regarding how does one go about, becoming more self-accepting. And if indeed you think that, uh, the two are connected. You know, it's, I mean it seems pretty obvious that it would (T: Mhm, hmm) but, it, I guess it's not that the two are connected because I know they are. But, um, if indeed by detaching from my mother, which, by that I don't mean not seeing her, (T: Mhm, hmm) or not keeping a connection. But really is more like an emotional adjustment. (T: Mhm, hmm) Um, by detaching from her, then self-acceptance would, would come about? Or, I don't know, or it would be easier for it to come about, I don't know. I don't know if my questions are clear.

T39: Mhm, hmm. Well, one question I think, I'm taking it you're asking is, if you were to fully succeed in this adjustment of yourself in relation to your mother, so that you didn't still ... have, I don't know if the word longing is right, but something, longing for what you remember. Which was of, was acceptance, (C: Mhm, hmm) from mother. If you changed, inside, some of that, that was past, I mean you just didn't have it. That you're wondering if that would be, if that would make the difference in terms of your self-acceptance. And that you would become (C: Sighs) so I guess you were, kind of asking if my, in my opinion there would be a significant shift in you, toward greater self-acceptance if you succeed in that, task, with your mother. Is that one?

C40: Yeah, yeah. Yes, yes. That's, that's the question. Mhm, hmm.

T40: Um, I would think it would help, (C: Mhm, hmm) um, a lot. I would, but

I would think, from what you've been telling me that, it probably, well, this is a general view about, s-, how to work on self-acceptance, or work to change self-hatred or pockets (C: Mhm, hmm. Mhm, hmm. Mhm, hmm) of self-hatred. I think it's very useful, sometimes I mean, to really, um, explore and spend time, uh, reflecting upon the pockets of self-hatred and what, what's involved, you know, the nooks and crannies of them. And, because usually when one does that, in my experience, huh, there is nothing valid there. (C: Mhm, hmm) One finds, that one doesn't believe (Phone rings) in what one has been believing in. (C: Mhm, hmm) And that, softens one's sense to one's self. (C: Mhm, hmm) So, this is based both, both on my experience, in relation to my self (C: Mhm, hmm) and also working with clients (C: Mhm, hmm) over the years. (C: Mhm, hmm) When people, choose to really focus on their self-hatred to get rid of that, uh it really does seem to have helped. So, definitely I, I, I think, the way in which you've been hoping for your mother to accept you, and though evidently she cannot, (C: Mhm, hmm) has um, has hurt you, (C: Mhm, hmm) uh, hurt your sense of self (C: Mhm, hmm, mhm, hmm) and to give up on that, probably would release you, free you to, to take more from your good experiences and from the ways in which you appreciate yourself (C: Ohhh) for that to, to expand and the other to diminish. (C: Mhm, hmm) That's probably saying too much, but ...

C41: No, no. You answered both questions. One is "Yes," you think there would be a connection. A freeing ... It makes sense to me, right? That it would. But the other is, how does one work on self-acceptance? (T: Mhm, hmm) And you're saying by, by exploring more, by focusing, by ... So when you say by, it, I don't know the word you used, was it exploring or focusing more on, on those areas of self-rejection, um ...

T41: Yeah, the specific areas, for example, on your, your color (C: Mhm, hmm) that you mentioned, probably, there might, there probably is, I don't know, but, more, more subtle feelings and experiences and thoughts and reactions about that. So, in a way I think it's easier to do it with someone, (C: Mhm, hmm) but one can do it just in reflecting in one's (C: So,) experience alone.

C42: Yes. So, um, so if I were to do, I really want to understand that this is crucial for me.

T42: Do I make sense, so far?

C43: Well, you see, yes, yes. I just want to get into it more. (T: Mhm, hmm) Um, because really it's, it's, the task at hand for me, right now, (T: I see) self-acceptance. And um, so, when you say the nuances, the subtleties, the uh, can you tell me a, more what you're talking about? Let's take the example of the color of my skin. (T: Mhm, hmm) If you were to speculate, what would you, how would you, how would you go about uh, reflecting on, more the nuances, the subtleties that you, (T: Mhm, hmm) that you're referring to?

T43: It's hard is to … It's hard to, do that.

C44: I just don't, I guess I'm not understanding quite, quite exactly –

T44: You're not understanding, concretely enough what I (C: Yeah) as a process. I'm suggesting a process of self, um, exploration and then you'd like to know (Laughs) exactly what I mean.

C45: Yes, yes. I guess that's it. Yes. (T: Mhm, hmm) (Pause)

T45: I, I, I can't imagine for your … trying to think if there's some example. In a way what I mean is, is probably very obvious and simple. It's when you think about yourself as brown, (C: Mhm, hmm) a brown person, a brown girl, (C: Mhm, hmm) then I would think as you reflect on that, there are associations and maybe memories, and q- qualities associated with (C: Mhm, hmm) the brownness … (C: Mhm, hmm) um … It could go in many different directions. (C: I see.) So it was like, whatever comes from within, associated with that and, and with the negative feelings about yourself. (C: Mhm, hmm) Does that help?

C46: I got it. I got it. I got it. I got it. (Sigh) Yes.

T46: So you see, I mean it's rather simple, (C: Right) yet not so easy necessarily to go through, but it's …

C47: Mhm, hmm. Mhm, hmm. Right. No, but it, it and you know one thing I, I know I can do, is, go into myself and explore and look around, (T: You're good at it, you do.) yeah, yes, yes, yes. So I, I, yes I, yes I can do that. I know how to, I know that if I said to myself, um well I'm going to uh, explore this in depth, and then remain quiet and silent, things would come to me. Memories (T: Mhm, hmm) and experiences that would help me. (T: Feelings, mhm, hmm) feelings, that would help me understand where this is coming from. (T: Mhm, hmm) OK, all right, um … the one strange thing however, you know, Barbara the one thing, well, like the brown, the color of my skin, my body, it's easy to understand. It, it comes readily. The one thing I haven't been able to pin down is for example my accepting my intelligence. (T: Mhm, hmm) Because at my house, uh, when we were, when I was eleven years old, my mom and I went to live with this, family, in Columbia. My mom didn't want me to um, be an adolescent and, and not have, she worked and she wanted some supervision. Well, in this house, and this is how, uh, this is this um, a huge chapter in my life, living with this family. It was very, very traumatic, very, very bad. But the one thing this family always did uh, was to uh, tell me that I was intelligent. (T: Mhm, hmm) You know, it, I mean, it was, they were – this woman, this particular woman that I'm talking about, um, always put me down, in many ways. But um, she used to say that I was intelligent. My mother doesn't say that one way or another, you know she never (T: Mhm, hmm) uh …

T47: She doesn't put you down and she doesn't praise you for a (C: Right) somewhat a neutral area. (C: Yeah, right, right, right) But this woman you lived with in the family (C: Yes) she, she was negative in many ways, and critical (C: Yes) but she also praised you. (C: Well,) praised your intelligence. (C: She always kind of, kind of,) or judged it .

C48: Where it, it, it um, said that I was. (T: I see.) Not so much like praise it, because that be, that's not, (T: Is … not the aspect) why am I, maybe a little bit of praising. No there wasn't an at,

T48: It was more an assessment. (C: Yeah) She would comment. (C: Yeah. That's it, that's it.) Make a comment. An assessing comment, to your intelligence.

C49: Yes. Exactly. Exactly. Because praising – there wasn't, (Laughing)

T49: That wasn't the feeling of it at all.

C50: No,

T50: From her.

C51: From her, no. And um, but anyway she, you know she said, she used to say that um, and I haven't, I haven't had many experience – or experiences that I can remember where people had make me feel dumb, you know. I, you know or when people commented and said things that I would feel "Oh my gosh, I'm so dumb!" (T: Mhm, hmm) Or, but I felt that dumb. Or you know like at the school, at the uh, graduate school, I used to think "Oh my God. Oh my God. All these bright people, what am I doing here?" (T: Mhm, hmm) You know like, um, (T: Mhm, hmm) So I was just …

T51: It's puzzling because it isn't as though you've been put down, that way.

C52: Right, right.

T52: Humiliated or anything like that, and not many, – and yet, it, it

C53: And yet it's in here.

T53: In the context of the school, you were, feeling it very vividly. (C: Mhm, hmm) You were not as smart as these other people. (C: Yes, yes, yes, yes.) What am I doing here? (C: Yeah, right. Yeah, right. Yeah, right. So, uh,) There's some, something mysterious about the feeling. (C: Right,

right) Where it, where it came from.

C54: Right, right. Exactly. Exactly. I just don't know, I just don't know um, why do I carry this dissatisfaction, um I don't know. I just don't know, um, I guess the task at hand would be the same wouldn't it? Even though it's not as readily apparent to me. It would be the same to just sit with it and see, what comes up (T: Mhm, hmm) and kind of explore it maybe with ...

T54: Well, I think that is a way that, (C: That might ...) can be helpful.

C55: OK. OK.

T55: The fact that you have more readily explanation for negative feelings in terms of of color or your body. (C: Mhm, hmm) The cultural, societal factors. (C: Mhm, hmm. Mhm, hmm. Right.) Then the intelligent issue, probably would get clearer. They'd all get clearer, (C: Mhm, hmm) I think. (C: OK) But, of course they, I guess I wanted to clarify the, (C: Mhm, hmm) to me the mechanism of, change isn't the um, isn't the understanding as much as other, I don't know, something in the process, uh I think self-comprehensibility helps our self-acceptance. If, if there are puzzling things that are connected with not feeling good about the self. Then to become more comprehensible to one's self, I think, does help. But, that, what I was getting at is that I di-, I may have misled you in my remarks. I didn't mean to imply that the mechanism in the way in which the exploration can help improve one's self-regard, (C: Mhm, hmm) is having explanation. It's somehow going through the process of having more, just ... I don't know. Something about the process of, of relating more to those feelings and thoughts. (C: Oh) And, and in a way the, the (C: Yeah) dispelling of, of their, their emotional impact. Their negative, emotional impact, is somehow a process in which the positive experiences just, (T Laughs) take over. I don't know. I can't explain it psychologically ...

C56: Mhm, hmm. Yeah. So, it's not just to know where these things are coming from. It's, that's only part of it, but ...

T56: That's only part of it.

C57: But it's more, uh can you, can you tell me, I mean, like, who, by self-comprehensibility I'm understanding my self better, (T: Yeah) but, but um,

T57: Making sense. "Oh, that makes sense," when I feel that way. (C: Mhm, hmm) Well, if it's simply if you've had a parent who's been really critical about your appearance, say, you say, "Well it makes sense that I, would feel that way." As opposed to, there being a mystery about it. (C: Hmmm)

I don't, I don't have the impression that, the negative feelings you have about your intelligence or dissatisfaction with it is necessarily particularly worse because you don't know the origin of it. (C: Mhm, hmm) But somehow in the process of understanding that better, probably it'd be a, that'd be part of the relaxing, (C: Hmmm) you know, inner relaxing, and of self-acceptance.

C58: Mhm, hmm. Yeah, right, right. (Pause, 8 seconds) Let me digest this a little bit. (T: Sure.) (Pause, 10 seconds) OK. Well, I don't know if I'm ready to use that much time. Uh, I didn't check the time. How, how,

T58: It was twenty to [the hour], I think, so …

C59: Twenty to. We have until 1:30? (T: Yeah) Is that helpful? You want to go, OK.

T59: Approximately there, a little more.

C60: OK. That's … um, uh I guess I, I want to talk about, I would really like to, spend more time on the self-acceptance thing. (T: Mhm, hmm) But, I don't know what else to say. (Laughs) Um, so I guess I can change the topic, so,

T60: Mhm, hmm. We could meet again if you, if you're (C: Oh, OK) willing to do this again, (C: OK) so we could do it, more of it, after you have, reflected on it. (C: OK) If you want to.

C61: OK, OK, OK. Well, but I'm not ready to move on. I'm not ready to really move, uh, because I really want to, I want to digest it for a moment so let me just, (T: Mhm, hmm) it'll take me a minute or two, to just see if there's anything else I want to say about this, um … (Pause, 20 seconds) I guess I want to spend more time exploring the um, the dissatisfaction with my, my intelligence. Because, I feel that the other two are much easier to tackle. Because I have a, more material readily, (T: Mhm, hmm) awa-, in my awareness, (T: Yes) to go with. The, the intelligence, I don't. (T: Mhm, hmm) So, uh, so I just don't know. But I don't know what to say, that's the thing. I don't know, um,

T61: This one's really puzzling.

C62: Yeah, yeah.

T62: Just in gener … How it got generated.

C63: Yes, yes, yes, yes.

T63: Where it is much more, and that there's much less data, at least you're aware as to …

C64: Mhm, hmm, mhm, hmm. Right, right. So um, so yes. I guess, but I, but the thing is I just don't know. Let me think, um, well, you know I'm thinking that, you know I'm thinking that part of it is, is the c-, is the culture, they, in the United States. I think that's part of it. Um, because in Columbia, I don't remember feeling this way in Columbia. It may be that I don't remember, but I just don't remember feeling that way. Um, I did feel the other two, (T: Yeah) in Columbia, but h-, I think it is here, that I have become, you know? Because I came to this country 14 years ago. And what I have noticed, oh you know and it could be, what I noticed, right, at first I couldn't speak English very well. And I could just barely make myself understood. And what happened was that people mistook my not being able to speak the language by, a, in, in, mistook it by my being dumb. And, you know, so they would, (T: Mhm, hmm) so I would speak and they would say, um, "What?" but in a way that clearly, conveyed to me that they were impatient with me, that, "This dumb Columbian" um, can't speak. (T: Mhm, hmm) You know and um, so that was one thing. And that's why I set out (Laughs) to learn English well, because I didn't want people giving me those looks, (T: Mhm, hmm) um …

T64: Mhm, hmm. So that is a, one of the sources that is, because you didn't have English at a high level people, were impatient and there was some message that you weren't smart. (C: Yeah) You were dumb. (C: Yes) In not communicating, (C: Yeah) coherently or clearly or adeq-, whatever, right. (C: Yeah) Mhm, hmm. (C: So, uh,) And you, we would have motivated you, you really worked on (C: On, on English) (Laughing) your English. (C: Mhm, hmm) Because it was so, it was such a distinct experience, uh being, looked down on, (C: Yes) intellectually.

C65: Yes, mhm, hmm. (Sigh) So,

T65: So that's a piece of it in terms of uh …

C66: That's a piece of it. That's a piece of it. I, I that's a piece of it, and I, I don't know, but maybe a big piece of it. I don't know, but maybe. Um, the other thing I've noticed is that, in this country, it's not OK to make mistakes. Um, so for example, if people make mistakes they usually apologize for it and, and make it an external cause. I mean in Columbia you can say um, "I don't understand. I don't get it. I forgot." (T: Mhm, hmm) I mean, it's OK. Here, when you make a mistake, people say, "Well, it's Monday" you know, or like, I was watching the news this morning (Laughs) and um, the, the co-anchor of the Today show made a mistake and said "Well, it's Monday. It's Monday morning." (T: Mhm, hmm) Rather than just accepting. (T: Yeah) But I made a mistake, you know, so big, big deal. Um, and, and here people usually give you …

(Tape change from side A to side B)

... an external explanation of why (T: Mhm, hmm) a person may have made a cognitive mistake.

T66: Mhm, hmm. It's not inside. "It's not because I'm dumb, it's because – something." (Laughs) (C: Yes, yes.) I didn't sleep enough or ...

C67: Right, right, right, exactly. And so, I began to notice that, being smart, or you know appearing smart, all the time, was a big thing. (T: Mhm, hmm) And that, forgetting, not understanding, those were not OK, you know, you were not (T: Mhm, hmm) a, a,

T67: You're not all right. You had to account for it in some way (C: Yeah) that didn't blame yourself for anything.

C68: Yeah, yeah. And so I, and so, so I guess I became more aware of the importance that people place in intelligence in this country. And it is not true in Columbia. In, and I've noticed that people say, for example, "Thomas so and so. He's so smart." You know, in Columbia, you usually you don't say that. Unless it's something remarkable, (T: Mhm, hmm) but usually the, the, the attribute that people look for is sincerity. And so they say "Yes, Thomas, that so and so, he's so sincere." (T: Mhm, hmm) And that's the thing, you know, oh, (T: That's a very positive virtue ...) yeah. Yes, yes, yes. (T: But not intelligence. Not commented on, unless it's extraordinary.) Yeah, yeah. I mean it's not a big deal. (T: Where here, people often comment "Very intelligent, very smart.") Yeah, yeah. It's a big thing. It's a big thing. Um, or witty, you know. They're quick-minded (snap) and witty. It's a big thing. It's funny. And, and since I'm not either, witty or quick-minded, um I feel that, like in a, in, in making small conversation, cocktail conversation, people joke a lot. And I don't know what to say and I feel awkward and inadequate and because and I don't have comebacks (T: Mhm, hmm) and, and you know, I'm just, I laugh at jokes but, (T: Yes) that's ...

T68: But you don't have that repartee, that, that's valued, (C: Yeah) that's valued (C: Yeah) here in this country.

C69: Right, right, right. So um,

T69: So then you're not so smart, is the implication ...

C70: Right, exactly. (T: Mhm, hmm) That's it. So, I think that's another piece, you know that um, the lack of wit, (T: Mhm, hmm) is another piece of this dissatisfaction. (T: Mhm, hmm) Um, because it's valued in this culture, very much, very much uh, and not in Columbia. In Columbia people are funny and that's great, but it's not something like ... you know, I get a letter of recommendation, in my letter of recommendation somebody said "Well, she has a good sense of humor." And I'm thinking, "I don't."

But it's strange that, that, (T: Would be put in.) Yeah. Or they say, I remember that they were talking about the candidate, one of the presidential candidates. And they were saying "Well he's so very funny." And I, he was, he's funny, he's witty and I'm thinking ... "So what?" (Laughing) (T: So what?) So what. You know, I mean how is that going to make him a better president?

T70: Mhm, hmm. But wittiness, quick-mindedness, being able to um, comeback, quick comeback and sharp. (C: Yeah) Those are the qualities, (C: Yeah) mhm, hmm (C: Yeah) valued here. (C: Mhm, hmm) And that's stood out to you and stood out as a contrast, to you.

C71: Yeah, right. Right, right, right, right. And um,

T71: So that's another piece of this (C: Mhm, hmm) vul-, sense of yourself as not being, (C: Good enough) good enough and intellectually (C: Yeah) good enough.

C72: Right, right, right. So, um, so yeah, I think that's another piece of it, um,

T72: The two you've mentioned are, the impact of coming to the United States, or the encounter (C: Yeah) with the United States (C: Yeah) from Columbia.

C73: Right, mhm, hmm, mhm, hmm. Maybe another part of it, I don't know if this is true or not, let me see how we're doing on time, maybe another part of it is that um, I have this, appeal, attraction, magnet towards very intelligent people, you know. Even in Columbia. I remember I used to do something very strange. (Laughs) I used to write to writers. And then make reunions to get to meet them. Because I thought "Oh my gosh, this is a wonderful book." And I would find a way to write to a writer and then have this, um these gatherings where this writer would come at someone's house. I mean, that in, in, in and it was just ex-,

T73: You were so drawn, you actually took action.

C74: I was so drawn, to bright, brilliant people. It's just, so appealing to me. (T: Mhm, hmm) And I guess maybe that's another piece, you know that I tend to gravitate to uh, people who are brilliant and then of course by comparison I don't measure up. Well, the point is why should I even compare, you know? I mean, I shouldn't have to compare myself; I should be able to enjoy these people's intelligence without feeling less, um, a person for it.

T74: That's what you would want, to gently say "I appreciate it. I enjoy it. I want to be close to it, to, to be enhanced by it" just as uh, someone listening or present. But, you add a comparison, that feels part of this. (C: Yeah, yeah, right) A comparison that puts you below,

C75: Beneath, below, (T: Mhm, hmm) below. Yeah. And I think that, for example, that is true in the network, um, in the person-centered network. (T: Yes) Yet um, (T: The email) mhm, hmm, email, because, of course, I mean people, I mean the, the, the post that come through (Laughs) are just amazing, you know. Um it, they're just amazing.

T75: The intelligence shines out, doesn't it?

C76: Yeah, and it's like "Oh my God." (T: Mhm, hmm) And I'm still thinking "And here I am in their midst." (Laughs)

T76: You're in the midst of some pretty bright people, yeah.

C77: Mhm, hmm. Yeah, and maybe that's,

T77: And you're saying, here I am in their midst.

C78: In their midst.

T78: Their midst. The smart ones.

C79: (Laughing) I snuck in. (T: Mhm, hmm) I snuck in here. Which is funny, but it's not really funny, not really.

T79: It's painful.

C80: It, well, it's, it's a put-down to myself. (T: Mhm, hmm) You know, um, um, I, I don't feel, of course, (inaudible) I mean, nobody makes me, they, they, they treat me as an equal, everyone there, you know. Which is also puzzling, you know. It makes me scratch my head, you know? (Laughs) In, in …

T80: This gesture, uh …

C81: Yeah. Like, "Oh, ah," (T: How can it be?) "now how can it be, this is …" And in a way of course, it's um, it's mostly puzzling. It's helped, some, a little flattering too, you know, to think "Oh, my gosh, these people accept me and treat me as an equal" um. But for the most part is, uh, hard to understand. But I think that might be another piece of it, um, that I do, gravitate to intelligence and brilliance. But of and, and then, and then um, (Pause) But, but the problem is then, then I compare. (T: Mhm, hmm) That, you know, then I (T: Mhm, hmm) then I, compare myself and then, you know.

T81: You're saying that you'd, you are drawn to people who are exceptional in their intelligence. (C: Yeah, yes) Who are really quite, the exceptional. (C: Yeah, yes.) And you're saying that you don't view yourself as exceptional, (C: Right, no, God no.) and (C: Right) but to be drawn to and interested in people who are exceptional could be simply something that you enjoy that, nurtures your own intelligence and your own understanding of things, whatever. (C: Yes) But somehow, you you give some emphasis to the, what you believe is the fact that you are not, as gifted, (C: Mhm, hmm) as these people to whom you are drawn. The, the writer, people who have accomplished things, where there's lots of evidence of their extraordinary ability, at least sometimes, right. (C: Mhm, hmm, mhm, hmm) So, but there's an objective truth to in fact, that in certain measures of ability, these people are, more (C: Outstanding) they're outstanding. (C: Mhm, hmm) But, you give a weight to the fact that you're not, (C: Yeah) in contrast, and that pulls you down.

C82: Yes, yes! Exactly, exactly. Um, you know, and even like, uh, I look at Maria's, uh, posts, you know, the way she expresses herself, the way she, her understanding of, many things. And, and I'm thinking "Oh, wow." And yet I have to say though, at the same time that, I also see that, I do have wisdom. Um, that even though, and that if I had to choose between brilliance and wisdom, I'd go for wisdom. Um, because it is also true that, the two don't necessarily go together obviously. (T: Mhm, hmm) But um, but, but that I do see that in myself, you know that I, and I think it stems from self-knowledge. That um, that emphasis I put on the intuitive life, the uh, my inner life in, in, in, contemplation, in, in solitude and self-understanding and all of that, has resulted in a greater wisdom about life itself. (T: Mhm, hmm) And uh,

T82: You value that and you, you, you value your development, (C: Yeah) where you've arrived. (C: Yeah) Where you are in that regard. (C: Mhm, hmm. Yeah, yeah.) That you've, you've cultivated from your experience you've cultivated wisdoms (C: Yeah) wisdom (C: Right, right) you really, (C: And I,) feel good (C: Yeah, I do, I do) about it, and you value that more than pure, brain-power.

C83: Right, right, right. And it's amazing too, and this is you know, this I discovered, I didn't know that about myself until I, came to the network. I didn't because um,

T83: You didn't know, or recognize, or appreciate your wisdom as much as you do now. (C: It, it,) Before that, so the network process (C: Has helped me) has helped you that way.

C84: Yes, because uh, because people, (Sigh) who have, you know PhDs and, and uh, write to me and say "Oh, Alejandra" like either publicly or privately, (T: Mhm, hmm) and say "Oh Alejandra, I really appreciated this that you said and," (T: Mhm, hmm) "and I really like your view on that." And I'm thinking, (Inhales) "Oh my God!" (T: Mhm, hmm) You know, again it's like,

T84: Surprise, (C: Yeah, yeah) you've been surprised, (C: Yeah) but it's also been adding up inside, (C: Right) a little.

C85: Yes, I like "Oh my gosh, I, I guess I do have this quality that is valuable." That I value and that other people value as well. And, and thank goodness I do you know, um it's wonderful (T: Mhm, hmm) I mean I'm glad for it, um so anyway, let me see, yeah our time's up on that. OK then. Um, but, um, I guess that's just it, you know that's, that's it as, you know as far as we can, I want to go with it at this point. (T: All right) So, we can end with that. We can end.

T85: Mhm, hmm.

## COMMENTS

T1: All right, thank you.

C1: Oh, you're welcome. Thank you.

T2: I guess um, it, it would be useful to have any comments you have about the interaction.

C2: Sure. Well, the main thing is that, (clears throat) you know, I mean I, I knew you wouldn't do it, but, the least helpful thing, would've been if you would have tried to give me evidence of, (T: Oh) intelligence (Laughs) (T: Mhm, hmm) or, or, or anything else, you know, um. (T: Mhm, hmm) Because that's, what I usually get, you know. (T: Mhm, hmm) It doesn't help.

T3: A direct reassurance with pointing to things that prove to the person that you are … (C: Mhm, hmm) That wouldn't have been helpful at all?

C3: No. No, because that's what um, because then that stops for me the exploration. (T: Mhm, hmm) It's like, well, you know, um … (T: Mhm, hmm) So, no. Even though, in, in some instances, like this girl said, the earth is beautiful and it's round, it was just so helpful and it was, it was a,

T4: … spontaneous, comment, that just connected for you.

C4: Yeah, yeah. But, but nonetheless, I think sometimes, um, therapists make the mistake of, reassuring. And I mean clients, and, and (Phone rings) I think that for me it would have been, um, not helpful, not helpful. I mean, what it does, what it would have done, is make me feel good about myself, for the rest of the day. (T: Mhm, hmm) You know, say, "Oh my gosh, Barbara thinks I'm s-, intelligent, smart, or …" And that's wonderful. (T: Mhm, hmm) But that's the end of it. Tomorrow I'm dealing with the same thing. (T: Yeah) So, um,

T5: So it isn't as though that wouldn't be pleasing. It (C: Yes) would be.

C5: It would've been wonderful. But it's, (T: Right.) but it's not,

T6: But not so therapeutic.

C6: Not, not, right. Doesn't, exactly, doesn't produce inner change. (T: Mhm, hmm) It just makes me feel good for the day. (Laughs)

T7: Mhm, hmm. Mhm, hmm. So it really stood out that I didn't do that because in a conversation about, your topic, it's very likely that, that people would, uh, reassure you and even many therapists would do that. (C: Right) You knew I wouldn't, or you thought the probability is that I wouldn't (C: Knowing your style) go anywhere. But, but still it's notable because it was a, you had an awareness that that was an alternative.

C7: Right, right, right. And um, so that was one thing. I was apprec-, I mean I appreciated and I was glad um, that you gave me some concrete things to answer to my questions. (T: Mhm, hmm) You know, that you said, "Well, this is something you could try," (T: Mhm, hmm) "and would help," you know that, so, oh, that's, that's helpful, you know that, um,

T8: That I, that I did answer your,

C8: Yeah, that you answered my questions, said "Well, try this." (T: Try this) And "This is what I think" and just give me your honest reaction and your, you know (T: Mhm, hmm) suggestions. So that was, that was good. Um,

T9: You didn't feel that stopped your process. I mean, (C: No) temporarily, (C: No) you were giving attention to me, in order to understand what I, was trying to say. (C: Right) So in that way it certainly interfered with a process that might otherwise have been happening but it was in response to your wanting, from me at the time (C: Right) or some in-, indicating you wanted my (C: Yeah) my point of view, uh …

C9: Exactly, because the thing is, I mean if um, what, what I needed at the time was something that would enhance the process even bef-, after I'm leaving, after I leave. (T: Ahhh) and so that's (T: Mhm, hmm) you know that's, you gave something to work with, even after. (T: Mhm, hmm) And so …

T10: So, behind the question was, in a way, "Barbara, can you give me something to take away" (C: Yeah) "that I can use" (C: Right) "on my own?" (C: Right) You know, and so then (C: Exactly) what I did was (C: That was,) along those lines.

C10: Right, right, right. Mhm, hmm. And um, and of course I felt understood. You know, the, the, the, the, the, the way you, (Pause) verbalize and, and um, you, you know the, the responses you gave me, let me know that you're getting it. That you're understanding (T: Mhm, hmm) what I was saying and I, and I'm glad, I was glad you did. Because um, when you were doing it in, in, it felt good that, uh, you know was um, (Sigh) there's some release there, (T: Mhm, hmm) in feeling understood. (T: Yeah) You know, there's …

T11: And actually hearing it (C: Yeah) specifically.

C11: Right. I mean just getting it, you get it. You get it, you know like, that's it, that's it. (T: Mhm, hmm) Thank you. (T: Mhm, hmm) (Sigh) So, I guess, the other thing Barbara, I have to say too, is that I felt your, your sensitivity. I felt that, um, that it mattered to you, you know that my feelings, (Pause) mattered, you know. (T: Mhm, hmm) It wasn't um, just an intellectual exercise for you, (Laugh and weak voice) (T: Mhm, hmm) that, (T: That I cared about what,) that you cared, (T: what you,) that you cared, yeah. (T: It came through?) Yeah, it came through, it came through. Um, and I guess that's it. That's all I, (T: Mhm, hmm) uh, want to say, (T: Mhm, hmm) about my experience.

T12: Mhm, hmm. May I just ask you, one more thing? (C: Sure) About the last part. Do you know, can you, can you say what, what it was in my behavior (C: Mhm, hmm) that gave you the sense of my caring about your feelings, not just having a good understanding (C: Right) um,

C12: Yeah, I can. Uh, it was in your body posture, was very present, leaning towards me. (T: Mhm, hmm) It was the expression of your eyes that um, that reflected, uh, a feeling you know, a, a, a concern and a sp-, perhaps, I don't want to say, necessar-, perhaps a sadness or a hurting with me at the moment, you know. That you (T: In my eyes, you could see) in my eyes, your eye, your expression of your eyes. (T: I see.) Um, in your, your emotional presence, (T: Mhm, hmm) at the moment, you know. Your expression. Your, your eyes, but al-, your facial expression was um, one of perhaps the word might be compassion. (T: Mhm, hmm) Uh, uh, and then your, there, your emotional presence was also, felt, you know. It was also, uh …

T13: My emotional presence I, I assume you mean by that, some kind of complex data that comes from body language, face, voice tone, other, uh, just a whole, 'cause you, you were referring specifically back to my eyes, and to my expression and then you said my presence. So I was guessing that there's something that's, some integration of different features in the therapist (C: Yeah) and what in myself in this case (C: Right) that feels like a presence, of one sort or another, (Laughs) (C: Right) and that my presence came across as, genuinely caring. (C: Yes, right, right.) I'm very interested in this. (C: Oh, right.) Rogers talked about presence and Chuck, who worked with Carl in the European programs a lot, emphasized presence and of course he wrote, Carl wrote, near the end of his life, about presence. He didn't write a lot, but he pointed to it.

And I'm just interested in any, (C: Yeah) reference to that. (C: Yeah) That's why I was asking. (C: Yeah, yes, right.) What this presence is, I, (C: Yeah, yeah) feel it's very important. (C: Yeah, oh yes, Mhm, hmm) Comes out of one being in one piece as a therapist (Laughs) and would-be therapeutic attitudes and, but then to understand, not that we can do it, not that we can make it happen, but just to understand it. I think it's very spontaneous.

C13: Yeah. But I, maybe in my view, it also comes out about an openness. About not, fearing, uh, pain, or not fearing, or not shying away from the, the person's feelings of uh, sadness, pain, or whatever those may be. (T: Mhm, hmm) You know hurt, and not closing one's heart. (Laughs) (T: Mhm, hmm) And um, you know I think it's, mentally, one needs to remain open, both, emotionally and, and, you know mentally to say "OK" (T: Mhm, hmm) "I'm willing to receive and contain your, your pain."

T14: Yes. To allow it in. The therapist allowing it in. (C: Allowing it in, exactly.) As opposed to kind of, knowing it at a distance.

C14: Exactly, protecting oneself, you know.

T15: So an unprotected, open, quality, (C: Mhm, hmm) you feel it, I mean, you're analyzing it and saying that's what you think is an important element in it. (C: Mhm, hmm) and I guess you saw that, or

C15: Yeah right, yeah right.

T16: Well, I appreciate both, your doing this, (C: Mhm, hmm) for the video and also your comments (C: Mhm, hmm) and um, I don't know if I have anything, I, I, felt interacting with you, for the most part, was very, um, flowing, or fluid. (C: Mhm, hmm) For me, uh, and that I, felt I was following, uh well. (C: Mhm, hmm) Um, but of course getting feedback from you that I was. (C: Mhm, hmm) When you asked me the question and then I clarified the first part of the question and then addressed that and then just sort of went into the, other part of your question, I felt like I wasn't being as clear as I would like to be. Um, and um, then I felt a little concerned, in taking too much of your time because I wasn't doing it as clearly (C: Mhm, hmm) as I like to. But I, (C: Mhm, hmm, mhm, hmm) did the best I could (Laughs) with it at the time. It's a very, um, what is it that one can do to change feelings of self-dislike, or self-hatred, or non-self-acceptance to, self-acceptance. (C: Mhm, hmm) Um, self-appreciation (C: Mhm, hmm) is, to me, a central question about what client-centered therapy d-, does and uh, how it does it and why it does it and so on. So, it's a big question. (C: Mhm, hmm) But of course I was addressing it in terms of, the specific of your question, "Do you have any ideas," (C: Mhm, hmm) "about how you might, address that?" And, (C: Mhm, hmm, mhm, hmm) so, I, I felt some, uncertainty, about that. Probably also because of the video (C: Mhm, hmm, mhm, hmm) that wasn't a theoretical presentation, it was a response (Laughs) to you. (C: Yes) I, I also felt good, about the fact that you did ask me a question. (C: Mhm, hmm) Because, because clients ask us questions. (C: Mhm, hmm) And, and there needs to be examples for discussion of how client-centered therapists, respond. (C: Respond, yes.) So I thought that was ... very ... could be very useful. (C: Mhm, hmm) Future use of this, video, (C: Mhm, hmm yes) for discussion.

C16: Yeah, and I guess in cl-, do you have anything else you want to say? (T: No) In closing I want to say that um, it was a helpful session, you know. It was, I, I was, it's, it was um, I feel some, I don't know the word, but ... some ver-, peacefulment right now. That I wasn't feeling when I started, so ... peacefulness, that's it. (T: Mhm, hmm) (Sigh) So, it, it was good.

T17: Thank you and I'm glad to hear that.

C17: Thank you, thank you too, yeah.

# Chapter 28

# Client-centered demonstration interview 3 with Alejandra

## Therapist: Barbara Temaner Brodley
### (Videotaped June 9, 1997)

C1: Yeah, uh, well, um ... I had said to you that I wanted to, talk about self-acceptance and that's what I want to continue to talk about. Um, um, I want to start out by telling you something that has been happening lately that um, (clears throat) has just exacerbated my sense of, self-rejection. And uh, what happens is that I have made some modifications in the relationship with my mother because the way it stood before was just much too painful to me. And what I needed to do was to create more distance between us. There is complete, um emotional distance. But, but, but I used to call her more frequently (T: Uhm, hmm) as you know, she lives in Columbia and I used to call her more frequently and, and the calls were, um sometimes tolerable and sometimes painful but never, huh, pleasant or gratifying.

T1: Uhm, hmm. They were more –

C2: Well, not nurturing.

T2: Yes. (C: Uhm, hmm) They were more of a duty than anything.

C3: They were a duty. They were a duty, yes. (T: Uhm, hmm) And so, (Sigh) at some but, but, but because sometimes she was actively hurtful, um, I, I, just needed to protect myself, you know? I just needed to say, "Um I can't put myself through this any longer, every week, or every other week. I just can't do it every other Sunday." So what I said to her is that, I wanted us to communicate by letter. And, she agreed. You know, she didn't say (T: Uhm, hmm) "How come?" or, she said "OK." (T: Uhm, hmm) You know, very matter of fact. (T: Uhm, hmm) Um, and so we

---

This is the third in a series of four videotaped therapy demonstration sessions with Barbara Brodley as therapist and a volunteer client, Alejandra [code name]. The first session, not included here, occurred August 2, 1996.

These session transcripts were chosen specifically because they illustrate a client-centered therapist's responses to client questions. For a discussion of this subject see Chapter 16 in this volume.

started communicating by letter. She wrote me a letter. I wrote her another letter. And for a while I didn't hear from her. And I thought that, that was not going – I, I had considered that possibility even before I had made that decision, (T: Uhm, hmm) but, but, I thought that I could handle it well and that it wouldn't affect me too much. (T: Uhm, hmm) But when I didn't hear from her for a while I was really very affected. I was, very upset. I wanted to hear from her. I wanted to know how she was doing. (T: Uhm, hmm) And um, that's one thing. But the, the other part of it is that, along with that I began to feel very, um self-hate and self-hating, um, (T: Uhm, hmm) I began to get in touch I think with, more with the effects of her rejection of me with um, with a shame that that causes in me. And I was just like, (T: Uhm, hmm) it was as if, I mean, um … (Pause) It, it, it, the concept that she, that she has of me is, is very, very painful. Just the image that she, which she believes to be true about me is painful. For one thing she thinks I'm totally untrustworthy and you know, totally untrustworthy and a liar. And that's not true. (T: Uhm, hmm) Um, and think, she thinks I'm a, a very bad daughter. (T: Uhm, hmm) Really that's not true, I'm, I'm an excellent daughter. (Laughs) I've been so dutiful. I've been so, loving and huh (T: Uhm, hmm) just, it's just not true (T: Uhm, hmm) it's not true.

T3: She has it all wrong. (C: Yes) But the way she has it, hurts you enormously.

C4: Yeah, yeah, yeah, yeah, yeah. So, so the thing is Barbara, even though I know this not to be true about me, I cannot extricate myself from, from it. I cannot, not – uh, (Sigh) deeply feel that there's something very wrong with me. Even though, rationally I don't think it's true. (T: Uhm, hmm) I, feel that "What is wrong with me that my mother rejects me?" (T: Uhm, hmm) At what, what, what is, is had to be (T: Uhm, hmm) so wrong with me, how, I mean I just feel … (T: Uhm, hmm) It's just …

T4: Rationally you, it doesn't make sense but the truth is that the rejection and the judgments that your mother has toward you, are in you. (C: Yeah) And you somehow believe there must be something to them. (C: Yeah, yeah) Even though rationally you'd (C: Right, right, right) say "No, I'm not." (C: Right, right, right, right) And this came out very much more when you made the arrangement for the correspondence and then she doesn't write. And then, somehow this flooded into you. Very clearly, how much self-criticism, self-hatred comes out of your mother's, rejection (C: Yeah) and judgment.

C5: Yeah, yeah. Right, yeah and um … (Pause) Well, I just don't know, do you see, I just don't know. Who – what's been happening since – and this is for a couple of weeks already, is that I, am so upset that I get, I wake up early in the morning around 3, 4 in the morning, can't go back to sleep. I wake up, insulting myself, (T: Uhm, hmm) just, (T: Uhm, hmm) and I hate to, I hate to treat my – I would never, ever, ever treat –

T5: Treat anyone the way you were treating yourself.

C6: You know, never, (T: Uhm, hmm) I mean never (T: Uhm, hmm) never would I tell (T: Uhm, hmm) anybody that. Not even my wor- , an enemy.

T6: Someone you hate.

C7: Not even an enemy. (T: Uhm, hmm) I would not (T: Treat,) treat an enemy like that. (T: Uhm, hmm) I just wouldn't.

T7: The way you're reacting to yourself.

C8: Yeah, right. (T: Uhm, hmm, uhm, hmm) I mean it's so, huh.

T8: Though it's really up in you. It's just very alive in you how, bad you feel toward yourself and how connected that is to mother's rejection. (C: Yeah, yeah, yeah) You're haunted. With it, I mean it sounds you're just haunted with what's in you, now. (Client softly chants "yeah" during T's last remarks)

C9: And so um, I just um, um I just think um ... (Pause) Um – (Sigh) Yeah, I mean it's just um ... (Pause, 6 seconds) hard not to implicate myself in her judgment of me. And it is, it's just not ... I do it, I just do it. Um, (Pause) and of course that causes me to be irritable with others you know, which is (T: Uhm, hmm) I don't like that. I don't ... (T: Uhm, hmm) (Sniffles)

T9: Where you're very upset and very hurt and then somewhat irritable and that comes out at your loved ones?

C10: Yes, yes. Or even (T: Those close to you.) at work, you know. At work I feel a little ... uh,

T10:   Uhm, hmm. A little irritable, uhm, hmm.

C11:   Edgy, yeah. So, (Sigh) but um,

T11:   But you can't fend this off. It's as if – her reactions to you just live in you somehow.

C12:   Yeah, yeah. Right. And that's why too also at the conference um, I, I couldn't cope with anyone's reassurance. I mean people were so reassuring to me (T: Uhm, hmm) throughout the conference. People were so nice, so generous in, in their feedback. (T: Uhm, hmm, uhm, hmm) And at some point I just couldn't cope with it. Because it was clashing with my self-concept. And so, so when I came back what I did was ask for negative reass-, negative feedback (Laughing) as if to you know, (T: Uhm, hmm) balance things or something like that. But the point of course, is that,

that, um, I cannot let in, very easily, people's good comments about me, (T: Uhm, hmm) you know, good feedback. I can't ... (Sigh)

T12: It really clashes with (T: Uhm, hmm) what you hold inside about yourself.

C13: Yeah, yeah, yeah, yeah. And so, um, I guess, I mean, I, I don't know. I mean I don't, this is the thing Barbara, what I, this is what I wanted to ask you. I, I mean it is clear to me and to many people but also to me that you have attained self-acceptance. And it's just, to me, a major, major accomplishment. A major, major psychological accomplishment. So what I wanted to ask you is two things. One is, what, if, if you can think of, what are some of the things that may have, that, that you have found to be more, most helpful, in your attaining this psychological state. The other one is, um, when it, what happens to you when you are in trouble. When you have hardship. When you have, let's say, uh, it ... hardship in your life (T: Uhm, hmm) or rejection from someone you love (T: Yes, uhm, hmm) or ... Does that, does that, does your self-concept remain, um intact? Or, or do you, when these things happen, that are painful to you, do you sometimes fall back into, and I say fall back because I do remember that one day at the Illinois school you said "I started out with a lot of self-hatred like most of us." (T: Uhm, hmm) So, I remember (T: Uhm, hmm) that this has been also a journey for you. (T: Yes, yes) So anyway, do you fall back into self-accusation, self-blame and self-shame and all of that. So, those are the things I wanted to ask from you.

T13: Uhm, hmm. Right. That, that second question is somewhat easier to answer. (C: Yeah) That is, the one about whether I fall back. Um, I don't really fall back. (C: Uhm, hmm) Which is kind of (C: Uhm, hmm)'amazing (C: Uhm, hmm) because I, my self-hatred was very, very strong. (C: Uhm, hmm) Um, I feel very aware of my thoughts, um, and although I, I'd like to develop further in certain respects, and be less flawed, I do accept and so it's painful when I see, um, some manifestation of um, what I consider a character weakness, or flaw. But I don't feel like putting myself down or, or I don't have those, self-hating reactions. And when some, I get rejection, which just last year I did from my husband over a long, I mean there were months and various critical and very, um very angry, disapprov- you know, negative, a whole bunch of negative (Laughing) Uh, I was, it struck me that it didn't, I just simply did not absorb it as um, in that way. And it hurt my feelings, (C: Of course) a lot. (C: Yes) It made me sad (C: Uhm, hmm) and I was worried, scared, and so on and so forth. But I uh, (C: You didn't take it in) I didn't take it in. I just feel like I know what's, what's wrong with me. Why didn't, what it would be better for it to be. But I do not hate myself for it. And um, and,

and anyway most of what he was criticizing what was wrong anyway it was distorted (Laughing) from my point of view, I mean. It, it, it, it could be something that's completely accurate, coming in, I mean (C: Uhm, hmm) someone's criticizing me for something that I feel critical about, it happened, and for the most part it wasn't there. (inaudible) So, that's ... so I guess, am I, clear?

C14: Yeah, yeah, that's just it. Really. You don't fall back into it.

T14: I don't seem to ...

C15: Into some flagellating attitude.

T15: I don't. I don't. I don't get depressed. I don't have responses that I used to have years ago (C: Yes, yes, yes, yes) Uh, I do have a, uh, what I consider not a character flaw, but a vulnerability which has to do with my upbringing. But I don't think it's the same thing that's, it's really something I'd like to be free of and that is a susceptibility to humiliation. I, it's important that I am treated in, within a certain range of respect. And it makes me very angry if I am not. (C: Uhm, hmm) Um, but ... Uh, uh, I don't turn against (C: Uhm, hmm) myself. (C: Wow!) I don't know, but it's, it does hurt and that came up in that problem with my husband. (C: Uhm, hmm) So, and do you have any reaction to what (C: Well) I've said now (C: Yes) I'll be glad to address (C: Yes) the other part (C: Yes, yes) of the question.

C16: Well to me, it's hopeful indeed, it's hopeful. It's just hopeful to hear this. (T: Uhm, hmm) Because it's attainable. (T: Uhm, hmm) I know that and you know what this is the thing. I'm gonna get there. (T: Uhm, hmm) I mean, I mean, I'm just, I'm not going (T: You're determined) I'm just not going to relent. I'm just not.

T16: Uhm, hmm. You're not going to give up on yourself.

C17: No, no, no. Because you know the other part of it is, (Voice quakes) I know I'm a good person. (T: Uhm, hmm) There's no reason, absolutely no reason, why I should, absorb this nonsense. (Voice breaking) (T: Uhm, hmm) Just absolutely no reason.

T17: It's not valid.

C18: It's not.

T18: You're, you're ab- rationally you're absolutely sure.

C19: I'm positive. I'm not those things. (T: Uhm, hmm) So I'm not going to, I'm going to, I'm going to purge them out of me. I'm going to somehow. (T: Uhm, hmm) So when I hear you saying these things, it makes me very hopeful that this is really possible. That even in the face of hardship of the rejection from, from the one I may love the most and I love the most in, in this case you know, from your own husband and in the case, in the one I love the most is my own husband. And so even in the face of – if that should ever happen (T: Uhm, hmm) you know that we went through a period of, of that, even then, I would not (T: Uhm, hmm) absorb (T: Uhm, hmm) this, this um ...

T19: The judgment against you.

C20: The judgment. No, no, no. And not to say, not to say also that I wouldn't that I am not going to continue to observe myself with as, as objective eyes as I possibly can to, to, to realize my flaws. You know, to (T: Uhm, hmm) not to say that, I'm not going to see – I'm going to try to see myself always as accurately as possible (T: Uhm, hmm) including my flaws. (T: Uhm, hmm) But,

T20: But that's different than hating yourself.

C21: That's different. That's very different. That's just very different.

T21: Uhm, hmm. Uhm, hmm. So you're absolutely determined you're also, well you just, you're determined that you're just not going to stop, to, to purge or free yourself from this contamination.

C22: This poison, you know.

T22: A kind of poison (C: Yes) that's got into you (C: Yes) Uhm, hmm. (C: No) Uhm, hmm. And then my remarks about my experience and the way in which I don't seem to fall back is supportive to, hope makes you feel, (C: Yeah) hope, you know ...

C23: That this is possible. You know, that it is not a transient state based on circumstances that this is really a, a, a psychological state to be attained.

T23: Uhm, hmm. The self-acceptance.

C24: Yes, yes. (T: is attainable) Yes, yes, yes. Even in the face of, rejection.

T24: Yeah. Unfortunate circumstances (C: Yeah) pull one down from, in one way or another (C: Yes) still don't have to get absorbed and, and tap into that old reaction. (C: Yes) Uhm, hmm (C: Yes, yes) and you had another question. The first question is –

C25: Yeah, the, the first question is um, if you can, can pin down some of the elements that help you get to this point. That were most helpful in getting you to this point of self-acceptance.

T25: I, uh, over the years I've had a lot of um, client-centered therapy. I mean, I was the client in client-centered therapy and I would say that the work in that context was a great deal of it. That's a general, uh, just the basic work of being understood and accepted, (C: Uhm, hmm) by people.

I, I really experienced as genuinely, appreciative toward me, accepting toward me, and understanding a strong woman. And it really was through a series of therapies over (C: Various therapists) yeah, different, points in time.

C26: And with different therapists.

T26: Yeah. Diff- several different client-centered therapists. (C: Uhm, hmm) And then the work that goes on in my own mind is in relation to the therapist but not in the presence of the therapist and I think there's a kind of way in which we take the therapist home with us, when it's good, (C: Uhm, hmm) when the relationship is working. Um, and I do feel that I, I have been fortunate in some of my relationships, people who accepted me. My third husband, the father of my children, uh he could be irritable and cranky, get angry at me, uh often, for good reason. Uh, his basic attitude toward me was very accepting and understanding. It, right in the center of my flaws there was a way which he was able to love me and accept me. (C: Uhm, hmm) You know, that's really more true with Jerry, my third husband (C: Uhm, hmm) than my present husband (C: Uhm, hmm) who is much more withholding. In fact that, in a way, love Bob as much as I do, he's not a very therapeutic presence. (C: Uhm, hmm) (T laughs) He's really not. (C: Uhm, hmm) 'Cause he, he's touchy himself and he's not very, very giving to me in that way. (C: Uhm, hmm) And um, sometimes it hurts me. (Laughs) (C: Sure, sure, sure) And I complain about it, (C: Sure, sure) and it's an issue between us that we're working on. (C: Uhm, hmm) But it's interesting because it really, it really doesn't, soak in. (C: Uhm, hmm) Uh, and I think I, I should have better and of course I wouldn't be with Bob if he didn't give me a great deal. (C: Uhm, hmm) And including a great deal of love. But, he, he – he could be a better interpersonal environment (C: Uhm, hmm) than he is. But the fact that he isn't doesn't, really does not undermine me at all. But my, my, my husband, Jerry, we, husband who is the father of my children, is emotionally extremely generous and very smart. And so he could understand me, very accurately (C: Uhm, hmm) and accept me. And also my second husband, who was a, was a client-centered psychologist, he was a brilliant therapist. And that relationship was, in many ways, a therapeutic relationship for me, because he really valued me. And so I was – I was, this is my 65th year of living and I mean it really, um, I uh, it, I guess I would say I was in my 40s before I felt really – had reached a solid level (C: Uhm, hmm) of self-acceptance. In the middle 40s I think. (C: Uhm, hmm, uhm, hmm) So, it took a long time. (C: Uhm, hmm) um ... more specifically I think, that the, the direct addressing of the experiences of self-hatred which I did mostly in the context of a therapy relation. But also just working on my, myself, was therapeutic and helped free me. It's like a differentiation of, that occurred between, something I felt was a um, a weakness in myself, or a flaw – something that I, I would like to be better, in a way, I would like to be better from the self-hatred. Instead of, when you have self-hatred I think the things that you have legitimate basis for being somewhat critical of yourself about, just – sort of, merge, you know?

C27: Yes. Yes. Yes. (Sigh)

T27: So a differentiation, I think, uh, occurred. So exploring the feeling of self-hatred and then just thinking about it. Relating myself to the things about myself that, you know come to mind, in the context of those hating feelings. Led to a differentiation and I don't know, somehow the, the myth, ah, the – the basis for the hatred just sort of gradually disappeared. (Laugh) So, I'm a flawed human being. (C: Uhm, hmm) Mostly, pretty decent, but sometimes not – so … (C: Yeah. Yes, exactly.) So, that work I, I think did a lot. (C: Yeah, right.) And then the luck and the, you know, I think that, I've been, I've been um, able, to – avoid bad experiences quite a lot during my adulthood. So for example (Phone rings in background) I would, oh, the machine's on, um (Phone rings again) which I think is another valid thing where in answering your question, in there. Um, I kind of instinctively, I think, (Laugh) because I was so hurt and so vulnerable, I, yeah some people go toward people who treat them the same way that they've been treated. And somehow I tended in my life to avoid people who were abusive. Scooted away, I just scooted away as fast, and I've been lucky because I haven't been in situations where I had to stay, around somebody. I mean that's whether it's socially or in work, or, in my selection of men, in my life, really. I mean when I say Bob I love so much and I'm glad we're married. But he's like my poorest choice in regard to that being uh, given. Uh, a sense of um, uncritical, um, love. (C: Yeah, yeah) And I mean, he's got other qualities I, so … (Sigh) I, I think probably it's wise if one can do it (C: Yeah) to, to um to, avoid. (C: Yes) And in regard to my mother (C: Yes) who was a source of, basically was the source of my self-hatred, I was um, moderately dutiful. (C: Uhm, hmm) Um, and um, I'm glad I was, somewhat dutiful. (C: Uhm, hmm) If I had loved her, I would have, behaved very differently. (C: Uhm, hmm) But she really did, kill it except for the sympathy, a little bit, so when she died, I was present when she died, and I, and I wept a few tears, um I felt sorry for her (C: Uhm, hmm) because I could, I knew ways in which her life had been difficult. But she'd been a real, she'd really fucked-up. And um, that's just the truth. She was hurtful and damaging to me. I feel like she almost destroyed me. And um, so, I, I did avoid my mother a lot. And it was in the, even though as she aged she got more neutral. Some of the intensity of her criticality and a meanness in her just sort of faded. So – she wasn't so bad, in the last years of her life when she was weak. But, still it didn't elicit too much. But I, you know, I did some duty by her. So I don't know, there may be something more but, maybe, maybe if, you could say what your reactions are, if you have anything that's not clear, you want me to say more about ... and then your own reactions, I'd be very interested. (Pause)

C28: (Sigh) Well, um, that what you said about, you started out by saying that you, you had done a lot of work on client-centered, with client-centered therapy, therapists. (T: Yeah, yeah) And I think that if you know, I, I work with Marge and um, but I also think that, it would be beneficial for me to talk to, also other people about this. Because, I feel right now and I have, I talked to Marge today even, but it, it even after I hung up I said I, I need to tell Marge this, that I feel I real – right now I'm at an impasse in terms of this particular issue. And I will address with her next Monday. But um, but the thing is, I, I, I, I think that, naturally, I mean obviously, working with other people bring out, brings out other aspects of it.

T28: Yes different personalities (C: Exactly) and even if they work almost the same way (C: Yes) yeah.

C29: So, so that's good to hear. That you know, she, she – you, you saw a few people and that was helpful, or several people – you know, various therapists, at, at different times, I understand.

T29: At different times. Right.

C30: Yeah, but nonetheless, right now I'm thinking about that the importance of that particular thing. (T: Uhm, hmm, uhm, hmm) Um, the other thing um, that was good to hear is that you've surrounded yourself with people who, you – that you avoided people who are critical and, and abusive and you know that you just, don't stay around. (T: Uhm, hmm) And um, I have too for the most part. At some point, you know. I mean I have been able to, more and more, remove myself from, in this case, my mother's family and you know, the, her family of choice and, and, who, who were also very abusive. And now even my own mother, um ... (T: Uhm, hmm) that I am really gaining distance and, and protecting myself. And then you talk about um, Jerry. (T: Uhm, hmm) You know, he, the father of your children and how therapeutic he was and I think that applies to Joseph as well. Um, Joseph's just so loving you know, just, he is so adoring of me, is the word. (T: Uhm, hmm) (C laughs) Just so adoring of me. I, I don't think anybody ever, has or will, ever love me that much. (T: Uhm, hmm) You know, just, and I, and it's wonderful. But he tends to be critical. I mean, he and I'm not, right, in small ways, and I'm going to give you an example what I mean. But the reason I think this is very important is because he must learn, he needs to, and he will learn. Because (T: Uhm, hmm) he is, he cares enough. (T: Uhm, hmm) But, he must learn that he must not be critical. He must not even in small ways. And a good example of this is that yesterday, I went grocery shopping and then I came home, put the groceries on the kitchen table and ran to the computer to get the email and left everything like that and (T: Uhm, hmm) he had cleaned the kitchen, right before. (T: Uhm, hmm) So he comes from the yard, looks at the, at the table and I'm doing yoga and he says "I had cleaned the kitchen. It was so clean. And look what you did. (T: Uhm, hmm) Look, you've left it a mess and blah, blah, blah, blah, blah" (T: Uhm, hmm) And I'm thinking "What is the big deal. Nothing's going to spoil. Everything (T: Uhm, hmm) I needed to be in the refrigerator was in the refrigerator. What was the big deal. He wasn't getting read- to have dinner. What is the big deal if he (T: Uhm, hmm) the table is full of groceries? What is the big deal?" So, I go upstairs angry and I start putting things away. And I get mad at him. I, you know, I started yelling, not that you know, that's my own character flaw, I start yelling and saying "Oh Joseph, what is, what is the big deal, and you blah, blah, blah, blah, blah." And then he defends himself and then we, we have an argument. And then later on he realizes that yeah, this was unnecessary and he apologizes and I apologize for yelling and so on. But the point is that I'm just too vulnerable. I, I cannot take any criticism, small as it may be (T: Uhm, hmm) like he wasn't saying "You're a slob." He just said "I left the kitchen clean, and look what you did." (T: Uhm, hmm) "I want you to clean it." But the thing is, I must, I have to tell, because, but he was upset, he was annoyed.

T30: He was upset and annoyed.

C31: That's the problem. (T: Uhm, hmm) So, the thing that he is going to have to learn is that if he, if he has a problem he needs to talk to me in a kind, in a pleasant tone of voice. In a, in a noncritical. He can say "Alejandra, you know it just truly bothers me when I see the kitchen like that. Would you mind putting things away just so I" then I say "OK Joseph, wait until I finish my yoga and I'll go right upstairs (T: Uhm, hmm) and do it, blah, blah, blah." But, little things like that. That he's so used to getting annoyed about things and, and … and talking to me in that tone of voice (T: Uhm, hmm) and you know what I, I just will not take it anymore. (T: Uhm, hmm) Just, I just won't. (T: Uhm, hmm) And so I need to um …

T31: Uh, improve your uh, in- interpersonal environment in that particular way of influencing your husband to find another way to address things that are annoying him or bothering him that you do that you're saying you feel you'd be willing to address and look at, but you can't, you can't take the critical tone and attitude (C: Exactly) that comes out because it, it seeps into you and, and I guess you're implying it, it undermines the development that you want. (C: Precisely) Which is to free yourself of that. So you need him to help you more in that way. (C: Yeah, exactly, uh,) So that's something you're saying I guess, you need to continue working on with him.

C32: Yeah. Yeah, yeah, yeah. And I think of it as I hear you saying (clears throat) talking about Jerry and talking about Bob (T: Uhm, hmm) and the differences, you know. That the importance of, a, a very accepting environment. (T: Uhm, hmm) In, especially with your you, you know, mate or your spouse (T: Yes) and so on. So, um, so that's another thing that I think from what you said. (T: Uhm, hmm) And the last thing, I mean it's just so, so, so important. You said that, um, you were "somewhat dutiful" with your mother but that you would have been very different had she been different with you. (T: Yes, I think so.) And that, you remained you know, somewhat dutiful (T: Uhm, hmm) and that, and that was OK. But that in, inside and that you said she killed it. (T: Uhm, hmm) What did, can you tell me what is it when you say it (T: It) ye-

T32: Well, I think it would have been natural, to love her, I mean she did give me – she did the best she could. For one thing. But she also had some strengths. And um, I, I really can see ways that I have good qualities that came from her and ways that she – we were very poor and she functioned in such a effective way that I really didn't feel poor. I mean it's amazing how poor we were and that I didn't feel that. I wasn't ashamed of being poor, or, uh frightened. I mean there were disappointments like "Well, we won't have, a Christmas tree (Laughs) for Christmas." Or there were, you know, concrete things that were disappointing, uh, because of the lack of money. But she managed so well and really admirable that discipline that she had, the resourcefulness and so on. (Sigh) (Pause) I, I guess, I feel that my mother loved me. She did love me. But, she was so fucked up herself, that, what came through to me was tremendous disapproval, and hatred, and disgust, and just very strong negative feelings. And that what would have been otherwise a natural feeling of love for her, just got wiped out. So, uh I, well some, I have sympathy for her because I know how she came to be, to a certain extent. I mean I know something about her origins and the way she was treated and the way she was I think, that's pretty understandable to me. But, she behaved so destructively toward me, created such fear in me, and such self-hatred and you know, it almost completely destroyed what were to me, to be natural love feelings for her. (C: Yeah) So I do feel a certain appreciation for her and I feel sorry for her. And I did feel sorry for her once I got over being afraid of her. Which didn't happen until I was about 35 only losing the fear of her came before I was free from the self-hatred. (C: Uhm, hmm) But ... so, I don't know, Alejandra, am I answering your questions?

C33: Yes you did. Yes you did. (T: I answered ...) Yes you did. Yes you did. Because you, that's what I wanted to, that's what I thought I, you meant, but you confirmed it when you say "It" you were talking about the love. (T: Yes) the love (T: The natural) the natural love. That would have existed ...

T33: ... for the woman who gave me life and who nurtured me and who took care of me, made clothes for me. She did do things. (C: Yeah) But she did other things that just ...

C34: Yeah, you know what's amazing to me is that you're just describing my situation, you know, it's just – (T: A replica.) It really is a replica. But the important part for me to hear is because I also think that my mother does at some level love me. That this is the thing – where, from the time I was born 'til I was 10 years, about 10 years old, she was adoring. (T: Uhm, hmm) You know, she was very loving (T: Uhm, hmm) very affectionate and warm and ... then when I became an adolescent she turned on me, forever. Forever, forever, forever. And then became extremely, extremely destructive and just did some very cruel, cruel things. She messed up big time. Big time, big time, big time. (T: Uhm, hmm) Without going into it. (T: Yes) She really, really, really, really, really made some very disastrous mistakes. Uh, tragic mistakes. (T: In relation to you) In relation to me. And she, for one thing she took me to live at a house where it was just – I just, you know with a family who, who was just, who were just abusing in every way there is. But anyway, so that was one. And, and you know she didn't see it, she didn't – but anyway. So all I'm, what I'm saying Barbara, what, why this is important, very important to me to hear is that, you are able to say without any, qualms about it, with any, without – clearly without guilt or shame, (T: Uhm, hmm) that, you just didn't feel the love that you would have otherwise. (T: Uhm, hmm) You know to just say "OK" (inaudible) and you're clear that she destroyed it. (T: Uhm, hmm) And uh, and so, (T: Uhm, hmm) so this is important to me because I sometimes get confused, you know, that, I'm at a point right now in my life where I want to continue to, you know be dutiful in some ways, which I am. And but there, re, really a little – det, they're detached really. (T: Uhm, hmm) They're detached. You know, this is out of, this is, these are things I want to do for you, (T: Uhm, hmm) and it's OK.

T34: Yeah, but you're not doing them out of a feeling of giving. (C: No) Feeling of wanting to.

C35: No, no. It's, it's a duty I choose to keep. (T: Uhm, hmm) And it's important for me to, you know, it's important for me to do so. (T: Yeah) It's important for me to remain somewhat connected. But I think the – also I need to become comfortable with the fact that, I know my feelings for her have drastically changed. That I was extremely loving of her. Just very really loving, very loving. And that um, and that has changed. You know, and that I need to, and that I need to say, you know, "You killed it. I'm sorry. You killed it." (T: Uhm, hmm) And you know, I am only human. And I'm not going to remain connected to this idea of filial love, ideal of filial love, that, that is just, it, you know.

T35: That hasn't been lived, lived adequately enough. Is that?

C36: Exactly, that …

T36: That it was lived. Your mother did, what you've told me is that you did get love from her, strong love from her, and you responded with strong love. And then, for whatever reasons she did it, at your pubescence or adolescence, she turned on you and against you. And that has just, killed, or almost completely killed your – your feelings (C: Yes) for her.

C37: Exactly, I mean (Sigh) that's just it. Almost completely killed, my feelings for her, at this point. It's just, huh. (T: Uhm, hmm) You know, I've tried for decades. (T: Uhm, hmm) I'm, I'm …

T37: You tried to, to love her or,

C38: Yes, I've tried for decades to show her my love. (T: Uhm, hmm) And at this point, I, I will not at, at this point, it's just not there anymore. I mean, I do have a bond. (T: Uhm, hmm) And I do have some, warmth. (T: Uhm, hmm) And I don't know exactly what it is – what to call it. But something's there, (T: Yes) because I was upset after all when I didn't hear from her. (T: Yes) I was worried. (T: Worried about her) So there's something there. But what, what it is exactly I don't know. But as far as the, the worry, the concern, the, the tenderness, the warmth, the affection, the love, – that's gone. (T: That's gone.) (C sighs) You know and I just need to become comfortable with it. (T: Uhm, hmm) So when I hear you say that, this is a fill-in reaction to what you're saying, to what you said. (T: Yeah, it –) When I hear you say these things, I said, "You know,

(Laughs) this is only natural that I feel this way." (T: Uhm, hmm) You know, I mean it's, this is in response to her actions. (T: Uhm, hmm) To, um ...

T38: Hearing from me that I, seem to be, and I think it's true, accept the fact that I, by the time she died I just had the smallest amount of, caring, for her. Because I feel that her behavior toward me, destroyed my love, almost completely. (C: Uhm, hmm) And I'll say almost since there was something. Hearing that from me, heck, you're saying helps you feel, a little more comfortable with the way in which it's very similar for you in relation to your mother. (C: Yes) Is that right?

C39: And hearing you say, say it so openly without any guilt, without any shame (T: Uhm, hmm) guilt and shame about it. (T: Shame, uhm, hmm) You know it's like, um, this is in response to that. This is just a natural phenomenon. (Laughing) It's not that you're a, an un- (T: Uhm, hmm) ungrateful person. (T: Ungrateful or bad or something) Yes. You're not an ingrate, you're not a, you know, like which I might sometimes worry about. (T: Uhm, hmm) And I, and it was helpful also to hear you say, "Yeah, there are some ways in which I am the way I am, that are good because of her." (T: Uhm, hmm) Because this is true for me as well. (T: Uhm, hmm) You know that, yes there are some things she gave me that are, important. (T: Uhm, hmm) And that, (T: You value in yourself.) Yes, but that, still the fact remains, I cannot be forever grateful for that. And, and still I have to say "Well this is true, but this is bigger and this is also true." (T: Uhm, hmm) Much, much bigger.

T39: Yes it doesn't negate, (C: Ultimately) bigger doesn't negate the truth of these aspects that were good for you from her. But the other really, you're saying, it's just more and bigger, (C: Oh, yeah) than, the damage, the, the mistakes (C: Oh, yeah) the hurt was, overrides ...

C40: The destruction, the destruc- the ways in which she's been destructive (T: Uhm, hmm) are much, are certainly override the ways in which she was, she was loving, (T: Uhm, hmm) way back then, you know, it's just (T: Uhm, hmm) uh ...

T40: The overriding is in terms of the overall feeling that you're left with toward her, that is, you can rationally point to ways she was good. And ways that she affected you. And you can say "Well, I'm grateful for that.' But, it, you, you're saying that you don't believe you have cause to feel uh, overall gratitude and love because she was so destructive. (C: Yes) Is that getting at it?

C41: That's, that's it. Well that's just it. But I, I don't need to cling to this. You know, (Laughs) (T: Uhm, hmm) and say "Well, but look at this, and she gave you this." (T: Uhm, hmm) I don't need to, I mean because the real, the reality is, she also gave me that. (T: Uhm, hmm) And that is powerful and massive and, and ... and it's much more of, in terms of even the length of time, you know. (T: Uhm, hmm) I'm 45 years old, so for 35 years, she's she, she's given me, um very destructive, (T: Uhm, hmm) interaction. So, for 10 she gave me, yes the 10 are important, (T: Yes) were, at critical age. But, the point however remains that, uh, I cannot, try to, justify, or, or I cannot try to base my feelings on that because it's unreal. This is what I feel. And it's based on what she's done for me the most, most of, largely, you know, the most of my life. And the, what I feel is detachment. I just want, (Sigh) as much distance as I can have, you know. I just I, I, I'm not, I'm not the way I was. I, I, I just don't feel this warmth and ... The uh, you should have seen me before. My friends used to say they wanted to be my daughters (Laughs) because I was so, no – they wanted me, they wanted to be my mothers, because I was so ...

T41: You were so (C: Uhm, hmm) loving and (C: Yes) devoted. (C: Yes, yes, yes) Uhm, hmm, uhm, hmm. And that was in the face of not any reciprocation or, the other side of that is to get love back (C: Yeah) and to have a sense of being loved and appreciated. You were getting the opposite of that. But you were still (C: Yeah) trying to express ... and now you're saying you just, – need to, I don't know if the expression should be, allow yourself to, to live out the way you, you do feel toward her which is, a, a, avoidant? (C: Yeah) Avoidant, and very little (C: Yeah) sin- sincerely, very little warmth. There's (C: Yes) some there like you can worry about her, (C: Yeah) when you didn't hear from her (C: Yeah) and ...

C42: Sincerely very little warmth. Sincerely very, sincerely very little warmth. (T: Uhm, hmm.) Very little warmth. Very little warmth. (T: Uhm, hmm.) It's just amazing. (T: And that's the truth.) Yeah, that's the truth, you know? Just, that's the truth. (T: Uhm, hmm) Um, it's amazing to me that this could happen. But it did. It did. It did. It did. It did. It did. I mean it's just amazing to me. It's just amazing to me that she could possibly kill my love for her but she has, she has, she has.

T42: It was strong.

C43: Oh my God ...

T43: You really loved your mother.

C44: Oh God, I loved her so, (T: So much.) very much. So very much, uhm, hmm, so very much. (T: It's really incredible for it ...) Yeah, (T: ... to be destroyed.) Yeah, yeah. I just didn't think, I just didn't think, I couldn't conceive, it could ever happen. So, um, the other thing that you said that was also important to me, is that, very important, is that oh, and, and with this we end, is that, yes, you know, you say, yeah that she had love. Your mother had love for you. But that she herself, but that the, you know because of her own mental s- emotional state, what came out was criticism and judgment and, and so on and so forth. But you said yeah, I know she loved me but what she gave me was this. For whatever reason. And you said yeah I know she had this, (T: Uhm, hmm) you know, background and so on. (T: Yeah) But whatever – but in other words you're not apologizing for your feelings. (T: Uhm, hmm) That's the point. (T: Uhm, hmm) But it's important for me. (T: I see) Because you said, because that is exactly the situation with my mother.

T44: You can understand a lot about her.

C45: Yes, she gave me love. She has love for me at some level. Y-yes she is a very emotionally, um, damaged woman. (T: Uhm, hmm) Very, very, very much so. (T: Uhm, hmm) Yes, she had a um, a, a, a difficult life. A difficult childhood. There are reasons for which she became the way she – she is. (T: Uhm, hmm) But you know what? It just doesn't matter. (T: Uhm, hmm) The fact remains, that this is what she gives me, and this is what I respond to. And I'm not going to make apologies or excuses for it. (T: Uhm, hmm) It doesn't matter.

T45: Uhm, hmm. It doesn't matter in regard to, how you, respond in your true self, to her. Even though intellectually you can understand her and if you thought of her as, or more objectively you could have compassion perhaps even, right? for her.

C46: I mean if she is a client, or she's, you know, another per ... (T: Uhm, hmm, yeah, another person) yeah, she's a kind, but, but if she's not dam- damaging, she's, but she's not dam- hurting me, or (T: Uhm, hmm) or, you know. Then I can see yeah, well wonderful. But the fact is, this is what she's giving me, and this is what I'm going to respond to. This is all I can do. In, and so I like how you phrase it. Uh, how you phrase it "in my true self." (T: Uhm, hmm) "This is how I feel." (T: Uhm, hmm) This is, this is how I feel. (T: Uhm, hmm) So, with, on that note we, our time's up Barbara.

T46: Is it, yeah, uhm, hmm, uhm, hmm.

## COMMENTS

T1: Hmm, when you feel like doing it, still keeping the video on. If you have any comments about the way we worked together, (C: Uhm, hmm) I'd be interested ...

C1: Well, you know, right off the bat I could tell you certain things. I mean, I'm just lucky, (Laughs) to be talking with you, because your situation resembles mine so much. I appreciate the fact that you've been so candid and open. I really, really, really appreciate that. Um ...

T2: But feeling you're lucky because it, uh, happens that there're some similarities (C: Great similarities.) in what happened to me and what happened to you.

C2: Yeah – great similarities, great similarities.

T3: It could be otherwise, I mean then that would be a different, completely different interaction.

C3: Yeah. But I appreciate the fact that you've, you know, you've said, that you've said what you've said. That you were free to, to, to tell me your story in a nutshell. Um, that you tell me candidly, um, you know, um what you've been through, what you went through. Because this is important and I'll tell you why. Because here you are having gone through what you went through, and here you are now. You know, in a state of, in a mature psychological state. Concerned about others. Treating others well. And treating yourself well. Which is a mature psychological state. So, it tells me, that um, this is what it tells me – it tells me that um, (Pause) again, you know it's, it's, it's, it's it's a reality, that it's not just a construct. That this is possible. (T: Uhm, hmm) That this – here you are. Here you are. To prove it, I mean to, not to prove it but to, to, to ...

T4: Illustrate it?

C4: Illustrate it, to confirm to me that this is possible. This is possible. And um, so that's one thing, one reaction I have. The other part of it is, I feel very free, for some reason, um, with you to, to, this is not to say that I haven't felt like this with other therapists or that I don't feel it with, like this with Marge, but (T: Uhm, hmm) but, but I do feel very free with you to ... to be as intense as I need to be. (T: Uhm, hmm) That if I am, that if my anger level is rising I don't need to, subdue it. (T: Uhm, hmm, uhm, hmm) And I think it is because you have a comfort with it. You know, that you're not, (T: Uhm, hmm) it's not, put off by it.

T5: I don't give any indication that it's difficult for me.

C5: That, "Whoa God, calm down, calm down."

T6: So you're free.

C6: I'm free to just, (T: To go) emote.

T7: Uhm, hmm. And that's good, right? Good.

C7: But, and that feels good. Um, and so I, I also felt that you really very accurately understood. Um, what I was saying ... and I was glad you verbalized it. Because I was, you know, I was – told me you did. Um ...

T8: Some, uh some of my responses were rather long. Uh, was that, makes a demand on the client, on you?

C8: Yeah. Well, no because they were very, very relevant to my point. Isn't that you were digressing. You were answering my questions. (T: Uhm, hmm) In a, in a, in an explicit, even generous way. (T: Uhm, hmm) As far as I saw it.

T9: I see, uh, you felt that way about it rather than, "When is she gonna stop?"

C9: No, right. Right, right. It would have felt that way, had it not been relevant, to what I was (T: Uhm, hmm) thinking. If you had digressed.

T10: I see, but I, (C: But you didn't) I didn't, (C: No you didn't) digress?

C10: No. No you didn't. So it was, instead, kind of riveting. (Laughs) (T: Uhm, hmm) So, um ...

T11: I wondered about that. How about the empathic response to some early, one of my empathic responses as rather long.

C11: I didn't observe it that it was long. (T: You didn't) I didn't even notice.

T12: You didn't notice it that way.

C12: No, no, no. So I didn't even know what you would be referring to because I didn't – never ...

T13: It wasn't the thought, (C: No, no, no) as we were (C: No, no) interacting.

C13: No. Um, the other thing I would say is that oh, oh, oh, oh. The certain phrases that you used, that solidified my feelings. For example, you said, at some point "And this is the truth" (T: Uhm, hmm) about my feelings for my mother. "And this is the truth" you said, (T: Uhm, hmm) and that cements it for me. (T: Uhm, hmm) You know, it's like, yes this is the truth. (T: Uhm, hmm) So your choice of words, was helpful in that it just connect the, you know, my, my gut with my mind, you know? (Laughing) (T: Right) It's just like, it just solidified it. I guess that's the best way to say that. It's just that, it made it to be true because it, it was, a, spoken and it was accurate. (T: Uhm, hmm) And it just ...

T14: It was accurate, you didn't, you didn't, you didn't feel I was imposing ... it I, I, because when I said those, that word or that phrase, I, uh, it came out of me because that seemed to be what you, part of what you were getting at "That's just true." And so it's, it formulated and in my mind that way. (C: Right) I didn't mean it to be an imposition.

C14: It wasn't. (T: No) I didn't feel it that way. I didn't feel that you were, that you were, um, adding to, adding anything to (T: Uhm, hmm) you didn't add anything to what I was saying. You just verbalized my feelings or my, what I was getting at. (T: Uhm, hmm) You just say "And this is the truth." (T: Uhm, hmm) And you know, I wanted to say "Yes, this is the truth!" um, so …

T15: So certain phrases like that, that were particularly, had … (C: Impact) impact, yeah.

C15: Yes, yes, yes, yes. Because, again, because they were accurate. They were just … (Sigh) But you used another phrase in the beginning and I can't recall what it was. But it was the same thing, you know. Um … Yes! Because what happens is that many times, excuse me, many times I was kind of um, excuse me, the, the feelings and the words don't necessarily match. I mean, the, I don't necessarily have um, a, a, a perfect articulation of what I'm trying to say. (T: Uhm, hmm) So when you catch it, (T: Uhm, hmm) it just makes a match between body and mind. (T: Uhm, hmm) And it just feels very right. (T: Uhm, hmm) You know, it feels as if, "Now this is true." You see now I can get, grab a hold of this concept. (T: Uhm, hmm) That's what I'm saying.

T16: Uhm, hmm, uhm, hmm. There's a, it doesn't, it's not adding anything to what you mean, or (C: No) what you're getting at (C: No) but it has some kind of psychological, emotional connecting effect.

C16: Yeah, connecting effect. (Phone rings in background) Connecting effect and reality effect. (T: Uhm, hmm, uhm, hmm) (Phone rings again)

T17: Get back again the truth of it. The truth of what you've been expressing, (C: Yeah) is, hmm …

C17: Is out there. Is now, it's real you know, it's see, you can touch it. We can call it, "this is the truth." (T: Uhm, hmm) You see, it's here. (T: Uhm, hmm) It's plain. (T: Uhm, hmm) It's out in the open.

T18: Uhm, hmm. It sounds like it's a feeling too, a feel- the, something is, it's, it's a validation, a verification, experience. Or something like that. (C: Uhm, hmm) I know it's hard to …

C18: It makes it real, really. (T: Uhm, hmm) It just makes it real. Because now I have the concept very clear in my mind. (T: Uhm, hmm, uhm, hmm) I can grab a hold of it. (Pause) So, overall, really – I mean this is, (Sigh) a very productive session. (T: Uhm, hmm, I'm glad) A very productive session. A very productive session. A very productive session. (T: Uhm, hmm) (Pause)

T19: Here's a question uh, (C: Yes) about my behavior (C: Yes) I'd like to check out with you. (C: Yes) I'm aware, of the, that I'm, I'm ex, ex, expressive, when I, make empathic responses. I mean I don't make them in an aloof, cool way. There's a way which, of course it depends on the material. It depends on the emotion of the client, it varies, a response to response. But, I feel like my empathic responses are, from my whole, my body. (C: Uhm, hmm) My whole self. (C: Uhm, hmm) And so, they just come out and I don't know exactly what my face does or so, but, but I feel like they're idiosyncratic. (C: Uhm, hmm) That is they're me expressing what I've thought I understood. (C: Uhm, hmm) And I just wonder if that, comes across, uh if it has any good or bad effect. (C: Uhm, hmm) I, I mean I've thought well, maybe it could be, distracting (C: Uhm, hmm) to someone. Because I'm such a um, I feel like I'm such a distinct personality, even though what I'm doing is following, that I'm still a very distinct personality. (C: Uhm, hmm) I'm not, I'm not minimizing myself, even though I'm not, I mean part of our interview I was talking about myself because you were asking me questions. So, I'm really, um referring more to the part where I'm purely empathically following, not the part where I was answering questions. Anyway, is my question clear at all?

C19: Yes it is, yes it is.

T20: I wonder if you have any thoughts.

C20: Yes, yes. Well at some point, (Laughing) at some point, I thought, I briefly smiled because I, at that point I noticed that we both speak with our hands!

T21: We both do! (Both C & T laughing)

C21: You know, I was going like that and you were going like that. (Laughter) I thought that was funny. It was like "Ooohhh, we're going to ..." and I really thought that was funny. Here we are, um, (T: Laughs) Um, so, but it didn't have a good or a bad effect. (T: Uhm, hmm) I just noticed it. (T: Yeah) And I thought it was funny, you know, (T: Uhm, hmm) that we, we express –

T22: We would have, both of us

C22: And that we speak with our bodies (T: Yes) you know, that, right. Um ...

T23: Yes, I'm aware that you do too, and everybody doesn't. (C: Yes, right, right) Not as much, that's strong in me and it's strong in you. (C: Yes, exactly) It is funny isn't it. (C: Yeah) We're waving! (C: Exactly! Uhm, hmm, uhm, hmm so) So you didn't feel, it was just there, you're saying.

C23: It was just there. That's what (T: Part of it) well, that's one thing. Um, the other thing again I notice and I said to, and I said this in the last interview we had, but, again I, I notice this presence that you do have that is very caring. And it comes across in your face. That, you really – it really matters to you what, what I was saying. That, that you were receptive to my pain. That it wasn't, you were not detached or removed from it. (T: Uhm, hmm) And that is apparent, (T: In my face – it shows?) in your face, shows that your eyes. Well, even, even I think that your, probably your, the body inclination. Yeah, that (T: Uhm, hmm) too. You're, you're, you know, you're um, mostly your face – facial expression and your eyes. So, (T: I see) uhm, hmm, yes. As far as the other, no it doesn't. In fact, if I think about it I, uh, that would be my preference. That you would respond with your body, your entire body. (T: Uhm, hmm) Because, (T: That's comfortable for you) because it's comfortable for me. It's how I am (T: Yeah) and so it's, feels compatible.

T24: Yeah. I can (inaudible) it might not be as comfor- comfortable for someone who is more, calm in their expressiveness.

C24: So. Could be. Could be. Could be. Could be. Right.

T25: But it's natural for you.

C25: For me, yes. But, but the reality of it is is that I just didn't really notice it. (T: Uhm, hmm) Except in that brief moment and it wasn't positive or negative. It was just there. (T: Uhm, hmm) So, yeah.

T26: Uhm, hmm. Uh, thank you.

C26: Yes. Well, thank you too. Thank you too. Thank you too Barbara, very much.

T27: So we, shall we?

C27: We can end.

# Chapter 29

# Client-centered demonstration interview 4 with Alejandra

## Therapist: Barbara Temaner Brodley
## (Videotaped July 21, 1997)

[The client began by mentioning several topics that she hoped to discuss during this session, then picked the one to start.]

C1: I want to talk about the relationship with my mother right now. How long ago? I think it was early in May, yes. That I told her that I wasn't going to be calling her any more regularly. I told her that I wasn't going to ... I used to call her every week for many, many years, every single Sunday. Every Sunday I used to just dread the call. My stomach shrunk.

T1: An ordeal.

C2: It was, it was, it was an ordeal every week because I never knew what was going to come up.

T2: What was going to come at you.

C3: Oh boy, it was just awful.

T3: But duty, duty, duty.

C4: Oh yes, exactly, exactly. Oh, I hated it. Oh, I hated it so much. It was awful, it was awful. It ruined my Sunday many times. (T: Uhm, hmm) And even Saturday I began to agonize because (T: Uhm, hmm) the call was coming. Then one day finally I told her that I was going to call her every other Sunday. And uh, and that was better. That was better. That was better. (T: Uhm, hmm) And up until April I was calling her every other Sunday. And so in April I told her that I was only going to call her once a month. And I said, "The reason is that because you're so rejecting

---

This is the fourth in a series of four videotaped therapy demonstration sessions with Barbara Brodley as therapist and a volunteer client, Alejandra [code name]. For confidentiality, the beginning and ending of this session have been excluded. The first session, not included here, occurred August 2, 1996.

These session transcripts were chosen specifically because they illustrate a client-centered therapist's responses to client questions. For a discussion of this subject see Chapter 16 in this volume.

of me and you're so cold to me that the calls are damaging to me." I told her the truth. (T: Directly) Which was a great accomplishment for me. (T: Uhm, hmm) I used to always kind of soften things and embellish. But no – I told her the truth and she said "OK." She didn't like it but she has great pride. So she wouldn't say anything else. (T: Uhm, hmm) She said "OK, fine."

T4: Uhm, hmm. No begging.

C5: Nothing, nothing. Or "How come?" (T: Uhm, hmm) Nothing, nothing. Just "Fine, that's what you want." Then in May, I said to her, "I don't even want to do these calls once a month." Oh God, I don't! I just want to know if she lives or dies. That's all that interests me at this point. (T: Uhm, hmm) I don't want anything else. So I said to her in May, "You know mother, I want to tell you that I don't want to call you anymore. All I want to do is write to you now. All I want to do is write to you." Um, and she said "OK," but her voice broke. She didn't like it. She didn't like it. And I said, "The reason is the way we relate, I can't do this anymore. From now on we're going to write to each other." Well, ever since we've been writing to each other her letters have become progressively more affectionate. She now calls me "daughter" which she never has. She signs her letters "love" or "kisses." And sometimes she writes things such as, "Please know that I love you with every beat of my heart." Or she writes, "Think of me, because I am always each and every day, I am constantly thinking of you." Or she'd say, I saw a girl seven years old and which reminded me of the time when you were seven and you danced in school and I cried reminiscing and so on. (T: Uhm hmm) One thing you must know is that my mother showed me her love up until I was about ten. (T: Uhm, hmm) She was so loving, (T: Uhm, hmm) so affectionate, so loving, so ...

T5: Uhm, hmm. I remember you told me that. And then it changed.

C6: Yes.

T6: So she's now becoming expressive, after all these years (C: Yeah) in the letters.

C7: Yes, yes.

T7: After you pushed her back.

C8: Yes, yes. (T: Uhm, hmm) So the thing is, it doesn't matter at this point. Really. (T: Uhm, hmm) I believe she is telling the truth. (T: Uhm, hmm) I believe she is accessing a deep, deep place in her heart that (T: Uhm, hmm) still has love for me.

T8: Uhm, hmm. But it doesn't, uh ...

C9: It doesn't matter. It just doesn't matter.

T9: It doesn't get ... (C: No) It doesn't get to you.

C10: No. It doesn't get to me. In other words it doesn't get to my tender feelings.

T10: Uhm, hmm. It doesn't bring out your ... You know it's true. You accept it. (C: Yeah, yeah) But it's, (C: But it, but ...) out there.

C11: Yeah, exactly. It's out there. It's out there. (T: Uhm, hmm) The thing is, it's hard for me to believe. In other words, I want to completely understand my feelings for my mother because at this point I don't. I cannot believe. (Pause) For a while in the letters I was continuing to be her therapist because the calls have always been me doing the listening, the understanding, the blah, blah, blah. (T: Yes) And her not even asking, "How are you?" Or being able to hear anything good about my life except, "The weather's good" and "There are squirrels in the back yard." Which is a fun thing for a person having grown up in a big city. (T: Uhm, hmm) I have an encounter with wild life. "Oh today I saw a squirrel and today I saw a deer." That she can tolerate and that's the extent of it. (T: Uhm, hmm) She would never let me talk about school. I was so excited to have had the opportunity to go to college here and so on. She would never allow me to talk about that. No, she wouldn't talk or let me talk about it. She wouldn't let me talk about how happy I was in my job. Once in a while. (T: Uhmm hmm) I cannot talk about Joseph [her husband]. He's not to be mentioned in our phone calls in 15 years. She doesn't know whether Joseph lives or dies. She will not allow that. I mean it. The calls were for her. The calls were not for me. The calls were not about how I was, about what's happening in my life. (T: Uhm, hmm) So I was hurt. I figured, "Well, I'm going to be her therapist." (T: Uhm hm) In the letters, for a while I started doing that. I started answering to each and every point and trying to understand and so on. (T: Uhm) It was fake. It was forced. It was dutiful again. (T: Uhm hmm) No way, no way, no way am I going to do this anymore! (T: Uhm, hmm) So, I started to I think, "No, no I'm doing this out of duty. I don't feel it. I don't care. I don't want to hear this." (T: Uhm, hmm) "I'm not interested if she's suffering." Really I'm not. I don't want to know if she's sick. I want to know if she lives or dies. That's all I care. (T: Uhm, hmm) That's all, that's all, that's all. (T: Uhm, hmm) So, it's just, for me Barbara, it's just so hard to believe that this is true. But it is true. (Uhm, hmm) It's true. But it is hard to believe that I am feeling this, that I'm saying it, that I'm not interested. I don't understand it. Not quite. I mean, I don't believe it, I just don't believe it.

T11: You don't believe it's possible (C: Yeah) even though it's before your eyes (C: It is!) and it is in you, but you don't believe it's possible that you could be so indifferent to (C: Yeah) your mother. (C: Yeah, yeah) You just can't ...

C12: I can't believe it's true.

T12: Somehow it doesn't make ... sense. Like the ground were suddenly up there or something. It's just (C: Yeah) out of possibility. And yet it's true.

C13: Yeah, exactly, exactly. (Short pause) Because I really loved her so deeply for so long. (T: Uhm, hmm) It's just unbelievable (T: How much) to me that this has happened. It's just inconceivable.

T13: Uhm, hmm. Because you loved her so much.

C14: Because I loved her so very much. (T: Uhm, hmm) I loved her, I loved her, I loved her so deep, so deep (sighs). (Pause) I was so grateful to her. I read a letter that I wrote when I turned 40. Just five years ago I still was worshipping the earth that she walked. I still was deeply grateful. I still was telling her, thanking her for all that she gave me. For having taught me how to love. I would go out of my way, Barbara, to show my love and affection to her. She was just rejecting and pushing me and pushing me and pushing me, pushing (sighs).

T14: So, recently (C: Oh) as the five years ago (C: Oh) you still adored her.

C15: Adored her. (T: Uhm, hmm) Adored her. Adored her. Adored her. I don't know. It's just amazing to me this has happened. (T: Uhm, hmm) It's just amazing. As recently as early last year in January I was there for her 81st birthday. The purpose of my trip was to celebrate her 81st birthday with her (T: Uhm, hmm) She got angry because she wanted me to pick her up Sunday morning. I have two friends in Columbia that are like my sisters, and I said to her "I won't be able to pick you up Sunday morning because I'm going to go out with Dolores and her mother." And she said, "But I wanted to go to the philharmonic." I said, "We won't be able to because if I don't see Dolores this Sunday then everybody goes back to work and I won't see her family. But I will pick you up for lunch and then we can go to a play." So it's not as if I wasn't going to see her on Sunday. (T: Uhm, hmm) I was going to see her a little later. (T: Later. Uhm, hmm) But she wasn't going to go to the philharmonic if we couldn't. And she said, "Well, I won't see you tomorrow." This was Saturday. "I won't see you tomorrow. I won't see you Monday." Monday was her birthday. "And I won't see you Tuesday either.'" I said, "But Monday's your birthday." Oh, I said to her, "You've got to understand Mother, that Dolores really is like my family. I have to make space to see her when I'm here." When I said that to her, she said, "Well I won't see you Monday." I said, "Monday's your birthday and I'm here for your birthday." She replied, "I'm gonna spend it with *my* family." Oh boy. (T: Uhm, hmm) So, she didn't see me. I was going to be there for a week out of which she didn't see me three days. (T: Uhm, hmm) Then after that she said to me that she was going to go to a 25th wedding anniversary. And that she didn't have an outfit. And I said, "Oh let's go get you an outfit." And we went to this department store and she got a lovely outfit complete with shoes and a purse. And she didn't thank me for it. This is nothing. This outfit is nothing. It's nothing, nothing, nothing compared to how much I lavished (T: Uhm, hmm) presents on her. It's just (T: Uhm, hmm) absolutely nothing. But it is the first time I really was very angry that she didn't even thank me for it. (T: Uhm, hmm) Not only that, the next day she said what a bad daughter I was. Of course that's extra because in addition to that – I want to give you a full picture. In addition to that, I have supported her. I mean, I have given her money from the very first paycheck I ever had up until now. Since I was 18 years old when I started working. Up until now she has money from me faithfully, faithfully, faithfully. I could be without a job. My husband could be without a job. But we figured it out. So, what I'm trying to tell you is (T: Uhm, hmm) that I have not been the bad daughter that she says I have been. I'm not. I have been an excellent daughter as a matter of fact. But anyway, that outfit was in addition to many other things that she had asked for that day. She had wanted new glasses, and she needed new glasses and she wanted medicine. She wanted this and she wanted that and of course, she didn't say, "May I have?" She just said, "We're going to the pharmacy. I need you to buy my medicine for the month." Which I resented. I don't resent buying her medicine. I resent the sense of serving. What's the word? "Entitlement." That she didn't even ask, "Can you buy me new glasses?" (T: Uhm, hmm) She says, "We're gonna get new glasses." So that day then I bought her her outfit, and she didn't thank me. And I was really mad. I was just so pissed. I'm thinking, "How ungrateful, how ungrateful." (T: Uhm, hmm) Just, (sigh) "How ungrateful."

T15: This is in the same vacation, same week (C: Same week) where she had already refused to see you obviously in retaliation (C: Yes) because you were seeing someone else in the morning.

C16: Exactly. In retaliation. Exactly. (T: Uhm, hmm) And then, yes it all happened in the same week and it happened even after she had done that. I was still (T: Still …) being generous (T: Uhm, hmm) and extending myself for her. Right!

T16: Yeah.

C17: Again, as recently as January of last year I said, "Mother why don't you go to have a nice haircut?" So we went to a place where she was going to have a nice haircut. And the woman who did her hair was considerate toward her because of her age. And I wanted to tip her profusely, I gave her a tip that was equal in the amount ...

T17: To the charge?

C18: To the charge. Because she was considerate with elderly people (voice breaking with emotion) ...

T18: Uhm, hmm. It was out of feeling for your mother ...

C19: I was just ...

T19: ... that you were generous to this ...

C20: Yeah, yeah. I was thinking "Thank you." (T: Uhm, hmm) Just "Thank you for treating my mother with consideration." (T: Uhm, hmm) My mother was so difficult with her, so difficult, so ornery. And this lady was patient with her. I know it was because of her age. Because she even said, "Oh, normally I see people upstairs but no, let me get another station."

T20: To make it easier for her.

C21: Yeah, and I was just so grateful for, for that (voice continues broken with emotion). And then when I left, when I left Columbia, I thought "God I wish I could live here, I wish I could, I wish I could, I wish I could protect her. I wish I c- you know she's 81 years old. She has to take buses, she has to take taxis. "I wish I could just be here to take her places. To take her to the doctor, to buy her groceries, to ... (sniffles) (T: Uhm, hmm) hire somebody to do her housework," and (pause) I don't remember if this is true, but I have a vague sense that I told her, "I really wish I could be here to ..." I'm almost positive that this is true.

T21: That you even *said* it.

C22: Yes, that I wanted to be there so that I could be there for her, help her. Then what she said was very dismissive, very dismissive and very, uh, (sniffles) oh, she put me down. Like she always used to. (T: Uhm, hmm) She always did. She (T: Uhm, hmm) *put me down*. She said, "No. I don't need you to be here." (T: Uhm, hmm) She dismissed my (T: Yes) tender feelings for her. (T: Yes) Just totally dismissed them. Not only that. She took the opportunity to dig at me (sniffs). So anyway, I guess the point that I'm trying to make, Barbara, is that as recently as last January I was still so open to her, so open. So it is hard for me to believe that I've turned the corner. (T: Uhm, hmm, uhm, hmm) That ...

T22: That she could be expressing the love, the affection she now is in the letters and you ...

C23: Be so indifferent.

T23: Be indifferent.

C24: Yeah, exactly, exactly! That she's now, "Oh daughter think of me." And "I love you with every beat of my heart." And I want to say ... uh, "I don't care!" And, "It's just too late! I don't care!" (T: Uhm, hmm) I want to say, "Ugh!" (T: Uhm, hmm) You know?

T24: It's too late.

C25: Yeah, it's just, "Ugh! Keep, keep your affection. Keep it. Keep it. It doesn't do me ... I don't want to hear this. These words are totally meaningless to me at this point." (T: Uhm, hmm) "So please spare me!" (Laughs) I guess that's it. "Just spare me, just spare me." You know, "Spare me." It's just so meaningless it makes me angry. It makes me just angry to ... But I guess because of my anger I realize I'm not resolved. (T: Uhm, hmm) Because (T: Uhm, hmm) I want to be totally at peace. Totally at peace is my goal, totally at peace. (T: Uhm, hmm) But if I'm angry I'm still, I'm still hooked somehow. (T: Uhm, hmm) (Pause)

[The cassette had to be turned at this point, so some dialogue was lost]

C26: She likes to very much likes to talk about politics and I'll respond to that.

T26: You can converse.

C27: We can converse superficially. (T: Uhm, hmm) Very superficially. And if she tells me that she's been ill, I'll say "I hope you feel better." (T: Uhm, hmm) And (sigh) if I feel like telling her something, I will. (T: Uhm, hmm) Although realizing of course (T: Uhm, hmm) that everything I say to her she's going to first of all distort (T: Uhm, hmm) and criticize. (T: Uhm, hmm) (Pause)

T27: So no ...

C28: It's a given.

T28: You know too well not to reach out and you don't want to reach out, and anyway it's been pure duty for a long while. (C: Yeah) You're telling me you're being civil with her. (C: Yeah) Being civil (C: Yeah) with her, and that might include sharing (C: Yes) something about yourself. But with no expectation because you know realistically that what you can expect is that she will punish you. She will respond in a hurtful way if you have any expectation of a reciprocation of affect ... But independently of that she may continue to pour out this love for you. (C: Yeah) But you are resolving not to get caught up in it in any way.

C29: Precisely. Exactly.

T29: You are still caught in some way because it makes you angry that she's now being so loving (C: Yeah) in her words in the letters after all these years of rejecting you and depriving you. Is that right?

C30: Right. Depriving me, depriving me. She was so withholding of any affection! Any affection! Any affection! It is so weird. It is so, so weird. You know, it just, it's just so weird.

T30: Her behavior (C: Yeah) has been weird.

C31: Her behavior, yeah. (T: Uhm, hmm) It's just so weird. When you say "depriving" it brings back a couple memories. One of them is that I remember one day – I was not living in the house any more. And so we sat, we had agreed to meet at a certain department store. We were going out to lunch. And so when I saw her I was so happy to see her. And I ran to her. I was already an adult in my twenties. I ran to her and I wanted to hold her and to hug her and to kiss her and she ... (voice breaking again with emotion). Like this (gestures).

T31: Squirmed away.

C32: Yeah, she just let go of me. That was so typical. She's so weird that she responded that way to my affection. It was just so weird. Just so weird. Just so weird (sniffles).

T32: Although you were so used to, so accustomed to this hurt for so long. I gather, given that she loved you so much earlier, you never fully understood what happened to her. (C: Yeah) Is that right, that it's weird. (C: Yeah, yeah) The whole thing is ...

C33: Why would she be so rejecting of my love? Why? It's just so weird (T: Uhm, hmm) that a mother would do that. (T: Uhm, hmm) It's just so weird to me. (Pause) Why would a mother ...

T33: Especially since she didn't start out that way. (C: Uhm, hmm) There are women who just don't have it.

C34: Don't have it.

T34: They don't have it.

C35: Right.

T35: But your mother, had it. (C: Uhm, hmm) And then where did it go? (C: Yeah) For years!

C36: Yeah, right. Right. Uhm, hmm.

T36: And it got worse, I mean not only the coldness but a kind of hostility.

C37: Oh, hostility, oh ...

T37: Is that right, the word?

C38: Hostility. Oh my God, yes! She is so contemptuous and critical and hostile to me, just so hostile. So hostile, distrusting. I mean *distrusting*, oh my

God! (Sighs)

T38: It's really strange, really weird.

C39: Oh yeah, oh yeah.

T39: And weird, now that she's ... you don't understand yourself now. After how open you remained for so long (C: Yeah) in the face of so much. (C: Uhm, hmm) And then, here you are.

C40: Yeah, yeah, yeah.

T40: She just doesn't get, it's not ...

C41: Yeah, it's not getting to me.

T41: (Inaudible) Honestly ...

C42: It's just not getting to me. (T: Uhm, hmm) In other words, it's not going to make me go back to her. It really isn't. It's futile. (T: Uhm, hmm) It's just futile at this point. I've turned the corner.

T42: You've turned the corner. (C: Sigh) It died.

C43: It died. It just died. (T: Uhm, hmm) It just died.

T43: The love died.

C44: She killed it, she killed it.

T44: She killed your love.

C45: She killed it. She killed it. I didn't think it was possible.

T45: Didn't think it would ... It hung on for an awfully long ...

C46: I didn't think it was possible. (T: Uhm, hmm) I just didn't think so. (T: Uhm, hmm) I used to always say "The bond between a mother and a daughter ..." I really thought it was a physical law. I guess that's it. (T: Hmm) I really thought it was. I'd always tell Joseph, because Joseph would say "Ugh!" "Oh Joseph, you just don't understand the bond between a mother and a daughter. It's indissolvable. It's for life. It's until death do us part" and "Blah, blah, blah." Well, there may be a thread of a bond, yes, but I don't even at this point I don't dare say that it's indissolvable. I don't dare say that anymore because I'd have to eat my words. (Laughs) (T: Uhm, hmm) I now have to eat my words. I can, I can see Joseph was right. He used to say "No, no it isn't. Not necessarily." (T: Uhm, hmm) And he was right. I know it. Anyway Barbara, I guess that's it. I like the words you said, "It's as if the earth was up right now," like gravity turned backwards. (T: Uhm, hmm) I guess that's it. I guess that's it. I guess that's it. I really thought this was not in the realm of possibility.

T46: Not in the realm of nature, not in the ...

C47: Nature even, in nature (sighs). And here I am.

T47: Uhm, hmm. And here you are.

C48: Yeah. I get her letters and I'll get to it when I get to it. I'll answer when I feel like it – if I feel like it. And I won't answer her questions. She has asked questions. Some of them I don't trust her to answer. (T: Uhm, hmm, uhm, hmm) She wants to know what my emblem means. Well, I have a logo and it's very meaningful to me. And I will not share it with her because she'll be critical and she'll say, "Oh ..." I will not share it with her. It's in my stationery, that's how she knows about it. (T: Uhm, hmm) But (pause) I will not share it with her. She's asked me twice, and I say "Oh this is blah, blah, blah." And she says "But explain to me what does it mean, what does it mean to you?" And I will not do it because I know that she'll put me down and criticize me. Even if, at this point she won't dare do it to my face because she knows. It's a predictable pattern. In the past sometimes I've kind of moved away. And she hooks me back and then I go back (loud clap) again (Loud clap). No more.

T48: No more.

C49: It's just not gonna happen anymore. Not again, not ever. So I don't know what the relationship will look like once I am more resolved. I don't know. I don't know. Um, I don't know what my feelings are going to be for her. I don't know. I really have no idea. Some sympathy or some (pause) benign neutrality (laughs) (T: Uhm, hmm, uhm, hmm) or some tenderness maybe, some compassion. I have no idea. Maybe some tenderness just because she's old. (T: Uhm, hmm) I don't know. Um, (Pause, 10 seconds.) I don't know.

T49: You don't know where this whole change is going to arrive. (C: Right) Or where it's going to go further than it is, whatever that is. (C: Yes) You don't have any idea.

C50: Yes, yes, yes. I guess I am very intrigued. (T: Uhm, hmm) I'm very intrigued as to what are my final feelings going to be. Because right now I know I'm still not resolved. I'm not there yet.

T50: Right.

C51: But what are my final feelings going to be for this woman? I don't know. I just don't know. Um, (T: Uhm, hmm) I'm very intrigued really. (T: Uhm, hmm) Very intrigued. Um, (sigh) um, (Pause) I'm just curious. Let me think. (Pause – 1 minute) Yeah, I don't know. I guess I will have to wait it out (clears throat). (Pause) Yeah, I guess I'll just have to wait it out.

T51: Uhm, hmm. You can't predict.

C52: Yeah, I can't predict, I can't predict, I can't predict. Maybe that's part of the reason I'm so intrigued. Because I wonder if she's going to die and

I'm gonna be angry with her. It is possible. And so be it if that's the case. She's 82 now. If that's the way we're going to say goodbye. In this space, (T: Uhm, hmm) which is bad for both of us. (T: Uhm, hmm) I know it's bad for her. I know she doesn't like it one little bit. (T: Uhm, hmm) She said in a letter she misses my calls. (T: Uhm, hmm) Um, (pause) I guess I would like to be a little more resolved, before she dies. But, I'm not going to push anything. Whatever happens, happens. If she dies tomorrow and I'm angry with her and cold, so be it. (T: Uhm, hmm) I'm not going to do anything out of fear, out of fear of guilt, fear of remorse. (T: Uhm, hmm) I'm not. I'm not. I'm not. So I guess maybe that is why I am so intrigued. I wonder if that's the way we're gonna say goodbye. In such a distant and cold fashion. (T: Uhm, hmm) Or in such a distant and cold space. That we're in. It's quite possible. It's quite possible (sighs). Umm. (Pause) And so be it, really. (T: Uhm, hmm) So be it. So be it. So be it.

T52: Uhm, hmm. (Pause) You – (pause) you'd like to arrive wherever you're going to arrive, so that you're truly or more truly free. And you don't know what the quality of your relating to her will be and so on. And she's old. She could die. She's at an age where people just die all of a sudden. (C: Uhm, hmm, uhm, hmm) And you're saying you don't feel an anxiety to make sure you've got it where it could go, to the optimal place. It may be hard in some ways, or …

C53: Unresolved. (T: Uhm, hmm) She may die when I may still be unresolved (T: Uhm, hmm) and I still may be angry, and so be it. I'm not going to try to push for some resolution, some reconciliation. (T: Uhm, hmm) No, I'm not. (T: Uhm, hmm, uhm, hmm) If it does happen, so be it. So be it. So be it. Fear of guilt, fear of remorse is not going to make me push into anywhere I'm not feeling (T: Uh huh) to go. So (sigh) I guess that's all I want to say about that.

[The client continues with another topic she had mentioned wanting to discuss during the session.]

# CLOSING SECTION

# Chapter 30

# Garden of women

Thirty-three years ago, while working in a large state mental hospital, I met Florence.[1] My assigned work included visiting wards to talk with people who might be getting close to leaving the hospital. My personal goal was to develop myself as a client-centered therapist so I viewed my ward visits as an opportunity for client-centered therapy encounters with patients, regardless of their readiness for pre-discharge services. I would talk with anyone who was willing to talk with me.

One of the patients I felt especially attracted to was Florence. So I visited her ward to talk with her as often as I could.

Florence was a tall woman, 24 years old. In these two ways we were alike, but otherwise we were quite different. She had short blond hair, I had long brown hair; her eyes were blue, mine brown; she weighed 150 pounds, I weighed 120. The important differences between us, however, came from the fact that she suffered from a serious and chronic illness then called "Schizophrenia, Hebephrenic type" and I did not.

Florence talked in a "word salad." As best I can express it, she said such things as "Frof a lay, gay, stay, what-cha ... bo-kow-pooh." She was animated as she said such things, making hand gestures and body movements. Often there was the appearance of a struggle within her to say what she meant while realizing she wasn't making sense.

I was certain she was trying to talk to me, to tell me things. Occasionally I thought I understood, but I was never sure, even when I had some information about an event or altercation on her ward. Sometimes there was a physical confirmation that we communicated. She would walk over to a bench and sit down after I asked "Would you like to sit down with me?" Or

---

1. Florence is a pseudonym.

We found this July, 1989 paper in Barbara's library after she died. According to Jerold Bozarth, she wrote it upon returning home from the annual meeting of the Association for Development of the Person-Centered Approach in Rock Eagle State Park, Georgia.

she would nod and walk away from me when I asked her "Do you mind if we stop now? I have to talk to some other patients." These were instances when she obviously understood me. I assumed that she always understood me because of instances like these. But I was not sure.

I believed Florence liked our relationship because she would hurry over to me and start talking to me as soon as she noticed I had stepped onto the ward. I assumed she liked me as well as the relationship, but she never made a direct gesture or sign of affection towards me.

While we sat together I would state what I thought she was telling me and ask her if I was right. Of course I was guessing most of the time. And she would usually respond by shaking her heard and then continue to talk as if she were trying to get me to understand. Sometimes she showed signs of frustration or, more rarely, annoyance. Usually she responded in a lively, even happy, manner while shaking her head "no."

Florence and I were basically attractive young women. Florence had a small straight nose, high cheekbones, a full mouth. She was, beyond the signs of her illness and circumstances, a Scandinavian beauty. But she did not appear beautiful. Her skin was pale and pasty. Her posture was slumped. She walked duck-like, in jerky movements, pushing her head forward and back as she lumbered. Her clothes were too small. She smelled of perspiration and old food.

She lived on a ward housing 250 women. She slept on a cot in one of the two huge dormitories. The beds were almost touching and there was only a small cubby for storage of personal things. She spent her days in a big common room with uncurtained windows, hard wooden chairs and benches. The lavatories had toilets without doors, no paper, soapless sinks, no towels. The other women on the ward were constantly raving or muttering or fighting or fussing or slumped over on chairs or on the floor or in frozen postures. Often a woman would be screaming or moaning for hours without stop.

Florence had no known living relatives. She had been institutionalized since she was 11 years old. As a result of her illness, her history, and her situation she looked like a very overgrown, awkward, weird child.

I had, of course, nice clothes that fit me, a shiny head of hair. I was clean. I stood up straight and walked with some grace. I was very conscious of the fact that circumstances outside of our control had created the dramatic and terrible differences between us. I felt akin to her even though it was a vivid fact that her potentiality for a happy life was cut off and mine was not. I felt identified with her. Although I doubt she felt identified with me.

There we were. We sat together three to five days a week for 15 or 20 minutes. She would usually chat with me in her incomprehensible way. Sometimes we sat silently. I gave my whole attention to her during our time together. Sometimes she would grasp my wrist, holding me as she talked. Sometimes she would jump up and disappear into her dormitory, returning to show me a piece of crumpled paper with incomprehensible writing on it, or with a dirty handkerchief to blow her nose.

The relationship lasted a year. One day near the end I got permission to take her onto the hospital grounds. They were pretty, like a college campus. It was a sunny, warm day. We wore cotton dresses. We walked arm in arm, for her support, Florence talking, reacting to the scenes or telling me something. We sat down on a bench close together.

I smoked at that time. Sitting together in that pleasant and almost normal environment, I asked Florence if she'd mind if I smoked. She nodded, so I took out the pack from my purse, pulled out a filter-type cigarette, lit it and inhaled. Florence seemed very interested so I asked her if she wanted to try it. She nodded with an excited expression on her face.

Florence selected a cigarette from the pack. I showed her the filter end and she put it into her mouth. I lit a match to the cigarette. She sucked in and it was lit. But then, suddenly, holding it between her thumb and forefinger, Florence took the cigarette from her mouth, turned it around, and thrust the burning end into her lips. She reacted immediately to the pain. I don't know if I or she pulled it away from her mouth, I reacted so quickly, too. I know I took the cigarette, threw it down and stamped on it.

Florence licked her lips. Her eyes watered and rolled around from the pain for a few moments. Then, suddenly, she acted as if nothing had happened. She was quiet for a moment then looked around and started chatting as before. I was panicked with anguish and guilt. I felt stupid and naive to have assumed that she could handle such a dangerous object without hurting herself. I had lost track of the meaning of her disability in my enthusiasm for giving her a normal experience with me.

I felt terrible that I had had a part in hurting her. I still feel awful when I remember the moment when she placed the burning cigarette end into her mouth. After that incident I did not arrange to take her out, but continued to see her on the ward. Florence didn't show a change in her interest in being with me.

Several weeks after the cigarette incident an aide told me Florence was going to be transferred. The next morning she was to be taken, with many other patients, to another state institution miles away where there was more room. The ward doctor told me not to tell Florence about the move and I didn't dare tell her because I was fearful about how she might be treated if she became very upset. And I didn't want to get in trouble.

I was with her awhile that afternoon knowing her life, such as it was, would be drastically disrupted the following day, that she would not be given the respect of being told about it, that she would not be seeing me again.

I remember I told her that day that I liked her and enjoyed visiting with her. She was quiet. Then she turned to me and said something that was clearer than anything she had ever said before. It made me believe she knew about the move.

Florence said haltingly, but clearly, "One day I shall fall from this garden of women."

I often think of that poetic line. That was the last time we were together, the last time I saw her.

# Historical bibliography of selected works of Barbara Temaner Brodley

This bibliography is intended to include all of Barbara's written publications as well as selected presentations. In the interest of representing the history of her thinking in relation to client-centered therapy, her works are entered in chronological order with the most complete versions of each entry based on the earliest known date of appearance of that work. Later entries of the same work are cross-referenced backwards in time to the earliest entry. Translations are not listed separately, but when known, they are described within the main entry. While two films in which Barbara played a role are included, DVDs of her demonstration sessions are not.

Through the years, Barbara wrote under different names, Propst, Temaner, and finally Brodley. We've listed her works below, as best we can determine, according to her name in the publication.

All references in this bibliography to the numbering of the annual meetings of the Association for Development of the Person-Centered Approach are corrected to reflect the most recent information available.

While compiling this bibliography, we relied heavily upon Alberto Segrera's International Archives of the Person-Centered Approach (http://www.bib.uia.mx/aiecp/default.html). In that archive, Barbara's presentations and articles are listed under her maiden name Scott. Most of her talks and presentations at conferences are listed there.

Propst, B. S. (1962a). *Openness to experience and originality of productions*. Unpublished master's thesis, Committee on Human Development, University of Chicago.

Propst, B. S. (1962b, March 30). *Why do I want to be a therapist?* Memo to John Shlien. This volume, Chapter 1.

Maddi, S. R., & Propst, B. S. (1963, September). Activation and personality. Unpublished manuscript prepared for symposium: *Some determinants and implications of activation level*, American Psychological Association, Philadelphia, PA, September 4.

Propst, B. S. (1964). A preliminary survey using a sexual experience questionnaire. University of Chicago Counseling Center. *Discussion Papers, 10*(5). (Presently unavailable.)

Maddi, S. R., Propst, B. S., & Feldinger, I. (1964). *Three expressions of the need for variety.* (Research Bulletin). Princeton, NJ: Educational Testing Service. Also, (1965) *Journal of Personality, 33,* 82–98.

Propst, B. S. (1966). Client-centered psychotherapy as a complex task. University of Chicago Counseling Center. *Discussion Papers, 12*(9).

Temaner, G., & Quinn, G. (Producers/Directors). (1966). *Home for life* [Motion picture]. B. S. Propst, (Research Coordinator). (Depicts treatment of the elderly person in a home for the aged.) (Available from Kartemquin Educational Films, 1901 W. Wellington, Chicago, IL 60657.)

Temaner, G., & Quinn, G. (Producers/Directors). (1970). *Marco* [Motion picture]. V. Scott, & L. Marrone (Executive Producers). (Music composed by P. Glass.). (B. Temaner appears as herself giving birth to her son Marco). Reissued (2010) as *Part 3 of the Kartemquin Collection: The early years, Vols. 1–3.* (Contains additional footage of family life and breastfeeding some years later.) (Available from Kartemquin Educational Films, 1901 W. Wellington, Chicago, IL 60657.)

Maddi, S. R., & Propst, B. S. (1971). Activation theory and personality. In S. R. Maddi (Ed.), *Perspectives in personality: A comparative approach* (pp. 434–439). Boston: Little, Brown & Co.

Temaner, B. (1975a). *Ethics in psychotherapy.* Unpublished outline for a January 8, 1975, presentation at the Chicago Counseling and Psychotherapy Center. This volume, Chapter 4.

Temaner, B. (1975b). *Unpleasant emotional stimulation and openness to experience in an imaginative task.* Unpublished doctoral dissertation, Committee on Human Development, University of Chicago.

Temaner, B. (1977a, March). The empathic understanding response capability. Lecture, March 9. Chicago Counseling and Psychotherapy Center. *Chicago Counseling Center Discussion Paper.*

Temaner, B. (1977b, March). The empathic understanding response process. Revision of paper presented to Changes on March 6. Chicago Counseling and Psychotherapy Center. *Chicago Counseling Center Discussion Paper.* This volume, Chapter 12.

Temaner, B. (1982a). Criteria for making empathic understanding responses in client-centered therapy. Chicago Counseling and Psychotherapy Center. *Chicago Counseling Center Discussion Paper.* Published (1984) under Brodley in A. S. Segrera (Ed.), *Proceedings of the First International Forum on the Person-Centered Approach.* México, Distrito Federal, Mexico: Universidad Iberoamericana. Excerpted (1985) in *Renaissance, 2*(1), 1–3. Also published (1986) as Los criterios para responder empaticamente en terapia centrada en el cliente (Nuria López Garcia, Trans.) *Revista de Psiquiatria y Psicologia Humanista, 17,* 36–42. Revision published (1998), Criteria for making empathic responses in client-centered therapy, in *The Person-Centered Journal, 5*(1), 20–28. This volume, Chapter 14.

Temaner, B. (1982b). The overt empathic understanding response. Chicago Counseling and Psychotherapy Center. *Chicago Counseling Center Discussion Paper.*

Brodley, B. T. (1984). Criteria for making empathic understanding responses in client-centered therapy. See 1982a.

Brodley, B. T. (1985). Criteria for making empathic understanding responses in client-centered therapy [an excerpted version]. See1982a.

Brodley, B. T. (1986a). A client-centered demonstration in Hungary. Transcript with commentary published (1999) in I. Fairhurst, (Ed.), *Women writing in the person-centred approach* (pp. 85–92). Ross-on-Wye: PCCS Books.

Brodley, B. T. (1986b, September). *Client-centered therapy – What is it? What is it not?* Unpublished paper presented at the first annual meeting of the Association for the Development of the Person-Centered Approach, Chicago, September 3–7.

Bozarth, J. D., & Brodley, B. T. (1986a). Client-centered psychotherapy: A statement. *Person-Centered Review*, *1*(3), 262–271.

Bozarth, J. D., & Brodley, B. T. (1986b, September). *The core values and theory of the person-centered approach.* A paper presented at the first annual meeting of the Association for the Development of the Person-Centered Approach, Chicago, September 3–7. Published (1993) as Les valeurs essentieles de l'approche centrée sur la personne. The core values of the person-centered approach (in French and English) in *Le Journal du PCAII*, pp. 1–25 (Person-Centered Approach Institute International – France).

Brodley, B. T. (1987). *A client-centered psychotherapy practice.* Paper prepared for the Third International Forum on the Person-Centered Approach, La Jolla, CA. Published (1998) in C. Wolter-Gustafson (Ed.), *A person-centered reader: Personal selections by our members* (pp. 59–87). Boston: Association for the Development of the Person-Centered Approach. Also (2002) C. Zabus-Baudart (Tr.), Une pratique de la psychothérapie centrée sur le client. (Available from the editors.)

Brodley, B. T. (1988a, May). CCT [client-centered therapy] and PCA [person-centered approach] definitions in *Responses to person-centered vs. client-centered?* Panel: J. Seeman, B. T. Brodley, N. J. Raskin, & J. M. Shlien. Revision of a discussion paper presented at the second annual meeting of the Association for the Development of the Person-Centered Approach, New York, May 26. *Renaissance*, *5*(3&4), 1–4. Barbara's contribution, pp. 1–2.

Brodley, B. T. (1988b, September). *Client-centered and experiential: Two different therapies.* Presentation at the First International Conference on Client-Centered and Experiential Psychotherapies, Leuven, Belgium, September 12–16. Published (1990) in G. Lietaer, J. Rombauts, & R. Van Balen (Eds.), *Client-centered and experiential psychotherapy in the nineties* (pp. 87–107). Leuven, Belgium: Leuven University Press. This volume, Chapter 23.

Brodley, B. T. (1988c). Concerning "transference," "countertransference" and other psychoanalytically developed concepts from a client/person-centered perspective. Originally a classroom lecture, Illinois School of Professional Psychology. Revision published (1992) *Renaissance, 9*(2), 1–2. Revision (2008) in French by F. Ducroux-Biass (Ed. & Trans.), Le point de vue de l'approche centrée sur la personne sur l'utilisation de notions issues de concepts analytiques, notamment celles de "transfert" et de "contre-transfert". *Approche Centrée sur la Personne: Pratique et Recherché, 2*(8). This volume, Chapter 24.

Brodley, B. T. (1988d, May). *Does early-in-therapy experiencing level predict outcome? A review of research.* Unpublished manuscript. Revision of a discussion paper prepared for presentation at the second annual meeting of the Association for the Development of the Person-Centered Approach, New York, May, 26–30. (Available from the editors.)

Brodley, B. T. (1988e). Why are there so few client-centered therapists when so many people around the world acknowledge Carl Rogers' influence? In Roundtable Discussion: Why do you think there are so few person-centered practitioners or scholars considering that literally thousands of persons throughout the world attest to the enormous impact Carl Rogers has had on their personal and professional lives? *Person-Centered Review, 3*(3), 353–390. Barbara's contribution pp. 357–360. This volume, Chapter 3.

Brodley, B. T. (July, 1989a). *Garden of women.* Unpublished manuscript. This volume, Chapter 30.

Brodley, B. T. (1989b). *An introduction to the application of client-centered theory to therapy with two persons together.* Unpublished manuscript. This volume, Chapter 19.

Brodley, B. T. (1989c). Letter to co-editors. *Renaissance, 6*(1), 3.

Brodley, B. T., Bozarth, J. D., & Cain, D. (1989). Power, decision-making and the future of ADPCA [Association for Development of the Person-Centered Approach]. Barbara's contribution, p. 1. *Renaissance, 6*(1), 1–2.

Bower, D. W., Brodley, B. T., Gold, C. L., Graf, C., Kahn, E., Khanna, M., Newton, K., Seeman, J., & Thompson, M. (1989). Responses to the 1989 ADPCA [Association for Development of the Person-Centered Approach] business meeting. Barbara's contribution, p. 1. *Renaissance, 6*(3), 1–4.

Brodley, B. T. (1990a). Client-centered and experiential: Two different therapies. See 1988b. This volume, Chapter 23.

Brodley, B. T. (1990b). *Instructions for beginning to practice client-centered therapy.* Unpublished classroom handout, Illinois School of Professional Psychology, Chicago. Revised 1991. (Chinese translation by J. Wu available from the editors). Further revision published (1993) as The therapeutic clinical interview: Guidelines for beginning practice. *Person-Centred Practice 1*(2), 15–21. Reprinted (2000) in T. Merry (Ed.), *Person-centred practice: The BAPCA reader* (pp. 103–109). Ross-on-Wye: PCCS Books. Also, *La entrevista clinica terapeutica guias para quien se inicia en la practica* (available from the editors). Slightly revised in French version (2009) (M. Sally, Ed., F. Ducroux-Biass, Trans.), Directives pour commencer à pratiquer la thérapie en approche centrée sur le client. *Approche Centrée sur la Personne: Pratique et recherché, 1*(9). This volume, Chapter 17.

Brodley, B. T. (1990c). *Uncharacteristic directiveness: A session with Dione.* Unpublished paper. Illinois School of Professional Psychology. Revision published (1996) as Uncharacteristic directiveness: Rogers and the "Anger and Hurt" client. In B. A. Farber, D. C. Brink, & P. M. Raskin (Eds.), *The psychotherapy of Carl Rogers: Cases and commentary* (pp. 310–321). New York: Guilford Press. (Book is translated into Chinese, *Luo jie si xin li zhi liao: JIng dian ge an ji zhuan jia dian ping.*) Reprinted (2004) in R. Moodley, C. Lago, & A. Talahite (Eds.), *Carl Rogers counsels a Black client: Race and culture in person-centred counseling* (pp. 36–46). Ross-on-Wye: PCCS Books.

Brodley, B. T. (1990d). 1. What are the greatest contributions of client-centered theory and practice to the field of psychotherapy? 2. What modifications in client-centered theory and practice are most essential to the evolution and effectiveness of client-centered psychotherapy? Roundtable discussion contribution. *Person-Centered Review, 5*(4), 467–469.

Brodley, B. T. (1990e). With Wolter-Gustafson, C., McCreesh, J., Pildes, S., & Temaner, N. Fourth annual meeting (1989) of ADPCA [Association for the Development of the Person-Centered Approach], Hebron, CT. *Renaissance, 7*(2), 1.

Brodley, B. T., & Brody, A. F. (1990, August). Understanding client-centered therapy through interviews conducted by Carl Rogers. Paper presented for the panel *Fifty years of client-centered therapy: Recent research* at the American Psychological Association annual meeting, Boston.

Brodley, B. T. (1991a). Instructions for beginning to practice client-centered therapy. See 1990b.

Brodley, B. T. (1991b). Responses to Cain's "concerns." *Renaissance, 8*(1), 1–4, 6. (Barbara's contribution, pp. 1, 3.)

Brodley, B. T. (1991c, May). *The role of focusing in client-centered therapy.* Unpublished paper. Presentation for a dialog with A. Weiser Cornell at the fifth annual meeting of the Association for the Development of the Person-Centered Approach in Coffeyville, KS, May 23–27. Slightly revised in French version (2008) (F. Ducroux-Biass & K. Moon, (Eds.), F. Ducroux-Biass, Trans.), Rôle du focusing dans la thérapie centrée sur la personne. *Approche Centrée sur la Personne: Pratique et Recherché, 1*(7), 79–91.

Brodley, B. T. (1991d). Seeking more data. *Renaissance, 8*(1), 2.

Brodley, B. T. (1991e, July). Some observations of Carl Rogers' behavior in therapy interviews. Published (1994) in *The Person-Centered Journal, 1*(2), 37–48. A revision of a presentation, *Empathic understanding in Carl Rogers' therapy interviews,* at the Second International Conference on Client-Centered and Experiential Therapy, University of Stirling, Scotland, July 1–6, 1991. This volume, Chapter 25.

Bozarth, J. D., & Brodley, B. T. (1991). Actualization: A functional concept in client-centered therapy. In A. Jones & R. Crandall, (Eds.), *Handbook of self-actualization. A special issue of the Journal of Social Behavior and Personality, 6*(5), 45–59. Reprinted (2008) in B. E. Levitt (Ed.), *Reflections on human potential* (pp. 33–45). Ross-on-Wye: PCCS Books.

Brodley, B. T., & Brody, A. F. (1991). *A rating system for studying client/person-centered interviews.* Unpublished manuscript. Also, 1993 and 1995 (Short summary). Final version published (2008) by Wilczynski, J., Brodley, B. T., & Brody, A. F. A rating system for studying nondirective client-centered interviews – Revised. *The Person-Centered Journal, 15*(1&2), 34–57. Slightly revised in French version (2008) (F. Ducroux-Biass, Trans.), Système révisé d'évaluation pour l'étude des entretiens non-directifs centrés sur la personne. *Approche Centrée sur la Personne. Pratique et Recherché, 2*(8).

Pörtner, M. [circa 1990–1991]. [Interview of Barbara Brodley.] [Cassette Recording] (Presently unavailable.)

Brodley, B. T. (1992a). Concerning "transference," "countertransference" and other psychoanalytically developed concepts from a client/person-centered perspective. See 1988c. This volume, Chapter 24.

Brodley, B. T. (1992b, July). *My experiences of long-term breastfeeding.* Paper written for presentation at the Fifth International Forum on the Person-Centered Approach on Terschelling Island, The Netherlands. As part of the presentation, Barbara showed the film *Marco.* See Temaner & Quinn, 1970.

Brodley, B. T. (1992c). (Incomplete version) Empathic understanding and feelings in client-centered therapy. *The Person-Centered Journal, 1*(1), 21–32. Corrected version published (1996) in *The Person-Centered Journal, 3*(1), 22–30. Also (2001) (R. Brites, Trans.) Compreencao empatica e sentimentos na terapia centrada no cliente. *A Pessoa Como Centro: Revista de Estudos Rogerianos, 5,* 71–83. This volume, Chapter 8.

Brodley, B. T., & Zimring, F. (1992). Person-centered practice: A therapy transcript. *The Person-Centered Journal, 1*(1), 77–90.

Brodley, B. T. (1993a, April 14–15). Letter to Dr. Carol Topping. Appendix F in C. Topping, *An unequal prizing: Couple therapy from a client-centered perspective* (pp. 167–173). Unpublished doctoral dissertation. University of Georgia, Athens, GA. Partial summary in 1996a. This volume, Chapter 20.

Brodley, B. T. (1993b). Response to Patterson's "Winds of Change." *Journal of Humanistic Education and Development, 31*(3), 139–143.

Brodley, B. T. (1993c). The therapeutic clinical interview: Guidelines for beginning practice. See 1990b.

Bozarth, J. D., & Brodley, B. T. (1993). Les valeurs essentieles de l'approche centrée sur la personne [The core values of the person-centered approach]. See Bozarth & Brodley, 1986b.

Brodley, B. T. (1994a, May). *The nondirective attitude in client-centered therapy.* Presentation at the eighth annual meeting of the Association for the Development of the Person-Centered Approach, Kendall College, Evanston, IL. Revision (1997) published in *The Person-Centered Journal, 4*(1), 18–30. This volume, Chapter 5.

Brodley, B. T. (1994b). Some observations of Carl Rogers' behavior in therapy interviews. See 1991e. This volume, Chapter 25.

Brodley, B. T., & Brody, A. (1994, September). *Can one use techniques and still be client-centered?* Presentation at the Third International Conference on Client-Centered and Experiential Psychotherapies, Gmunden, Austria, September 5–9. Published (1996) in R. Hutterer, G. Pawlowsky, P. F. Schmid, & R. Stipsits (Eds.), *Client-centered and experiential psychotherapy: A paradigm in motion* (pp. 369–374). Frankfurt am Main: Peter Lang. This volume, Chapter 18.

Rose, J., & Brodley, B. T. (1994). Notes on the ADPCA [Association for Development of the Person-Centered Approach] business-focused community meetings. Contribution. *Renaissance, 11*(4), 6.

Brodley, B. T. (1995a). *Client-centered therapy: Not a means to an end.* Unpublished manuscript. Paper presented at the Fourth International Conference on Client-Centered and Experiential Psychotherapy, Lisbon, July 7–11, 1997. Published (2000) as Client-centered: An expressive therapy. In J. E. Marques-Teixeira & S. Antunes (Eds.), *Client-centered and experiential psychotherapy* (pp. 133–147). Linda a Velha, Lisboa, Portugal: Vale & Vale. Revised version (2002) in *The Person-Centered Journal, 9*(1), 59–70. A further revised version, this volume, Chapter 13.

Brodley, B. T. (1995b). *Considerations when responding to questions and requests in client-centered therapy.* Unpublished manuscript. This volume, Chapter 16.

Brodley, B. T. (1995c). Designated facilitators. *Renaissance, 12*(1), 9.

Brodley, B. T. (1995d). The name of the Association [for the Development of the Person-Centered Approach]. *Renaissance, 12*(1), 9.

Brodley, B. T. (1995e). Response to Suzanne Spector concerning predesignated facilitators at the ADPCA [Association for Development of the Person-Centered Approach] annual meeting. *Renaissance, 12*(1), 3–5, 7.

Brodley, B. T., & Merry, T. (1995). Guidelines for student participants in person-centred peer groups. *Person-Centred Practice, 3*(2), 17–22. Reprinted (2000) in T. Merry (Ed.), *Person-centred practice: The BAPCA reader* (pp. 110–115). Ross-on-Wye: PCCS Books. Related but different version available (from the editors) in Spanish by B. T. Brodley & C. Stuart, Lineamientos para participantes en los grupos centrados en la persona.

Brodley, B. T. (1996a, May). *Client-centered couple therapy.* Presentation at the tenth annual meeting of the Association for Development of the Person-Centered Approach in Kutztown, PA, May 23–27. See also 1993a. This volume, Chapter 20.

Brodley, B. T. (1996b). *Client-centered demonstration interview transcripts: Alejandra. Sessions 1 through 4.* (Videotaped August 2, 1996, January 13, 1997, June 9, 1997, and July 21, 1997). Session 1, unpublished. Sessions 2 through 4 in this volume, Chapters 27, 28 and 29.

Brodley, B. T. (1996c). Empathic understanding and feelings in client-centered therapy. See 1992c. This volume, Chapter 8.

Brodley, B. T. (1996d). Uncharacteristic directiveness: Rogers and the "Anger and Hurt" client. See 1990c.

Brodley, B. T., & Brody, A. (1996). Can one use techniques and still be client-centered? See Brodley & Brody, 1994. This volume, Chapter 18.

Brodley, B. T. (1997a). Brief report on the Kutztown community meeting study. *Renaissance, 14*(1), 4.

Brodley, B. T. (1997b). A client-centered demonstration interview with Ms. S. *The Person-Centered Journal, 4*(1), 61–74.

Brodley, B. T. (1997c). The nondirective attitude in client-centered therapy. See 1994a. This volume, Chapter 5.

Brodley, B. T. (1998a). A client-centered psychotherapy practice. See 1987.

Brodley, B. T. (1998b). Congruence and its relation to communication in client-centered therapy. *The Person-Centered Journal, 5*(2), 83–116. Reprinted (2001) in G. Wyatt (Ed.), *Congruence.* (pp. 55–78). Ross-on-Wye: PCCS Books. This volume, Chapter 7.

Brodley, B. T. (1998c). O conceito de tendencia actualizante na teoria centrada no cliente. The actualizing tendency concept in client-centered theory. (Portuguese and English) *A Pessoa Como Centro, 2,* 37–49. English reprinted (2000) in D. Bower (Ed.), *The person-centered approach: Applications for living* (pp. 81–106). San Jose: The Writers' Club Press. Revision published (1999) in *The Person-Centered Journal, 6*(2), 108–120. This volume, Chapter 11.

Brodley, B. T. (1998e). Criteria for making empathic responses in client-centered therapy. See Temaner, 1982a. This volume, Chapter 14.

Brodley, B. T. (1998f, June). Email to Maureen O'Hara on brief therapy (June 26). This volume, Chapter 22.

Brodley, B. T. (1998g). More on exclusion. *Renaissance, 15*(2), 9.

Brodley, B. T. (1998h, May). *Reasons for responses expressing the therapist's frame of reference in client-centered therapy.* Presentation at the twelfth annual meeting of the Association for the Development of the Person-Centered Approach, May 21–25, Wheaton College, Norton, MA. Published (1999) in *The Person-Centered Journal, 6*(1), 4–27. Slightly revised in this volume, Chapter 15.

Brodley, B. T. (1998h). A client-centered psychotherapy practice. See 1987.

Brodley, B. T. (1999a, July). *About the nondirective attitude.* Paper presented at the Second International Congress on Psychotherapy, Vienna, July 8. Published (1999) in *Person-Centred Practice, 7*(2) 79–82. Revised version published (2005) in B. E. Levitt (Ed.), [as] Introduction: About the non-directive attitude. *Embracing non-directivity* (pp. 1–5). Ross-on-Wye: PCCS Books.

Brodley, B. T. (1999b). The actualizing tendency concept in client-centered theory. See 1998c.

Brodley, B. T. (1999c). A client-centered demonstration in Hungary. See 1986a.

Brodley, B. T. (1999d). Interview with Mrs. H concerning her therapy with Carl Rogers. *Renaissance, 16*(2), 1–8, 11.

Brodley, B. T. (1999e, October). *Personal presence in client-centered therapy.* Paper prepared for the Workshop on Presence, Bratislava, October 5–9, and for Lecture Series at the Chicago Counseling and Psychotherapy Center, October 29. Published (2000) in *The Person-Centered Journal, 7*(2), 139–149. (Slightly different emphasis and title from the (2003) version in *A Pessoa Como Centro*) This volume, Chapter 10.

Brodley, B. T. (1999f). Proposal for discussion at ADPCA [Association for Development of the Person-Centered Approach] 1999. *Renaissance, 16*(2), 8.

Brodley, B. T. (1999g). Reasons for responses expressing the therapist's frame of reference in client-centered therapy. See 1998h. This volume, Chapter 15.

Brodley, B. T., & Bradburn, W. M. (1999). *Did Carl Rogers' positive view of human nature bias his psychotherapy?* (Based on a doctoral clinical research project (1996)

428   *Practicing Client-Centered Therapy: Selected writings of Barbara Temaner Brodley*

by Wendy M. Bradburn). Unpublished paper presented at the Second World Congress for Psychotherapy, Vienna, Austria.

Brodley, B. T. (2000a). The actualizing tendency concept in client-centered theory. See 1998c. This volume, Chapter 11.

Brodley, B. T. (2000b). Client-centered: An expressive therapy. See 1995a. This volume, Chapter 13.

Brodley, B. T. (2000c). Memories of Fred Zimring: Contribution 1. *The Person-Centered Journal,* 7(2), 175.

Brodley, B. T. (2000d). Memories of Fred Zimring : Contribution 2. *The Person-Centered Journal,* 7(2), 181–182.

Brodley, B. T. (2000e). *Observations of empathic understanding in two client-centered therapists.* Paper presented at the International Conference on Client-Centered and Experiential Psychotherapy, Chicago. Revision (2001), Observations of empathic understanding in a client-centered practice, published (2001) in S. Haugh & T. Merry (Eds.), *Empathy* (pp. 16–37). Ross-on-Wye: PCCS Books. A different revision (2002) published in J. C. Watson, R. N. Goldman, & M. S. Warner (Eds.), *Client-centered and experiential psychotherapy in the 21st century: Advances in theory, research and practice* (pp. 182–203). Ross-on-Wye: PCCS Books. This volume, Chapter 26.

Brodley, B. T. (2000f). Personal presence in client-centered therapy. See 1999e. This volume, Chapter 10.

Brodley, B. T. (2000g). The therapeutic clinical interview. See 1990b. This volume, Chapter 17.

Brodley, B. T. (2000h). When CCT [client-centered therapy] is misrepresented by professionals of other therapy schools. *Renaissance,* 17(2), 15.

Brodley, B. T., & Merry, T. (2000). Guidelines for student participants in person-centred peer groups. See Brodley & Merry, 1995.

Brodley, B. T. (2001a). A client-centered approach to religious and spiritual experiences. In S. King-Spooner & C. Newnes (Eds.), *Spirituality and psychotherapy* (pp. 148–156). Ross-on-Wye: PCCS Books.

Brodley, B. T. (2001b). Congruence and its relation to communication in client-centered therapy. See 1998b. This volume, Chapter 7.

Brodley, B. T. (2001c). Observations of empathic understanding in a client-centered practice. See 2000e.

Brodley, B. T. (2001d). Summary of guidelines for participation in client/person-centered groups. *Renaissance,* 18(1), 15–16. For a related but different Spanish version, see Brodley & Merry, 1995.

Brodley, B. T. (2001e). Report on the summary of guidelines for participants in a client/person-centered group. *Renaissance,* 18(2), 10–11.

Brodley, B. T., & Bozarth, J. D. (2001). An informal dialogue: Barbara Brodley tests her understanding of some of Jerold Bozarth's writings. *Renaissance,* 18(2), 1, 6–7.

Brodley, B. T., & Schneider, C. (2001). Unconditional positive regard as communicated through verbal behavior in client-centred therapy. In J. D. Bozarth & P. Wilkins (Eds.), *Unconditional positive regard* (pp. 155–172). Ross-on-Wye: PCCS Books. This volume, Chapter 9.

Brodley, B. T. (2002a). Client-centered therapy: An expressive therapy. See 1995a. A further revised version, this volume, Chapter 13.

Brodley, B. T. (2002b). Observations of empathic understanding in two client-centered therapists. See 2000e. This volume, Chapter 26.

Brodley, B. T. (2002c). Notes on community meetings: Views for discussion. *Renaissance,* 19(3&4), 12–13.

Brodley, B. T. (2002d, August). *The relation of research to psychotherapy: A question for discussion.* Paper presented at the 16th annual meeting of the Association for the Development of the Person-Centered Approach, Cleveland, OH. Published (2003c) in *Person-Centred Practice, 11*, 52–55. Revision published (2005) as Client-centered values limit the application of research findings: A question for discussion. In S. Joseph & R. Worsley (Eds.), *Person-centred psychopathology* (pp. 310–316). Ross-on-Wye: PCCS Books. This volume, Chapter 6.

Brodley, B. T., & Merry, T. (2002). The nondirective attitude in client-centered therapy: A response to Kahn. *Journal of Humanistic Psychology, 4*(2), 66–77.

Metevier, D. J. (2002). [Interview of Barbara Brodley] in *On client-centered clinical supervision: Its attitudes, processes and dilemmas.* Unpublished doctoral clinical research project, Illinois School of Professional Psychology (now Argosy University, Chicago).

Brodley, B. T. (2003a). *Consultation guidelines: Some important features of client-centered therapy to keep in mind when a situation with a client is problematic.* Unpublished manuscript.

Brodley, B. T. (2003b). Presence in client-centered therapy. *A Pessoa Como Centro: Revista de Estudos Rogerianos, 6,* 48–77. (Slightly different emphasis and title from the (2000f) version in *The Person-Centered Journal.*) Barbara referenced this paper as in press in 2002 and cited it as 2003. Other sources suggest 2000 or 2001. See 1999e.

Brodley, B. T. (2003c). The relation of research to psychotherapy. See 2002d.

Lietaer, G., & Brodley, B. T. (2003). Carl Rogers in the therapy room: A listing of session transcripts and a survey of publications referring to Rogers' sessions. *Person-Centered & Experiential Psychotherapies, 2,* 274–291.

Brodley, B. T. (2004a). Postscripts to "Uncharacteristic directiveness": A note on multicultural counseling and Rogers' sessions with African-American clients. In R. Moodley, C. Lago, & A. Talahite (Eds.), *Carl Rogers counsels a Black client* (pp. 47–51). Ross-on-Wye: PCCS Books.

Brodley, B. T. (2004b, July). *Rogers' responses to clients' questions in client-centered therapy: Some findings from a dissertation research study by Claudia Kemp (2004), Chicago School of Professional Psychology.* Unpublished paper prepared for presentation at the 18th annual meeting of the Association for Development of the Person-Centered Approach, Anchorage, AK, July 14–18.

Brodley, B. T. (2004c). Uncharacteristic directiveness: Rogers and the 'Anger and Hurt' client. See 1990c.

Brodley, B. T., & Kemp, C. M. (2004, July). *Some differences in clients' questions and Rogers' responses to questions between the Mr. Bryan sessions and Rogers' post-Bryan therapy sessions.* Unpublished paper prepared for presentation at the eighteenth annual meeting of the Association for Development of the Person-Centered Approach, Anchorage, AK, July 14–18. Based upon the doctoral clinical research project of Claudia Kemp (2004), Chicago School of Professional Psychology.

Motomasa, N. (2004). Summary of an interview with Barbara Temaner Brodley: Views of the nondirective attitude in couple and family therapy. In N. Motomasa *Client-centered couple and family therapy: Experienced therapists' views of theory and practice* (pp. 129–134). Unpublished doctoral clinical research project, Illinois School of Professional Psychology, (now Argosy University, Chicago). This volume, Chapter 21.

Brodley, B. T. (2005a). Client-centered values limit the application of research findings. See 2002d. This volume, Chapter 6.

Brodley, B. T. (2005b). Introduction: About the nondirective attitude. See 1999a as About the nondirective attitude.

Levitt, B. E., & Brodley, B. T. (2005). "It enlightens everything you do": Observing non-directivity in a client-centered therapy demonstration session. In B. E. Levitt (Ed.), *Embracing non-directivity* (pp. 96–112). Ross-on-Wye: PCCS Books.

Brodley, B. T. (2006a, July). *A Chicago client-centered therapy: Nondirective and nonexperiential.* Paper presented in Fargo, ND on July 24, during the 20th annual meeting of the Association for the Development of the Person-Centered Approach. This volume, Chapter 2.

Brodley, B. T. (2006b). Client-initiated homework in client-centered therapy. *Journal of Psychotherapy Integration, 16*(2), 140–161.

Brodley, B. T. (2006c). Non-directivity in client-centered therapy. *Person-Centered & Experiential Psychotherapies, 5,* 36–52.

Brodley, B. T., & Lietaer, G. (Eds.). (2006). Transcripts of Carl Rogers' therapy sessions. Email publication available from Germain Lietaer <Germain.Lietaer@psy.kuleuven.be> and Kathryn Moon <kmoon1@alumni.uchicago.edu>.

Fairhurst, I. (2007). [Interview of Barbara Brodley]. In *Person-centred approach, past, present and future: Memories and conversations* [Motion picture]. (Film to be made available as part of a project sponsored by the British Association for the Person-Centred Approach – for further information see www.bapca.org.uk.)

Bozarth, J. D., & Brodley, B. T. (2008). Actualization: A functional concept in client-centered therapy. See Bozarth & Brodley, 1991.

Wilczynski, J., Brodley, B. T., & Brody, A. (2008). A rating system for studying nondirective client-centered interviews – Revised. See Brodley & Brody, 1991, A rating system for studying client/person-centered interviews.

Temaner, G., & Quinn, G. (Producers/Directors). (2010). *Part 3 of the Kartemquin Collection: The early years, Volumes 1–3.* See Temaner & Quinn, 1970, *Marco.*

Moon, K. A., Witty, M., Grant, B., & Rice, B. (Eds.). (2011). *Practicing client-centered therapy: Selected writings of Barbara Temaner Brodley.* Ross-on-Wye: PCCS Books.

# Index of names and places